Public Personnel Management

Public Personnel Management
Current Concerns, Future Challenges

Third Edition

Edited by

Carolyn Ban
University of Pittsburgh

Norma M. Riccucci
University at Albany, State University of New York

New York San Francisco Boston
London Toronto Sydney Tokyo Singapore Madrid
Mexico City Munich Paris Cape Town Hong Kong Montreal

Publisher: Priscilla McGeehon
Senior Acquisitions Editor: Eric Stano
Associate Editor: Anita Castro
Marketing Manager: Megan Galvin Fak
Production Manager: Mark Naccarelli
Project Coordination, Text Design, and Electronic Page Makeup: WestWords, Inc.
Cover Designer/Manager: Wendy Ann Fredericks
Cover Photo: © Jim Wehtje/Brand X Pictures
Manufacturing Buyer: Lucy Hebard
Printer and Binder: The Maple-Vail Book Manufacturing Group
Cover Printer: Lehigh Press, Inc.

Library of Congress Cataloging-in-Publication Data

Public personnel management: current concerns, future challenges / edited by Carolyn
Ban, Norma M. Riccucci—3rd ed.
     p. cm.
  Includes bibliographical references and index.
  ISBN 0-321-08562-0
    1. Civil service—United States—Personnel management. I. Ban, Carolyn. II. Riccucci,
  Norma.

JK765 .P947 2001
352.6'0973—dc21

                                                                        2001038992

Please visit our website at http://www.ablongman.com

ISBN 0-321-08562-0

1 2 3 4 5 6 7 8 9 10–MA–04 03 02 01

Contents

Contributors

Margo Bailey is an Assistant Professor in the Department of Public Administration at American University. She teaches courses in management analysis, managing nonprofit organizations, and human resource strategies. Dr. Bailey's research interests include organizational effectiveness within nonprofit organizations, strategic human resource management, and public sector careers.

Carolyn Ban is the Dean of the Graduate School of Public and International Affairs at the University of Pittsburgh. She received her Ph.D. from Stanford University, and her career has spanned the public and private sectors as well as academia. She has written broadly on issues of civil service reform and public management. She is currently serving as President of the National Association of Public Affairs and Administration.

Sergio Fernandez is a doctoral student in the D.P.A. program at the University of Georgia and a recipient of the Carl Vinson Institute of Government Graduate Research Assistantship. His primary research interests are public management, privatization and program evaluation. He has served in positions involving contract administration for the Florida Department of Revenue and the City of Coral Gables, Florida, and recently served as a research associate in the Metropolitan Center, Florida International University. His recent article in *Public Performance and Management Review* (with Ross Fabricant) analyzed methodological issues involved in assessments of privatization and in comparisons between public and private service delivery.

Charles Gossett is an Associate Professor of Political Science at Georgia Southern University and Director of the MPA program. He worked for four years as chief of the Employee Benefits Division of the District of Columbia government and for two years in the Evaluation Management Division of the U.S. Office of Personnel Management. In addition to research on gay and lesbian issues in human resources management, he conducts research on gay and lesbian politics at the state and local levels of government and state civil service reform.

Patricia Wallace Ingraham is Distinguished University Professor at the Maxwell School of Citizenship and Public Affairs, Syracuse University. She was the Founding Director of the Alan K. Campbell Public Affairs Institute and the first director of the Government Performance Project, a multi-year study of management at all levels of government in the United States. She has lectured and written extensively on the topics of public management and bureaucratic reform. She is the author or editor of nine books; the most recent is *Putting Management in the Performance Equation*.

J. Edward Kellough is an Associate Professor in the Department of Political Science at the University of Georgia where he teaches in the graduate programs in public administration. His major area of academic interest is public personnel management. His research has addressed such topics as equal employment opportunity and affirmative action, representative bureaucracy, reinventing government, and civil service reform. He is the author of numerous book chapters and articles in scholarly journals.

Carol E. Lowman is currently a procurement analyst for U.S. Army Forces Command, Department of the Army and has 10 years of experience in the awarding and administration of contracts in support of privatization initiatives. In 1998, she received the prestigious Secretary of the Army Award for Excellence in Contracting. She holds a Masters of Public Administration degree and is currently a doctoral candidate in public administration at the University of Georgia, working on a dissertation on the skills and human capital required for effective contracting by federal agencies.

Dr. Barbara Nunberg is Lead Specialist, Public Sector, East Asia and Pacific Region, at the World Bank. She received her Ph.D. in Political Science from Stanford University and has published broadly on issues of administrative reform. She is the author of *The State After Communism: Administrative Transitions in Central and Eastern Europe*.

B. Guy Peters is Maurice Falk Professor of American Government and Senior Fellow of the Canadian Centre for Management Development. He holds a Ph. D. from Michigan State University and honorary doctorates from universities in Finland and Sweden. Among his recent publications are *The Politics of Bureaucracy*, 5th ed., *The Future of Governing*, 2nd ed., *Governance in the 21st Century* (co-edited with Donald J. Savoie) and *Institutional theory in Political Science*.

Joan E. Pynes is the Director of the Public Administration Program at the University of South Florida. She is the author of *Human Resources Management for Public and Nonprofit Organizations* (1997) published by Jossey-Bass, Inc. Her research interests include public and nonprofit human resources management.

Hal G. Rainey is Alumni Foundation Distinguished Professor at the University of Georgia. His research concentrates on organizations and management in government, with emphasis on performance, change, leadership, incentives, privatization, and comparisons of governmental management to management in the business and nonprofit sectors. He recently coedited *Advancing Public Management* (Georgetown University Press, 2000) with Jeffrey L. Brudney and Laurence J. O'Toole. He is preparing a third edition of his book, *Understanding and Managing Public Organizations* (Jossey-Bass, 1997).

Norma M. Riccucci is Professor and Director of the Ph.D. Program of Public Administration and Policy at the Rockefeller College, University at Albany, SUNY. She has published extensively in the areas of public management and public personnel administration. One of her recent books is *Managing Diversity in Public Sector Workforces* (Westview Press).

David H. Rosenbloom is Distinguished Professor of Public Administration in the School of Public Affairs at American University. He is the 2001 recipient of the American Political Science Association's John Gaus Award for Exemplary Scholarship in the Joint Tradition of Political Science and Public Administration. He writes extensively about public administration and democratic-constitutionalism.

Sally Coleman Selden is an Associate Professor of management at Lynchburg College. Her major areas of research interest include human resource management, representative bureaucracy and public management. Her recent work has appeared in *Public Administration Review, Journal of Public Administration Research and Theory, Administration and Society, American Journal of Political Science*, and *Review of Public Personnel Administration*.

Myra Howze Shiplett is the Director of the National Academy of Public Administration's Center for Human Resources Management. Prior to joining the Academy in 1999, Ms. Shiplett spent more than 30 years as a federal executive working for both the executive and judicial branches of the federal service. In addition to her federal career, Ms. Shiplett has taught at the high school and college level, is the author of a number of articles, and does extensively public speaking. She holds a Masters Degree in Urban Affairs from the Virginia Polytechnic Institute and State University in Blacksburg, VA and a Bachelor of Arts Degree in English and Journalism from the University of South Florida in Tampa, FL. She is a graduate of the Department of State's Senior Seminar in American Diplomacy.

Ronald R. Sims is the Floyd Dewey Gottwalld Senior Professor in the Graduate School of Business at the College of William and Mary. He is the author or co-author of seventeen books and more than seventy-five articles that have appeared in a wide variety of scholarly and practitioner journals. His most recent books are: *Reinventing Training and Development* (1998), *Accountability and Radical Change in Public Organizations* (1998), Keys to Employee Success in the Coming Decades (1999), *The Challenge of Front-line Management: Flattened Organizations in the New Economy* (2001), *Organizational Success through Effective Human Resources Management* (2002), *Changing the Way We Manage Change* (2002). His research focuses on a variety of topics to include change management, human resources management, employee training and management development, learning styles, experiential learning, and business ethics.

James D. Slack is Professor and Chair of the Department of Government and Public Service at The University of Alabama at Birmingham. He is a Senior Scientist in the Medical School's Center for AIDS Research, and he is a Senior Scholar in the School of Public Health's Lister Hill Center for Health Policy. His research centers on anti-discrimination policies and workplace issues. Slack has published extensively in public administration journals. His most recent book is *AIDS/HIV in the Public Workplace* (University of Alabama).

George T. Sulzner is Professor of Political Science at the University of Massachusetts, Amherst. He has published extensively on the subject of public sector labor relations in the United States and Canada. Currently, he is researching the work of the "Task Force on Modernizing Human Resources Management in the Public Service of Canada," and the efforts of the Canadian Federal Government to develop a gender neutral position classification system. He is also the elected Vice President of the Association of Canadian Studies in the United States.

Glenn Sutton is Principal Consultant with Federal Management Partners, Inc., a small human resources (HR) and management consulting firm focusing on the public sector. His experience includes more than 15 years as a human resources practitioner and 12 years as a senior project manager and information technology executive. Prior to entering the consulting field, Mr. Sutton was Deputy Chief Information Officer for the U.S. Office of Personnel Management (OPM), and also served on the federal Chief Information Officers Council as Co-Chair of its Education and Training Committee, leading the Council's initiatives on IT workforce issues. Mr. Sutton received both a BA degree in Economics and an MBA from George Washington University.

Chapter 1

Public Personnel Management: Where Has it Been, Where is it Going?

Carolyn Ban and Norma M. Riccucci

The ten years since we published the first edition of this book have confirmed the need for a reader that reflects the most current issues in public personnel administration. It has been a decade of rapid change in government as a whole as well as in the broader society, and many of those changes have been played out in the area of public personnel administration. This third edition reflects, then, what we consider to be many of the most important current issues. This book is not designed to be a "how-to" manual but rather a supplement to a public personnel text, one that gives the student a broad understanding of the key policy and management issues in the field today.

To put the specific discussions contained in this book into a broader context, it is important to address two interrelated issues. First, what makes public personnel management "public;" that is, what differentiates *public* personnel management from approaches in the private or nonprofit sectors? Second, what is the historical background of current public personnel practices? Understanding how we got to this point will help us to think about where we are going, and where we should go, in the future.

WHAT IS DIFFERENT ABOUT *PUBLIC* PERSONNEL MANAGEMENT?

As most personnelists or human resource (HR) specialists will tell you, many of the tasks they perform and challenges they face are similar across sectors. All personnel staffs are concerned with the "people part" of management, including hiring and promotion, training and development, compensation and benefits, retirement, and related issues, and most HR offices see working with managers on broader "people issues" as part of their job. These might include organizational design, organization climate, workforce planning, and related issues.

The sectors, however, differ in ways that have profound effects on the goals and processes of personnel/HR systems. The goals of private personnel managers are the goals of the firm: to increase the long-term profitability of the firm. This means not just hiring and retaining staff with critical skills, but also development of strategic HR systems linked to the firm's immediate needs and also to its long-term strategic vision.

Nonprofit organizations' HR systems are, in technique, roughly similar to those of private-sector firms of comparable size, but nonprofits are often working with a smaller or less predictable resource base (Pynes, 1997). They function within a different accountability system, as well. Both private and nonprofit organizations have boards of directors. But private firms' managers are ultimately accountable to their stockholders. Those nonprofits with membership bases are accountable to those members. But all are accountable to their boards, and all nonprofits, large or small, require personnel systems that support the mission of the organization (see Pynes, Chapter 17).

The public sector is different from both the private and nonprofit sectors. The differences are based primarily in law and politics. With respect to public personnel, the U.S. Constitution serves as the fundamental framework for public employment (see Rosenbloom and Bailey, Chapter 11). It sets parameters around the rights and responsibilities of both public employers and employees. In terms of politics, both the public and private sector are certainly affected by small "p" politics (e.g., in the form of office politics). However, big "P" Politics in the partisan sense is relevant only to the public sector. In fact, as will be discussed shortly, the evolution of public personnel systems clearly illustrates this.

Public personnel systems, normally termed civil service systems, were developed to support goals that are central to the concept of public administration in a democracy. The concept of a professional civil service was still relatively new when it was first implemented in the United States in 1883. Among the key values embodied in the system are:

- Selection by merit
- Neutral competence
- A high level of job security for all except political appointees
- A workforce that is representative of the citizens

More recently, the focus has shifted to more managerial values, and the civil service system has been exhorted to meet additional goals. These include:

- Efficiency and cost effectiveness of the personnel system itself
- Strategic HR management in support of the agency's mission

These new values may conflict with more traditional values, particularly around the definition of merit. To understand that conflict, we need to look at the history of the civil service system.

THE CULT OF MERIT

When the first national civil service law, the Pendleton Act, was enacted in this country in 1883, the preeminent force behind the nation's system of personnel was merit. Driven by the desire to hire the most competent workers or, alternatively, to keep politics out of the hiring process, the key value behind the public service was to ensure the pursuit of merit. This concept was not an idle invention to be dealt with superficially; rather, it was politically and pragmatically motivated and tied to a fundamental value underlying the American way of life—democracy. Mosher (1982: 217, emphasis in original) wrote that the

> people of the United States built an ideology which related the public service to their indigenous concepts of democracy.... The ideology came to be known as "merit principles." ... *Merit* became the administrative expression and foundation of democratic government.

Merit's lofty association with democracy has not only enshrined it as an American icon, but it has virtually assured its perdurability throughout the history of the civil service. It is perhaps the one value with a lasting legacy. Today, civil service systems continue to be driven by the notion of merit, if not in practice, at least in theory. Performance appraisal systems, pay schemes, and other personnel functions continue to operate on the notion that merit is being promoted, even though in actuality it may not be the end result.

In practice, there are perhaps three important functions served by merit in contemporary public personnel management: One is the symbolic value it confers on civil service. As noted earlier, merit was seen as a way to preserve and promote a paramount value in our society—democracy. In effect, one is hard pressed to negotiate away a concept that has been built on such a high ethical, moral, and, indeed, constitutional foundation.

The second function of merit in today's civil service is that it continues to protect employees from managerial or systemic abuses. Public employees who believe that their employment rights have been abridged have several types of protections offered by civil service or "merit" systems. In fact, the creation of the U.S. Merit Systems Protection Board (MSPB) in 1978, with passage of the Civil Service Reform Act, was intended to provide an appeals board, separate and distinct from the main personnel agency—the Office of Personnel Management, formerly the U.S. Civil Service Commission—for federal employees to redress alleged violations of merit.

A third, less positive function of merit is that serving as a subterfuge for public managers when they seek expressly to abuse if not the letter, the spirit of civil service laws—that is to say that public managers may continue to gripe that relying on merit hamstrings their managerial capabilities, but that they will also hide behind the veil of merit when it is convenient to do so. Managers may claim to be upholding merit when, in fact, they are manipulating the "rule of three" to hire their preferred candidate who is actually number twenty-five on the civil service hiring list.

In sum, public personnel management, for better or worse, continues to embody the concept of merit. Notwithstanding, the nature of civil service and the personnel practices which sustain it have changed considerably since 1883. From passage of the Civil Service Reform Act in 1978 to Executive Order 13087 issued in 1998, which prohibits discrimination on the basis of sexual orientation in federal employment, we've come a long way in terms of the policies, programs and values that underlie the U.S. civil service.

Those reforms have, however, made only marginal changes in the process of hiring, promoting, paying, and motivating government employees in many jurisdictions. As a result, new political appointees, who come from outside the government, are often taken aback at the extremely complex and rigid systems within which they must now learn to operate. As Ingraham and Selden make clear in Chapter 15, some states and local governments have taken drastic steps to reinvent their civil services systems or even, in a few cases, to abolish them. But the issue of how to balance the need for managers to have more flexibility and for the systems to be simpler and more transparent with the ongoing need to protect individual employees from abuse and to protect the underlying value of merit is probably the key issue currently facing the personnel field. When *merit* is defined only as numerical ranking on a written test (especially when it is scored in the fraction of a point), then we have created a straight jacket that may actually make it much harder for organizations to hire the most talented employees and the employees who are committed to the values of the organization.

WHERE ARE WE NOW?

The last ten years have seen rapid change, and the articles in this book reflect on the implications of those changes, which span the political arena, the economy, social and demographic changes, and the impact of new technology. Let us look briefly at each.

Political Change. The past decade has been marked by dramatic change at the federal level with the Clinton administration's National Performance Review (NPR—later renamed the National Partnership for Reinventing Government) and with the passage of the Government Performance and Results Act (GPRA) in 1993. Several of the chapters detail the far-reaching impact of the NPR on federal personnel management. The National Performance Review proposals were controversial among public administration scholars. Although many supported its calls for decentralization, deregulation, and empowerment of government employees, others critiqued its emphasis on customers rather than citizens, its focus on increased managerial flexibility (which was seen as threatening to employee rights), and its deemphasis on the role of political appointees and the Senior Executive Service.

Some also saw within the NPR staff a battle of emphasis between those who wanted to focus on improving management systems and others who emphasized cutting the size of government as the key goal. Within the field of personnel management, it was clearly the latter who had the greatest impact. While there was some deregulation, massive cuts in the size of the personnel workforce had far-reaching implications for how personnel offices carried out their work. The National Partnership Council, formed under the auspices of the NPR, appeared to create a new vision of labor-management partnership, and even of shared governance, in the 1990s, but it was one of the first structures dismantled by the new Bush administration, and it remains to be seen to what extent existing partnerships will be supported.

GPRA's emphasis on performance management and accountability systems have also had a direct impact on HR systems in government, as they, too, struggle to find ways to measure what they do and to demonstrate how it supports the overall strategic goals of the agency.

The Clinton years were also, after 1994, a period of divided government, with Congress controlled by the Republican Party. Such a division of power did not provide a political environment supportive of broad legislative reform of the current system, so changes had to be made within the existing legal and regulatory structure.

State governments have, in some cases, been much more willing to make bold changes. As a result, state practice in the U.S. is remarkably diverse, with a range from very traditional civil service systems to more flexible or decentralized systems, with a few states actually abandoning central civil service systems altogether.

Economic Changes. The 1990s were a period of economic growth in the United States. The impacts on government were twofold. First, the competition for employees became fiercer than ever, and government agencies faced increasing difficulties in hiring and holding on to their top employees, particularly in technical fields. That competition has spurred calls for reform of the hiring system and for compensation systems that allow governments to compete in the market for qualified employees. Second, the growing economy led to an increase in tax revenues at all levels of government. But, given the current political environment, growing revenues have not, in most cases, led to increasing workforces. At the federal level, increasing demand for services, coupled with a political commitment to cut the size of government, has driven an increase in contracting out to other entities (nonprofits, private firms, or state governments) to do the actual work of government. The same trend was evident in many state governments as well.

Both effects of economic growth have had direct impact on personnel systems. First, traditional hiring and pay systems have often been found wanting by managers dealing with an overheated job market, and they have struggled to work within or to find ways around these systems, as is discussed in Chapter 12. Second, managers and personnelists face the dilemma of how to manage a contractor workforce that does not have the same rights and benefits as civil service employees and that cannot be directly supervised by the government manager responsible for the program. These challenges are explored in more depth in chapter 16.

Social and Demographic Changes. The continuing demographic shifts in the U.S. population have led to considerable changes in the social composition of both public and private sector workforces. As Riccucci illustrates in Chapter 7, there have been notable increases in the number of women, people of color, foreign-born or immigrant workers, and older workers in government workforces. This creates both challenges and opportunities for public-sector employers not only to be truly representative of the American people, but also to manage effectively the delivery of public services.

Technological Changes.   Technology has changed how all organizations do business and how we, as people, communicate with each other. The effects have been pronounced in the personnel field, from use of the web for job listing and job searches to computerized systems for record-keeping and analysis to different ways for personnel offices to communicate with their clients. Shiplett and Sutton provide an overview of the many uses of new technology in HR management in Chapter 3.

WHERE TO, WHAT NEXT?

Prognosticating about the future is always difficult, and predictions about dramatic change in government structures have often been wide of the mark. It is particularly challenging to try to make predictions about the federal workforce at the beginning of a new administration. We do, however, have some expectations about future challenges and the directions of future policy.

Defining Merit: An On-going Dilemma.   As we discussed above, the entire civil service system is based on the principle of merit-based selection. There is, however, increasing dissatisfaction among managers with an overly narrow definition of *merit* that undercuts attempts to focus on quality. Expect more dialogue and more attempts either to reform the system or to opt out of it at the federal level. At state and local levels, expect more experiments with decentralization but probably not much support for the drastic step of abolishing merit systems.

Human Capital and Workforce Planning.   The human capital approach, which builds on strategic human resources management, will become more common, at least as a goal. Its focus on workforce planning will become increasingly important as agencies deal with both turnover and retirements.

Sector Blurring.   The trend towards contracting out for delivery of government services will not slow down. If anything, there will be pressure to increase contracting out by governments at all levels. That will result in increased blurring of the distinctions between the public, nonprofit, and private sectors. Personnel specialists and managers in each sector need to understand how their counterparts in the other sectors work and where management styles and formal systems are currently incompatible. We reflect that trend by including, for the first time, a chapter on personnel in nonprofit organizations (see Pynes, Chapter 17).

Internationalization of HR Reform.   Internationalization is reflected not only in the movement of people across borders, discussed above, but also in the movement of ideas. The rapid sharing of information, via conferences, publications, and personal contacts, has led to a worldwide movement of public management reform models, and many of those reforms have dramatic effects on personnel management. As a result, we have also internationalized this edition, with new chapters by B. Guy Peters on reform in developed countries (See Chapter 4) and by Barbara Nunberg on the challenges of reform in developing and transitional countries (Chapter 5).

Trying to keep up with a field that is changing so rapidly is a challenge for scholars and students. The one thing we can be certain of is that public personnel administration will continue to reform and reinvent itself. One would expect no less from such a dynamic field, especially in its ability to keep up with the changing political, social, legal, technological, and economic demands of this nation.

REFERENCES

Mosher, Frederick C. 1982. *Democracy and the Public Service,* 2nd ed. New York: Oxford University Press.
Pynes, Joan. 1997. *Human Resources Management for Public and Nonprofit Organizations.* San Francisco: Jossey-Bass.

Chapter

2

The Changing Role of the Personnel Office[1]

Carolyn Ban

INTRODUCTION

For well more than twenty years, personnel offices have been exhorted to change their roles. From the Civil Service Reform Act of 1978 and before to the reports of the National Performance Review in the 90s, reformers have argued that personnel offices should move away from their traditional role, with its focus on routine processing of personnel transactions and on control and enforcement of arcane civil service laws, to new roles more aligned with management and more responsive to management's needs. This chapter explores the reasons for these calls for change and the specific critiques of the traditional personnel office roles. It then presents three related models for reform. Finally, it looks at specific attempts to implement change and at the sources of resistance to change.

Before we turn to the issue of new roles for the personnel office, it is useful to look briefly at the context for this discussion—the structure of the personnel process in the public sector. In the private sector, each business or organization is free to establish its own personnel procedures, although it must work within the constraints imposed by a growing body of employment law governing such issues as affirmative action, labor relations, rights of the disabled, and family leave. In the public sector, in contrast, individual agencies typically have little freedom to design their own personnel systems; they must operate within civil service laws. Although there are variations between states and between municipal governments, most civil service systems are complex and highly formalized, and they stress uniformity rather than flexibility. Further, in many jurisdictions an external body—a civil service commission or, at the federal level, the U.S. Office of Personnel Management—sets the rules. That external organization may actually do much of the work, developing and administering civil service examinations for hiring or promotion, and it typically has the responsibility of oversight for agency personnel offices. However, this chapter focuses not on the role and functions of those central personnel organizations but on the operating personnel offices within government agencies or departments, offices that work on a daily basis with managers and employees.

WHAT IS THE PROBLEM? NEGATIVE IMAGES OF THE PERSONNEL OFFICE

The traditional role of the personnel office in government, as it evolved since the creation of civil service systems in the late nineteenth century, emphasized two functions: routine processing of administrative tasks relating to payroll and retirement benefits and the like and enforcement of an increasingly convoluted set of laws, rules, and regulations governing the civil service system. Although agency managers recognize the need for both functions, they are increasingly dissatisfied with how personnelists handle them. They critique the inefficiency with which routine processing is managed. More important, they are strongly critical of the negative stance of personnelists, their heavy focus on compliance, and their tendency to be naysayers, that is, to tell managers that they cannot do what they want rather than helping them to find a way to meet their goals within the system.

Managers interviewed by the U.S. Merit Systems Protection Board (MSPB) (1993) gave a variety of explanations for their dissatisfactions with personnelists. Many recognized that the problems they encountered were rooted in the civil service system itself—in the complexity and rigidity of personnel policies and procedures. But almost an equal number (69 percent in each case) perceived the problems as stemming from "personnel staff's excessive concern with strict compliance with the rules and procedures rather than results" and from "lack of sufficient staff resources in the personnel office." Finally, more than half the managers interviewed blamed "lack of sufficient skill in the personnel staff" for the problems they encountered (21).

Such critiques of the traditional personnel role are not new. They reach back well more than twenty years. Alan Campbell (1978), who spearheaded the effort for the Civil Service Reform Act of 1978 and became the first head of the U.S. Office of Personnel Management, excoriated personnelists for "rigidity, inflexibility, and a turn of mind . . . that thinks in terms of protecting the system; can't do, rather than can do" (61). The same message was echoed by scholars, who called for personnelists to abandon their traditional focus on the "compliance officer" role. (Nalbandian, 1981).

At the root of the problem is a deep-seated role conflict between personnelists and line managers. As I have said elsewhere:

> Personnel staff saw themselves as the 'keepers of the flame,' charged with preserving merit in the merit system—a probably accurate reflection of congressional

intent. This view of their role was also instilled by their socialization, both inside most agencies and particularly in training given by the office of Personnel Management (OPM) and its predecessor which reinforced in budding personnelists an adversarial view of the system. They were conditioned to see managers as the people asking them to break the rules—to violate the merit system (Ban, 1995, p. 91).

In addition to the conflict between personnelists and managers that is rooted in this traditional compliance function, conflict arises because personnel offices must serve multiple clients. They work for managers but also for employees. Thus they risk being seen as either "management tool or employee advocate" (Straus, 1987).

THREE MODELS OF REFORM

Although reformers' descriptions of the problem with the traditional system have much in common, the new personnel office roles they have suggested over the years differ among three dimensions. First, reform proposals may focus on how the personnel office does its work. The model for this reform, which I term the *customer-service model*, assumes that the personnel office will perform most or all of the same functions it currently handles but exhorts it to do what it does better and faster, recognizing that the manager is its key customer.

Second, reform may focus on what the personnel office actually does. Thus the second model, the *organization development or consulting* model, urges personnelists to take on new functions within the organization, serving as internal consultants to managers on a wide range of organizational issues. This proposal is sometimes combined with the suggestion that personnel offices give up some of their traditional functions.

Finally, reform can focus on where the personnel office sits within the organization—on its power and role in organizational policy. The third model, the *strategic human-resource management model*, focuses in this issue, urging the personnel staff to act as full members of the management team, linking personnel and human-resource (HR) policy to agency mission, goals, and policy.

Although it makes sense to separate out these strands of reform for analytic purposes, in reality they are often intertwined, with organizations pursuing reform along two or three of these dimensions simultaneously. Thus, as we examine each model, it is important to look at the ways that strategies for change reinforce or conflict with each other.

MODEL 1: CUSTOMER SERVICE

The customer-service model for reform has existed in the literature for more than twenty years (Balk, 1969; Campbell, 1978; Nalbandian, 1981). Quite simply, it urges personnelists to do what they do better and faster and to be more responsive to the needs of their primary clients, managers. More specifically, this means improving accuracy and speed in processing routine administrative actions. It also means taking a more positive attitude toward managers' requests, helping them to find creative ways to do things within the constraints of the system instead of simply saying no to them.

MODEL 1 CHANGE STRATEGIES:

As we have seen, both managers and scholars have recognized that much of the problem they see in personnel offices is inherent in the rules and regulations within which personnelists are forced to work. Thus, a key thrust of reform proposals is to deregulate civil service systems. At the federal level, the National Performance Review report critiqued the excessive complexity and rigidity of civil service regulation and argued that "[w]e must enable all managers to pursue their missions, freed from the cumbersome red tape of current personnel rules" (NPR, 1993a, p. 22). Indeed, one of the first actions taken under the NPR was to abolish the federal government's ten-thousand-page *Federal Personnel Manual*. Similarly, the National Commission on the State and Local Public Service (chaired by former Mississippi governor William Winter, and also known as the Winter Commission) decried "rule-bound and complicated systems" and argued that "[w]e must not be so hidebound in order to protect against failure that we quash the spirit of innovation" (1993, p. 25).

In addition to deregulation, proposals to implement the customer service model call for increasing reliance on new technology to improve efficiency and responsiveness. This includes use of computers for rapid scoring of civil service tests and for drawing up lists of eligibles and use of telephone hot lines or the internet for distributing information about vacancies. The federal government has even implemented a system for applying for some jobs directly by push-button telephone.

But simplifying the formal rules and providing new technology will not of themselves change the traditional culture of personnel offices. A number of efforts have focused on the structure and style of work, linking reform to culture change. In the early 1990s, the introduction of Total Quality Management (TQM) in personnel offices both in the federal government (Ban, 1992) and in state and local governments (Berman, 1997) was seen as an important tool for culture change. TQM encourages personnel staff to examine their relationships with their customers and to set measurable goals for their work. It is often linked to a restructuring of work, with a movement away from narrow specialization, with one group handling hiring and another classification, toward a more generalist approach, with cross-training so that one staff person or a team can follow through on all the related steps of a complex personnel action. In fact, some personnel offices that have implemented TQM have moved to the use of self-managed teams. Barzelay's description of reform in the state of Minnesota encompasses this combination of approaches:

The new organizational structure—involving agency service teams—signaled the change in emphasis from performing a set of separate technical functions to providing a unified service to a segment of the customer base. As part of the same strategy, operating-level staffing professionals were given the intellectual tools to respond proficiently to whatever problem customers brought to their attention. Through cross-training, for example, employees who had known only about position classification learned how to deal competently with recruiting and examining. Conversely, specialists in the hiring process learned how the system of position classification worked (Barzelay, 1992, pp. 58–59).

As Barzelay makes clear, improving the quality of customer service may also require upgrading the skills of personnel staff. The MSPB study of the personnel function found that "more than half (56 percent) of managers and almost half (48 percent) of personnelists thought that either 'to a large extent' or 'to some extent' carrying out their personnel management responsibilities was more difficult than it ought to be because of a lack of sufficient skill among personnelists." What is particularly striking here is that the personnel staff agreed; in fact, when asked, "To what extent do you feel that you know enough and are skilled enough to provide excellent service?" more than half (57 percent) responded, "To a small extent; there's a lot I don't know," and 9 percent responded, "To no extent; I'm overwhelmed and need a lot more development" (1993: 28).

These skill deficits are exacerbated by the fact that many personnel offices are short staffed. But increasing personnel staff is not a viable option in most jurisdictions. Indeed, in the federal government, personnel staff (along with other "overhead" staff) were targeted for significant cuts during the Clinton administration. Although the rationale for such cuts was that in a deregulated environment fewer control staff would be needed, the cuts have far outstripped the process of deregulation and delegation, putting even greater pressure on the staff who remain and contributing to a growing skills gap in federal HR offices (U.S. Office of Personnel Management, 1999a). Based on a survey of managers, OPM reports that "an unfortunate result of this lack of skill may be the dramatic decline in HR customer service cited by line managers" (U.S. Office of Personnel Management, 1999c).

A final issue in implementing the customer-service model is more controversial. Many proposals for change have stressed the need to decentralize personnel in large organizations down to the operating level to give managers the service they need. Both the NPR and the Winter Commission expressly called for decentralization. In the area of hiring, the NPR called for giving "all departments and agencies authority to conduct their own recruiting and examining for all positions, and abolish[ing] all central registers and standard application forms" (National Performance Review, 1993a, p. 23). Yet some research has found that centralized personnel offices may actually give superior service (Ban, 1995), and a report by the National Academy of Public Administration (1996a) showcased reinvention efforts that included extreme centralization, with a single central personnel office, often combined with smaller offices that could provide some face-to-face service. The Department of Defense, which took the largest cuts in personnel staff in recent years, has, according to an OPM report, "undertaken HR regionalization on a grand scale. In 1994, DoD made the decision to regionalize its HR delivery system" (U.S. Office of Personnel Management, 1999b). DoD's goal was to increase efficiency, and OPM reports that projected annual savings in personnel and other costs are approximately $150 million.

MODEL 2: ORGANIZATION DEVELOPMENT AND CONSULTING

The second model goes beyond improving customer service to advocate that the personnel office take on broader functions, serving as an internal organizational consultant to management, not just on narrow personnel issues but in such areas as organizational design, organizational development (OD), employee motivation, and productivity. Advocates of this role see personnel staff acting as change agents, helping to introduce new management approaches. For example, in many organizations it is the personnel office that is charged with implementing Total Quality Management in the organization (Berman, 1997). Terminology becomes important here; advocates of a broader role also often support use of the term *human resource management* (HRM) rather than personnel management. As a General Accounting Office (GAO) report explained it:

> The term "human resource management" was introduced in the 1950s to expand the focus of personnel management from its emphasis on traditional functions such as recruiting, selection, and pay and benefits. HRM introduced additional strategies to address the needs of increasingly complex organizations, the changing work force, advanced technology, and the external environment. According to the literature, an organization employing an HRM strategy:
>
> - emphasizes the integration of its mission and future direction with the planning and management of its work force,
> - fosters a collaborative relationship between management and employees and encourages employee involvement, and
> - addresses not only the development and motivation of individual employees but also the development of work units and the organization as a whole (U.S. General Accounting Office 1987, p. 6).

Indeed, in 1987, the GAO found that over half the agency HR offices surveyed offered organizational assessment and diagnosis or OD services to management.

MODEL 2 CHANGE STRATEGIES:

Moving to model 2 poses even greater challenges than we saw with model 1. First, the personnel staff must offer these new services on a voluntary basis, relying in requests from their customers, that is, from managers. This requires a very different relationship with management than does the old oversight function and thus a far greater culture change for personnel staff. Additionally, model 2 requires staff with a whole new range of skills and knowledge. Staffing and classification specialists do not automatically know how to do employee surveys or how to counsel managers on strategies for improving productivity.

The potential for conflict with traditional roles is, of course, also greater with model 2. A recent report on civil service reform points up the difficulty of reconciling personnel's roles of "auditor and consultant" and quotes a personnel director who explains the dilemma vividly:

> I assure you that when folks have a difficult question about a financial decision, they don't call the state auditor. They call somebody who will help them decide what the state auditor might say. Balancing performance review with being consultative is difficult because it will mean that it will be in the agencies' best interest to hide all difficult or questionable decisions instead of seeking advice (Carnevale, Housel, and Riley, 1995, p. 25).

One argument, then, is that the two functions should be separated in some way. One approach is that of the U.S. Environmental Protection Agency, which has two connected units: a personnel unit performing the traditional functions and an HR unit providing consulting services to managers (Ban, 1995). Another approach is the franchising or outsourcing of the routine personnel functions. The argument is that outsourcing will save money via economies of scale and will free internal resources to provide consulting services.

Another strategy linked both to improved customer services and to changing personnel office roles is to delegate greater authority over personnel decisions to line managers themselves. The intention is to empower managers by giving them authority over such personnel decisions as classifying positions. At the same time, in theory, such delegation of authority should lead to a changed role for personnelists, who are no longer controllers but consultants who help managers exercise their new authority. As Nigro (1990, p. 195) has put it, this approach "imposes extraordinary demands on administrators while saying very little about how they should go about meeting this challenge." Particularly at a time when federal managerial ranks are being thinned and spans of control broadened, asking managers not only to supervise more people but also to take on responsibility for personnel functions may make them feel overburdened and resentful. Indeed, there is already evidence that some managers given authority over classification will reject it (Ban, 1995).

MODEL 3: STRATEGIC HUMAN-RESOURCES MANAGEMENT

The third model focuses on a strategic human-resources management approach. This model envisions not only a changed role for the personnel or HR office but a changed way of thinking about that office's primary responsibility; no longer should the focus be on carrying out the rules and regulations. The new charge is to support the mission of the organization. The Office of Personnel Management equates strategic human-resources management (SHRM) with "alignment," which "means to integrate decisions about people with decisions about the results an organization is trying to obtain" (U.S. Office of Personnel Management, 1999d,p.1).

This model also entails a new power relationship within the organization, with the HR senior staff functioning as part of the management team, sitting at the table with top management when major policy or program decisions are being made and considering their HR implications. In sum, in this view HR is no longer simply handling routine tasks or providing consulting services on a voluntary basis; it is a major player—an integral part of the strategic planning process.

MODEL 3 CHANGE STRATEGIES

Model 3 differs from model 2 in both level of involvement and scope of issues covered. The consulting provided under model 2 is targeted to operating levels, with personnel specialists working with individual line managers to solve organizational problems. Under model 3, HR staff are working at the very top of the organization, hand in hand with senior managers. The scope of the issues covered also varies; model 2 personnelists are typically working on short-term operational planning and consulting. Under model 3, the focus is longer-term and proactive, with HR specialists charged with avoiding problems via strategic planning, including projecting future staffing needs.

The concept of strategic resources planning originated in the private sector. As Schuler (1992, p. 18) describes it:

> Strategic human resources management is largely about integration and adaptation. Its concern is to ensure that: (1) human resource (HR) management is fully integrated with the strategy and the strategic needs of the firm; (2) HR policies cohere both across policy areas and across hierarchies; and (3) HR practices are adjusted, accepted, and used by line managers and employees as part of their everyday work.

In a business environment, becoming a *strategic partner* means, in the words of one business leader, that "HR must become bottom-line valid. . . . The HR function must perform in a measurable and accountable way for the business to reach its objectives" (Caudron, 1994, p. 54).

That "bottom-line" focus is difficult to transfer to the public sector, but some agencies are succeeding in linking HR to the strategic concerns of the organization. An interview with Barbara Sundquist of the Minnesota Department of Transportation, winner of an Agency Award for Excellence from the International Personnel Management Association (Minnesota Department of Transportation, 1993, p. 1), gives a good sense of the dynamics of this approach:

The Human Resource Planning Board (HRPB) is the strategic human resource planning body . . . responsible for identifying, prioritizing, and strategically planning for emerging human resource issues, trends, and opportunities which will impact the agency. The focus of the HRPB is on longer term, strategic, human resource planning rather than tactical or operational human resource planning. The HRPB is composed of managers from each division within the agency and supported by a working team of human resource professionals from within the Office of Human Resources. . . . I consider our major accomplishment to be obtaining the involvement of management in addressing human resource issues on a long-term strategic basis. . . . With the HRPB we have a partnership with managers as human resource staff that are directly involved along with the managers. This will prevent the "dumping" of ideas on the human resource office without any input from us. It also will give managers a better understanding of the many varied human resource issues and the difficulty in solving some of the resultant problems.

Many federal agencies are attempting to move toward a more strategic approach to HR. In 1987 the General Accounting Office found that less than half of (39 of the 71) agencies studied were doing some strategic HR planning, but only 36 percent of that group thought it contributed significantly to operations. Both the NPR and the Government Performance and Results Act of 1993 (GPRA) have led to increased emphasis on SHRM. GPRA requires agencies to develop five-year strategic plans with measurable goals. Its intention is to hold agencies and managers accountable for results. As a report of the National Academy of Public Administration (NAPA) points out, GPRA holds great potential for encouraging strategic HR—potential which is not yet being tapped:

GPRA allows agencies to propose waivers to administrative requirements. In return for the waivers, agencies are to be held accountable for achieving the promised performance improvements. This allows agencies to propose flexibilities to improve HR programs and processes to more closely align HRM with organizational goals and strategic plans. A review of a sample of agency plans submitted under GPRA pilot tests does not demonstrate that agencies have fully recognized the human component of improving organizational performance. Nor do [the plans] . . . reflect clear emphasis on the linkage between effective human resources management and achievement of mission objectives (National Academy of Public Administration, 1995).

By 1999, OPM's study of SHRM found that, "of the 31 [agency] strategic plans reviewed, 87 percent had addressed HRM in some way" (U.S. Office of Personnel Management, 1999d). Further, agency HR staff were playing an active role in the planning process; "seventy-nine percent of the agencies we talked to indicated that they do play a role in the overall agency strategic planning process" (p. 9) although those roles varied from integrated team member to peripheral consultant. On the other hand, few agency plans had any outcome measures for human resources management. And in only a few agencies has HR "been able to develop strong working relationships with management in which HR is a full member of the agency decision-making body" (p. 21).

The recent focus on human capital issues, particularly by the General Accounting Office (GAO), builds on the strategic human-resource management model. GAO has identified strategic human-capital management as a "government wide high-risk challenge" (U.S. General Accounting Office, 2001) and, based on a series of studies, has concluded that "serious human capital shortfalls are eroding the ability of many federal agencies—and threatening the ability of others—to economically, efficiently, and effectively perform their missions" (2001, p. 2). The human-capital approach views employees as assets to be valued, rather than costs to be cut. Like the strategic human-resources management model, it focuses on linking HR planning to organizational planning, in a "strategic and results-oriented approach to human capital planning" (2001, p. 4). Central to human-capital planning is succession planning, ensuring that agencies can project turnover and ensure that their workforces have the skills needed to meet agency goals. There are obvious links to GPRA in this approach, which also emphasizes development of measurable standards and linking employee performance goals to agency results. Whether it is called strategic human-resource management or human-capital management, there is consistent pressure, at the federal level, for HR professionals to partner with management in addressing critical human-resource issues.

CHALLENGES TO REFORM

Each of the three models presented above is controversial, and each will encounter some resistance if personnel leadership chooses to implement it, either singly or in combination. To some extent the sources of resistance will be common to any of the three approaches, although each raises some specific issues. This section discusses challenges in four areas: cultural and legal issues, management attitudes, personnel staff competencies, and resources.

CULTURAL AND LEGAL ISSUES

Each of the three models requires a major change in the culture of the personnel office away from the traditional compliance and control orientation. A customer-service approach means that personnelists need to let go of the assumption that their main function is to uphold the integrity of the merit system. Although many personnel staff welcome this change, they point to some enduring problems. Even within a somewhat deregulated environment, the civil service law remains the basis on which they must act, and they have no desire to expose themselves to charges that they have been so flexible that they have violated the law. Further, some complain that no matter how helpful they are, managers will push them to do even more, making demands that are patently unreasonable. As a personnelist in an agency that was implementing TQM explained to me, "The TQM focus on the client doesn't deal with clients who have unreasonable demands. You can't go to Burger King and ask for a Big Mac" (Ban, 1995, p. 101). As we saw earlier, the conflicts over role and culture are even greater in agencies implementing the organizational development model of reform because the continuing compliance role makes it difficult for managers to accept personnel staff as helpful consultants.

Finally, the strategic human-resources approach poses some potentially serious values conflicts. There has been considerable debate in the public administration literature about the applicability of private-sector administrative reforms to the public sector. Making top human-resources staff part of the management team raises quite different problems in government agencies than in private companies. Personnel staff are typically career civil servants. Further, as Nalbandian points out, "Historically . . . the development of merit personnel systems went hand in hand with government reform, and consequently took on an anti-political, moralistic spirit, which by and large endures" (Nalbandian, 1981, p. 40). Personnelists imbued with that spirit have long struggled against pressure from political appointees. Those pressures will be even greater under strategic human-resources management, but advocates have failed to recognize this values conflict. For example, the report, *Reinventing Human Resources*, issued by the National Performance Review (1993b, pp. 3–4) states that "in the future . . . HRM staff adviser should be viewed as part of the management team, not servants of management or the system's police." But it then argues that "the ideal system is free of political influences and embodies merit system principles." Meeting both of these goals simultaneously may be difficult, given the likelihood of pressure from political appointees to put loyalty to the team above maintaining merit system principles.

MANAGEMENT ATTITUDES

Attitudes of managers toward a changed role for personnelists are also problematic. This source of resistance is compounded by the reformers' calls for related changes in managers' HR role. Models 2 and 3 assume that managers actively desire or will at least accept a different conception of the role of the personnel office. But it is not clear that senior political appointees will, in fact, accept and trust personnel staff as full members of the management team. The level of acceptance may depend to a great extent on the philosophical posture of the administration and its stance in relation to political-career relations. Under the Reagan administration, for example, senior officials argued for *jigsaw puzzle management* as a way of dealing with career staff, in which staff members were given only the information they needed for their narrow areas of responsibility, but never allowed to see the big picture (Sanera, 1984).

At the operational level, it is evident that line managers are very supportive of the customer-service model. But it is not clear that line managers want to turn to the personnel office for broad consulting assistance in areas outside of personnel. Public and private managers surveyed for a study of HR roles (King and Bishop, 1994) thought that the three top-ranked purposes of HR from their perspective were to advise the line, maximize use of HR, and assure legal compliance (in short, rather traditional role definitions). An interesting private-sector study examining how multiple constituencies assessed the effectiveness of their HR departments found a difference by level of management: "The constituencies in the operating levels have a strong preference for their HR departments to perform administrative and employee support activities, while the constituencies at the corporate level tend to emphasize planning and development activities or activities that have organization-wide implications" (Tsui, 1987, p. 64). Tsui concludes from her findings that "the HR department should first satisfy existing needs before creating new needs" (p. 67). In sum, although some agencies' HR staff have been successful in developing a clientele for their consulting services, organizations considering such an approach need to recognize that acceptance by managers is far from automatic; managers may be more interested in an improved customer service focus.

Perhaps a more serious problem is the issue raised above, under model 2, which is that changing the role of the personnel office may also entail expanding line managers' roles vis-à-vis the personnel process. It is far from clear that the majority of managers would buy into that change.

PERSONNEL STAFF COMPETENCIES

Certainly one of the challenges for personnel offices taking on new roles is that new approaches require different competencies of staff. As we saw in our discussion of managers' dissatisfaction with their personnel staff, not only do many managers feel that staff do not have the skills needed to do their current jobs but many personnelists have admitted that they feel they lack competence and need additional training.

The resource issue has become increasingly serious in recent years as the full effect of the cuts in HR staff resulting from the NPR have been felt. As OPM has documented, "from 1991 to 1998, the HR field experienced a 17.5 percent drop. . . . Excluding the Equal Employment Opportunity . . . series, the HR workforce dropped by one-fifth (20 percent)" (U.S. Office of Personnel Management, 1999b). Cuts in defense agencies were even more severe; the DOD HR workforce decreased by over 25 percent (U.S. Office of Personnel Management, 1999c).

OPM's study also makes clear that most vacancies in HR professional positions have been filled from within, primarily by staff moving up from clerical and administrative positions. As a result, even though there have been repeated calls for upgrading the educational levels and skills of HR staff so that they can take on new roles, the percent of new HR staff who have completed a BA degree actually declined, from 55 percent in 1994 to 52 percent in 1998 (U.S. Office of Personnel Management, 1999b).

New roles, particularly those required by models 2 and 3, require not just upgrading skills but acquiring some quite different competencies. There is a considerable body of private-sector literature concerning HR competencies. For example, Ulrich and his colleagues conceptualized HR competencies within a "three-domain framework: . . . knowledge of business, delivery of HR practices, and management of change processes" (Ulrich et al, 1995). The National Academy of Public Administration, in its report, *A Competency Model for Human Resource Professionals* (1996a, p. 9), focuses on five key roles and competencies: business partner, HR expert, change agent, advocate, and leader. Figure 2.1 illustrates these roles in more detail and shows how they are interrelated:

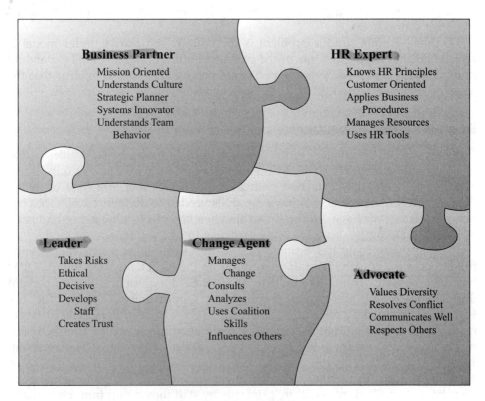

FIGURE 2.1   Competency Model for HR Professionals.

SOURCE: National Academy of Public Administration, 1996a, p. 9.

The Office of Personnel Management has also encouraged agencies to adopt a competency approach to HR, as a way to help "meet organization needs with fewer HR professionals" (U.S. Office of Personnel Management, 1999c, p. 1) and to cope with the early retirement of many "seasoned personnelists," which left significant skills gaps.

Personnel offices, then, face a dilemma. The NAPA report argues that "a wide gap appears to exist between the potential and actual performance of the federal HR community in delivering services needed to accomplish the agency mission" (National Academy of Public Administration, 1996a, p. 4). The same can be said of personnel/HR staffs at the state and local levels. To acquire the new competencies they need, they can either upgrade the skills of current staff or hire new staff. Neither will be easy.

RESOURCES

The dilemma underlying any reconceptualization of personnel roles is that resources are tight and are likely to become even tighter. This is particularly true at the federal level, where, as discussed earlier, personnel took a disproportionate share of the cuts as a result of the National Performance Review.

Yet even before those reductions in staff size, both managers and personnelists agreed that their personnel offices were understaffed (U.S. Merit System Protection Board, 1993). One personnelist quoted in the 1993 MSPB study pointed to the relationship between understaffing and lack of competence: "We're so understaffed that we can't get away to take the training. There just isn't anybody to handle the work while you're gone, so we aren't developing at all" (U.S. Merit System Protection Board, 1993, p. 31). The NPR argued that deregulation will lessen the burden on personnel staff, but realistically, even if staff do not choose to take on new roles, they will continue to find resources very tight for the foreseeable future.

Personnel offices, like other organizations, have been looking for ways to cope creatively with scarce resources. The National Academy of Public Administration has compiled many of the creative approaches taken by both public and private organizations to cut costs and improve productivity, focusing on three areas: reengineering, information technology, and alternative service delivery (National Academy of Public Administration, 1996b). The reengineering cases presented provide concise descriptions of both the process and the results of restructuring HR in both public and private organizations. As noted previously, several organizations that were profiled moved to extremely centralized HR structures, with dramatic cuts in HR staffing. For example, Sears reduced the number of employees working in HR and payroll "from over 700 to approximately 200 working in a single service center" (National Academy of Public Administration, 1996b, p. 7). Similarly, the Small Business Administration consolidated its five regional personnel offices into two locations and moved from a specialist to a generalist concept, cutting overall staffing levels from ninety-one full-time equivalent positions to sixty-one. One of the lessons that SBA learned was that "procedures should be streamlined and standardized prior to consolidation so the organization is not trying to do the same amount of work with fewer staff" (National Academy of Public Administration, 1996b, p. 16).

The NAPA study also explores the links between reengineering and new technology, with consolidated service centers using service kiosks, phone systems, and computer-accessed systems to offer greater self-service for employees and managers. The study also notes that "the general effort to increase efficiency and effectiveness of HRM has led to the use of increased automation of processing through the use of workflow technology, increased attention to the integration of payroll and HRIS [human resource information systems], and the use of automation tools to support functions that may not be part of a shared service center such as training, succession planning, and strategic planning (National Academy of Public Administration, 1996b, p. 23). Additionally, NAPA explores the range of alternative service delivery approaches, including franchising (i.e., hiring another federal agency to manage some or all HR functions) and outsourcing (i.e., contracting out to private-sector firms).

Although it is clear that each of these approaches, separately or in combination, can be a useful strategy for dealing with resource scarcity, such broad structural changes as reengineering or using alternative service delivery approaches should be driven by decisions about the appropriate roles for the personnel office, not just by a desire to cut costs.

CONCLUSION

In some ways, it is depressing to review the literature and to be reminded that we have been calling for similar reforms in the role of the personnel office for over twenty years. It appears that the private-sector organizations are far ahead of the government agencies in accepting new roles for their HR staffs. Certainly, the failure to change may be due to inertia or to resistance on the part of personnel staff who are set in their ways. But it is also apparent that fundamental change in the role of government personnel offices faces a number of challenges that private organizations do not encounter, foremost among them the structure of the civil service system itself. Agencies that wish to streamline hiring, for example, do not have the discretion to throw out the existing system and design their own. Even though increased delegation of hiring authority may have given agencies greater flexibility, they are still forced to work within the confines of the system. At the federal level this means enforcing the rule of three and veterans' preference, for example.

Further, the fact that public-sector top management comprises political appointees, who are often short-timers and sometimes ideologues, limits the potential for personnel directors to be full partners of management. And, as we have seen, line managers may also be resistant to accepting personnel staff as either partners or consultants.

The key question, then, is whether it is possible for the federal government to address its very real human resource, or human capital, challenges within the current political and legal framework. The National Academy of Public Administration, which has, in the past, published a report on innovations and flexibilities possible within the existing laws (National Academy of Public Administration, 1997), has called this approach "making the civil service system work in spite of itself" (National Academy of Public Administration, 2000, p. 41). Although cuts in the size of the HR workforce and the limited competency of HR staff to handle new roles remain key barriers to change, equally important are the restraints of managing within a civil service that remains archaic. Working within a system that is overly rigid and complex is extremely wasteful of staff and management time and effort and limits greatly the ability of HR professionals to move to a more strategic approach. The 1990s were a period of reform in many management areas, including procurement, financial management, and information management. As David Walker has pointed out, "In contrast, human capital management has yet to find the broad conceptual acceptance or political consensus needed for comprehensive legislative reform to occur, and in this sense, human capital management remains the missing link in the federal management framework" (U.S. General Accounting Office, 2001, pp. 2–3). As Ingrahams and Selden make clear (see chapter 16), some states have led the way in reforming their civil service system, sometimes quite drastically. At the federal level, however, HR professionals who wish to adopt any of the three roles discussed in this chapter, as well as managers who want to take an active role in human-capital management, must do so by finding ways around the system, rather than being able to work within a system that supports truly strategic human resources management.

NOTES

1. An earlier version of this chapter appeared in Stephen E. Condrey, ed. *Handbook of Human Resource Management in Government*. San Francisco: Jossey-Bass, 1998. Reprinted with permission.

REFERENCES

Balk, Walter. 1969. "A Harsh Light on the Personnel Function," *Public Personnel Review*, 30, 3 (July).

Ban, Carolyn. 1992. "Can Total Quality Management Work in the Federal Government? The Politics of Implementation." Presentation at the American Political Science Association Annual Meeting, Chicago, September.

———. 1995. *How Do Public Managers Manage? Bureaucratic Constraints, Organizational Culture, and the Potential for Reform*. San Francisco: Jossey-Bass.

Barzelay, Michael. 1992. *Breaking Through Bureaucracy*. Berkeley: University of California Press.

Berman, Evan. 1997. "The Challenges of Total Quality Management." In Carolyn Ban and Norma M. Riccucci, *Public Personnel Management: Current Concerns, Future Challenges*, 2nd ed. Reading Mass.: Addison Wesley Longman.

Campbell, Alan K. 1978. "Revitalizing the Federal Personnel System." *Public Personnel Management*, 7 (6), 58–63.

Carnevale, David, S.W. Housel, N. Riley. 1995. *Merit System Reform in the States: Partnerships for Change*. Norman: Programs in Public Administration, University of Oklahoma.

Caudron, S. 1994. "HR Leaders Brainstorm the Profession's Future," *Personnel Journal*, 73 (8), 54–61.

Civil Service Reform Act of 1978. U.S. Code, Title 5, sec 1101 et seq.

Government Performance and Results Act of 1993. U.S. Statutes at Large 107 (1993) 285.

King, Albert S., and Terrence Bishop. 1994. "Human Resource Experience: Survey and Analysis," *Public Personnel Management* 23, 1 (Spring), 165–180.

"Minnesota Department of Transportation: Recipient of IPMA's Agency Award for Excellence: Medium Agency," *Public Personnel Management* 22, 1 (Spring), 1993, 1–6.

Nalbandian, John. 1981. "From Compliance to Consultation: The Changing Role of the Public Personnel Administrator," *Review of Public Personnel Administration*, 1 (2), 37–51.

National Academy of Public Administration. 1995. *Strategies and Alternatives for Transforming Human Resources Management*. Washington, D.C.: NAPA.

National Academy of Public Administration. 1996a. *A Competency Model for Human Resources Professionals*. Washington, D.C.: NAPA.

National Academy of Public Administration. 1996b. *Improving the Efficiency and Effectiveness of Human Resources Management*. Washington, D.C.: NAPA.

National Academy of Public Administration. 1997. *Innovations and Flexibilities: Overcoming HR System Barriers, Phase III, Practical Tools*, Washington, D.C.: NAPA.

National Academy of Public Administration. 2000. *The Case for Transforming Public-Sector Human Resources Management*. Washington, D.C.: NAPA.

National Commission on the State and Local Public Service (Winter Commission). 1993. *Hard Truths/Tough Choices: An Agenda for State and Local Reform*. Albany, N.Y.: Nelson A. Rockefeller Institute of Government.

National Performance Review. 1993a. *From Red Tape to Results: Creating a Government That Works Better and Costs Less*. Washington, D.C.: U.S. Government Printing Office.

National Performance Review. 1993b. *Reinventing Human Resource Management. Accompanying Report of the National Performance Review*. Washington, D.C.: U.S. Government Printing Office.

Nigro, Lloyd G. 1990. "Personnel **For** and Personnel **By** Public Administrators: Bridging the Gap." In Naomi B. Lynn and Aaron Wildavsky, eds. *Public Administration: the State of the Discipline*. Chatham, N.J.: Chatham House Publishers.

Sanera, Michael. 1984. "Implementing the Mandate." In S.M. Butler, M. Sanera, and W.B. Weinrod, eds. *Mandate for Leadership II*. Washington, D.C.: Heritage Foundation.

Schuler, R.S. 1992. "Strategic Human Resource Management: Linking the People with the Strategic Needs of the Business," *Organizational Dynamics*, Summer, 18–32.

Straus, Stephen K. 1987. "Municipal Personnel Department: Management Tool or Employee Advocate?" *Popular Government*, Fall, 21–26.

Tsui, A.S. 1987. "Defining the Activities and Effectiveness of the Human Resource Department: A Multiple Approach," *Human Resource Management*, 26 (1), 35–69.

Ulrich, Dave, Wayne Brockbank, Arthur Yeung, and Dale Lake, 1995. "Human Resources Competencies: An Empirical Assessment," *Human Resources Management Journal*, 34, 4, 473–496.

U.S. General Accounting Office. 1987. *Human Resource Management: Status of Agency Practices for Improving Federal Productivity.* GAO/GGD-87-61FS. Washington, D.C.: USGAO.

U.S. General Accounting Office. 2001. *Human Capital: Meeting the Governmentwide High-Risk Challenge.* Testimony of David M. Walker, Comptroller General of the United States, before the Subcommittee on Oversight of Government Management, Restructuring, and the District of Columbia, Committee on Governmental Affairs, U.S. Senate. GAO-01-357T, Washington, D.C.: USGAO.

U.S. Merit Systems Protection Board. 1993. *Federal Personnel Officers: Time for Change?* Washington, D.C.: USMSPB.

U.S. Office of Personnel Management. 1999a. *An Occupation in Transition: Part 1, Federal Human Resources Employment Trends.* Washington, D.C. USOPM, MSE-99-5, September.

U.S. Office of Personnel Management. 1999b. *An Occupation in Transition: Part 2, Looking to the Future: Human Resource Competencies.* Washington, D.C. USOPM, MSE-99-6, September.

U.S. Office of Personnel Management. 1999c. *An Occupation in Transition: Part 3, The HR Workforce: Meeting the Challenge of Change.* Washington, D.C. USOPM, MSE-99-7, September.

U.S. Office of Personnel Management. 1999d. *Strategic Human Resources Management: Aligning with the Mission.* Washington, D.C. USOPM, Office of Merit Systems Oversight and Effectiveness, September.

Chapter 3

Technology and Human Resources

Myra Howze Shiplett and Glenn Sutton

INTRODUCTION

Like all tools, information technology for human resources management functions only to the extent that it contributes directly to the organization's ability to carry out its mission and its strategic goals and objectives. Within this context, the promise of information technology (IT) is great, but it is not yet totally proven. Public organizations are spending millions of dollars to develop and install a variety of IT systems to support the full range of HR functions. However, only when the HR staff, line managers and others in the organization come to understand and to use these systems to their full capacity will the organization realize an appropriate return on its investment in information technology.

This chapter will describe how information technology changes the HR function itself, as well as the way it changes the relationship between HR and its customers. It will then cover how modern technology is used in various components of public-sector HR, benefits of the technology, and potential problems and issues created by the technology.

Today, many public-sector HR departments are using information systems to support their daily activities. The next few years will bring an explosion of high-impact technology solutions throughout the HR community. Technologies that will have the most dramatic impact on the HR function are Web-enabled applications running on the Internet and intranets and multimedia technologies including virtual reality. The concept of knowledge management (KM), although not a technology itself, will help enable the movement of organizations from traditional hierarchies to networked models. In that environment, HR will have an expanded and strategic role in dealing with issues brought about by the interaction of people and technology.

Many organizations use the Web for HR-related activities, including information distribution and relatively simple self-service transactions, but few use Web technology for complex transactions such as benefit calculations. Web-based technology is maturing, and HR departments are learning how to overcome the difficult implementation obstacles. As a result:

- Web-enabled applications will drive vast increases in the use of employee self-service, manager self-service, and HR workflow systems. Web-based expert systems will proliferate.
- The trend toward reengineering the HR function will continue. Centralized service centers, already becoming commonplace, will be the norm. Web-based services will be supplemented by interactive voice response (IVR) and multimedia technology, as well as by links to external resources such as financial analysis and counseling tools.
- Application service providers will deliver HR technology over the Web. Small organizations in particular will be able to use a state-of-the art HR information system to provide the latest technology to managers and employees without a huge capital investment, hardware maintenance cost, or in-house IT support. Larger organizations may choose to outsource selected processes to application service providers via the Internet while maintaining data control within their own HR systems.

Multimedia technologies will facilitate major changes in approaches to employee training or, more accurately, organizational learning. This will support the shift from a top-down training model, in which the organization prescribes a set of lessons, to a network-based learning model, in which individual workers and work teams engage in self-directed educational experiences.

Knowledge management and related technologies will create major changes in the way HR departments do business. Knowledge management (KM) is not a technology. It is a blend of strategy, technology, and people.

Most significantly, though, a new strategic role for HR will evolve from the need to resolve issues created by the interaction of technology and people, such as privacy concerns, issues around telecommuting, or the lack of clear boundaries between personal and work life. In the longer term, HR departments should become a valued part of the team effort needed to transform organizations radically.

For the public sector organization of the future, this role might mean using KM to share knowledge across external organizational boundaries, creating networks for leveraging skills and expertise. HR should have a role in teaching managers and employees how to function effectively in "virtual" work groups that cross organizational and geographic boundaries. Sector managers should look for ways to adapt to an environment of uncertainty and continuous change. In this scenario, close-networked relationships will need to be maintained among all participants: employees, managers, and such nontraditional contributors as contractors and consultants.

HR's role, then, will be to facilitate the "people" dimensions of these new relationships. Although the information technology function will provide the infrastructure (networks and communications) to support this role, HR will be focused on the intellectual capital held by the workers within, or networked with, the enterprise. To the extent they create systems to retain and update this corporate information in a user-friendly manner, public-sector entities will not only enhance mission accomplishment, but also facilitate their movement from today's hierarchy to tomorrow's network model.

RECRUITMENT AND STAFFING

The public-sector manager begins the recruitment and staffing process by creating a job requisition. This document, which may be in either paper or electronic form, contains the duties and responsibilities as well as the knowledge, skill, or competency requirements of the position to be filled. When approved, the job requisition provides the information that HR staff needs to begin its portion of the hiring process, which includes some or all of the following steps:

- Posting vacancy announcements,
- Receiving and processing resumes or application forms,
- Evaluating applicants—screening for minimum qualifications and ranking candidates,
- Referring candidates to the hiring manager,
- Acting on the results—notifying applicants of offers or nonselection and hiring or placing the selectees, and
- Analyzing data to evaluate program effectiveness.

Information technology is used in each of the above-listed stages. Automated job-requisition systems enable the hiring manager to create the job requisition electronically and forward it to the HR department through any required approval channels where electronic signatures are affixed along the way. This can be accomplished via an electronic form, filled out by the manager and transmitted to the HR department. Tools are also available to help the manager with the substance of the requisition, such as a competency or knowledge/skill database. Such a database would contain a catalog of competency statements, including those for similar positions in the agency, from which the manager could choose and insert into the job requisition document. Web-based or other automated job-posting systems mean that the organization's need for an employee with a particular skill set can be quickly and widely publicized. Techniques include posting vacancies on the agency's own web site or public job boards and transmitting vacancy information to employment service offices operated by the states under Department of Labor guidance.

Once the vacancy is posted, the agency can receive resumes or applications through online application processes. Among the options available are accepting electronic copies of the applicant's resume or providing on-screen forms to be filled out and submitted electronically. Some organizations may also use scanning technology to automate data from paper resumes or application forms. In either case, the HR staff will create a searchable database of applicant information from which to select the most qualified candidates. They will typically use *expert systems* to aid in screening and evaluating applicants. In the next step, an electronic referral list is sent to the hiring manager together with electronic copies of the applicants' resumes. Finally, the HR staff may use *database queries* for program evaluation. For example, HR can evaluate the quality of candidates attracted from different sources and marketing methods by searching databases containing information on the performance level of employees who were hired through on-campus recruiting, as compared to those hired through Internet advertisements.

Some of the benefits of these applications of technology are obvious, including faster processes that are more applicant-friendly than typical paper-dependent procedures. The fact that there is less paper and manual processing also means lower labor costs for the HR function. But other important benefits accrue. They include the automatic creation of records and audit trails. These are especially important in public-sector staffing because of the likelihood that hiring actions will be reviewed for consistency with public-policy goals such as affirmative action or veterans' preference.

Another benefit is better and fa≠≠fiˇ≠≠fiˇ≠≠fiˇ≠≠fiˇiimˇiimˇiimˇiimˇs permits identification of problems and adjustments to the staffing process. For example, a recruitment approach that is not attracting highly qualified applicants can be identified and quickly corrected.

Automation is not without problems and issues, however. Online application and screening processes may seem impersonal to some people, and there is always the potential for errors in automated screening and evaluation. Finally, these techniques must be used where they work and not forced into situations where they do not. For example, expert systems work well for entry-level administrative occupations but may not be effective in screening applicants for some highly specialized technical or scientific jobs.

Performance Management and Awards

Every organization must have a way of managing the performance of its employees, assessing the degree to which employees meet performance requirements and rewarding performance that meets or exceeds the stated performance standards. Performance management goals and standards should be directly linked to the organizations' strategic goals, objectives, and plans. Current theory on performance management assumes that employees should be assessed on both their organizations' performance as well as their individual performance. Although this is the desired state, the public sector's actual achievement of these goals is a mixed picture. Some organizations are placing significant focus on linking performance to organizational outcomes, but this is difficult, especially when the outcomes themselves are not readily measurable.

The typical process is to establish organizational and individual performance goals and standards at the beginning of the performance period (usually a year). The employee and supervisor meet to discuss the degree to which the employee is meeting or failing to meet performance expectations several times during the performance period. At the end of the period, the employee's performance is officially assessed. Depending upon the performance management philosophy of the organization, employees whose performance meets or exceeds the stated standards are given cash or other awards in recognition of their accomplishments.

Although most emphasis is focused on employees who are at or above satisfactory, performance management systems are also important in identifying and correcting performance deficiencies. Relatively few organizations understand the importance of managing such information strategically, much less having in place a strategy to manage the information and supply appropriate automated support. Consequently, information technology is used primarily to perform the administrative support functions of identifying:

- when performance management activities are due (e.g., interim rating, final rating);
- who must be involved (e.g., employee, immediate supervisor, reviewer);
- what rating is actually received and recorded, and
- what additional related actions such as promotions, awards, and salary adjustments are suggested or required.

These functions are found in either a "stand-alone" system, or more frequently as a component of an enterprisewide Human Resources Information System (HRIS). Because performance decisions are frequently tied, either directly or indirectly, to financial decisions of promotion or award, the administrative component of the performance management system is linked directly to the organization's financial system(s). In the case of an employee whose performance does not meet an acceptable standard, IT applications are also available to track a trial performance period and may link directly to employee relations, grievance, or appeals systems.

Equally important, information technology is used to distribute and collect the actual performance rating. Web-based applications provide the appraisal form directly to the rater and to the employee being rated. Most appraisal systems require the employee as well as the supervisor to complete an initial rating. In the more comprehensive appraisal methodology, such as the 360-degree system, colleagues, customers, and others who interact with the employee are also asked to provide input to the rating process. Web-based applications allow this information to be completed and assessed by the computer, thereby providing anonymity, as well as significantly reducing the resources invested in the performance appraisal process.

Finally, performance management systems can provide useful statistics about appraisal patterns. Organizations need to know such things as:

- Appraisal patterns of managers;
- Appraisal patterns by organization;

- Appraisal patterns by various demographics such as occupational group, male/female, minority group, grade level, and the like.

Such data is invaluable in assisting individual managers, the HR staff, and the organization as a whole in maintaining a performance management system that is fair, equitable, and supportive of the organization's strategic goals.

As with other HR applications, the performance management applications are useful in supporting the rater and the employee being rated, but they are not a substitute for the human interaction, the discussion(s) that must take place between the employee and his or her supervisor. All users of this technology must learn how the system works and be willing to use the system for it to be worth the investment made by the organization.

LEARNING SYSTEMS

This section will cover traditional training as well as electronic learning and distance learning. The public sector HR department's training-related functions typically include:

- Planning, including training needs assessment and analysis;
- Identification of sources to provide the needed training;
- Obtaining training services from sources outside the agency (including universities, technical schools, and other training vendors;
- Training delivery using in-house instructors, online courseware, computer-based training (CBT), or other media;
- Training administration, including processing and tracking requests for employee training, updating individual training records, and tracking training-cost information.

Training planning and administration functions are typically covered by full-service HRIS software packages. These systems help set up training programs and associate particular courses with individual positions. Workflow solutions enable maintenance of course requirements and facilities, instructor, equipment, and materials information for employees and vendors; individual record updates and course-completion certificates; and tracking cost data such as tuition reimbursement costs.

The greatest potential benefits of technology, however, are in the delivery of training to public-sector employees. Examples of this technology, known as "e-learning," are:

- Computer-based training (CBT), in which the student accesses the training material either on-line (web-based) or via other media such as CD-ROM. Most computer-based training requires the student to reach a certain level of proficiency or knowledge before going on to more advanced material. Proficiency or knowledge testing is built into CBT software so that the student can move at his or her own pace but will not miss important material before moving on.

- "Smart" classrooms that give instructors or facilitators the ability to deliver training at multiple locations from a single classroom; present instructional material from a variety of sources (such as video and real-time internet access); provide selected information to each student; and monitor student progress through an automated student-response system.
- Distance learning, enhanced by multimedia interactive technologies such as hybrid CD-ROMs with Internet connections. In this environment, the CD-ROM loaded on the student's PC contains the basic training program and embedded Internet links. Concurrent Internet connectivity allows interaction among participants (e.g., a work team) and the instructor/facilitator.

Trends are likely to produce significant improvements in the value and effectiveness of technology in the training function; for example, web-based training delivery, already proliferating, will grow and improve. New video compression techniques will remove current limitations of narrow communication bandwidth, making it possible to provide television quality video over the Internet and intranets.

Both classroom and workstation-level virtual reality capability will present realistic simulations for group learning experiences. In technical subjects, for example, students could use virtual reality to create and manipulate abstract conceptual representations, like data structures and mathematical functions.

CLASSIFICATION AND COMPENSATION

Fundamental to every human-resources management program is the classification of the work to be done and equitable compensation in return for work performed. Classification is the methodology used to identify units of work, group work units into jobs, and group jobs into career ladders or paths. Compensation is the methodology used to identify the dollar value of each job. Compensation may include only direct salary, or it may include a variety of other components such as recruitment and retention bonuses, awards, benefits, work-life programs, developmental classes and opportunities, and the like. Whatever methodology is used for classification and compensation, it is one of the more complex and labor-intensive functions in the human resources management program.

Information technology supports the classification program by providing software that prepares the written position description, and then performs the analytical process of actually classifying the position(s). The position-description writer software is loaded with descriptions of the work to be performed, the complexity of that work, the level of supervision required, and any other information critical to describing positions in an organization. When managers or the HR department want to describe and classify a position, they look among the descriptive materials in the database on duties, complexity, and supervision and select those items that most closely match the job to be done. This type of database would contain competency statements, typical tasks, knowledge or skill requirements, or training needed. The software then produces a written description. These systems are structured so that if the position does not fit the typical information contained in the database, the manager or the HR department may insert the description need-ed to reflect the requirements of the position accurately. Once the position is prop-erly described, the software can classify the position based upon the rules of the organization's classification system.

The value of position-description writers and the associated classification tools include standard language, greater consistency among like positions across an organization, ease of use, greater efficiency, and usually both the perception and the reality of greater fairness and equity. The statistics that the application gathers can be used by the organization to manage the classification program more effectively; for example, statistics can show which positions are used most or least often, which descriptions are the most or the least accurate, how frequently the basic description must be altered, and metrics for how long it takes to produce position descriptions. In today's world of shrinking resources and demands for greater efficiency in public-service organizations, the position-description writer can be an invaluable tool. A potential drawback, however, is that as changes occur in the nature of work, the technical systems must also be changed to avoid obso-lescence. A position-description library, even if available online, is useless if it con-tains outdated descriptions of work.

In most public organizations, compensation costs represent 70 percent to 90 per-cent of the organization's budget. The compensation system can include base pay, overtime, periodic increases, bonuses, awards, and promotions, as well as the mech-anism to update the compensation system as the dollar values of the various com-pensation tools are periodically adjusted. As with classification, compensation is among the most complex of the HR functions. The information technology that sup-ports compensation decisions and compensation management either can be a stand-alone system or, more typically, is a component of the organization's HRIS. It functions both to remind managers and employees when compensation decisions are due and to produce statistics that managers and the HR department can use to ensure consistency and equity between compensation decisions. This system com-ponent is directly linked to the pay and benefits administration described later in this chapter.

DIVERSITY AND EQUAL EMPLOYMENT OPPORTUNITY

A cornerstone of today's well-managed public organization is the principle that the organization's workforce must reflect the diversity of the population served. This belief is founded both upon laws relating to equal treatment of individuals regardless of race, gender, religion, color, disability, or other nonmerit reasons, as well as cost-benefit analyses that demonstrate that organizations with diverse workforces tend to be more effective and more able to meet the strategic goals of the organization . These fundamental concepts are supported by information technology applications that track workforce demographics, EEO activities, affirmative action, and EEO complaints. As with other HR applications, diversity and EEO functions can be stand-alone or components of an enterprisewide HRIS. As organizations revamp their automated systems, these functions tend to be included in the enterprisewide HRIS. Because of the sensitivity of the data, there are special considerations about data security. Most diversity and EEO components of the HRIS have limited access for the employee-specific data but allow full access to the demographics and statistics, which the system can compile.

The diversity profile of the entire organization and all its subcomponents is an invaluable management tool. Most well-done strategic plans contain mission-related goals and objectives concerning the diversity of the workforce. The diversity profile allows the organization and its managers to know whether the stated goals and objectives are being achieved by the organization as a whole, as well as by its subcomponents. This HRIS system component is frequently linked to other components such as recruitment, retention, classification, complaints, compensation, and the like. It is essential to know whether other decisions that directly affect individual employees are being made fairly and equitably or whether there are conscious or unconscious patterns that favor one category or group of employees over another. These patterns could show that men are more favored than women; it could as easily show that lawyers or engineers are more favorably treated than those in administrative support functions. Statistics alone do not determine whether or not there is a problem, but they do serve as an indicator of areas in which a closer examination is warranted. The important goal is to be sure that there are not unintended consequences of managerial decisions and actions that can have negative effects for individuals or for the organization. The organization's statistical and demographic profiles can be analyzed to identify areas of success, as well as areas which need attention.

PAYROLL AND BENEFITS ADMINISTRATION

Technology is the backbone of public-sector payroll and benefits administration because these functions have high-volume, transaction-intensive business processes. Payroll functions include time and attendance, and paycheck calculations, including tax computations and deductions, savings allotments and other direct deposits, and tax/financial reporting.

Benefits processes include health benefits, life insurance, retirement, and savings plans, for example, 401(k). In each benefit area, organizations carry out the following functions:

- Enrollment
- Records maintenance
- Benefit calculations
- Management and financial analysis of benefit programs
- Employee inquiries and changes in benefits and payroll status, for example, tax withholding or insurance coverage.

The principal technology used for payroll and benefits functions is full-service processing using off-the-shelf HRIS and payroll packages. Although many public sector agencies have and continue to operate self-developed "legacy" systems, most have adopted or are moving toward modern HRIS. A full-service HRIS will provide automated support for pay calculations, tax processing, garnishments, audit reporting, and interfaces to the agency's accounting system. On the benefits side, HRIS features include employee enrollment, flexible spending account management, and benefit calculations.

Possibly the most significant technology-driven change in the payroll and benefits area is employee self-service (ESS). ESS tools include use of the *Internet and agency intranets* for web-based employee access to information and initiation of transactions such as pay deduction changes and enrollment. Often, *electronic forms* are used to simplify and speed these types of transactions. *Interactive voice-response (IVR) systems* give employees similar access and functionality, using a telephone keypad to obtain information or process transactions and changes. IVR systems are usually linked to *call centers,* staffed by HR specialists who can answer questions or process more complex transactions. These specialists may be aided by an automated *knowledge base,* using expert systems technology to solve individual employee problems. Another method for accessing employee information is the use of *kiosks*. These devices, usually equipped with a touch-screen computer, are especially well suited to work environments, such as a hospital laundry facility, in which most employees do not have a desktop workstation.

Self-service technology gives employees a way to administer their own data and processes without paperwork or administrative support. They make it easy to walk employees through all the steps necessary to complete whole processes rather than just single transactions. For example, employees who marry may need to change their name, address, emergency contacts, dependents, beneficiaries, and tax-withholding status. Furthermore, these technologies provide an easier link with outsourcing providers. This allows HR to outsource selected processes while maintaining data control within the agency's HR management system.

There are, however, potential problems and issues with self-service technology. First, one cannot always assume that employees are technologically literate, so the HR department must provide ongoing training in use of the technology, online help, and access to human assistance. Further, technology is often not intuitive—applications need to be engineered and tested for usability, not just technical correctness. *Usability engineering* is an emerging field precisely because the systems cannot deliver services and benefits if they are not designed with the user in mind. Security and privacy may be issues of major concern for some employees, so safeguards and assurances are essential.

RELATED ISSUES

Because the application and impact of information technology is relatively new to the human-resources management function (except in the basic processing of personnel transactions such as pay and benefits), there are a number of related issues that must be understood and considered before the organization will realize the full benefit of its very substantial information-technology investment. These issues include:

Process Reengineering. After the basic system requirements are identified, but before actual design begins, the organization must examine the way it does its business to assure that the work processes and information flow are efficient and effective. It must also examine its policies to be sure that they are up to date and support the strategic plan goals and objectives. This will help ensure that the new automated system will contribute to more efficient and effective organization, and that the organization is more likely to recoup its substantial dollar investment in the development and implementation of automated systems.

Build or Buy. The organization must also decide whether it will build the system using its own IT resources or buy the software or service via contract with another public-sector organization or a private vendor. This issue is frequently one of the most hotly debated issues encountered. In deciding what is the most effective and efficient route to pursue, the organization needs to consider such issues as:

- What is the organization's capacity to develop and maintain automated systems?
- What is the most cost-effective alternative?
- How does the organization maintain the skills of its current IT workforce? How will it do so in the future?
- Are there economies of scale to be gained by purchasing off-the-shelf software?
- Are the organization's system requirements truly unique or just the result of decisions that have been made over the years?
- How rapidly is the underlying technology changing? What does this mean for system maintenance?
- How rapidly will the program (e.g., recruitment, performance management) change? If it changes rapidly, will the organization have the resources to change the IT system supporting the program?
- Are the HR systems integrated with other administrative systems within the organization (e.g., finance)?

Culture Change. One of the least understood phenomena accompanying the design and implementation of new IT systems in an organization is the culture changes that must occur if the organization is to realize a reasonable return on its IT investment. These include the following:

- The business processes must be examined and frequently reengineered. (See discussion above.)
- Systems users must acquire new skills, understand and accept new policies and workflow procedures, and understand how this new tool

contributes to the organization's ability to accomplish its strategic goals and objectives.

- The organization must make a long-term commitment in development and training to assure that user skills continue at peak level.

- Managers and supervisors must find ways to ensure employees whose work is now done by the new system that they are still valued and must find ways to ensure that these employees have whatever new skills are needed to perform effectively.

- Productivity improvements, which are frequently cited as the justification for new IT systems, seldom come easily or early. Depending on the complexity of the system, it may take six to eighteen months and sometimes longer for system users to become sufficiently proficient to actually increase organizational productivity.

- New IT systems frequently set off intergenerational conflicts within organizations. Younger workers who tend to be more IT literate also tend to be impatient with workers (usually older) who are not as conversant with information technology or who are frightened of the changes.

Data as a Management Tool. The justification for investment in information technology frequently cites that "more accurate, relevant data will be available to make better informed management decisions." However, this result does not come without a price. Those who must use the data to make better decisions must be educated about the system and its data capabilities and then held accountable for using the new tools in their decision making. Without this investment, it is highly unlikely that organizations will, in fact, use the data capabilities of the system.

CONCLUSION

Information technology is an indispensable tool for today's HR department, as well as for the organization's managers and employees. It allows discrete functions such as recruitment, performance management, classification, and compensation to be linked directly to each other and to accomplishment of the organization's strategic goals and objectives. IT provides invaluable demographic and statistical information. The demographics and statistics can then be used to analyze patterns of decisions to assure that these decisions are fair, equitable, and support the organization's stated principles, goals, and objectives.

In the end, however, information technology is just a tool to support strategic organizational goals. The successful HR department must recognize its power, its limitations, and the very substantial investments that must be made in the organization's human capital to ensure that investment in information technology actually pays a return on investment.

REFERENCES

Graduate School of Business, University of Texas at Austin. 1998. "KM: Answers to Frequently Asked Questions About Knowledge Management." February 1. www.bus.utexas.edu/kman/answers.htm

Hansen, Morten T., Nitin Nohria, and Thomas Tierney. 1999. "What's Your Strategy for Managing Knowledge?" *Harvard Business Review,* March-April, 106–16.

The Hunter Group. 1999. "How Knowledge Management Drives Competitive Advantage" White Paper. www.hunter-group.com/THG/ART/white_km.htm

———. 1999. "Information Technology Status in the Human Resources Function" White Paper. www.hunter-group.com/THG/ART/white1.htm

Le Tart, James F. 1998. "A Look at Virtual HR: How Far Behind Am I?" *HR Magazine,* June. www.shrm.org/hrnews/articles/0698webtr.htm

Martin, Alexia. "Electronic Service Delivery: Ratcheting Up the Value of HR," The Hunter Group, www.hunter-group.com/thg/ART/art47.htm

Mullins, Craig S. 1999. "What is Knowledge and Can it Be Managed?" *The Data Administration Newsletter,* December. www.tdan.com/i008fe03.htm

Rivenbark, Leigh. 1999. "Technology Requires a Shift in HR's Focus." *Society for Human Resources Management,* November. www.shrm.org/hrnews/articles/111899b.htm

Ulrich, Dave. 1999. *Human Resource Champions,* Harvard Business School Press, 1997. Quoted in "HR Imperatives: The Future of the HR Organization." The Concours Group.

Venkatraman, N. 1994. "IT-Enabled Business Transformation: From Automation to Business Scope Redefinition," *Sloan Management Review,* Winter, 73–87.

Chapter 4

Administrative Reform and Public Personnel Management

B. Guy Peters

The ubiquitous administrative reforms of the past several decades have influenced all aspects of public administration (Peters, 2001; Pollitt and Bouckaert, 2000), but have affected few areas of government as much as personnel administration. If we were writing about public personnel administration two decades ago, the principal focus of the discussion might have been on civil service systems and the mechanisms by which senior officials (who now are styled *managers* in most of the literature) are able to motivate personnel and to make organizations effective despite the rigidities imposed by civil service laws. Likewise, most personnel within the public sector were permanent, tenured employees who had accepted the implicit bargain (Schaffer, 1973) of relatively low wages and anonymity in exchange for tenure and often good retirement benefits, not to mention real opportunities to influence public policy behind that veil of anonymity.

The numerous reforms implemented within the public sector have produced a very different style of personnel management for most industrialized democracies (see Hesse, Hood and Peters, 2001; Klingner and Lynn, 1997) than that characterizing the traditional civil service systems found in those systems. Rather than being controlled through a compilation of general rules and regulations, public employees are now often employed on individualized contracts with very different rewards and expectations. Further, public servants generally have, willingly or unwillingly, renounced the "Schafferian bargain" of low wages and anonymity in exchange for job security (Hood, 2000). Civil servants have become more subject to dismissal and also more open to being blamed publicly for program failures. Public employees (especially at the highest levels) also have become able to earn much larger salaries than they might in the past, although those salaries are likely to be paid on a performance basis and therefore to be much more variable. Further, the accelerating levels of pay for senior public officials has opened them to even greater criticism about being overpaid relative to their contributions to society (see Hood and Peters, 1994; Sherman, 2001) and may have further undermined public confidence in the public sector.

Another way in which to think about the shift in personnel management is that there has been a shift away from thinking about the public service as an entity and toward managing diversity within the system (Tihonen, 2000). That diversity has some normative importance as governments continue in many countries to attempt to be model employers and to employ perhaps larger numbers of women, minority group members, and difficult-to-employ people than might be true in the private sector. The other dimension of diversity, more relevant for the arguments here, is that there has been a marked shift from managing the civil service as a collectivity toward managing it as a set of individual actors. In some countries, for example, Canada, that have had a strong collective sense of the public service, this change has damaged morale and recruitment (Ingraham, Murliss, and Peters, 1998). Especially from the perspective of the market reformers, this change has numerous advantages, but it also has some problems for personnel. Thus, this chapter will look at the implications for the continuing disaggregation of the public sector and the movement away from a corporate sense of the public service.

The basic argument of this chapter is that the continuing reforms of public personnel management, and with them the acceptance of greater diversity within the public sector, have created greater opportunities for career public servants. At the same time, however, or at least shortly thereafter, these changes also have reduced the desirability of working in many positions within the public sector. The logic of the argument we will present is that there was a first round of reforms, implemented mostly during the 1980s and into the 1990s, that created a number of apparent, and some very real, benefits for public employees. These improvements were primarily in terms of greater freedom for all employees, as well as some economic advantages primarily for the upper echelons of public organizations. There has also been a second round of reforms, to some extent in reaction to that first spate of change. This second set of reforms has reversed some aspects of the first (at least in some countries) and also has demonstrated to many public employees some of the dangers created in the initial reforms, as well as some of the virtues of "old-fashioned" public personnel management.

There appears little probability of public employees returning to those halcyon years (at least for them) of civil service systems, and they are in many ways left with the worst of both worlds. Despite reformers' attempts to reduce formal controls over the public sector and its employees, there are still numerous rules governing the recruitment, retention, promotion, and rewarding of public officials. Further, for the majority of employees, salaries and conditions of work have been little improved, despite some major financial incentives for the top of the public service hierarchy. There is also a tendency to reregulate (Hood et al., 1999) in this and other aspects of the public sector. This reregulation is in some ways worse for public servants than was the previous regime simply because much of the current regulatory style focuses on individuals rather than on collectivities and involves sanctioning after the fact rather than controlling actions *ex ante*. Therefore, public employees are left with greater exposure to personal blame for failures while gaining relatively little from that exposure.

THE DEVELOPMENT OF PERSONNEL MANAGEMENT REFORM

I have already alluded to the impacts of administrative reforms during the 1980s and 1990s but should detail those changes and the particular consequences for personnel administration. These reforms have a wide range of intentions and various targets for change, but all of them have substantial implications for public personnel, although some of those implications were designed into the reforms and others are more unintended. There are a number of ways to describe and explain the New Public Management (Hood, 1991; Pollitt, 1993), all of which capture some elements of the reality of that now familiar style of public administration. Not surprisingly, I will use the categorizations that I developed (Peters, 1996) to describe these reforms, arguing that there have been four basic varieties of change adopted and implemented in the industrialized democracies. Although I find these categories useful for analytic purposes, it should be clear that there is some overlap among them, and the reform efforts of the past several decades represent to some extent a mélange of ideas and styles.

MARKET REFORMS

The dominant approach to reforming the public sector during the past several years has been to attempt to make the public sector function more according to market principles. The dominant assumption of advocates of this approach to changing the public sector is that the failures of government are a function of the monopoly status of many public programs, as well as the insulation that individuals within government have from competitive pressures. Therefore, the obvious solution (within the confines of this approach) to any perceived problems in governing was to instill some form of competition into the public sector, whether that is competition between organizations or competition between individuals. Structurally, this has involved disaggregating large government departments in favor of numerous small organizations—often referred to as agencies—that are given substantial latitude in implementing policies and, in some cases, also in making policies (Hogwood, Judge, and McVicar, 2000). These reforms have been most evident in the Australia and New Zealand (Halligan, 2001) and in the United Kingdom administrative systems, but there are some elements of this style of changes in almost all administrative systems.

For personnel management, the implications of market-based reform have been to move the public sector away from formal, egalitarian civil service pay and grading schemes toward pay for performance and individualized contracts and to abolish most conceptions of tenure within the public service. Individuals working for government have become treated increasingly like individuals working in private-sector organizations, with many of the same pressures on individual performance and with many of the same possibilities for punishments and rewards commonly found outside the public sector. The evidence is that the implementation of pay for performance is often less than successful in the public sector (Perry and Petrakis, 1988) and that many employees have become demotivated rather than motivated by these market-oriented changes. Those findings have not, however, deterred the advocates of markets as the solution to public management problems; these advocates appear to believe that these problems with their pet theories in the public sector say more about the inadequacies of public employees than about the inadequacies of the theories. Further, there are some notable successes of pay for performance, even in countries such as Sweden, where one would not expect a market-oriented reform to be so successful (Sjolund, 1994).

One of the more paradoxical elements of the implementation of pay for performance is that it has been implemented to a great extent in those positions in the public sector where it is most difficult to measure performance, while those positions within government that are more repetitive and correspond to what Mintzberg has called "machine bureaucracies" less often have effective pay for performance. So, top managers in government commonly now are rewarded by individualized contracts and have large bonuses and raises, while the more routine workers have much less of that type of differentiation of reward. Comparatively, this seeming disjuncture between jobs and assessment is often a function of the power of trade unions that prevent the implementation of performance-based pay and that defend the prerogatives of lower-level employees.

PARTICIPATIVE REFORMS

A second, and almost antithetical, approach to administrative reform stresses participation. The central diagnosis of the ills of the public sector motivating this approach is that hierarchy is the root cause of failures. Hierarchy produces top-down decision making, denies employees involvement in their organizations, and also denies clients any opportunities for affecting their benefits and many other aspects of their own lives.[1] The assumption is that programs would work better if the people most affected were provided more opportunities to shape both their work and the benefits being offered. Given that diagnosis, the obvious way in which to make the system perform better is to permit both employees and the clients of programs enhanced opportunities to influence the decisions made by their organizations. Just as the market-based reforms were characteristic of Australia, New Zealand, and the UK, these more participative reforms tend to have been found more commonly in the North American countries and in Scandinavia.

The term *empowerment* is used to capture this direction of administrative reform (Kernaghan, 1992). The concept is that both workers and clients should be empowered to make more decisions and to have greater influence over policy decisions. In the extreme, empowerment has come to mean client management of public facilities such as schools and public housing estates, practices especially common in Scandinavia (Sorenson, 1997). Also, there has been some return to concern with street-level bureaucracy and the impact that the lowest echelons of public organizations can, and should, have on programs (Vinzant and Crothers, 1998). As well as being concerned with some general managerialist aspects of running public organizations, the market-based reforms also talk about empowering higher level managers to make more decisions, often attempting to provide that segment of government greater autonomy with respect to their nominal political masters.[2] All of this empowerment is intended to provide greater involvement and commitment and also to provide the organizations with the information and expertise possessed by the personnel.[3]

As well as involving public employees more directly in organizational decisions, this approach to administrative reform implies that decisions concerning personnel should also be more open and transparent. The shift toward teams in place of hierarchy implies that some decisions about the performance of members of the team and therefore about their retention, promotion, or dismissal will also have a more collective element. The market approach discussed above tends to conceptualize performance as a more individual attribute, while the participatory approach may look more at performance in collectivities while still attempting to assess the contribution of individuals to that collectivity, always a difficult managerial task.

FLEXIBLE GOVERNMENT

The third approach toward reforming the public sector argues that what is wrong with government is the permanence of government organizations and of public employment. The tradition of tenure of employment and the notion (especially in the Anglo-American and German administrative traditions) that public employment should be largely separate from private employment have produced (in the view of advocates of this approach) a public service that is perceived to be too expensive and also as being unresponsive to public and political pressures. At the organizational level, permanence is also deemed to institutionalize policy solutions that may or may not be appropriate for changing circumstances, given that organizations tend to be "path dependent," and that may therefore tend to perpetuate existing solutions.[4]

The solution for the perceived problem of excessive permanence in the public sector is, again rather obviously, to create greater flexibility for individuals and for organizations. For individual employees, this flexibility implies organizations using more temporary employees and also making it easier for employees to move in and out of more-established positions in the public sector. Permanent organizations may constitute a more difficult problem for the public sector to solve, given the existing commitments of these organizations to their clients as well as their role in implementing public laws. Likewise, many citizens may prefer predictability and permanence for the programs providing them services, even if that permanence may create some inefficiencies. Even with those problems, the advocates of greater flexibility believe that creating temporary, flexible organizations will solve many problems in government.

DEREGULATION

The final version of administrative reform, and perhaps the most important for changing public personnel management, is deregulation. This concept is not economic deregulation but rather the internal deregulation of the public sector itself. The argument of this approach is that what is wrong with government is the dominance of rules and regulations within the system. These regulations prevent public sector managers from exercising their talents and therefore produce suboptimal outcomes within government. For example, all the rules concerning the use of public money prevent public sector managers from using their resources effectively and may create perverse incentives for their behavior.

The civil service system typical of public employment in most industrialized democracies is a clear example of the use of regulations that constrain the capacity of managers to make their own decisions on personnel within their organizations. Therefore, to reduce the number of rules and open up personnel management to greater influence by managers appears to advocates of deregulation to be central to making government perform better. For example, the National Performance Review (1993) in the United States called for eliminating many of the formal constraints on personnel recruitment and retention, provided that general principles of the merit system were followed. This change in the civil service system permitted much greater managerial freedom but also opened the system to some questions about fairness. In other administrative systems, the deregulation of the civil services has been associated with a perceived increase in corruption.

SUMMARY

The administrative reforms of the 1980s and 1990s moved governments very far from their traditional "bureaucratic" pasts but did so in a number of different ways and therefore did so with a number of different goals in mind. In some countries, each of these four styles of reform was implemented in some form or another. For example, Australia and New Zealand have almost completely transformed their public management systems, using market and deregulatory ideas for much of top management but also attempting to empower lover echelons. The general outcome was to produce public sectors that have much less formalized control over the actions of their participants, especially over senior managers in government. The tendency toward reform was not, however, universal, and countries within the Germanic tradition have tended to maintain their adherence to stronger legal norms about managing within the public sector. This diminution of controls within the public sector in many ways lessened the accountability of government and also created problems of coordination and coherence that required further consideration. The formality and rigidity that had become the stereotype of the public sector was, in most political systems, relaxed, and governments became less predictable, both for employees and for citizens.

The consequences for personnel management were similar to those for other aspects of public management. The numerous rules and hierarchical controls that had characterized traditional public personnel management were abolished or at a minimum were softened in favor of greater managerial and personal autonomy. Further, personnel management was made to appear much more like that characteristic of the private sector, with less security and greater differentiation of rewards. Again, while this reformed personnel management had numerous virtues, it also seemed to make public control and accountability less certain than it had been under that older, and perhaps not totally unlamented, management system.

THE SECOND ROUND OF REFORM

One of the virtues of administrative reforms, at least for those of us who make careers of following them, is that one change will quickly beget another. The reforms implemented in the first round of change produced significant changes in the public sector, but they also created the perceived need among many practitioners of government for more change. Some of the second round of change was an attempt to reverse some of the excesses of the first, while other aspects of the second round merely built on the first and extended the change process already begun. There are no particular dates at which we can argue that there was a clear shift from the first to the second spate of reform, but yet there does seem to be a shift in emphasis and some change in the overall tenor of the changes.[5]

In particular, this second round for reform appears to be characterized by four problems within the public sector that were not so readily apparent during the first round. The first of these concerns arising in the continuing reform of government is coordination and coherence. As already noted the first round of change tended to exalt the freedom of individual managers and their organizations to make more choices That was in many ways a laudable change in the public sector, but it also tended to weaken the capacity of government to coordinate its activities; the type of hierarchical control implied by coordination became very unfashionable in the face of demands for greater empowerment for managers and employees. It soon became apparent, however, that some greater coherence was demanded in government and that empowerment and decentralization had gone somewhat farther than was optimal for the performance of government as an entity.

Further, as public personnel management was made more individualized, there also was a need to think again about the public service as a corporate resource, rather than just a set of individuals who happen to work for government. For example, Finland has moved perhaps as far as any other country down the road toward individualization in public personnel management but has come to recognize the need to think abut the civil service more collectively and to coordinate the careers of the individuals involved in government.

Accountability has been another of the major thrusts of change during the second series of reforms. We have already noted that accountability was to some extent undermined by deregulation, as well as by empowerment and also by some market reforms (see Gregory, 1998). This is perhaps the essential value in public administration, and therefore a number of political and administrative leaders have recognized the need to reassert the fundamental point that public organizations and public servants must be held to account for their actions. The methods for dealing with restoring accountability within government generally have not been the traditional ones of parliamentary or even judicial controls, but the fundamental principle has returned to a central position in governing (Aucoin and Heintzman, 2000).

Related both to the demand for greater coordination and the demand for greater accountability has been a tendency to reregulate the public sector (Hood et al., 1999); that is, after the initial reforms abolished a number of rules and regulations during the first set of changes, the second generation of reformers has found it necessary to create new sets of rules. That having been said, it is crucial to understand that the second generation of regulations differs from the first in several important ways. The most important is that the second generation regulation is *ex post*, while the first generation was *ex ante*. Managers now face the wrath of regulators for any failures, but they are allowed to make their decisions about how to reach policy goals and then be judged on performance. In *ex ante* controls, managers had to get approvals—for hiring, for purchasing, for using money—in advance. This *ex post* checking on the actions of administrators is certainly one form of accountability that has become increasingly crucial for control within the public sector. In addition, reregulation addresses issues of coordination through the use of the powers of central agencies to regulate and force organizations to cooperate (see Bardach, 1999).

The final, and probably the most important, style of reform in this second round has been the increasing centrality of performance and quality in public management. This emphasis on performance is an outgrowth of the first round of reform, especially the market-based idea of "serving the customer," but also stems to some extent from the quality ideas found in some of the participatory approaches to reform. The idea motivating this style of reform is that the fundamental purpose of reforming government is to provide better services to citizens. The initial round of market reforms focused attention on saving money and on efficiency, while this next round addresses the even more fundamental question of what is being produced. The market idea of monitoring the performance of individual public employees is extended in this approach to include organizations as well as individuals. Again, some of this style of thinking about government was included in the first round of reform, but that has been expanded and has become perhaps the motivating force for the most recent rounds of change. Further, in the second round of change, the performance of organizations and their programs has been linked directly to the budget (Radin, 1998) so that the assessment of performance has very real and significant consequences for the organizations involved.

The performance idea for driving reform is closely linked with the concept of reregulation mentioned above. A significant portion of the reregulation of the public sector is conducted around the performance of organizations. Again, the implementation of the primarily *ex post* controls is designed to permit managers to make decisions about how to reach policy goals and then judge them on how well they have reached their goals. This judgment of performance can be achieved in a variety of ways, such as utilizing publicity, and "naming and shaming" poorly performing managers and their organizations (Gosling, 2000), generally through providing comparative measures of performance among a set of schools, hospitals, or other public facilities A related method of assessing performance is using "organizational report cards" that provide somewhat more standardized objective measures of the performance of the organizations (Gormley and Weimer, 1999). Both of these performance systems amount to a form of regulation over government organizations.

CONTINUING REFORM AND PUBLIC PERSONNEL

The various styles of reform found in this continuing second round of change have a number of implications for personnel management. It is important to note, however, that this second round of reform has a more systemic than individual focus. The initial reforms addressed ways in which individual public employees were recruited, rewarded, and involved in the operations of their organizations. The drive to enhance the efficiency of the public sector meant that considerable time and energy was devoted to ensuring that managers were given the tools to make their organizations efficient and effective, with comparatively less emphasis on the outputs of those organizations or their connections with political authority. During these initial sets of reforms "serving the customer" was interpreted rather narrowly in efficiency terms, rather than as a question of quality, albeit with some ideas that the customer should have some greater capacity for identifying problems and complaining about them.

As implied above, the performance and quality approach is perhaps the most crucial aspect of the changes adopted during the second round of reforms, not only for changing government activities in general, but also for exerting pressures for change on public personnel management. The market-based reforms implemented during the first round focused on the individual performance of public servants and attempted to make them perform better by providing differential incentives. This pattern of rewarding (or punishing) individual performance continues and to it has been added a more collective dimension of performance. Not only is it important to assess how the individual is doing his or her job, but it is also crucial to measure how well his or her organization is doing and to relate rewards to that type of service quality as well.[6]

The emphasis on performance management tends to highlight the need for assessment criteria that are useful for both managers and for citizens. Given that a good deal of accountability has now been displaced to the public through performance criteria and reregulation, the criteria that are used to measure performance become crucial. Of course, in the political world, the criteria used for assessment can always become subjective, but having some sense of agreement over what government programs and their employees are supposed to be doing makes the process fairer and ultimately more effective. Even the most advanced systems of performance management appear to find it difficult to reach agreement, as indicated in part by the long period of time needed for reaching agreement on criteria for the Government Performance and Results Act of 1993 in the United States, and the number of escape clauses built into that process (Peters, 2001).

The ambiguity of the criteria used for assessment of performance by public servants and the apparent increases in the politicization of the performance assessment process raise a number of problems for public managers. On the one hand, these managers are often asked, or virtually required, to buy into a process about which they have numerous reservations, using criteria over which they may have rather little effective control. This process will be used to assess their performance and that of their organization, but they may have little capacity to shape the terms and hence are placed in some jeopardy by the process. Further, even if there is some agreement on the criteria for performance, most evaluative and legislative bodies feel free to alter the terms of any agreement largely at will. Especially in the case of legislatures they may feel (with some justification) that this is their sovereign right.

If formalized systems of performance management place substantial pressures on public managers as well as on the lower-echelon employees of organizations, then the less formal "naming and shaming" version of accountability may be even more damaging to morale and (paradoxically) to performance. The underlying logic of this approach to accountability is that if programs fail, it is almost certainly the problem of the managers and/or other employees of government. Such an approach fails to take into account all the other possibilities for failure, such as poorly designed programs and inadequate resources or even clients who are poorly prepared for receiving the benefits of the program. For example, the emphasis on accountability in schools in the United States and several other countries appears to assume that schools fail because of poor teachers and principals rather than because of inadequate spending or inadequate parental support.[7] In this version of personalized accountability, the administrator or service provider may be left with little protection and little opportunity for rebuttal.

Finally, the individualization of public personnel management may not be as advantageous to individuals as imagined, and it certainly has had some negative consequences for the public service as an institution. Movement in and out of government has seriously weakened many public service values such as probity and fairness, given that individuals not inculcated with those values may not see their value in managing. Further, the public service has ceased to be a corporate resource for government that could be employed as the government of the day believed most appropriate. Because of the loss of control through rules and hierarchy, political considerations have come in as alternative controls in many systems (Peters and Pierre, 2001). In addition, we have noted that career tracks within government are not nearly as well defined as in the past, so that the public service can not easily shape the careers and values of its members.

CONCLUSIONS

The two rounds of reform of the public sector have changed dramatically the way in which public personnel are managed. As already noted there has been a marked shift away from a corporate, public service conception toward a more individualized and generally more marketized conception of being a public employee. This means that public employees may have greater latitude in defining their own careers but that government may lack the service of a clearly defined workforce with a continuing commitment to government. This is a particular problem for the upper echelons of the public service where the movement in and out may be more significant, with individuals taking with them experience and perhaps also creating conflicts of interest when they move to private firms regulated by, or doing business with, government.

Although many employees may benefit economically from the market-based changes that have been implemented, they also face some significant losses. These losses include the elimination of security of tenure and also the blurring of clearly defined career paths that have been beneficial to government as an employer. By being defined as "just" employees, public servants are to some extent devalued and are further exposed to greater demands for personal accountability, given that more collective anonymity has been reduced if not abolished entirely. Thus, any improvements in the conditions of public employees may have been bought at some considerable costs. Further, these benefits and costs are not distributed equally throughout the public service. Indeed, most of the benefits and costs have accrued to the senior positions of government. The major exception to that statement would be the greater latitude that some lower-echelon employees have received in making policy decisions.

In summary, administrative reform often has focused on structural elements and formal reorganizations. Reforms in both rounds of reform discussed here have a much stronger managerial and personal element than most in the past. That managerial and individualistic element of these changes has, in turn, engendered the need to rethink government as an entity and to consider how the system as a whole coordinates its actions. Likewise, the initial round of reforms forces some rethinking of how the public service as an entity performs, both in serving its clients and in managing its own personnel. This dialectic between individualistic and corporate responses to managerial questions is one of the numerous dichotomies found in public administration and one that is likely to continue to shape governance.

NOTES

1. This is hardly a novel idea in the study of organizations. Going back at least to the Hawthorne Study, there is strand of human relations management that has stressed the importance of involving workers in their organizations.
2. Of course, some of the reforms implemented are also designed to disempower the career service and to return greater powers to those politicians (see Savoie, 1994).
3. The danger is that attempting to empower everybody may in the end empower nobody and may only engender greater conflict within the organization. See Peters and Pierre (2000).
4. Those solutions may have been successful at their inception, but their utility may be exhausted as conditions change.
5. Indeed, some of the earlier pattern of change continues even as some of what I am arguing characterizes the second round is being implemented. Still, there does seem to be a real and meaningful change.
6. There is, as yet, relatively little that has been done to square the circle and attempt to relate individual contributions to overall performance. To the extent that this is done, the assumption is that the manager at the top is responsible for all that occurs within the organization. This is an oddly hierarchical assumption, given that there have been so many other changes in the ways in which organizations are being managed.
7. This is a very useful assumption for politicians because it enables them to escape blame for their budgetary and taxation decisions.

REFERENCES

Aucoin, P., and R. Heintzman. 2000. "The Dialectics of Accountability for Performance in Public Management Reform," in B. G. Peters and D. J. Savoie, eds., *Governance in the Twenty-first Century*. Montreal: McGill/Queens University Press.

Bardach, E. 1999. *Getting Agencies to Work Together; The Practice and Theory of Managerial Craftsmanship*. Washington, D.C.: The Brookings Institute.

Gormley, W. T., and D. Weimer. 1999. *Organizational Report Cards*. Cambridge, Mass.: Harvard University Press.

Gosling, P. 2000. "An Inspector Calls," *Public Finance*. March 24, 5–9.

Gregory, B. 1998. "A New Zealand Tragedy: Problems of Public Responsibility," *Governance* 11, 231–40.

Halligan, J. A. 2001. "Australia and New Zealand," in J. J. Hesse, C. Hood, and B. G. Peters, eds., *Paradoxes of Public Sector Reform*. Berlin: Duncker & Humblot.

Hesse, J. J., C. Hood, and B. G. Peters. 2001. *Paradoxes of Public Sector Reform*. Berlin: Duncker & Humblot.

Hogwood, B. W., D. Judge, and M. McVicar. 2000. "Agencies and Accountability," in R.A.W. Rhodes, ed., *Transforming British Goverment, Vol 1: Changing Institutions*. Basingstoke: Macmillan.

Hood, C. 1991. "A Public Management for All Seasons?" *Public Administration*, 69, 3–19.

Hood, C. 2000. In B. G. Peters and D. J. Savoie, eds., *Governance in the Twenty-first Century*. Montreal: McGill/Queens University Press.

Hood, C., C. Scott, O. James, G. Jones, and T. Travers. 1999. *Regulating Inside Government*. Oxford: Oxford University Press.

Hood, C., and B. G. Peters. 1994. *Rewards at the Top*. London: Sage.

Ingraham, P. W. 1993. "Of Pigs and Pokes and Policy Diffusion: Another Look at Pay for Performance," *Public Administration Review* 53, 348–56

Ingraham, P. W., H. Murliss, and B. G. Peters. 1998. *The Higher Civil Service in Britain, Canada and the United States*. Paris: Organization for Economic Cooperation and Development.

"Is Ofsted Right To Attack Local Education Authorities?" *The Guardian*. July 1, 2000.

Kernaghan, K. 1992. "Empowerment and Public Administration: Revolutionary Advance or Passing Fancy?" *Canadian Public Administration*, 35, 194–214.

Klingner, D. E., and D. B. Lynn. 1997. "Beyond Civil Service: The Changing Face of Public Personnel Management," *Public Personnel Management* 26, 157–78.

National Performance Review. 1993. *Creating a Government That Works Better and Costs Less* (The Gore Report). Washington, D.C.: Government Printing Office, March.

Olivera Rocha, J. A. 1998. "The New Public Management and its Consequences in the Public Personnel System," *Review of Public Personnel Administration* 18, 2, 82–87.

Perry, J., and B. A. Petrakis. 1988. "Can Pay for Performance Succeed in Government," *Public Personnel Management* 17, 359–58.

Peters, B. G. 1996. *The Future of Governing*. Lawrence, Kans.: University Press of Kansas.

Peters, B. G. 2001. *The Future of Governing*, 2nd. ed. Lawrence, Kans.: University Press of Kansas.

Peters, B. G., and J. Pierre. 2000. "Citizens Versus the New Public Managers: The Problem of Mutual Empowerment," *Adminstration and Society* 32, 9–28.

Peters, B. G., and J. Pierre. 2001. *The Politicization of the Public Service*.

Pollitt, C. 1993. *Managerialism and the Public Service*, 2nd. ed. Oxford: Basil Blackwell.

Pollitt, C., and G. Bouckaert. 2000. *Public Management Reform: A Comparative Analysis*. Oxford: Oxford University Press.

Radin, B. A. 1998. "The Government Performance and Results Act (GPRA): Hydra-Headed Monster or Flexible Management Tool?" *Public Administration Review* 58, 307–16.

Savoie, D. J. 1994. *Reagan, Thatcher, Mulroney: In Search of the New Bureaucracy*. Pittsburgh: University of Pittsburgh Press.

Schaffer, B. 1973. *The Administrative Factor*. London: Frank Cass.

Sherman, J. 2001. "Union outrage at bonus for mandarins," *The Times of London*, January 17.

Sjolund, M. 1994. "Transition in Government Pay Policies," *International Journal of Public Administration* 17, 1907–35.

Sorenson, E. 1997. "Democracy and Empowerment," *Public Administration* 75, 553–67.

Tihonen, S. 2000. *From Uniform Administration to Governance and the Management of Diversity*. Helsinki: Ministry of Finance.

Vinzant, J. C., and L. Crothers. 1998. *Street-Level Leadership: Discretion and Legitimacy in Front-line Public Service*. Washington, D.C.: Georgetown University Press.

Chapter 5

Exporting Administrative Excellence: Adapting Advanced-Country Models to Developing Contexts

Barbara Nunberg

A global revolution is in progress in many advanced-country public administrations. Public human resource management has been radically altered in those governments where new managerialism has been introduced. In other countries, traditional bureaucracies have retained basic systems of personnel administration but are slowly modernizing selective features. As experience with these new approaches accumulates, agreement about what constitutes best practice in developed settings remains elusive.

Meanwhile, less-advanced countries confront their own thorny administrative dilemmas. Increasingly, government administrative capacity—in particular, the ability of the civil service to carry out its assigned tasks—is understood to be crucial to achieving key economic and social development goals in poor and middle-income countries. This understanding has energized efforts to strengthen public human resource management to improve overall civil service performance in third-world countries. So as not to reinvent the wheel, developing-country governments have long sought solutions to their civil service problems that combined home-grown approaches with appropriately adapted advanced-country experience. Now, in the midst of the ongoing global debate on administrative reform, third-world governments face hard choices about which civil service models or which elements of models should be introduced into their often resource-scarce, politically fragile environments. Can advanced country administrative approaches be successfully exported to less-developed country contexts? What works best where—and under which conditions? What should countries consider when contemplating adopting a public human resource management model with exogenous origins? This chapter probes some of the complexities associated with efforts to transfer advanced administrative models to poor and middle-income country contexts.

PUBLIC HUMAN RESOURCE MANAGEMENT IN DEVELOPING COUNTRIES—DIVERSITY RULES

The wide range of country circumstances and administrative conditions around the developing world defies simple characterization, but a broad typology may be helpful in identifying the main types of civil service problems found in developing countries. Although problem types tend largely to coincide with a particular region or income level, a given country may present a blend of problem characteristics.

- *Type One: Low-Income, Low-Capacity Countries—Dysfunctional Pay and Employment Policies.* This set includes low-income, low-capacity countries, characterized by a very thin human resource skill base and, frequently, by dysfunctional government pay and employment policies that have produced bloated but, on average, underpaid bureaucracies. Typically, type-one administrations may be found in sub-Saharan Africa but are also characteristic of some poor countries in other regions, where the state is commonly viewed as the legitimate employer of first resort and the provider of essential social welfare in the midst of widespread poverty. In type-one countries, restoring fiscal soundness to government through wage bill and employment rationalization is fundamental to moving on to reforms that focus on getting better civil service performance and improving the delivery of basic services linked to economic development (Lindauer and Nunberg, 1994).

- *Type Two: Transition, Post-party Bureaucracies.* This type refers to transition countries emerging from communist, party-dominated bureaucratic structures, such as those predominating in Central and Eastern Europe and in Central Asia. The main challenge confronting public administrations in these countries—many of which are endowed with staff who had been well educated, if narrowly or inappropriately skilled, under the communist system—is to transform state *apparatchiks,* selected on the basis of ideological loyalties, into professionalized civil servants, recruited and promoted according to meritocratic criteria (Nunberg, 1998).

- *Type Three: Middle-Income Countries Reaching for a Global Standard.* This set describes middle-income country administrations, endowed with reasonably well-prepared human resource bases and a set of established administrative rules and systems, that have been functioning moderately well but are now under increasing pressure to raise performance levels and to deliver services more effectively to citizens. Such administrations are particularly sensitive to the increasing weight of external demands for internationalized standards of accountability, transparency, efficiency, and integrity. Various of the civil services in countries once considered to be East Asian "tigers" fall into this category. Historically, these public sectors were considered relatively high performers. But the financial crisis of the late 1990s coupled with a new set of demands imposed by democratization and globalization laid bare the fundamental weaknesses in civil service management in many East Asian governments (Newfarmer and Nunberg, 2000).

- *Type Four: Opening Up Public Personnel Management in Emerging Democracies.* This type contains countries that have undergone dramatic political transformations and are especially driven to introduce equitable, depoliticized, merit-based practices inside government. Type-four administrations are also under pressure from civil society and from international donors to "democratize" their interface with their citizen public and to enhance the accountability, transparency, probity, and effectiveness of public service. Type-four issues clearly overlap with the other problem types described here. Emerging democracies in Latin America, Asia, transition Europe, and, to a limited extent, Africa are being pressed to solve type-four problems.

- *Type Five: Governmental Decentralization and Constitutional Restructuring.* This category applies to countries in which the structure of government—in particular, the relationship of central to local tiers of government—is undergoing a significant dislocation of power, functions, and resources that affects the work venue, responsibilities, and employment conditions of civil servants. In the main, these structural shifts are associated with a program of decentralization that involves either massive deconcentration of government activities or devolution of powers to subnational government units. In transition countries, modifications in government structures may reflect postcommunist constitutional rearrangements that create the separation of powers among executive, judicial, and legislative spheres of government. In new democracies, the need to enhance citizen voice by opening up access to government at lower levels may motivate restructuring. In some countries, decentralization may be part of an effort to hold together a national government that has been weakened by ethnic or regional tensions or other destabilizing cleavages.

The Advanced Administrative Menu: The Pros and Cons of What's Being Offered to Developing-Country Governments

OECD country administrative practice has been swept up in a dramatic global revolution in recent years. Many advanced industrialized-country governments have sought to reshape centralized, hierarchical bureaucracies that originated in the nineteenth century or before into more flexible, decentralized, client-responsive organizations, compatible with late twentieth-century technological and economic requirements. This wave of reform has left, in its wake, considerable convergence in public personnel practice in advanced countries; many administrations have been experimenting with the same or similar innovations, but there has also been significant variance among different public administrations. For some, reforms have been bold and comprehensive, representing programs of radical, systemic transformation. Others have pursued more modest strategies of incremental improvements in specific aspects of civil service management while conserving the basic core of administrative structure and practice. Most advanced countries can be situated along a continuum of change between these two poles. New Zealand, Australia, the United Kingdom, and Sweden, for example, cluster at the systemic, reformist end of the scale while the Asian cases, the United States, and Germany have taken more incrementalist approaches. France, the Netherlands, Canada, and Italy fall in the middle. Associated with each public administration model, a specific set of public personnel arrangements govern the civil service (Nunberg, 1995).

The range of administrative possibilities—and the uncertain outcomes associated with each of them—has left developing-country consumers of advanced administrative models with a dizzying array of options. What, then, are developing- or transitional-country "shoppers" likely to encounter when browsing this global supermarket of administrative models and public personnel approaches? What potential benefits and costs are associated with the adoption of one choice over another? Are there preferred mechanisms for transferring advanced-country approaches to developing-country government environment? The rough outlines of the public administration options and the associated human resource management approaches being pursued in advanced-countries today fall into three broad idealized models: (1) Classic Weberian, (2) New Public Management, and (3) - Modest Managerialism.[1]

Classic Weberian Model.   Classic Weberian administrations have provided the basic template in OECD countries upon which recent changes have been crafted. Initially introduced as a means to assure impartial application of personnel policies, Weberian bureaucracies have managed human resources through centralized, largely uniform systems, stressing merit-based regulations to enforce probity and impartiality. This model ushered in newly professionalized, largely honest civil services in many countries during the late nineteenth and twentieth centuries. In most countries, the emergence of these civil services coincided with rising levels of educational attainment, legal and constitutional reforms, wider suffrage, and the strengthening of mechanisms of parliamentary oversight and accountability. Weberian bureaucracies famously emphasize vertical accountabilities and routinization, discouraging customization and flexibility. By the end of the last century, many argued that classical bureaucracies, awash in procedures and red tape, also sacrificed efficiency by overly complicating otherwise simple transactions. Better performance might be achieved through the application of market surrogates to administrative practice, these critics conjectured.

New Public Management.   Disillusionment with uniform, centralized control of civil service management began to pervade advanced countries in the 1970s and 1980s. Governments came under increasing pressure to improve administrative efficiency and to render faster, better, and more responsive services to a client public whose demands were becoming more intense and more direct. Tightly centralized Weberian bureaucracies were attacked for failing to provide effective service delivery at affordable cost. The antidote to the Weberian problem came in the form of the New Public Management (NPM), which took root in one country after another. NPM began as simple "cutback management," seeking staff and expenditure reductions in search of lower government costs. It soon evolved into a broader set of input-focused reforms that gave departmental managers greater accountability and control over operating costs, subject to close financial supervision facilitated by advances in information management technologies. Over the next several years, reforms deepened to focus on outcomes, promoting even greater autonomy and flexibility to agencies delivering services. Following New Zealand's lead, some countries spun off such agencies from policy departments of core government, increasingly subjecting their personnel functions to market signals.

Modest Managerialism.   Many OECD countries, however, moved much more cautiously down the managerialist path. Various traditional administrations, such as those in France, Germany, and the Netherlands, pursued policies of administrative modernization without fully adopting a new public-management orientation. With enhanced information technology, they started to devolve greater autonomy to managers at lower bureaucratic levels, increased the focus on performance, and introduced greater flexibility in human resource management, but unlike the NPM reformers, civil services that pursued more modest managerialism retained centralized authority over core financial and personnel functions, keeping in place national standards for establishment controls and for staff recruitment, discipline, and promotions (Trosa, 1995).

Public Human Resource Management Approaches

These broad administrative models and technology developments provide the context for the more specific public personnel approaches currently applied in advanced countries, which governments in the developing and transitional world contemplate transplanting to their own environments. Among the many public personnel choices that need to be taken by countries trying to build strong civil service systems, there are two particularly crucial ones: (1) how to organize the overall civil service management and establishment control function;[2] and (2) how to recruit, promote, and reward civil servants. When developing-country governments are considering their options, they need to pay close attention to the types of issues discussed below.

Civil Service Organizational Structures and System Management.   In their purest form, Weberian administrations and NPM models offer developing-country civil services starkly different ways of organizing human resource management. Classic administrations centralize control but often with some degree of deconcentration. Usually, several central entities exercise shared authority with clear division of responsibility for policy guidance, merit over-sight, and financial control and monitoring. Nationally determined staffing tar-gets are often maintained through a coordinated effort by the central personnel authority and the finance ministry with heavy reliance on scrutiny techniques such as staffing audits or inspections.

In contrast, NPM governments decentralize detailed authority over virtually all personnel matters—recruitment, promotions, dismissals, position classifica-tion, staffing controls, and most training—to line managers, leaving only broad policy guidelines to be worked out at the center. Operating budgets determine optimal staffing levels, and money is fungible among different expenditure types. Salaries are largely determined by the market, subject to standardized guidelines and ceilings.

In principle, decentralizing civil service management (CSM) functions allows managers to tailor staffing to real requirements with more flexibility. In advanced-country practice, decentralization of personnel management functions has been implemented only when elaborate systems of computerized information and financial management to maintain tight reins on expenditures are in place. Techni-cal training and skill upgrading of staff throughout government are needed to make such arrangements work. Managers at decentralized levels must be pre-pared to make a range of financial and personnel decisions; line staff need to be capable of administering routine personnel movements and of feeding requisite human resource information up through the system (Schick, 1998; Kettl, 1997).

Frustrated by the same deficiencies that Weberian human resource manage-ment models present in advanced countries, a number of middle income, and even some lower income, countries have been attracted to the possibilities of enhanced flexibility and responsiveness that the increased managerial autonomy offered by the NPM models promise. The slogan "letting managers manage" that accompanies the NPM reforms has had particularly powerful appeal in settings where overall political liberalization has increased the call for civil service accountability.

Such autonomy also increases system susceptibility to fraud, patronage, and corruption, however. These are clear worries in developing and transitional countries of all types. Moreover, the technical requirements and skill-upgrading needs demonstrated in the advanced-country NPM experiences have shown that, to the extent that requisite skills do not exist down the line and throughout the organization, the tendency of central organs to "micromanage" through excessive information requests can actually result in an even greater role—and heavier management burden—for the center than in an initially centralized sys-tem. It goes without saying that the skill and technical gaps in most developing countries are that much greater.

But some selective deconcentration of personnel functions with limited devo-lution of authority makes sense for those middle-income countries with negligible establishment control problems, better personnel-management capacity, and high-er requirements for flexibility. But the feasibility of even modest delegation needs to be carefully assessed, as any devolution requires sufficient depth of skills in key points in the system to function successfully. In the end, centralized models of civil service organization and establishment management offer indisputable advantages for many developing countries—enhanced control and coordination as well as capacity for longer-term staff planning. These benefits probably outweigh the costs associated with rigidity and lack of managerial responsiveness for most countries. This is especially so for those governments with high pay and employment dysfunction. To ensure that the fundamentals of sound human resource practice are in place, these governments need to keep civil service numbers in tight check through central, uniform controls, at least in initial phases of civil service reform. Even relatively well-functioning, higher-income developing countries need to weigh carefully the potential costs and merits of NPM personnel management arrangements, perhaps moving gradually toward looser central controls, as human resource technological capacity becomes sufficiently developed to assume the burden of such complex systems.

Institutional Mechanisms for Staff Recruitment, Advancement, and Rewards. For all the developing-country types categorized earlier in this chapter, perhaps the most pressing challenge is how to attract, retain, and motivate well-qualified professional staff. This is all the more difficult for type-one countries, where societal educational attainment levels are low and the best and brightest are siphoned off by the private and, often, the international donor sector. In these settings, targeting recruitment, promotion, and rewards policies to capture the highest-quality staff is the key imperative for civil-service personnel management.

Mandarin or Market?   In contemplating the available advanced-country options for recruitment, promotion, and rewards, developing civil services face two main choices: (1) closed-entry, elite systems by which a "mandarin" class is selected, often from designated "feeder" educational institutions, to serve as leaders in a steeply stratified structure, with limited horizontal and vertical mobility and highly selective entry requirements; and (2) more open systems with lateral entry, greater vertical and sometimes horizontal movement, and more flexible, eclectic, entrance arrangements (Ridley and Blondel, 1969; Kim, 1988; Linde and Ehn, 1990).

Mandarin systems help countries address a number of public personnel problems. For very low capacity countries, the extreme dearth of qualified professionals argues for the urgent development of an elite cadre, even at the expense of a more comprehensive approach to staff development that also encompasses lower civil-service echelons. Mandarin systems provide an intensive means to marshal and groom a small, carefully selected, administrative caste. Even in the absence of competitive remuneration, these systems offer prestige, interesting and influential career opportunities, and access to international training and travel. These and other nonmaterial incentives can go a long way to attracting and retaining talent in government. Mandarin mechanisms that stress rigor in selection may also be a boon to type-two and -three administrations, where the merit basis for bureaucracies needs particular strengthening after long periods of excessive politicization.

There are, to be sure, serious problems in applying mandarin recruitment mechanisms to developing countries. Mandarin exclusivity can become exclusionary and may be vulnerable to attacks by those who see elite selection as a violation of egalitarian civil-service principles. Moreover, in many poor countries, the absence of credible educational institutions to furnish rigorously selected candidate pools can undermine the actual and perceived quality of the elite cadre.

There are ways to address these concerns. Steps may be taken to ensure that entrance into the selected cadre or designated feeder institutions takes place at multiple points along the career path and that meritocratic criteria are fairly enforced. Where general education-system weaknesses threaten mandarin cadre quality and raise suspicions of cronyism in selection, tightened recruitment criteria, possibly with external, even international, oversight, may be put in place. In the end, a hybrid approach may work best for many developing countries. Elite recruitment systems may need to be complemented by other selection mechanisms. Countries can compensate for education-system deficiencies through preinduction education programs as a means to targeting civil servants with customized training, or a mixed human resource management model may mean that some NPM market-recruitment approaches are paired with mandarin systems in developing countries. For example, generalist recruits inducted through a closed selection process can be hired alongside technical and professional specialists brought into service through more open, market-based competition on a decentralized basis.

But although such decentralized recruitment may be useful on a limited, supplemental basis, more comprehensive adherence to NPM's market-based approaches poses its own risks in developing contexts. This is particularly true for countries where the market for professional skills is dominated by international donor organizations that, in their quest to staff their own funded projects, compete among one another to bid up the price of scarce talent. The result in many developing countries has been a relentless brain drain that devastates efforts to build a qualified human resource base in government. The introduction of greater recruitment flexibility and managerial discretion also raises the potential for abuse and patronage in allocating civil service jobs. Of course, such infractions are still possible in systems of uniform standards, but the chances of abuse are lowered if standards can be made transparent and can be strictly and equitably enforced.

Tweaking the Elite Approach. Some developing countries have tried other means of building elite cadres through adaptation of senior executive service mechanisms, such as those operating in the United States, Canada, or Australia. The advanced-country experience has been mixed, and efforts to build strong, well-remunerated, interdepartmental senior executive corps have sometimes been stymied by fiscal constraints. Still, for the most part, SES experiences have succeeded minimally in establishing self-contained corps with superscale pay categories, introducing separate performance criteria and cross-agency training programs, and laying the basis for interagency rotation (Huddleston, 1991; Hunn, 1990; Dixon, 1990). The limited success of SES mechanisms in advanced countries notwithstanding, this is an approach worth exploring in developing countries, where the persistent pauci-ty of qualified higher-level civil servants argues powerfully for the development of a cross-service executive class. Moreover, the tepid advanced-country results may even provide useful lessons about how and how not to introduce SES schemes. For example, developing countries would do well to exclude political appointees and should be concerned to provide adequately long terms of service to ensure continuity. Governments should take care to keep salaries at high enough levels to provide attractive incentives. But the SES needs mainly to be identified with nonmaterial incentives, such as enhanced career and training opportunities and distinguished status.

Transplanting Modern Civil Service Pay Systems to Developing Countries.   Efforts to provide motivating but affordable financial rewards to government personnel have been at the heart of most developing-country civil service reforms. Ques-tions about how much to pay whom are hotly debated by national governments and have been central to internationally sponsored reform programs in poor and middle-income countries. A discussion of wage determination and distribution is beyond the scope of this chapter. But questions about the systems by which civil service employees are classified and paid are worth touching upon briefly, as they are key to setting the incentive framework for civil service performance. Advanced government systems for classifying and paying civil servants range from classic Weberian approaches, which emphasize centrally determined stan-dards with little room for individual deviation, to increasingly flexible and decentralized approaches. At their most pristine, classic civil services have relied mainly on unified pay scales with automatic, fixed step increments based on seniority and determined on a servicewide basis.

Many developing countries still operate with uniform pay and classification systems inherited from previous colonial eras. A powerful rationale for perpetu-ating such systems is that they appear to require less administrative intensity to maintain. Administrative simplicity is an important, perhaps overwhelming con-sideration for countries with severely constrained human resource management capacity. But experience in many developing administrations suggests that uni-fied classification and pay structures end up being anything but simple. Indeed, the basic tendency of uniform systems in developing contexts is to grow increas-ingly complex, with a steady proliferation in the number of steps and grades and the accumulation of a wide array of non wage benefits and allowances that serve to differentiate in practice what is intended, in principle, to be a standardized salary and classification structure. Such distortions stem, in part, from tensions between the managerial need to reward different attributes differently and the larger political imperative to suppress these distinctions. Circumvention of for-mal standardization is the consequence (Lindauer and Nunberg, 1994; Nunberg and Nellis, 1990).

Some solutions may be available even within largely standardized systems. One is to authorize more flexible pay and classification mechanisms that acknowledge the variegation and discretion that is already occurring in the system, introducing ways of injecting better professional bases for pay determination. One such approach would be broad-banding, which, in advanced countries, has tended to reduce the number of classification and grading categories and has afforded governments greater versatility in rewarding scarce skills. Locality pay has been another advanced-country approach that a number of developing countries have adopted to allow for greater customization of civil service pay to different conditions of employment. This has been an important element in civil services with national rotation systems that move staff among regional posts around the country (OECD, 1990).

The greatest flexibility on view at present in advanced countries is that associated with the most radical NPM regimes, where pay is largely determined by market factors for individual skills, subject only to loose guidelines from central personnel bodies. Some suggest that decentralized classification and pay arrangements offer significant financial efficiencies and promote better line management—potentially important benefits for developing-country governments hoping to enhance civil service performance at lower costs. But a complete relaxation of centralized pay controls poses unacceptable risks in countries where the fiscal balance is delicate and political patronage and corruption are commonplace. The acknowledged gaps in enforcement of the current uniform pay systems in many administrations notwithstanding, countries need to move cautiously toward non-standardized arrangements. Flexibility and decentralization should probably be introduced only on a limited basis, in direct relation to the management capacity of public personnel institutions at various levels of the system. Underlying more-flexible pay and classification systems must be a reasonable confidence that control over the overall wage bill and establishment numbers is reasonably close at hand.

Should Performance Matter?   A topical issue in public human resource management is how best to relate rewards to performance in motivating civil servants. To what extent are performance-based pay and promotions conducive to improving civil service staff productivity? Are there lessons from advanced-country approaches to this question that make sense for developing countries?

For many advanced countries, remuneration policies traditionally have operated on the basis of automatic, seniority-related increases rather than performance criteria. Various governments have now introduced some performance-based features into basically traditional pay systems (OECD, 1988). Singapore's civil service is now paid through a system that combines fixed annual seniority-based increments with minimally satisfactory efficiency bars that must be passed to ascend the salary scale. One-time bonuses have also been used. A few countries, such as the NPM reformers, have moved to install full performance pay systems in their civil services (Quah, 1991).

The claim for performance pay is that it underpins the concept of accountability, allows the public sector to compete better with the private sector for scarce skills, builds morale, and provides a rational means for allocating scarce personnel expenditures. Critics of performance pay claim that it overemphasizes short-term performance, produces more demotivated losers than happy winners, and biases rewards unrealistically toward quantitative measures, encouraging spurious, standardized norms that inadequately capture differences in civil service jobs. It also requires careful and, frequently, expensive management attention (OECD, 1988; Perry, 1991; Binder, 1990).

The debate about public-sector performance pay still rages in advanced countries. While this debate goes unresolved, what should developing countries do? Performance pay may be worth pursuing in the longer run, but it is not a top priority currently for most developing countries. For poor countries, the practical argument against performance pay stems from its cost and management intensity. Developing-country civil services are considerably less well equipped to deal with the implementation difficulties and unclear benefits that have been associated with performance pay programs in developed administrations. Given these capacity constraints, attention to performance pay must be seen as a trade-off against improvements in other parts of developing-country administrations. For example, nurturing a rigorous recruitment system or building a solid establishment control system may have greater medium-term returns than installing performance-pay mechanisms.

The case for investing heavily in performance-related pay is thus a weak one for most developing countries. At the same time, poor and middle-income countries might reasonably decide to incorporate advanced-country experiences with performance-related promotion in their civil-service human resource systems. Indeed, the use of some form of performance appraisal as a basis for career advancement and promotion, an approach that is now widespread in advanced countries, is well worth pursuing. Most performance appraisal-based promotion mechanisms are, of course, imperfect, with many of the same measurement problems as performance-linked pay (Daley, 1990; Glen, 1990; Fox, 1991). But in many developing countries, the alternative bases for upward mobility—unrestrained nepotism, mindless seniority, and pervasive cronyism—are undoubtedly far worse. In countries where standards have been perverted or have broken down, introducing performance-based criteria into promotion offers a good starting point from which to build a strong framework of merit principles. While informal, ascriptive practices of long standing are exceedingly difficult to curb, structured performance-appraisal procedures can be useful in professionalizing parts, if not all, of the career advancement system.

With all their flaws, then, centralized civil service models provide the most solid basis for public personnel management in many developing country administrations. Such centralization may well take place, however, through an arrangement in which power is shared and coordination is maintained among a limited number of organs, ensuring requisite checks and balances in the system. Sparely resourced developing countries need to weigh priorities in personnel management more carefully than advanced countries. They therefore need to focus on key functions such as establishment control and recruitment. In considering options for the latter, developing countries should develop approaches that emphasize elite recruitment but that work creatively to minimize the well-documented deficiencies in such programs. Such approaches offer developing administrations an important instrument for building a professional class in the context of weak human resource endowments. Likewise, countries should be slow to jettison uniform-pay procedures but should work to match them with more flexible approaches on a gradual basis. The case is weak for transplanting performance-pay approaches currently applied in advanced-country administrations to developing administrations, where measurement problems and management intensity offset potential advantages. But, at the same time, the benefits of performance evaluation as the basis for promotion offer a potentially better pay-off in countries where clientelist criteria for career advancement often prevail. That most developing countries will find adapting elements of classic administrative models most appropriate to their resource-constrained settings should not imply, however, that some of the higher-capacity developing administrations should not at least consider adopting some NPM approaches. Such civil services need, though, to be mindful of the substantial technological and human resource requirements that this model places on government administrative capacity.

TRANSNATIONAL INDUCEMENTS TO CIVIL SERVICE REFORM— PROCESSES AND INSTRUMENTS

The fit between a given human resource management approach and particular developing-country circumstances is, of course, key to the successful adaptation of an externally derived model. Perhaps as important as techniques themselves is the means by which the adaptation occurs, however. Indeed, the intrinsic difficulties and complexities in achieving civil service reforms—in any context—raise particular challenges for transnational adaptation. Civil service reforms may be the most complex and difficult to achieve of all types of public-policy reforms undertaken by governments. They require both high-level policy changes as well as intricate administrative and behavioral shifts throughout the bureaucratic system. Even if piloted in one sector or sphere, they must ultimately permeate through the governmental apparatus more broadly, placing a substantial burden on overall government capacity. Civil service reforms, often linked to changes in the larger political and constitutional framework, require political commitment at multiple points within the polity. National leaders must push reforms, and politicians throughout the system need to agree to support changes that could curtail their ability to distribute patronage. Political support is also needed from middle- and lower-level bureaucrats who—often themselves the target of draconian reform measures—must sign on to reforms or at least must agree not to sabotage them. Moreover, civil service reforms often need a boost of political support from the citizen public, whose pressure spurs reformers to make government more efficient or responsive (Nunberg, 2001).

In advanced countries, civil service reforms often evolved over centuries, mediated through many iterations of interest-group demands and government responses and through slow but steady institutional development. Many take the view that, given the importance of administrative performance to overarching goals of economic and political development, developing countries can ill afford this glacial pace of change. This urgency prompts questions about shortcuts to reform that may allow countries to bypass or "leapfrog" some phases of the complicated change process just described. Perhaps the most pressing query—whether and how such accelerated transformation can be successfully induced from outside—is discussed below.

National civil service reforms succeed to the extent that there is adequate motivation to push them through and sufficient capacity to carry them out. The three dominant types of transnational inducements that are widely used to catalyze the process of civil service reform and to facilitate the adaptation of advanced-country models to third-world settings vary in their powers of motivation and capacity building. First, there is the *global demonstration effect,* by which countries voluntarily emulate reform measures that have been successful elsewhere. The global demonstration effect assures high motivation and ownership but does not guarantee internal capacity to execute reforms. The *enticement of community,* through which a regional or international regime establishes administrative eligibility standards for prospective members, is another vehicle for transferring administrative models. This mechanism provides high motivation and, with additional external assistance and resources, medium to high capacity. *International development assistance,* which provides loans and grants to governments to reform their public administrations, sometimes under financial and political pressure, is a third transnational instrument of reform. International development assistance can help boost country capacity but has difficulty in inspiring reformer motivation (Nunberg, 1999).

Global Demonstration Effect—The Administrative Zeitgeist.   The global demonstration effect of the public management revolution occurring in advanced countries has been an important external influence on domestic civil service reform. Both radical NPM approaches as well as more modest shifts toward devolved authority and performance orientation in the classical administrations have found admirers among developing-country governments. Costa Rica's Ministry of Planning has experimented with a performance management budgeting and planning system patterned after elements in the anglophone models. Other countries as diverse as Latvia, Jamaica, Brazil, Mongolia, and Thailand are exploring ways to incorporate NPM practice into their administrations. Even lower-income countries are trying out managerial solutions: Zambia's government launched an autonomous management system in the health sector that pares down policy functions to a small central ministry and spins off managerial discretion to boards that, in turn, devolve hands-on decision-making responsibilities to service delivery agencies.

In each of these countries, reform measures have been taken not as a response to international development assistance but as a result of the exposure of top policy makers to worldwide currents of administrative reform and the resulting interest in trying out innovations in their own countries. In designing Brazil's recent civil service reform legislation, the minister of state reform consciously modeled the design of autonomous social entities on the U.K.'s Next Steps program, which he had studied at great length, having met one of its key architects at an international symposium. Thailand explicitly emulated New Zealand's reform programs when it conceived its own autonomous agency law. In Mongolia, a group of private New Zealand consultants captured the attention of a state minister who spearheaded a radical reform movement that bore many hallmarks of the most radical NPM reforms.

Disseminated through the force of ideas rather than direct intervention, such initiatives reflect a kind of "zeitgeist" of administrative reform. This spontaneous, demand-driven approach to importation of foreign administrative models reflects a considerable degree of country "ownership" and highly motivated policy makers. It also poses dangers. Countries enamored with a particular foreign model may be inclined to apply it without careful attention to the prerequisite conditions and capacity for doing so. In Thailand, for example, the absence of financial management safeguards to keep autonomous agencies in fiscal check raised concerns about the timing of the new legislation. In Zambia, decentralized health-sector hiring threatened to undermine overall government establishment control, already in extreme disarray for the civil service as a whole. Proceeding down the radical NPM route also requires considerable political consensus. Implementation of Mongolia's bold and comprehensive NPM reform legislation was stalled when a new government rejected the reform's basic premise. In postconflict Lebanon, national architects of the new public administration designed a system with a proliferation of departments, an arcane web of human resource regulations, and a complex approach to financial inspections. The system was modeled after the French administrative apparatus but was ill matched to the war-torn Lebanese government's own constrained managerial capacity.

Emulation is not the only response to the global demonstration effect. For many countries, the reception to advanced country models has been largely negative. New approaches, such as the New Public Management, have been spurned not only for their administrative maladroitness, but also for their lack of fit with local political, cultural, and historical circumstances. For example, New Public Management approaches should logically have resonated strongly with many countries in Central and Eastern Europe. Such countries possessed many of the prerequisites for successful transplantation of NPM: high human resource endowments, good technical capacity, and well-developed technology infrastructure. Moreover, many countries in the region actually had a legacy of decentralized human resource management that would have made adaptation to decentralized arrangements implicit in the NPM model relatively painless. Indeed, "branch ministries" under the communist system had had surprising autonomy in personnel management matters, but with the exception of Latvia, most transition countries actively rejected NPM. In addition to their cultural affinity with more classical, legal-formal traditions associated with neighboring countries in continental Europe, CEE administrations were also concerned that loosening central personnel management controls would not help solve—and, indeed, might even undermine remedies to—their critical problem: building a depoliticized merit system with standardized application of rules (Nunberg, 1999).

The Enticement of Community: Reaching for Transnational Organization Membership.
Another increasingly important transnational inducement to administrative
reform is the prospect of accession to membership in a common economic or political framework. Clearly, these mechanisms have, so far, held the greatest sway in
Europe. In Central and Eastern Europe (CEE), reforms of both local government
electoral and administrative institutions have frequently been guided by precepts
set forth in the Council of Europe, which inducted a number of CEE countries
early in the transition from communism to democracy. The increasing conformity
to COE standards has been reinforced by technical assistance and participation in
international conferences. But the basic impetus toward standardization comes
from the common reference point provided by COE membership to the countries
of the East.

The prospect of European Union accession is probably the most powerful
inducement to administrative reform in those countries for which membership
looms largest. Countries preparing for EU membership were initially prompted to
undertake those administrative reforms most closely tied to meeting EU member
standards for particular types of procedures that bear most directly on joint
arrangements for intermember interactions through travel and customs. In some
cases, this coincided with functions that had significant interface with citizens
who were demanding better, more "user-friendly" services. Hungary's Ministry of
Interior—once an ominous symbol of the iron hand of the communist police
state—was transformed into a client-oriented organization by revamping passport
services to meet EU requirements, opening up travel for a broad spectrum of Hun-
garians.

The "carrot" of EU membership has played an important part in motivating a
number of Central and Eastern European governments to initiate even more far-
reaching administrative and human resource management reforms to shape their
civil servants in the image of current EU member states. Estonia and the Czech
Republic built special units of carefully selected, highly internationalized staff to
establish a competent interlocutor on EU matters (Nunberg, 2000). Such units had
the effect of creating a core elite that is being extended gradually to other parts of
the state administration. Hungary vastly expanded training programs and introduced a salary supplement program to attract personnel with the requisite technical and managerial skills to handle the new norms that would come with EU
accession in every government sector. Prospective EU membership had perhaps
its most dramatic impact on Poland's civil service reform process. Different political factions had long been embattled over the eligibility requirements for a new
civil service and the transition process by which the communist employment
arrangements would be phased out. Reforms seemed permanently stalled when
the promise of EU accession helped opposing parties quell long-standing, divisive
wrangling over these issues. In 1996, a long awaited Civil Service Act, containing
compromises on the merit criteria underlying the new civil service, was approved
with multipartisan support.

Admittedly, it may be difficult to replicate the powerful regional and commu-
nitarian incentives associated with the European Union in other parts of the devel-

oping world. But it is not too farfetched to predict that the application of a common set of transnational standards is likely to play an increasingly important role in pushing countries to strengthen human resource management in their civil services. In East Asia, for example, civil services once viewed as relatively competent and meritocratic, such as Korea's or Thailand's, have come under increased scrutiny for their possible role in the widespread cronyism and corruption reputedly associated with the 1997 financial crisis. Many of the global pressures to raise government transparency and accountability in financial reporting have spawned analogous demand for greater probity and better performance in the civil service. This has energized both countries to undertake far-reaching civil service modernization programs. These programs have specifically sought to inject elements of performance management into human resource procedures that, for years, had been based on uniformity and automaticity.

Development Assistance for Administrative Reform: Does It Work?   For most developing countries, the principal transnational inducement mechanism for administrative reform remains that of international development assistance, which cannot, of course, offer the kinds of carrots provided by promises of EU accession to prospective members. But can development assistance perhaps provide incentives that can simulate those of community enticements? Or, in the absence of such "sweeteners," can international development assistance find alternative instruments to promote civil service improvements? Below, some recent international development assistance experience in supporting civil service reform suggests that some approaches work better than others and that some new ways of thinking may offer more promising outcomes.

Two Approaches.   Over the last several decades, efforts to reform civil services have used one of two approaches. A large number of multilateral and bilateral donors, nongovernmental organizations, academic institutions, and independent consulting services have provided assistance on administrative reform to developing countries through programs that provided advice, technical support and training in a kind of *"slow drip,"* which financed limited, low-level ongoing reform initiatives but did not apply conspicuous leverage or powerful incentives to exhort countries to make fundamental or radical changes. Although definitive evaluations of such programs have been largely absent, the anecdotal picture suggests that this mode of assistance has had at best very modest effect in raising civil service capacity.

An antidote to the slow drip approach is the *big-buck-big-bang, fast-burn* approach to administrative reform that emerged in the era of structural adjustment lending (Nunberg, 1999). Fashioned mainly by the World Bank and other International Financial Institutions, support was provided for civil service reform through policy-based lending that required significant structural reforms, primarily of civil service pay and employment practices, in exchange for significant balance of payments support directly provided to the national treasury. Such adjustment lending tended to be quick disbursing, focusing on discrete government actions rather than longer-term institutional changes. As adjustment lending evolved, however, it was increasingly accompanied by technical assistance loans to provide some institutional support for implementation of required policy reforms.

Policy-based adjustment lending for civil service (and other structural policy) reforms has been used successfully to provide support for difficult measures in the context of severe economic crisis, where governments facing hard realities have already demonstrated the will to act. Thus, adjustment lending was useful in supporting civil service downsizing reforms in Argentina and Hungary during their respective economic contractions. Indeed, policy-based lending appears to be most effective at reinforcing decisions already taken and at supporting short-term initiatives such as employment cutbacks. Despite its conditionality, policy-based lending has been less helpful in pressuring governments to undertake reforms lacking in indigenous political support. Moreover, its quick-disbursing nature makes it a poor instrument for sustaining reform efforts over the medium or long term.

Lately, international development institutions have been rethinking their approach to civil service reform. They are struggling to move beyond support for short-term, one-shot, civil service downsizing measures through adjustment lending, and they no longer see much promise in isolated assistance that does not emphasize larger political, institutional, and financial incentive frameworks. The new approach emphasized in international development financing has begun to target more comprehensive institutional programs that can be designed, discussed—and even changed—over a longer time period. Programmatic lending for civil service reform is likely to include a constellation of human resource management reforms geared toward achieving mutually agreed goals over several years (World Bank, 2000). Recent World Bank support for civil service reform in Latvia and Zambia has taken this approach, for example. In Thailand, a programmatic loan for public-sector reform is now the basis for a looser agreement framework where reforms are financed independently by government but retain access to advice and dialogue with the World Bank and other international centers of expertise. Such programs are of recent origin and have yet to bear fruit, so they should by no means be seen as a panacea to all the problems raised in this chapter. To the extent that they aim at pairing capacity enhancement with national incentives for reform, they represent a potential analogue for countries across the developing world to the powerful example of the community principle being played out among the European Union accession countries (Nunberg, 1998; World Bank, 2000).

CONCLUSIONS

Developing-country governments find themselves in a difficult quandary as they attempt to effect "administrative catch-up" upon entering the new century. In some respects, civil service reform in the third world should be growing easier. After all, the centrality of public personnel management to successful achievement of middle-income-country economic- and social-development agendas is now widely understood and accepted. This means that domestic support for such reforms should be more readily mustered, and international financing of civil service reforms should be more forthcoming. It could also be argued that developing countries are facing these dilemmas at a propitious moment, when the global administrative revolution has produced a wellspring of new approaches and technologies that can boost human resource efficiency and effectiveness dramatically, allowing less-well-off countries to profit from the experience of the advanced world.

This chapter has argued that things are not that simple. Grabbing the brass ring of administrative excellence requires preconditions that many developing countries lack. Many advanced-country approaches work well in environments where human resource capacity is high, political and cultural traditions are conducive to responsible and responsive administration, and technologies and financial resources are ample. The converse is true for most poor and even middle-income settings where advanced models might be transplanted. In some cases, the political, cultural, or historical fit may be wrong.

Finally, questions about the nature of the transfer mechanism itself continue to plague efforts to modernize civil-service human resource management in developing countries. Countries may embark on reforms because they wish to emulate models that have captured their attention and admiration. But the capacity to replicate such models has proven elusive. Among the luckier developing countries are those that aspire to membership in a larger community—such as the EU. Such administrations have a powerful incentive to match their own administrative reforms with those of current members, and they are likely to receive substantial community support to do so. Less fortunate are those developing countries that must depend on international aid to institute reforms. The international development-assistance record on supporting civil service reforms has been checkered. Support has either been too anemic and gradual to energize comprehensive reforms, or it has been too externally driven and short lived to sustain prolonged institutional change. Emerging approaches, emphasizing domestic ownership, longer-range incentive-based programs with substantial support show promise, but the experience is too new to know what the impact will be. The challenges facing developing-country civil services are daunting. Perhaps their best hope for attaining administrative excellence lies in the accelerated pace at which global knowledge is being diffused about innovative approaches—and about what works—and what does not—under which conditions.

NOTES

1. Another product in this global marketplace is E-government. The application of electronic techniques to public personnel functions has emerged in a range of advanced countries of late, with potentially important implications for developing-country administrations (OECD 1996). This trend transcends any particular administrative model, however, and is not analyzed in this chapter.
2. Establishment control (or establishment management) refers to the systems and procedures governing the wage and employment arrangements for the main body of staff

working for the civil service (commonly referred to as the "establishment" in British parlance). Establishment management controls include payroll systems, staff planning and budgeting processes, and wage-bill management. Key hallmarks of good public personnel management include: the degree to which governments keep establishment numbers in check and the degree to which civil service pay is set at levels that are sufficient to attract the right talent to government. Good establishment management also means that aggregate personnel spending is kept within an affordable envelope in line with overall government revenues as well as other public expenditures.

REFERENCES

Binder, Alan S. 1990. ed., *Paying for Productivity.* Washington, D.C.: The Brookings Institution.

Daley, Dennis M. 1990. "The Civil Service Reform Act and Performance Appraisal: A Research Note on Federal Employee Perceptions." *Public Personnel Management* 19, 3 (Fall 1990): 245–51.

Dixon, Daryl. 1990. *Senior Executive Service: Gaining Most Advantage from Your Remuneration Package.* Sidney: Premier's Department, 1990.

Fox, Charles. 1991. "Employee Performance Appraisal: The Keystone Made of Clay." In *Public Personnel Management: Current Concerns, Future Challenges,* Second Edition. Carolyn Ban and Norma Riccucci, eds. New York: Longman, pp. 58–72.

Glen, Robert. (1990) "Performance Appraisal: An Unnerving Yet Useful Process." *Public Personnel Management* 19, 1 (Spring 1990): 1–10.

Hood, Christopher. "Exploring Variations in Public Administration Reform of the 1980s." In *Civil Service Systems in Comparative Perspective.* Hans A. G. M Bekke, James L. Perry, and Theo A.J.Toonen, eds. Indiana University Press.

Huddleston, Mark W. 1991."The Senior Executive Service: Problems and Prospects for Reform." In *Public Personnel Management: Current Concerns, Future Challenges,* Second Edition. Carolyn Ban and Norma Riccucci, eds. New York: Longman, pp. 175–89.

Hunn, D.K. 1990. "New Zealand Senior Executive Service: Contract or Career Service." Canberra: *Canberra Bulletin of Public Administration* 61 (July 1990): 158–60.

Kettl, Donald F. 1997. "The Global Revolution in Public Management: Driving Themes, Missing Links." *Journal of Policy Analysis and Management.* Vol. 16, no. 3, p. 446–62.

Kim, Paul. 1998. *Japan's Civil Service System: Its Structure, Personnel and Politics.* Westport: Greenwood Press.

Kraus, Ellis S., and Michio Muamatsu. 1990. "The Japanese Administrative Elite." Paper presented at the Annual Meeting of the American Political Science Association, San Francisco, August 30.

Lindauer, David, and Nunberg, Barbara. 1994. *Rehabilitating Government: Pay and Employment Reform in Africa.* Washington, D.C.: World Bank.

Linde, Claes, and Peter Ehn. 1990. "The Swedish Administrative Elite." Paper prepared for Annual Meeting of the American Political Science Association, San Francisco, August 30.

Meyers, Ronald, and Robert Lacey. 1994. "Consumer Satisfaction, Performance and Accountability in the Public Sector." Paper presented at the International Institute of Administrative Sciences Annual Meetings, United Arab Emirates, July.

Newfarmer, Richard, and Nunberg, Barbara. 2000. "Responding to the Governance Challenge." In *East Asia Recovery and Beyond.* Ch. 5., Washington, D.C.: World Bank.

Nunberg, Barbara. 2001. "The Politics of Administrative Change: Reforming the State in Hungary." In *The Politics of Administrative Reform,* Blanca Heredia and Benjamin Schneider, eds. Forthcoming.

———. 2000. "Ready for Europe? Public Administration Reform and European Union Accession in Central and Eastern Europe." Washington, D.C.: World Bank Technical Paper No. 466.

———. 1999. "Leading the Horse to Water: Transnational Inducements to Administrative Reform." In James L. Perry, *Research in Public Administration*, vol. 5. Stamford, Conn.: JAI Press, Inc., pp. 19–38.

———. 1998. *The State After Communism: Administrative Transitions in Central and Eastern Europe*. Washington, D.C.: World Bank.

———. 1996. "Rethinking Civil Service Reform: An Agenda for Smart Government." Washington, D.C.: World Bank Discussion Paper.

———. 1995. "Managing the Civil Service: Reform Lessons from Advanced Industrialized Countries." Washington D.C.: World Bank Discussion Paper No. 204.

———. 1990. "Public Sector Management Issues in Structural Adjustment Lending." World Bank Discussion Paper No. 99. Washington, D.C. :World Bank.

Nunberg, Barbara, and L. Barbone. 1999. "Breaking Administrative Deadlock in Poland: Internal Obstacles and External Incentives." In Barbara Nunberg, *The State After Communism: Administrative Transitions in Central and Eastern Europe*. Washington, D.C.: World Bank.

Nunberg, Barbara, and John Nellis. 1990. "Civil Service Reform and the World Bank," Washington, D.C.: World Bank. PRE Working Paper 422.

OECD. 1996. *Governance in Transition: Public Management Reforms in OECD Countries*. Paris: OECD.

———. 1990. *Flexible Personnel Management in the Public Service*. Paris: OECD.

———. 1988. "Recent Trends in Performance Appraisal and Performance-Related Pay Schemes in the Public Service." Paris: Public Management Studies No. 4.

Perry, James L. 1991."Linking Pay to Performance: The Controversy Continues." In *Public Personnel Management: Current Concerns, Future Challenges*, First Edition. Carolyn Ban and Norma Riccucci, eds. New York: Longman, pp. 73–86.

Quah, Jon S.T. 1991. "Administrative Reform: Singapore Style." *International Review of Administrative Sciences* 57: 85–100.

Ridley, F., and J. Blondel. 1969. *Public Administration in France*. 2nd ed. New York: Barnes and Noble.

Schick, A. 1998. "Why Most Developing Countries Should Not Try New Zealand's Reforms."*The World Bank Research Observer*, 13 (1) (February), 123–33.

Trosa, Sylvie. 1995. *Moderniser L'Administration: Comment font les autres?* Paris: Les Editions D'Organisation.

World Bank. 2000. *Reforming Public Institutions and Strengthening Governance: A World Bank Strategy*. Washington, D.C.: World Bank.

Chapter 6

The Immortality of Affirmative Action

Norma M. Riccucci

INTRODUCTION

As we move into the twenty-first century, the contours of affirmative-action law continue to be reshaped by the courts. Moreover, voters across the country are initiating referenda to dismantle affirmative action in public-sector employment, contracting, and education, similar to what the voters of California did with Proposition 209 in 1996. To complicate matters even further, the politics surrounding affirmative action suggest that imminent changes to the composition of the federal courts, including the U.S. Supreme Court, can lead to a pendulum swing in an opposite direction in terms of the legality and constitutionality of affirmative action. To say the least, such ambiguity and volatility create significant challenges for personnel and human resources managers.

Interestingly enough, in the wake of voter initiatives and court rulings against the way in which affirmative-action programs operate, both the public- and private-sector employers have opted to continue their reliance on affirmative action. Whether to diversify their workforces or stave off future lawsuits by protected-class persons, employers are not willing to scrap their long-standing affirmative-action programs.

This chapter begins by discussing the current legal status of affirmative action as defined by the courts as well as voter referenda.[1] It then illustrates that, despite the regressive court rulings and voter initiatives, affirmative action continues to prevail and indeed may have reached a point of immortality.

AFFIRMATIVE ACTION AND THE COURTS

Affirmative action has been defined in many ways (see Rosenbloom, 1977; Kellough, 1991; Nalbandian, 1989; Klingner and Nalbandian, 1985; Riccucci, 1997). For example, affirmative action refers, in part, to proactive efforts to redress past discriminations in the workplace. In this sense, it has been viewed as a legal tool to ensure equal employment opportunity. From a managerial standpoint, it has also been viewed as a tool to diversify the workplace in terms of race, ethnicity, gender, physical abilities, and so forth.[2] Its emphasis on proaction has been the cause of endless controversy and public debate over its use as an employment tool or social policy. Indeed, opponents to affirmative action very early on were quick to label it "reverse discrimination."

Its reformative and compensatory emphasis has also led to myriad lawsuits, challenging its legality and constitutionality.[3] A lengthy discussion of the entire set of case law goes beyond the scope of this chapter, but Table 6.1 provides a chronological summary of the legal actions around affirmative action since the U.S. Supreme Court's landmark *Regents of the University of California v. Bakke* ruling in 1978.

As can be seen in the table, a year after the *Bakke* ruling, there were a series of U.S. Supreme Court decisions upholding the legality of affirmative action when certain criteria had been met. By 1989, however, the Court, now comprised by new members, issued a number of decisions that were not only unfavorable to affirmative-action programs, but that also sought to reshape equal employment opportunity and employment-discrimination law (see, for example, *Martin v. Wilks*). In response to these negative rulings, the U.S. Congress enacted in 1991 the Civil Rights Act, which essentially restored affirmative action to its pre-1989 legal status.

Since 1991, however, as seen in Table 6.1, the courts have continued to issue decisions that have further eroded affirmative action. Perhaps the most important legal developments around affirmative action as of this writing include the following cases: *Hopwood, Piscataway, Smith,* and *Lesage.*[4] A brief discussion of these cases is in order because they represent key augmentations around the current legal status of affirmative action. For example, as indicated in Table 6.1, the U.S. Supreme Court let stand the U.S. Court of Appeals for the Fifth Circuit's decision in *Hopwood v. State of Texas* (5th Cir., 1996). The Fifth Circuit Court in *Hopwood* struck down the constitutionality of an affirmative-action program at the University of Texas's Law School aimed at increasing the number of African-American and Mexican-American students. In reversing the district court's decision, the appeals court issued a ruling that did not necessarily evaluate the actual admissions program of the law school, but rather ruled more broadly on the constitutionality of using race as a criterion in admissions decisions. In effect, the ruling called into question the continued validity of the Supreme Court's 1978 *Bakke* ruling.

The appeals court in *Hopwood* began by applying the first prong of the strict-scrutiny test[5] to the law school's use of race in admissions decisions. More specifically, the court asked (a) whether relying on race for the nonremedial goal of

TABLE 6.1   The Chronology of Legal Actions Around Affirmative Action.*

1978	*Regents of the University of California v. Bakke*. U.S. Supreme Court upholds the principle of affirmative action but strikes down its operation by the University at California under the Fourteenth Amendment and Title VI of the Civil Rights Act of 1964.
1979	*United Steelworkers of America v. Weber*. U.S. Supreme Court upholds legality of voluntarily developed affirmative action plan under Title VII of Civil Rights Act of 1964.
1980	*Fullilove v. Klutznick*. U.S. Supreme Court upholds constitutionality (under Fifth and Fourteenth Amendments) of federal set-aside programs enacted by the U.S. Congress.
1984	*Firefighters Local Union and Memphis Fire Department v. Stotts*. U.S. Supreme Court upholds, under Title VII of the Civil Rights Act, as amended, the use of a seniority system in layoff decisions, despite its negative impact on affirmative action.
1986	*Wygant v. Jackson Bd. of Ed.* U.S. Supreme Court strikes down, under the Fourteenth Amendment to the Constitution, the use of affirmative action in layoff decisions.
1986	*Sheet Metal Workers' International Association v. EEOC*. U.S. Supreme Court upholds, under Title VII and the Fifth Amendment to the Constitution, a court-ordered affirmative-action program to remedy past discrimination by a union and apprenticeship committee against people of color.
1986	*Int'l Assoc. of Firefighters v. City of Cleveland*. U.S. Supreme Court upholds, under Title VII, affirmative-action consent decree that provided for the use of race-conscious relief in promotion decisions.
1987	*Johnson v. Transportation Agency, Santa Clara County*. U.S. Supreme Court upholds, under Title VII, voluntarily developed affirmative-action program intended to correct gender and racial imbalances in traditionally segregated job categories.
1987	*U.S. v. Paradise*. U.S. Supreme Court upholds, under the Fourteenth Amendment to the Constitution, a court-ordered affirmative-action plan aimed at remedying discrimination against African Americans in hiring and promotion decisions in Alabama Public Safety Department.
1989	*City of Richmond v Croson*. U.S. Supreme Court strikes down the constitutionality, under the Fourteenth Amendment, of a local government's set-aside program because it could not satisfy the criteria of the strict scrutiny test.
1989	*Martin v. Wilks*. U.S. Supreme Court allowed white firefighters to challenge, under Title VII, a consent decree to which they were not a party, years after it had been approved by a lower court.
1990	*Metro Broadcasting v. F.C.C.* U.S. Supreme Court upholds the constitutionality (under the Fifth Amendment) of F.C.C.'s set-aside policy, which bears the imprimatur of long-standing congressional support.
1990	Civil Rights Acts vetoed by President Bush. Congress fails to override veto.

(continued on the following page)

(continued from the previous page)

1991	Civil Rights Act passed. Restores affirmative action to its pre-1989 legal status.
1995	*Adarand v. Peña.* U.S. Supreme Court rules that the Equal Protection Clause of the Fifth Amendment requires that racial classifications used in federal set-aside programs must undergo strict scrutiny analysis.
1995	*In re Birmingham Reverse Discrimination Employment Litigation* (*BRDEL*). U.S. Supreme Court let stand, without comment, a decision by the U.S. Court of Appeals for the Eleventh Circuit that invalidated a promotion plan aimed at promoting African-American firefighters to the position of lieutenant.
1995	*Claus v. Duquesne Light Company.* U.S. Supreme Court let stand, without comment, a decision by the Third Circuit Court of Appeals, which awarded a white engineer for a utility company $425,000 in damages because, according to the court, he was "passed over" in favor of an African American for promotion to a managerial job.
1996	*Hopwood v. State of Texas.* U.S. Supreme Court let stand a ruling by the U.S. Court of Appeals for the Fifth Circuit, which struck down the constitutionality of an affirmative-action program at the University of Texas Law School.
1996	President Clinton suspends, for a minimum of three years, all federal set-aside programs.
1997	*Taxman v. Piscataway Township Board of Education* is dropped from the U.S. Supreme Court's calendar, because parties settled. Thus remains, the 1996 opinion of U.S. Court of Appeals for the Third Circuit: the goal of achieving or maintaining diversity cannot be a justification for a race-based employment decision.
1999	*Lesage v. Texas.* U.S. Supreme Court throws out a reverse discrimination suit against the University of Texas's Department of Education.
2000	*Smith v. University of Washington.* Relying on the *Bakke* ruling, the Ninth Circuit Court of Appeals upholds a race-based affirmative-action program for admissions, stating that a properly designed and operated race-conscious admissions program would not be in violation of Title VI or the Fourteenth Amendment.

*Actions around EEO or employment-discrimination law (e.g., the U.S. Supreme Court's *Griggs v. Duke Power Co.* ruling) are not addressed here.

having a diverse student body could serve as a compelling governmental interest, and (b) whether the use of racial classifications could be justified as a remedy for the present effects of past discrimination by not only the law school, but by the Texas educational system as a whole.

In assessing point (a) of the first prong of the strict-scrutiny test, the appeals court ruled that diversity, in and of itself, cannot serve as a compelling state interest in higher education. Interestingly, the court invoked the *Bakke* decision to support its ruling here. The *Hopwood* court reasoned that only one member of the Supreme Court—Justice Powell—had found that diversity could serve as a compelling governmental interest. The Fifth Circuit flatly rejected this aspect of the *Bakke* decision, opining that:

> Justice Powell's argument in *Bakke* garnered only his own vote and has never represented the view of a majority of the Court in *Bakke* or any other case. . . . Justice Powell's view in *Bakke* is not binding precedent on this issue (1996: 944).

The appeals court concluded that

> the use of race to achieve a diverse student body, whether as a proxy for permissible characteristics, simply cannot be a state interest compelling enough to meet the steep standard of strict scrutiny *(Hopwood,* 1996: 948).

The appeals court next assessed point (b) of strict scrutiny's first prong and determined that it was unconstitutional for the law school to employ racial classifications to remedy the present effects of past discrimination by the entire Texas school system. The appeals court rejected the lower court's argument that past, pervasive discrimination by the Texas primary and secondary educational systems against African Americans and Mexican Americans impeded their ability to compete fairly on the tests and other tools used in admissions decisions to the law school. The appeals court concluded that

> the use of racial remedies must be carefully limited, and a remedy reaching all education within a state addresses a putative injury that is vague and amorphous. It has no logical stopping point *(Hopwood,* 1996: 950).

It is interesting to note that even if the case turned on whether the use of race could be justified as a remedy for the effects of discrimination *solely* by the law school, the appeals court would have struck down the constitutionality of the program because it took the further step of saying that the law school no longer discriminated against African Americans. It said that

> While the school once did practice *de jure* discrimination in denying admission to blacks, the [U.S. Supreme] Court . . . struck down the law school's program [in a 1950 decision]. Any other discrimination by the law school ended in the 1960's . . . when the school . . . implemented its first program designed to recruit minorities . . . *(Hopwood,* 1996: 953).

In short, the *Hopwood* appellate court ruled that the law school's affirmative-action program could not meet the first prong of the strict-scrutiny test. As such, the court went on to say, it need not apply the second prong of the test, which examines whether the program was sufficiently narrowly tailored to meet its goals *(Hopwood,* 1996: 955).

For now, the *Hopwood* ruling governs at least the three states comprised by the Fifth Circuit—Texas, Louisiana, and Mississippi—because the U.S. Supreme Court, in July 1996, said it would not hear the appeal by the state of Texas from the Fifth Circuit's ruling.[6]

In another critical case, *Taxman v. Piscataway Township Board of Education* (1996), the school board in this New Jersey district was forced to lay off teachers because of budget problems. In an effort to maintain racial diversity in its teaching staff, the school board dismissed Sharon Taxman, a white teacher, rather than the equally qualified African-American teacher, Debra Williams, the only person of color in the Business Department out of ten other teachers. Both had accrued an equal amount of seniority. Taxman filed suit, claiming that her rights under Title VII of the Civil Rights Act of 1964 as amended had been violated. The appeals court examined whether Title VII permits the use of affirmative action to promote racial diversity. As the trial proceeded, Taxman was rehired by the school board, and so reinstatement was not an issue.

The U.S. Court of Appeals for the Third Circuit ruled in *Taxman* that the goal of achieving or maintaining diversity cannot be a justification for a race-based employment decision under Title VII of the Civil Rights Act. The court looked at the purposes of Title VII and stated that "we are convinced that unless an affirmative action plan has a remedial purpose, it cannot be said to mirror the purposes of the statute" (*Taxman*, 1996: 1557). Thus, the court opined that affirmative action could be justified as a remedy for past discrimination. The court also examined the legislative history of Title VII and concluded that Congress did not intend for the law to promote racial diversity.

The U.S. Supreme Court agreed to hear an appeal to the case,[7] but before the case went before the Supreme Court, the parties settled. Taxman received $186,000 in the settlement, and her lawyers received $247,500. Thus, the Third Circuit's opinion stands, and the Supreme Court did not have the opportunity to issue what some feared would have been a broadly worded opinion on affirmative action.

In contrast with the *Hopwood* and *Piscataway* decisions is the Ninth Circuit Appellate Court ruling in *Smith v. University of Washington* (2000), where the appeals court upheld an admissions policy at the University of Washington's Law School that effectively takes race into account. In *Smith*, three white applicants to the law school sued for the school's use of affirmative action in admissions decisions. The applicants claimed that they were denied admissions to the law school because racial preferences were granted to people of color. Race was considered as one of several diversity factors in making admissions decisions at least until November 1998 when Washington's voter Initiative Measure 200 was passed. Similar to Proposition 209 in California, Washington's I-200 bans the use of affirmative action in state and local hiring, contracting, and education.

Subsequent to passage of I-200, the university's law school developed a new admissions policy that retained a "diversity clause." The policy stated that "important academic objectives are furthered by . . . students . . . from diverse backgrounds" and then went on to set out a list of factors that would promote diversity including:

> persevering or personal adversity or other social hardships; having lived in a foreign country or spoken a language other than English at home; career goals; employment history; educational background; . . . geographic diversity or unique life experiences (*Smith*, 2000: 1192).

Because the terms *race, color* and *national origin* were not included in the list, the appeals court upheld the policy. The Ninth Circuit court stated that

> [t]he district court correctly decided that Justice Powell's opinion in *Bakke* described the law and would require a determination that a properly designed

and operated race-conscious admissions program at the law school of the University of Washington would not be in violation of Title VI or the Fourteenth Amendment. It was also correct when it determined that *Bakke* has not been overruled by the Supreme Court. Thus, at our level of the judicial system Justice Powell's opinion remains the law (*Smith*, 2000: 1201).

One of the most recent cases as of this writing is *Lesage v. Texas* (1998). In this case, Lesage, an African immigrant of Caucasian descent, applied for admission to a Ph.D. program in the Education Department of the University of Texas at Austin. Of the 233 applications received, about 20 students were admitted to the program. Lesage was not admitted, but one person of color out of the 20 was offered admission. Lesage discovered that race was a factor at some stage in the admissions review process and filed a "reverse discrimination" suit, claiming that his rights under the Equal Protection Clause of the Fourteenth Amendment had been violated.

The district court in *Lesage* ruled that there was "no evidence that race was a factor in the decision to deny [Lesage's] admission to the . . . program" and that there was "uncontested evidence that the students ultimately admitted to the program had credentials that the committee considered superior to" Lesage's (*Lesage v. Texas*, 1997: 7). The district court, thus, ruled against Lesage and in favor of the university.

On appeal, the Fifth Circuit Appellate Court reversed the lower court's decision. However, the court did not review the district court's conclusion regarding whether Lesage would have otherwise been admitted to the program (i.e., if there was no affirmative action or race-based consideration). The appeals court instead ruled that the university violated Lesage's constitutional rights by "rejecting his application in the course of operating a racially discriminatory admissions program (*Lesage*, 1998: 222). It may be recalled that it was the Fifth Circuit that struck down the affirmative-action program at the University of Texas in *Hopwood*; its decision in *Lesage*, then, was somewhat anticipated.

The U.S. Supreme Court, however, in a surprising decision, reversed the judgment of the appeals court (*Lesage*, 1999). Although the Court did not decide whether the university's admissions process was discriminatory, it ruled that the Court of Appeals erred in its judgment that it was "irrelevant" as to whether Lesage would have been admitted to the university in the absence of an affirmative-action program. The Supreme Court stated that the Appeals Court of the Fifth Circuit failed to adhere to the Supreme Court's well-established framework for analyzing claims similar to the ones arising in *Lesage*. Referring to earlier decisions, the Supreme Court said that

> even if the government has considered an impermissible criterion in making a decision adverse to the plaintiff, it can nonetheless defeat liability by demonstrating that it would have made the same decision absent the forbidden consideration (*Lesage*, 1999: 468).

This suggests that public employers and universities can avoid liability in constitutional challenges to their affirmative-action programs by demonstrating that they would have made the same decision (e.g., to hire or admit a person of color) without the affirmative-action program. The *Lesage* decision also leads to questions as to how the Supreme Court might have ruled on *Hopwood*, had it agreed to review the case.

In sum, the contours of affirmative action law continue to be reshaped by the courts. But it is important to note that, although affirmative-action programs have been hard pressed to meet certain constitutional challenges or standards (e.g., the strict-scrutiny test), employers can certainly mount defenses along the lines of demonstrating that they would have made the same decision to hire a protected-class person even in the absence of an affirmative-action program. This is a well-established approach in cases involving the liability and immunity of public officials and organizations facing constitutional challenges.[8] Indeed, this is the implication of the Supreme Court's opinion in *Lesage*, as discussed above. It is also worth noting that the courts continue to be willing to uphold the legality of affirmative-action programs under Title VII if used as a remedy for past discrimination, as the Third Circuit Court of Appeals made clear in its *Piscataway* decision. Some courts, such as the Ninth Circuit court in *Smith*, are also willing to go even further in upholding race-based affirmative-action programs.

AFFIRMATIVE ACTION AND VOTER REFERENDA

In addition to court rulings that affect the operation of affirmative-action programs, voters in some states and localities are mounting initiatives to dismantle affirmative action, as the voters in California did in 1996 with Proposition 209.[9] In fact, Ward Connerly, the African-American business person from California who wrote Proposition 209, was instrumental in getting Initiative 200 passed in the state of Washington in November 1998. Initiative 200 bans the use of affirmative action in state and local hiring, contracting, and education.

Connerly and other opponents to affirmative action are working to mount similar initiatives in a number of other jurisdictions around the United States, including Michigan, Nebraska, and Florida. Parenthetically, such an effort in Florida coincides with the agenda of Governor Jeb Bush, who recently implemented Talent 20, which prohibits the use of affirmative action in university admissions.

Yet, despite these ballot initiatives, many state and local government officials and managers continue to rely on affirmative action as well as other tools and techniques to rectify employment discrimination or to diversify their workforces. Indeed, it is sometimes the case that state and local laws, executive orders, or ordinances compel them to do so.

Perhaps one of the best examples of government employers' continued use of affirmative action, despite voter as well as court action, is in California. As noted, the voter initiative, Proposition 209, was passed in 1996. It forbids the use of affirmative action in public employment, public education and public contracting. Opponents of Proposition 209 challenged its constitutionality shortly afterward in

Coalition for Economic Equity v. Pete Wilson (1996). In this case, a federal district court judge ruled that Proposition 209 was unconstitutional, opining that the controversial measure violated the equal protection guarantees of California's women and people of color. The judge effectively blocked the enforcement of Proposition 209 by issuing a preliminary injunction, concluding that the law discriminated against women and people of color by banning "constitutionally permissible" affirmative-action programs.

A year later, the U.S. Court of Appeals for the Ninth Circuit reversed the district court's decision and ordered the district court judge to lift the temporary injunction (see *Coalition for Economic Equity v. Pete Wilson*, 1997). The appellate court's ruling, in effect, upheld Proposition 209. The Ninth Circuit ruled that Proposition 209 was constitutional and that it did not violate the equal protection guarantees of women and people of color. Parenthetically, the panel of circuit court judges in *Coalition for Economic Equity* differed from that panel that presided over the *Smith v. University of Washington* decision, discussed earlier. It may be recalled that in *Smith*, the Ninth Circuit panel upheld an affirmative-action program in university admissions that takes race into account.

In November 1997, the U.S. Supreme Court declined to hear a challenge to the appellate court's ruling in *Coalition for Economic Equity*, thereby leaving the Ninth Circuit's ruling in place and paving the way for the enforcement of Proposition 209.[10]

Notwithstanding the Ninth Circuit's decision in *Coalition for Economic Equity*, however, city, county, and state agencies in California continue to rely on affirmative action to curb discriminatory practices and to promote diversity.[11] It would appear that the only way to enforce Proposition 209 is to file a lawsuit against the government employer who continues to rely on affirmative action.

For example, in one such legal action, *Cheresnik v. City and County of San Francisco* (1999), the Pacific Legal Foundation filed suit against the San Francisco International Airport on behalf of three white males who alleged they were denied a chance for promotions because of the airport's diversity plan. The leadership at San Francisco's airport remains committed to diversity and was unwilling to scrap its plan, despite Proposition 209. As of this writing, the case is pending in the San Mateo County Superior Court.

In another case, *Schindler Elevator Corp. v. City and County of San Francisco* (1999), a company's bid for a city contract was rejected because it had not demonstrated good faith outreach efforts to minority subcontractors as required under San Francisco's Minority Business Enterprise/Women's Business Enterprise (MBE/WBE) ordinance. The company sued, asserting the MBE/WBE outreach provision violated Proposition 209. The case was decided on appeal in May 1999 in the city's favor, thus upholding the use of affirmative action in contracting decisions.[12]

In *Hi-Voltage Wire Works, Inc. v. City of San Jose* (1999), the city argued that Proposition 209 does not prevent public entities from requiring contractors to outreach to minority- and women-owned subcontractors. The California Court of

Appeals disagreed; it ruled for the plaintiffs, thus finding that San Jose's outreach program violates Proposition 209. The case is now on appeal with the California Supreme Court.

Notwithstanding the actual outcomes of the lawsuits discussed above, the important point made from this brief analysis is that public- and private-sector employers are not willing to scrap their affirmative-action programs even though ballot initiatives seek to force them to do so. As Kelly and Dobbin (1998) point out from their survey research, human resources managers continue to see affirmative action as an added "business" argument for attracting a diverse workforce, so they are simply unwilling to abandon these efforts even when government policy seeks to compel them to do so. Their findings show that organizations view affirmative-action practices as an essential management tool that reinforces accountability and maximizes the utilization of the talents of [the firm's] entire workforce (Kelly and Dobbin, 1998; *cf*, Feild, 1984: 49).

They go on to say that employers, especially in the business community, continue to see affirmative action as a policy that benefits organizations in terms of new ideas, opinions and perspectives, thus resulting in key competitive advantages. It may be that affirmative action has become so integral to public personnel and human-resources practices, and perhaps overall management policy, that employers across the country are not willing to end its use, even when voters have made the decision for government to do so.

CONCLUSIONS

One of the most important points to be made from this review of affirmative action is that, despite the legal rulings around affirmative action and the ballot initiatives, public- and private-sector employers continue to rely on affirmative action as well as other programs and techniques in an effort to prevent employment discrimination or to create greater diversity in their workplaces, as will be seen in the next chapter. They may also, from a purely financial standpoint, maintain their affirmative-action programs to avoid costly employment litigation advanced by women or people of color. Also, given the mercurial nature of court decisions around affirmative action, it may be the case in general that public-sector employers are not willing to abandon the affirmative-action programs that have taken them decades to institute.

In short, as we continue to move into the twenty-first century, governments and corporations across the country are holding on to their affirmative-action programs. This seems somewhat ironic, given the strong resistance to affirmative action when it first emerged. In any event, affirmative action may be around for a long time or at least until it is truly no longer needed, that is, when discriminatory practices cease to exist and when diverse workforces become the norm in this nation.

NOTES

1. It should be noted that this chapter addresses solely affirmative action, and not equal employment opportunity (EEO). EEO refers to policies aimed at preventing employment discrimination and was developed in response to discriminatory practices against persons based on race, color, gender, religion, national origin, disability, age, and other characteristics.
2. As will be seen later in this chapter, however, the courts have been unwilling to uphold affirmative action as a way to achieve social or demographic diversity in the workplace.
3. For review of the legal history of affirmative action, see, for example, Riccucci (1997).
4. There are a number of other federal district and appellate court cases addressing affirmative action that are, as of this writing, pending, being argued, or have not been (and perhaps will not be) appealed to the U.S. Supreme Court. Such cases are not addressed in this chapter. See, for example, *Gratz and Hamacher v. Bollinger, Duderstadt, and the Board of Regents of the University of Michigan* (2000), where a federal district court in Detroit upheld the University of Michigan's affirmative-action program on the grounds that racial preferences in admissions enhance the educational experience of not only people of color, but of whites as well. Also see *Majeske v. City of Chicago* (2000), where the Court of Appeals for the Seventh Circuit struck down a reverse discrimination suit by white police officers in Chicago's Police Department. The appeals court went on to uphold the constitutionality of the department's use of affirmative action in promotions for African Americans and Latinos. In rendering its decision, the appeals court applied the strict scrutiny test (see *infra*, note 5). The court found that there was a compelling governmental interest for the affirmative-action program because of evidence of past discrimination. The court next found that the second prong of the strict scrutiny test was met in that the department's affirmative-action plan was sufficiently narrowly tailored.
5. Strict scrutiny is a two-pronged test that asks: (1) whether there is a compelling governmental interest for the program (e.g., to redress past discrimination) and (2) whether the program is sufficiently narrowly tailored to meet its specified goals (e.g., whether there are alternative programs that could be employed that do not classify people by, for instance, race).
6. Also see *City of Dallas v. Dallas Fire Fighters Association* (1998), where the Fifth Circuit Court of Appeals struck down the constitutionality of the fire departments use of affirmative action in promotions. The court found that there was insufficient evidence of past discrimination on the basis of race and gender to justify the affirmative-action program. The court applied what it called a "less exacting intermediate scrutiny analysis" and found "little evidence" of racial discrimination and "even less" evidence of gender discrimination. The U.S. Supreme Court refused to review the case (*City of Dallas*, 1999).
7. *Piscataway Township Board of Education v. Taxman* (1997).
8. See, for example, Rosenbloom (1983; 1997).
9. The city of Houston, Texas, is a notable exception. Voters in Houston rejected an initiative similar to California's Proposition 209 that would have ended affirmative action in contracting and hiring.
10. See, http://www.ci.sf.ca.us/cityattorney/prop209/prop209.htm. It should further be noted that the California courts have not yet ruled on whether Proposition 209 is valid under the U.S. Constitution.

11. See, "Plaintive About Prop 209," *The Recorder* (on-line news service, December 5, 1997).
12. It should be noted that the court based its decision on contracting principles and did not reach the Proposition 209 issues. Also see *Taber v. City and County of San Francisco* (2000), where an employee of a graphics company and several taxpayers challenged the set-aside provision of the MBE/WBE ordinance. The employee maintained that his employer was denied the opportunity to bid on city contracts because under certain circumstances, the ordinance unconstitutionally authorized contracts to be set aside for minority- and women-owned firms. The city argued that it continued to rely on the MBE/WBE ordinance, despite Proposition 209, in an effort to prevent discrimination in contracting. In April 2000, the state Court of Appeals upheld a trial court decision dismissing the case.

REFERENCES

Cheresnik v. City and County of San Francisco, 99–4109 (1999).
City of Dallas v. Dallas Fire Fighters Association, 885 F. Supp. 915 (1995); *aff'd* in part, *rev'd* in part, 150 F. 3d 438 (1998); *cert. denied*, 526 U.S. 1046 (1999).
Coalition for Economic Equity v. Pete Wilson, 946 F. Supp. 1480 (1996); *vacated* and remanded, 122 F.3d. 692 (1997); *cert. denied*, 522 U.S. 963 (1997).
Feild, J. 1984. "Affirmative Action: A Fresh Look at the Record Twenty-Two Years After the Beginning." Washington, DC: Center for National Policy Review.
Fullilove v. *Klutznick*, 448 U.S. 448 (1980).
Gratz and Hamacher v. Bollinger, Duderstadt, and the Board of Regents of the University of Michigan, 97–CV–75231–DT (December 13, 2000).
Griggs v. Duke Power Company, 401 U.S. 424 (1971).
Hopwood v. State of Texas, 861 F. Supp. 551 (W.D. Tex. 1994), *rev'd* and remanded in part, *diss'd* in part, 78 F. 3d. 932 (5th Cir. 1996), *cert. denied*, 1996 WL 227009 (1996).
Hi-Voltage Wire Works, Inc. v. City of San Jose, 72 Cal. App. 4th 600 (1999).
Johnson v. Transportation Agency of Santa Clara County, 480 U.S. 624 (1987).
Kellough, J. Edward. 1991. "The Supreme Court, Affirmative Action, and Public Management: Where Do We Stand Today?" *American Review of Public Administration*, 21:255–269.
Kelly, Erin, and Frank Dobbin. 1998. "How Affirmative Action Became Diversity Management." *American Behavioral Scientist*, 41 (7):960–985.
Klingner, Donald E., and John Nalbandian. 1998. *Public Personnel Management: Contexts and Strategies*, 4th ed. Englewood Cliffs, NJ: Prentice-Hall.
Lesage v. Texas, A–96–CA–286, 1997 (unpublished); *rev'd*, 158 F.3d 213 (1998); *rev'd* and remanded, 120 S.Ct. 467 (1999).
Lorance v. AT&T, 490 U.S. 900 (1989).
Majeske v. City of Chicago, 2000 U.S. App. LEXIS 15839 (3d Cir. 2000).
Martin v. Wilks, 490 U.S. 755 (1989).
Memphis v. Stotts, 104 S.Ct. 582 (1984).
Metro Broadcasting v. F.C.C., 111 L.Ed. 2d 445 (June 27, 1990).
Nalbandian, John. 1989. "The U.S. Supreme Court's Consensus on Affirmative Action." *Public Administration Review*, 49 (January/February): 38–45.
Patterson v. *McLean Credit Union*, 491 U.S. 164 (1989).
Piscataway Township Board of Education v. Taxman, 521 U.S. 1117; 117 S.Ct. 2506 (1997), *cert. granted*.
Price Waterhouse v. Hopkins, 490 U.S. 228 (1989).

Regents v. Bakke, 438 U.S. 265 (1978).

Riccucci, Norma M. 1997. "Will Affirmative Action Survive into the 21st Century?" In Carolyn Ban and Norma M. Riccucci (eds.), *Public Personnel Management, Current Concerns-Future Challenges*, 2nd ed. White Plains, NY: Longman, 57–72.

Richmond v. Croson, 488 U.S. 469 (1989).

Rosenbloom, David H. 1997. "Public Employees' Liability for Constitutional Torts." In Carolyn Ban and Norma M. Riccucci, (eds.), *Public Personnel Management: Current Concerns, Future Challenges*, 2nd ed. White Plains, NY: Longman, 237–252.

Rosenbloom, David H. 1983. *Public Administration and Law.* New York: Marcel Dekker, Inc.

Rosenbloom, David H. 1977. *Federal Equal Employment Opportunity* New York: Praeger.

Schindler Elevator Corp. v. City and County of San Francisco, A081811 (unpublished) San Francisco County Super. Ct. No. 991956 (1999).

Smith v. University of Washington, 2 F. Supp. 2d 1324 (W.D. Wash. 1998); *aff'd*, 233 F. 3d 1188 (9th Cir. 2000).

Steelworkers v. Weber, 443 U.S. 193 (1979).

Taber v. City and County of San Francisco, A087636 (unpublished) San Francisco County Super. Ct. No. 300–548 (2000).

Taxman v. Piscataway Township Board of Education, 798 F. Supp. 1093 (1992); 832 F. Supp. 836 (1993); *aff'd*, 91 F.3d 1547 (1996); *Piscataway Township Board of Education v. Taxman*, 521 U.S. 1117; 117 S.Ct. 2506 (1997), *cert. granted*.

United States v. Paradise, 480 U.S. 149 (1987).

Wards Cove Packing Co. v. Atonio, 490 U.S. 642 (1989).

Chapter 7

Managing Diversity in the Government Workplace

Norma M. Riccucci

In the last decade or so, many organizations have been going to great lengths to prepare for and manage diverse workforces as a matter of competitive survival. This is due to the fact that America's workforce looks markedly different than it ever has before. In a way, it can be described as polytypic. Compared with even twenty years ago, more white women, people of color, disabled persons, new and recent immigrants, gays and lesbians, and intergenerational mixes (i.e., baby boomers, Generation Xers and Generation Nexters) now work in America. To say that this has created challenges for managing the workplace is an understatement. The way in which government employers embrace this opportunity of diversity will clearly distinguish effective and efficient organizations from those that are unproductive and unable to meet the demands and necessities of the American people in the twenty-first century.

Today, public and private sector employers are poised to create productive workforces that are truly representative of not simply the national, but the *global* population. This chapter begins with a brief examination of the demographic changes and forecasted changes to the labor force and workplace. It then looks at how "diversity" is being approached or defined by government employers. Finally, it looks at some of the general management strategies that government employers could rely on or are relying on to manage the imminently diverse populations that now fill public sector jobs. Workforce diversity will prevail in public- and private-sector organizations in the twenty-first century. To the extent that the demographics of the workforce reflect that of the general population that it serves and that the workforce is being effectively managed, the delivery of public services will be greatly enhanced.

THE DEMOGRAPHICS OF THE LABOR FORCE AND WORKPLACE

Predictions and estimates during the past twenty years or so suggest that because of demographic changes to this nation's population, the composition of public- and private-sector workplaces are contemporaneously changing. The workforce changes that have already begun to occur include:

1. increases in the number of women.
2. increases in the number of people of color.
3. increases in the average age of workers.
4. increases in foreign-born or immigrant workers.
5. increases in the number of contingent workers (e.g., part-timers, tempo- rary workers).

A very simple, yet striking way to portray the demographic shifts at least as they pertain to white men, white women, and people of color is presented in Fig- ure 7.1. As the data show, women will account for about 48 percent of the work- force by the year 2008. White men will account for about 37 percent, and men of color around 15 percent.

Table 7.1 provides greater detail on important demographic changes that have implications for employment. It illustrates changes in the workforce based on gender, race, and ethnicity from 1978 to 1998 and projected changes to 2008. The table shows a decline in the participation of white men in the workforce and an increase of white women (12.1 percent). In addition, the table shows remarkable increases of women of color in the workforce, while the projections

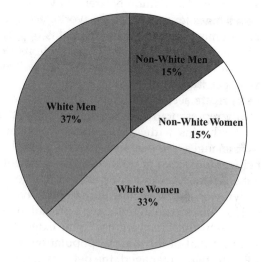

FIGURE 7.1   The Complexion of the United States Workforce by 2008.

SOURCE: Based on data obtained from the Bureau of Labor Statistics (BLS) website, http://stats.bls.gov/

TABLE 7.1 Workforce Participation Rates, 16 Years and Older, by Gender, Race, and Ethnicity, 1978, 1988, 1998, 1998, and Projected 2008.

Group	Participation Rate (percent)					Percentage Point Change (percent)
	1978	1988	1996	1998	2008	1978–2008
White	63.3	66.2	67.2	67.3	67.9	**4.6**
Men	78.6	76.9	75.8	75.6	74.5	**−4.1**
Women	49.4	56.4	59.1	59.4	61.5	**12.1**
African-American	61.5	63.8	64.1	65.6	66.3	**4.8**
Men	71.7	71.0	68.7	69.0	68.3	**−3.4**
Women	53.2	58.0	60.4	62.8	64.6	**11.4**
Asian and other[1]	64.6	65.0	65.8	67.0	66.9	**2.3**
Men	75.9	74.4	73.4	75.5	74.0	**−1.9**
Women	54.1	56.5	58.8	59.2	60.5	**6.4**
Hispanic origin[2]	. . .	67.4	66.5	67.9	67.7	**0.3**
Men	. . .	81.9	79.6	79.8	77.9	**−0.4**
Women	. . .	53.2	53.4	55.6	57.9	**4.7**

SOURCE: Bureau of Labor Statistics (BLS) web site: http://stats.bls.gov/
[1]The "Asian and other" group includes (1) Asians and Pacific Islanders and (2) American Indians and Alaska Natives. The historical data are derived by subtracting "black" from the "black and other" group; projections are made directly, not by subtraction.
[2]Data by Hispanic origin are not available before 1980. Percentage point change is calculated from 1988 to 2008.

for men of color show slight decreases in their workforce participation. Figure 7.2 shows a clearer picture of the changes in workforce participation of women from 1978 to the year 2008.

Table 7.2 illustrates the aging of the labor force. As we can see, there is a steady increase in the age group, forty and older. By 2008, this age cohort is expected to represent a majority share of the civilian labor force for both women and men. Although there are drops in labor-force participation of the younger-age cohorts, the changing *values* of younger generations (e.g., the Generation Xers and Nexters) will create challenges for government managers to the extent that younger and aging persons will be working alongside one another.

Changes to the labor force and workforce go well beyond race, ethnicity, gender, and age. As noted, there will be greater diversity based on such characteristics or factors as ability, sexual orientation, foreign-born status, and so forth. For example, greater protections offered to disabled persons under the Americans with Disabilities Act (ADA) of 1990 has increased their representation in public and private sector workforces. Also, the ADA has relatively strong provisions requiring employers to make "reasonable accommodations" for disabled persons; this includes making modifications or adjustments to a job or the work environment to enable the worker with the disability to perform the job.

Likewise, there are increasing numbers of gays and lesbians in the workplace, perhaps due to state and local laws and regulations that prohibit discrimination based on

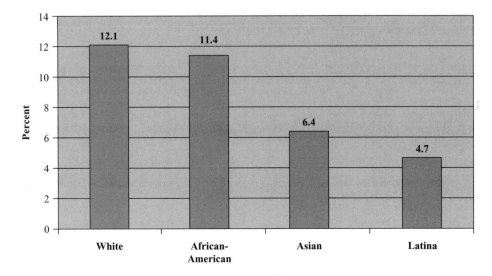

FIGURE 7.2 Percent Change in Women's Workforce Participation, 1978 to Projected 2008.

TABLE 7.2 Distribution of the Labor Force by Age and Gender, 1978, 1988, 1998, and Projected 2008 (Percent).

Group	Labor Force			
	1978	1988	1998	2008
Total, 16 years and older	100.0	100.0	100.0	100.0
16 to 24	24.5	18.5	15.9	16.3
25 to 39	36.0	42.3	37.6	31.9
40 and older	39.6	39.2	46.5	51.7
65 and older	3.0	2.7	2.8	3.0
75 and older	0.4	0.4	0.5	0.5
Men, 16 years and older	100.0	100.0	100.0	100.0
16 to 24	22.6	17.6	15.5	16.1
25 to 39	36.6	42.6	38.0	32.2
40 and older	40.8	39.9	46.5	51.8
65 and older	3.2	2.9	3.0	3.4
75 and older	0.5	0.5	0.6	0.6
Women, 16 years and older	100.0	100.0	100.0	100.0
16 to 24	27.1	19.7	16.4	16.6
25 to 39	35.1	41.9	37.1	31.7
40 and older	37.8	38.4	46.6	51.7
65 and older	2.7	2.4	2.5	2.5
75 and older	0.3	0.3	0.4	0.4

SOURCE: Bureau of Labor Statistics (BLS) web site: http://stats.bls.gov/

sexual orientation (Gossett, 1997). There is no federal law that prohibits discrimination against gays and lesbians in the workplace. Data on the percentages of gays and lesbians in public-sector workforces are extremely difficult to collect. Employers are not allowed to inquire about sexual orientation, nor are employees required to disclose their sexual orientation. Notwithstanding, the number of gays and lesbians "coming out" in the workplace is growing, and, in fact, we are seeing more and more employers offering domestic partnership benefits that serve the needs and interests of not only the partners of gays and lesbians, but the partners of heterosexual workers as well.

The contingent workforce (e.g., part-timers, temporary workers and retirees returning to work) has also been growing steadily since the 1980s due to a variety of factors, such as the changing needs and interests of workers. From 1980 to 1988, the number of part-time workers increased to 21 percent of the workforce, and for the same time period, the number of temporary workers increased by a staggering 175 percent (Khojasteh, 1994). The contingent workforce is also part of the "new workplace" and will require attention by government employers, particularly because these workers are sometimes found to be less dedicated and motivated, with lower levels of overall performance or productivity.

The U.S. Census Bureau reports a steady increase in the population of immigrants to the United States. Between 1970 and 1980, almost 4.5 million immigrants legally entered the United States, and in the 1980s, legal immigrants accounted for 30 percent of the nation's population growth (Khojasteh, 1994). Labor statistics indicate that legal immigrants comprised 7 percent of America's workforce in the mid-1980s and has increased to more than 20 percent as we move into the twenty-first century. In addition, employment analysts estimate that as of 1999, about a third of the 15.7 million immigrants in this country were here illegally. Most of the immigrants have settled in the South and the West, and they represent a broad spectrum in terms of socioeconomic status. It seems clear, based on past and current trends that the United States will continue to be a strong magnet for Latin American, Asian, and Eastern European populations.

Finally, it should be noted that rapid technological change in our society creates challenges for how work is done and the skills required to do it. Innovations in computing, telecommunications, and information technology have implications for all workers in the public and private sectors. The challenge for government employers is to ensure that *all* of their workers possess the tools and skills to perform the new jobs.

In sum, the nature of public- and private-sector workforces has undergone considerable change in the last several decades and will continue on this trajectory into the twenty-first century. Public-sector employers are challenged to seize the opportunities presented by the new workplace to better serve the American people.

WHAT IS MEANT BY *DIVERSITY*?

As noted in Chapter 6, because of the Supreme Court's gradual erosion of affirmative action, at least as a concept or, indeed, as an appellation, government employers have found other ways to maintain and continue their efforts to diversify their workforces. It is quite common today, for example, for government and private organizations to refer to their diversity programs, when in actuality, they are implementing their erstwhile affirmative-action programs. Although this is important in organizations' efforts to promote and value diversity, government agencies should not ignore or overlook the next critical step in diversity programs: the development of strategies to manage and accommodate effectively diverse peoples in the workforce. This includes harnessing the available diverse human resources to create a productive and motivated workforce. Key here is management's ability to develop ways to address such challenges as communication breakdowns, misunderstandings, and even hostilities that invariably result from working in an environment with persons from highly diverse backgrounds, age cohorts, and lifestyles (Carr-Ruffino, 1999). But the opportunities are abundant, and the efficacy with which they are seized by public employers will determine the ability of governments to serve the needs and interests of the American populace successfully.

GENERAL STEPS FOR EFFECTIVELY MANAGING DIVERSITY

This chapter is not intended to provide specific strategies for developing programs aimed at managing diversity. This has been done extensively elsewhere (see, for example, Riccucci 2001; Best Practices, 2000). Instead, important initial steps for developing diversity-management programs are outlined here. For example, as public-policy analysts, managers, and researchers have submitted, one of the most important ingredients to setting up successful diversity programs is strong commitment from not only agency leaders, but also from CEOs, such as mayors, governors, and the president. If the top-level leaders communicate that a program to manage diversity is a critical goal for the agency and that it is *integrated into the overall strategic goals* of the organization, the stage is set for commitment by lower-level managers, supervisors, and the employees themselves. The expression of commitment by leaders, however, must be backed by resources. Adequate resources in the form of both funding and staff are essential to achieving diversity goals. But more than this, if top-level leaders are genuinely committed to diversity objectives, those persons responsible for implementing the diversity programs must be held accountable for goal attainment. In other words, to the extent that managing diversity is a priority for the agency, it should be afforded the same weight as other important organizational goals. In this sense, managers and supervisors would be held accountable for reaching the diversity goals.

One of the most important areas that must be targeted for generous funding is training. Training is generally relegated to a back burner during fiscal crises, but keeping training as a primary activity will ensure that efforts to manage diversity are successful. Training programs and policies are crucial to fostering multicultural awareness among managers, supervisors, and employees, to instilling a sense of value around diversity, and to improving the overall management of diversity in the workplace.

The success of training programs may lie in the organization's ability to target the programs and policies to specific organizational needs. For example, if the organization is faced with an aging workforce, then training would, in part, be geared toward dispelling myths around older workers.

It is essential that a sense of "ownership" be instilled in managers and supervisors, as well as employees. Because everyone in the workplace represents a challenge to managing diversity successfully, everyone must be involved to varying degrees and capacities in developing ways to manage diversity in the workforce effectively. This may ultimately foster greater and *shared* commitment to achieving the diversity goals.

Organizations must assess and understand the current demographic complexion of their individual workforces and, in conjunction with projected forecasts for change, develop workforce planning models to target areas for recruitment, hiring, training, and retention. Such planning will not only help determine skills' gaps and targets of opportunity, but it will also help management in the allocation of agency resources so that a high-quality workforce is ultimately realized.

In addition, assessing the cultural environment of the existing workforce can identify challenges and barriers to managing diversity successfully. The U.S. Office of Personnel Management (OPM), which is responsible for the management of personnel and human resources at the federal level of government, suggests the use of "cultural audits" or "organizational needs assessments." These are surveys distributed to employees to assess their views on diversity; the feedback can help the agency target potential strengths and weaknesses in its efforts to manage diversity.

Golembiewski (1995) makes the important point that traditional, bureaucratic infrastructures serve as major impediments to successful diversity programs. As he and other organizational theorists have repeatedly told us, the culture of organizations tends to be male, white, and Eurocentric in orientation. This is due mainly to the fact that the culture of organizations reflects those who run and control them. It is axiomatic that such a culture will work against efforts to manage diversity.

An organization culture that supports flexibility is necessary so that supervisors can manage effectively in a diverse environment. Efforts must be made by governments to modify organizational policies (written and unwritten) to incorporate the cultural perspectives of those other than the majority group. Although it is impossible to consider every situation and policy that may have an adverse effect on women, people of color, the disabled and older workers, realizing that views other than those commonly held by white males exist in the workforce will allow managers and workers to be more productive. In other words, in a culturally diverse workforce, there cannot be "one best way" to manage; management styles will depend on the workplace over which a supervisor is responsible.

Government employers have been relying increasingly on the services of temporary employees to meet shifting workloads, and at the same time they strive to maintain continuous, effective services to the public. In the broader context of managing diversity, government employers need to ensure that they are effectively managing the "contingent workforce" and the "indirect and alternative work-force," as the U.S. Bureau of Labor Statistics refers to workers without an employ-ment contract and temporary workers, respectively. This is critical, especially because women and people of color, as Workforce 2020 reports, represent high concentrations in these jobs (see Table 7.3 for contingent workers in government).

Temporary employees work without any promise of permanent employment, and they also receive very few employee benefits. In the federal government, where the number of temporary employees ranges from 7 to 10 percent,[1] agencies are permitted to extend temporary appointments in one-year increments up to a total of four years for any given temporary employee. (In reality, research has shown that temporary appointments can last up to 10 years or more.[2]) It is important for government employers to ensure that these workers are not abused because their merit protections are limited as temporary workers, and, as the U.S. Office of Personnel Management (OPM) points out, "Employees who believe they are being treated unfairly are likely to evidence a lower commitment to the job and their employers—the American public."[3] Government employers must also seek to minimize conflicts between full-time permanent workers and part-timers. The reliance on temporary workers limits the potential job and promotion opportunities for full-time workers. Moreover, employers are able to convert temporary employees to permanent status, which can also threaten the job opportunities and status of full-time job incumbents. Whether or not race and gender conflicts are also imminent here, it would seem that government employers would find it in their best interest to manage the contingent and alternative workforce to maintain harmony in the workplace and, ultimately, efficient and effective service provision to the American people.

Employers will also need to balance the need to accommodate immigrant or foreign-born workers on the one hand, with training efforts for incumbent workers. Researchers and policy analysts have been warning for some time that if women and people of color are not trained with the technological and informational tools that are increasingly dominating the jobs of today, labor from abroad will be

TABLE 7.3   Percentage of Contingent Workers in Government, by Gender and Race, 1995.

	Contingent Workers
Total	2.7*
Men	0.6
Women	2.0
White	1.0
African American	1.8

SOURCE: Calculated from tables in Anne E. Polivka, "A Profile of Contingent Workers." *Monthly Labor Review A2* (October), 1996, pp. 10–21.
*Polivka estimates that in February 1995, there were 2.7 million contingent workers in the United States. This estimate is restricted to wage and salary workers who expected their jobs to last for an additional year or less and who had worked their jobs for one year or less. As noted above, 2.7 percent, or 72,900 contingent employees, worked in government occupations. This figure does not include temporary workers.

imported to fill the understaffed jobs. Indeed, the U.S. Congress in October of 2000 passed a bill that increases significantly the number of visas available for educated foreign-born persons to fill highly specialized jobs in the United States temporarily, especially those in the computer and technology industry. The measure was spurred by the great demand for jobs in high-tech industries and the low supply of American labor with the requisite skills (Alvarez, 2000). Of course, this raises questions around why the United States is not preparing Americans for these highly specialized jobs or why public and private organizations are not training existing workers to fill these high-technology jobs.

Finally, it is critical to point out that those public-sector organizations that perfunctorily develop diversity programs solely for the purpose of avoiding liability in potential lawsuits not only completely miss the point about the importance of diversity programs, but they will fail to adequately plan for their own successful performance as well as the future governance of the American people.

In sum, there are several initial steps for public-sector organizations to take to prepare for the development and implementation of diversity programs. Beyond these initial measures, the various management strategies embraced by agencies in organizing and developing diversity programs must obviously be geared toward each specified dimension of diversity—race, ethnicity, gender, physical ability, age and sexual orientation.

CONCLUSIONS

Diversity programs are becoming increasingly popular as part of government organizations' overall management of human resources. As discussed at the beginning of this chapter, diverse workforces are becoming a reality of the twenty-first century. Certainly, the way in which public sector employers manage this diversity will affect the overall ability of governments to meet the needs and demands of the American people.

But, as cautioned in this chapter, many government employers, in the wake of negative court rulings against affirmative action, seem to be mounting "diversity programs" that are mere relabelings of their old affirmative-action programs. Although this may be an important strategy for organizations to continue with their efforts to promote and value diversity, government agencies should not ignore or overlook the next critical step in diversity programs: the development of strategies to manage and accommodate diverse peoples in the workforce effectively. This will ensure that the organization is harnessing the available diverse human resources to ultimately create a hostile-free, productive, and motivated workforce.

NOTES

1. See www.opm.gov/.
2. See U.S. Office of Personnel Management (OPM), 1994.
3. Ibid., p. ix.

REFERENCES

Alvarez, Lizette. 2000. "Congress Backs Big Increase in Visas for Skilled Workers." *The New York Times* (October 4), pp. A1/A24.

Best Practices in Achieving Workforce Diversity. Washington, D.C.: U.S. Department of Commerce and the National Partnership for Reinventing Government Benchmarking Study, October, 2000.

Carr-Ruffino, Norma. 1999 *Diversity Success Strategies.* Boston: Butterworth Heinemann.

Golembiewski, Robert T. 1995. *Managing Diversity in Organizations.* Tuscaloosa, AL: University of Alabama Press.

Gossett, Charles W. 1997. "Lesbians and Gay Men in the Public Sector Work Force." In Carolyn Ban and Norma M. Riccucci, (eds.), *Public Personnel Management: Current Concerns, Future Challenges,* 2nd ed. New York: Longman, Inc., pp. 123–138.

Khojasteh, Mak. 1994. "Workforce 2000: Demographic Change and Their Impacts." *International Journal of Public Administration,* 17 (3&4): 465–505.

U.S. Office of Personnel Management (OPM). 1994. *Temporary Federal Employment.* Washington, DC: OPM.

Chapter 8

Lesbians and Gay Men in the Public-Sector Workforce

Charles W. Gossett

Most public-sector organizations already have a diverse workforce with respect to the sexual orientation of their employees; however, they are unaware of this fact or are unwilling to acknowledge it. Ironically, although government agencies struggle to increase the representation of historically underrepresented racial and ethnic groups and women, many have, until very recently, actively sought to prevent lesbian, gay male, and bisexual job applicants from being hired or to remove such employees from their jobs. This contradictory situation—success in recruiting and promoting personnel that the organization, in many instances, would prefer not to have—makes the issue of lesbians, gay men, and bisexuals in the public workplace substantially different from the problems faced by historically underrepresented groups. At the same time, however, the struggle between advocates and opponents of laws that would provide legal protection against discrimination on the basis of sexual orientation makes remarkably similar use of the strategies and rhetoric of the supporters and enemies of the civil rights movement of African Americans and the women's movement. Thus, personnel administrators, who will inevitably face questions concerning sexual orientation and employment, need familiarity with the historical experience of lesbians and gay males employed in the public sector, the current status of legal protections (or lack thereof) for lesbian and gay male employees, and some of the ways that traditional aspects of personnel administration are affected by the increasingly open presence of lesbians and gay men in the workforce.

HISTORICAL OVERVIEW

Though the written record of sexual relations between persons of the same sex indicates that such practices are hardly a new phenomenon, the concept of such persons as a "class" different from persons who have sexual relations with persons of the opposite sex is usually traced to the latter half of the nineteenth century. At that time, homosexual behavior moved from being a "sinful" act to being viewed as an "illness," more specifically a psychiatric abnormality (Katz, 1995). Despite the characterization of homosexuality as a disease, however, it retained an identity as a sin as evidenced by the fact that in the United States, all states had laws that criminalized sexual relations between persons of the same sex for most of this century (Nice, 1994), though between 1960 and 2000, 34 states and the District of Columbia decriminalized such behaviors. Only in 1973 did the American Psychiatric Association voted to remove homosexuality from its list of psychological disorders (Bayer, 1987). Most recently, scientific investigations into a biological origin for homosexuality have become prominent in discussions of whether or not sexual orientation is a personal characteristic more appropriately compared to race, ethnicity, or gender or whether comparison to some voluntary behaviors like religious choice is more suitable. The very fact that the term *sexual orientation* has replaced *sexual preference* in the discussion of this topic suggests that the arguments in favor of at least a partial biological explanation have gained fairly wide acceptance (Burr, 1993; LeVay, 1993; Hamer & Copeland, 1994). This brief discussion of how homosexuality has been conceptualized is important because, as in all policy matters, how the "problem" is stated has great influence on how "solutions" are developed.

In the United States, there is evidence that from its founding, persons engaging in sexual activity with persons of the same sex have been dismissed from public service (Shilts, 1993). For the most part, such dismissals were focused on the acts allegedly committed and not because the accused was a particular "type" of person. With the development of the concepts and terms of *homosexual* and *heterosexual* in the late 1800s and early 1900s, shorthand labels that purported to predict everything from sexual desires to fitness for particular types of employment became available to society. Public employers now had available scientifically-defined "groups" that could be favored (heterosexuals) or discriminated against (homosexuals) (Katz, 1995).

The Military.   Perhaps the best-known efforts at using the criterion of homosexuality to make employment decisions are in the military. Shilts (1993) recounts the long history of "gays in the military," but his story clearly demonstrates that the use of this classification as a tool of personnel management really accelerated during World War II. Until 1993, the question as to whether or not a person was a homosexual appeared on military application forms; it was dropped only as part of a compromise between the president and the Congress over the issue of officially allowing lesbians and gay men to serve in the armed forces (Aspin, 1993). This "don't ask, don't tell" compromise policy says that homosexual conduct, including the mere statement that one is a gay male, lesbian, or bisexual, is still grounds for discharge from military service, regardless of performance. The rationale offered in defense of this policy, given that several studies have demonstrated no perceptible differences in ability or performance between homosexual and heterosexual military personnel (Dyer, 1990), is that military readiness is harmed by the fact that many military personnel are made uncomfortable by the knowledge that homosexuals are serving with them. This argument is strikingly similar to the arguments raised when President Truman ordered the integration of armed forces units rather than continuing to segregate different races in separate units (Keen, 1992; Kauth & Landis, 1996). In the current case, however, gay male and lesbian soldiers are already integrated into all units, which makes it not surprising that some opponents of homosexuals serving openly in the military proposed segregation of homosexuals and heterosexuals as a compromise solution. To date, however, federal courts have not found discrimination against homosexuals by the branches of military service to violate any constitutionally protected rights (*Able v. United States*, 1998) and the number of military personnel discharged for homosexuality has increased since the "don't ask, don't tell" policy went into effect (D'Amico, 2000).

Federal Civilian Employment. In the post-World War II period, especially during the early years of the cold war, civilian government employees who were lesbians and gay men were also targeted for removal from public employment. Although the early 1950s are better known for the McCarthy hearings that sought to identify and remove alleged Communist Party members and sympathizers from government positions, homosexuals were also a major target of congressional investigating committees (Lewis, 1997; Katz, 1992: 91–105). Despite a variety of epithets and accusations of moral weakness, the "official" reason given as to why homosexuals were unfit for public service was that they posed a "security risk" to the nation. The logic behind this claim was that lesbian and gay male employees, being members of socially despised groups and, almost by definition, engaged in criminal acts every time they had sexual relations, would not want their employer or family members to know of their homosexuality. Thus, according to this logic, homosexual employees were highly susceptible to blackmail by foreign agents who would either threaten exposure or simply prey on the fact that they were morally weak. That there was no evidence of any homosexual U.S. government employee having engaged in espionage or betrayal of government secrets was irrelevant, nor did the circularity of the argument—homosexuals must be dismissed from employment because they could be blackmailed because they would lose their jobs if it was known that they were homosexuals—have any effect on the policy. Not surprisingly, given the nature of the "security risk" argument, most of the dismissals of homosexual employees occurred in the State Department and among civilian employees in defense agencies (Lewis, 1997). It wasn't until August 1995 that President Clinton issued an executive order prohibiting government agencies from denying security clearances simply because the person is a lesbian or gay man (Chibbaro, 1995; Lewis, forthcoming).

While specific numbers are hard to come by, it appears that during the late 1950s and throughout the 1960s, the number of dismissals of lesbian and gay male employees seems to have declined from the heights reached during the McCarthy era. In addition to the security risk argument, Lewis (1997) identifies three other reasons used to justify the dismissal of homosexual employees from civilian federal service: (1) Homosexuality is an example of the "criminal, infamous, dishonest, immoral, or notoriously disgraceful conduct" that always justifies a refusal to hire or a dismissal; (2) the presence of homosexuals impaired "the efficiency of the service" because some employees would be so upset working with known homosexuals that they could not perform their own jobs; and (3) employing homosexuals would "embarrass" the agency and impair its standing in the public's eyes. Over the years, the courts struck down each of these reasons for dismissing or refusing to hire openly lesbian and gay male personnel, although never completely closing the door to the possibility that in some circumstances a dismissal or refusal to hire on the basis of sexual orientation might be legitimate. Relying on the "nexus" arguments developed during the 1960s and 1970s, absent a clear connection between a person's sexual orientation and the ability to perform a particular job, discrimination against lesbians and gay men is not permissible. Of course, whether or not there is a connection is left to the judge reviewing the discriminatory claim.

As the social climate changed, particularly in the period following the historic Stonewall rebellion, which is often cited as the beginning of the current press for equal rights for lesbians and gay men (Duberman, 1993), the now defunct Civil Service Commission (CSC) began to modify its official policies in response to both court decisions and political pressure. In the mid-1970s, the CSC advised agencies that "merely" because a person is a homosexual, absent a showing that conduct affects ability to perform the job, there was insufficient grounds for a finding of "unsuitability." In 1980, the first director of the Office of Personnel Management, Alan Campbell, reemphasizing the importance of a nexus between off-duty behavior and job performance, issued a memorandum that stated "applicants and employees are to be protected against inquiries into, or actions based upon, non-job-related conduct, such as religious, community or social affiliations, or sexual orientation." (Lewis, 1997). This policy was also consistent with language in the 1978 Civil Service Reform Act that outlined "merit principles" that required selections to be made "solely on the basis of of relative ability, knowledge, and skills" and that employee retention should be based only on "the adequacy of their performance" (P.L. 95–454, §2301(b)(1) and (6), 1978). Despite a change in administration, this policy remained in effect throughout the 1980s.

In the 1992 election campaign, the question of lifting the ban on "gays in the military" was a clear policy difference between the Democratic and Republican candidates, and while the victory of Bill Clinton did not lead to a repeal of this particular prohibition, there was hope that a presidential order prohibiting employment discrimination on the basis of sexual orientation in the civilian branches of government would be issued. However, a different strategy emerged based on concerns that the antigay frenzy that had been whipped up over the military debate would lead to congressional action that would overturn an executive order covering civilians. Instead of a single order, the White House encouraged each cabinet department and independent agency to issue its own nondiscrimination policy. By mid-1995, thirteen of fourteen cabinet departments and more than fifteen agencies had issued such statements. In 1998, President Clinton amended the executive branch's equal-employment-policy statement, originally issued in 1969, Executive Order 11478, by adding the words *sexual orientation* to the list of categories protected from discrimination in federal civilian agencies (Executive Order 13087). Some members of Congress sought to overturn this executive policy legislatively but were unsuccessful. In the 2000 election, Vice President Al Gore, the Democratic candidate, pledged to support the policies adopted by President Clinton and to continue to appoint openly lesbian and gay male persons to positions of high visibility in his administration. Texas governor George Bush initially expressed doubt that he would find any lesbian or gay person who would share his political philosophies, although later in the campaign he indicated that he would not inquire into the sexual orientation of any potential appointees, nor would he actively seek to ensure their representation in his administration.

Current Federal Activity. In 1995, a bill known as the Employment Non-Discrimination Act (ENDA) was introduced into the U.S. Congress. Similar bills had been previously introduced in Congress since 1974 (Rutledge, 1992), although in 1995 the bill had a record 138 sponsors on the day of its introduction. The bill was reintroduced in both the 105th and 106th Congresses with more sponsors each time (35 senators and 153 representatives in 1999). This bill would prohibit employment discrimination in the public and private sectors on the basis of sexual orientation in a manner similar to, but more restricted than, the way such discrimination is prohibited by the Civil Rights Acts of 1964 and 1991 for the categories of race, color, national origin, religion, and sex. In addition to exemptions for small employers and religious organizations that can be found in other civil rights laws, ENDA also includes some unique features designed to disarm potential critics but of great importance to personnel managers who would be responsible for seeing that the law was followed in their organizations. First, the act does not apply to the provision of employee benefits to an individual for the benefit of his or her partner, an issue discussed in greater detail below. Other sections of the proposed law forbid both the use of statistics to establish disparate impact as prima facie evidence of discrimination and establishment of quotas or preferential treatment for lesbians or gay men. Also, the law makes clear that the nondiscrimination requirement does not apply to the armed forces, nor will it "repeal or modify any Federal, State, territorial, or local law creating special rights or preferences for veterans."[4] The latter statement recognizes that the issue of veterans' preference, a policy employed by many government jurisdictions, becomes problematic if the military is allowed to arbitrarily exclude lesbians and gay men. In *Personnel Administrator v. Feeney* (1979), the Supreme Court found that providing veteran's preference in employment decisions did not constitute illegal sex discrimination because women could join the military. Lesbians and gay men prohibited from serving in the armed forces will be unable to earn veterans' preference. Without this specific protection guaranteeing "special rights and preferences for veterans," a decision quite different from *Feeney* would be likely should the bill become law.

State and Local Government. Although no legal protections against discrimination based on sexual orientation have been enacted at the federal level, 140 local governments had passed laws or adopted personnel policies covering public employees by 1995 (Riccucci and Gossett, 1996) and a dozen or more cities have adopted similar policies since then (Human Rights Campaign, 2000). By the end of 2000, there were ten states with laws and another nine with executive orders by the governor protecting state employees from sexual orientation discrimination.

The forms and types of discrimination against lesbian and gay male public employees historically practiced by the federal government were often repeated at the state levels, as well. Even the congressional hearings of the 1950s attempting to root out homosexuals from federal service had their counterparts in state legislatures, the best known being the Johns Committee hearings in Florida in the 1960s (*Government versus Homosexuals*, 1975). However, because one consequence of American federalism is that the national and state levels of government have somewhat different responsibilities, the concerns of state and local governments about homosexuality were not exactly the same as the concerns of political leaders in Washington, D.C. Rather than using "national security" as the core element of an antihomosexual campaign, state and local leaders focused on the issue of education and an alleged danger to children from lesbian and gay male teachers. As was true with fear of the national security risk, fears of teachers molesting or "recruiting" students were based less on evidence than on emotion. The articulation of specific fears about homosexual teachers is a development of the post–World War II era when courts began to demand that public employers show a "nexus" between an employee's behavior off duty and job performance. Courts were somewhat lenient in accepting evidence of a nexus when cases involved school board decisions to dismiss lesbian and gay male teachers largely because of the traditional "role model" responsibilities of teachers and acceptance of the unsupported claim that homosexual teachers pose a danger to children. (Harbeck, 1992; Rienzo, Button, & Wald, 1999) Although teachers were the primary focus of antigay discrimination at the state and local levels, the general negative climate affected employees in other types of jobs as well.

As indicated earlier, however, some state and local governments have decided to treat sexual orientation as a category similar to race, sex, and religion in laws prohibiting employment discrimination. Unlike the federal government, however, most jurisdictions have not set about writing special legislation in the style of ENDA. Instead, where such laws have been adopted, the term *sexual orientation, sexual preference,* or *affectional preference* was simply added to the list of all protected categories. The city first credited with adopting such a law was East Lansing, Michigan, in 1972; the first territory was the District of Columbia in 1973; the first county was Santa Cruz, California, in 1975; and the first state was Wisconsin in 1983 (Singer and Deschamps, 1994).

Although there is great variety in the extensiveness of coverage of such laws, where they exist, public employment, at a minimum, is covered. However, due to the nature of multiple types of governments found in American states, laws passed by one jurisdictional unit do not always apply to other overlapping juris-dictions. For example, although a city council may have passed a sexual orienta-tion nondiscrimination ordinance, such a law may not apply to the employees of that town's school system, which is under the authority of a separately elected school board. Obviously, personnelists must be aware of whether or not the juris-diction in which they work provides such protections to perform their jobs effec-tively. Several gay rights advocacy organizations maintain web-based listings of such localities including the Human Rights Campaign (http://www.hrc.org/), Lambda Legal Defense and Education Fund (http://www.lldef.org/), and the National Gay and Lesbian Task Force (http://www.ngltf.org/).

IMPLICATIONS OF NONDISCRIMINATION LAWS FOR PERSONNEL FUNCTIONS

If a jurisdiction adopts a law that prohibits discrimination on the basis of sexual orientation—especially if that protection is achieved by adding the term *sexual ori-entation* to the list of other criteria rather than developed as a separate law similar to ENDA with a series of exceptions to the traditional interpretations of such laws—there are a number of corollary issues that must be faced by personnel administrators. These include issues involving recruitment, selection, and affirma-tive action; discrimination complaints; terminations; sexual harassment; diversity training; compensation and employee benefits; and several miscellaneous related tasks.

Recruitment, Selection, and Affirmative Action.   For many people, two of the most important contributions to personnel management coming out of the move-ments for civil rights for African Americans and women have been the focus on (1) expanding the number and variety of sources from which job applicants are recruited, and (2) improving personnel selection methods by insisting that jobs be carefully defined and the methods for selecting people be validly related to identi-fying the necessary skills for each job. Expanded outreach helps organizations attract previously underutilized or overlooked talent, while better selection tools are supposed to weed out "irrelevant" considerations such as race or sex or reli-gion in determining whether or not a person was qualified for a particular job. In jurisdictions that prohibit sexual orientation discrimination, that characteristic is also to be treated as irrelevant.

As noted earlier, because the sexual orientation of a job applicant or an employee is not usually apparent, it is probable that most lesbians and gay men do not face the blatant discrimination faced historically and currently by per-sons of color and women. This is particularly true with respect to recruitment and access to job information because sexual orientation is a characteristic that overlays other demographic (and legally protected) characteristics such as race, ethnicity, sex, and religion. To the extent that information and recruitment activities are targeted toward one of those groups, many lesbian and gay men will receive the information as well. However, organizations that have historically discriminated against lesbians and gay men may find, just as agencies that discriminated against African Americans or women have found, that positive, specifically targeted, and sustained recruitment efforts are necessary to overcome the resistance to working for previously hostile organizations. Thus, police departments in some cities have set up recruitment booths at lesbian and gay male festival sites or have established community liaisons to overcome negative perceptions earned after years of antigay harassment.

There are two specific situations in which discrimination against homosexuals may occur at the selection stage also. One is that popular stereotypes often associate certain physical and behavioral characteristics with homosexuality, for example, men who exhibit mannerisms society views as feminine and women who exhibit mannerisms considered masculine. Such a person may or may not be a homosexual but is much more likely to face discrimination based on perceived sexual orientation than lesbians and gay men who exhibit socially defined gender-appropriate behaviors. Although there are no federal court decisions specifically on this issue, the principle identifying gender stereotyping as a basis for employment decisions, such as illegal discrimination in *Price Waterhouse v. Hopkins* (1989), may become the basis for such claims (Harvard Law Review Association, 1989).

The second exception is for lesbians, gay men, and bisexuals who make known their sexual orientation to potential employers. For a variety of reasons, more and more lesbians and gay men and bisexuals are choosing to identify their sexual orientation publicly and do so in a variety of ways. Application forms provide a number of opportunities for people to reveal their sexual orientation. Perhaps the most obvious is the application forms question about organizational memberships. Required listings of organizational memberships have been used by public employers to screen out certain job applicants (Shelton v. Tucker, 1960). Failure to list a particular organizational membership became grounds for dismissal on the basis of having submitted a fraudulent application. This catch-22 scenario has been replicated with respect to the hiring of lesbians and gay men (*Acanfora v. Board of Education of Montgomery County*, 1974), although in the absence of a nondiscrimination law, this method of identifying and discriminating against people may still be used.

A second feature of the application form that is relevant here is the marital status box. Many jurisdictions prohibit discrimination on the basis of marital status, but some do not, including several which prohibit discrimination on the basis of sexual orientation. Marriage is both a legal and a religious ceremony, and although no American jurisdictions currently legally recognize marriages between two people of the same sex some religious denominations do perform such unions (Sherman, 1992: Sullivan, 1997). In any event, a person who considers him- or herself married to someone of the same sex may very well choose to indicate that by checking the "Married" box on an application form as the most honest representation of his or her relationship status. (Shahar v. Bowers, 1993) In a similar manner, lesbian and gay male employees may reveal their sexual orientation informally, though not inadvertently, in the course of an interview (Woods, 1993; McNaught, 1993).

The issue of affirmative action in the context of sexual orientation is somewhat more complex than it is in the case of race or gender. First, there is no reliable, statistical way to determine whether or not lesbians and gay men are proportionally represented, overrepresented, or underrepresented in a particular type or level of a government job. This is not surprising given that there continues be a dispute over what proportions of the total population should be classified as homosexual, bisexual, and heterosexual (Singer and Deschamps, 1994), and although there have been very few people calling for affirmative-action programs similar to those in place for historically underrepresented groups, there have been regular calls by activists for the appointment of "openly gay" officials at the highest levels of each political jurisdiction.

Discrimination Complaints. For most employees, bringing a complaint of discrimination to the attention of the appropriate authorities is not easy. Such a complaint formalizes a conflict by bringing in a third party, often from the personnel department in the form of an employee relations specialist or an equal employment opportunity officer. Employees who believe they are being treated in a discriminatory manner because of their race, gender, age, or disability must reach a point where the personal psychic and physical costs of the discriminatory behavior outweigh the costs of the tension in the work environment that are likely to result from filing a formal complaint. But for many lesbian and gay male employees, particularly those who have not discussed their sexual orientation in the workplace but who receive discriminatory treatment based on people's perceptions that they are gay, the decision also involves making a public record of their sexual orientation. This is an additional cost not usually borne by people for whom the discriminatory treatment is based on a visible characteristic such as skin color or gender or on a less visible but also socially less stigmatized characteristic such as certain physical disabilities or religion. As a consequence, it is not surprising that even when jurisdictions adopt nondiscrimination laws that include sexual orientation, the use of such protective provisions is relatively low. (Riccucci and Gossett, 1996; Button, Rienzo & Wald, 1997) Although several explanations are possible for the low number of complaints, the stigma still given to homosexuality in American society remains the most likely factor leading to a reluctance to file a complaint.

Terminations. In the past few decades, as noted earlier, the courts have been forcing public employers to demonstrate how any particular off-duty behavior has an impact on the job performance of an individual employee before using that off-duty behavior as justification for a termination of employment. At the federal level, *Norton v. Macy* (1969) was the first case involving homosexual activity to apply this standard in a way that overturned NASA's decision to terminate. Although this standard is now fairly well entrenched, application of the standard does not automatically lead to a finding of no relationship between sexual orientation (or a related aspect, such as a declaration of sexual orientation) and the requirements of a particular job. Several cases, for example, *Singer v. United States Civil Service Commission* (1976) and *Shahar v. Bowers* (1995) have found that an individual could be denied a job because of some factor closely related to his or her sexual orientation.

The key element in much of the discussion about sexual orientation and the suitability for particular jobs is related to the fact that in eighteen states, sodomy is a criminal offense. Although the definition of *sodomy* or *unnatural acts* varies among the states that have such laws, all include sexual contact between people of the same sex as a criminal activity. Despite the fine legal distinctions between *sexual orientation* and *sexual activities* being made in the course of the gays-in-the-military court proceedings, most public employees in states with sodomy laws who say that they are gay or bisexual are confessing to a criminal offense.

Sexual Harassment. The distinction that courts make between quid pro quo sexual harassment and harassment created by a "hostile environment" is proving to be particularly important to lesbians and gay men as the federal courts develop case law in this area. In *Oncale v. Sundowner Offshore Services* (1998), the U.S. Supreme Court unanimously found that Title VII of the Civil Rights Acts of 1964 and 1991 included protection against being sexually harassed by a person of the same sex. Previously, lower courts had been divided with some saying same-sex sexual harassment was not covered, some saying it was only covered if the harasser were a homosexual, and others saying that the issue was the sexual nature of the harassment, regardless of the orientation of the harasser (Turner, 2000; Paetzold, 1999). The *Oncale* case was ultimately settled out of court, so whether or not the alleged victim could have established that he had been harassed in violation of Title VII became a moot point.

Even though the Supreme Court has made clear that same-sex sexual harassment is possible, federal courts have been equally clear that the discrimination must be on the basis of sex and not the sexual orientation of the victim (Zalesne, 2001). Specific claims of sexual orientation discrimination in the U.S. Postal Service were rejected by the U.S. Court of Appeals (*Simonton v. Runyon*, 2000). Applying the principle from *Price Waterhouse*, however, a different U.S. Court of Appeals has found that sex-stereotyping of male appearances and behaviors may have led to the sexual harassment of a summer youth employee (he wore an earring) in a municipal public works program (*Doe v. City of Belleville*, 1997). On the other hand, establishing that the person accused of sexually harassing someone of the same sex was a homosexual could be used to support a charge of sexual harassment in such cases (Zalesne, 2001).

In what many consider a rather bizarre twist, federal courts have created what amounts to a "bisexual safe harbor" when the accused harasses men and women equally, or, in the words of the court, the victims are subject to an "equal opportunity harasser" (*Holman v. Indiana*, 2000). The reasoning is that because both sexes suffer ill treatment, there is no discrimination against one sex or the other, hence no violation of Title VII. It should be noted, however, that discrimination against an employee because of his or her bisexuality is not prohibited (Colker, 1993).

State and local governments that prohibit discrimination in employment based on sexual orientation, however, and state courts are making different decisions because, if sexual orientation discrimination is prohibited and if creation of a hostile environment is a form of discrimination, then an antigay hostile environment would not be defensible (*Murray v. Oceanside Unified School District*, 2000).

Compensation and Employee Benefits. Government entities, like private businesses, are governed by the Equal Pay Act of 1963. Lesbians, gay men, and bisexuals are not paid different wages or salaries based specifically on their sexual orientation, though there is some evidence that earnings of gay men are somewhat lower than comparable heterosexual men in society at large (Badgett, 1995). Of more immediate relevance, however, is the fact that the concept of *compensation* has in recent years been broadened beyond the idea of base pay and take-home pay to an idea called total compensation (McCaffery, 1992). Total compensation attempts to recognize that the value an employee receives from his or her employer in exchange for work includes more than just wages and salary, but a variety of monetary and nonmonetary benefits as well. Thirty or forty years ago, such benefits made up a relatively small proportion of total payroll expenses, but by the 1980s, such benefits comprised up to 40 percent of payroll costs (Gossett, 1994). Unlike actual wages and salaries, however, many employers distribute benefits of different value to different types of employees. The most common distinction made that results in differential benefit treatment is between married and unmarried employees. Although technically this is a distinction between single and married employees, the fact that gay male and lesbian employees are prohibited from marrying a same-sex partner who they see as the equivalent of a legal spouse makes this an issue of particular concern to them. Differences in treatment can be seen in a wide variety of benefits, including sick leave, bereavement leave, life insurance, health insurance, disability compensation, and retirement benefits.

Leave benefits are important because they usually include allowances for an employee to take leave to care for an ill family member or to attend the funeral of a deceased family member. *Family member*, however, is usually defined as a blood relative or someone related by marriage. Even when lesbian and gay male employees are willing to make known to their employers that they are in a relationship with someone of the same sex, a person who is their family, existing rules generally do not enable an employee to take leave to care for or grieve for such partners (or the children of such partners). Employee life insurance programs many times permit employees to purchase additional group coverage on the lives of their spouses and children, a benefit denied to unmarried employees. Disability (or workers') compensation in some jurisdictions provides different levels of benefits for employees with a spouse and/or dependent children than it provides for "single" employees, and pension programs, particularly defined benefit programs, usually include an option for an employee to elect a reduced annuity to provide a survivor's annuity for his or her spouse or minor children, another benefit denied to unmarried employees except in unusual circumstances (District of Columbia, 1990).[2]

For gay male and lesbian activists, the issue of unequal access to health benefits for the same sex partners of homosexual employees is often the focus once legal protection against employment discrimination has been obtained. In the United States, access to health insurance is, for all practical purposes, tied to employment. Most government employers offer their permanent employees the opportunity to purchase subsidized health insurance for themselves and for certain members of their family, namely their legal spouse and their own minor children and any minor children of their spouse. Given that employers may subsidize family health benefit plans at a higher dollar value (even if it is at the same percentage rate) than the subsidy given to single employees, an argument can be made that single and married employees are receiving unequal pay for equal work. More common, however, are complaints that the partners of heterosexual employees are being treated differently from the partners of homosexual employees. Technically, however, courts and human relations commissions that receive such complaints in a formal manner usually argue that the distinction made is not on the basis of sexual orientation but on the basis of marital status; that is, the difference in treatment is not because the employee is homosexual but because he or she is not legally married to his or her partner; the fact that the law prevents the homosexual partners from marrying is not a concern of the employer. (Riccucci and Gossett, 1996).

In addition to seeking redress through the legal system, lesbians and gay men have also used the political process to secure such benefits. In nearly thirty local governments (municipalities, counties, school boards, special districts), laws have been passed, collective bargaining agreements negotiated, or executive orders issued that provide for access to health benefits and various leave benefits by employees with same sex partners on the same or similar terms available to employees who have opposite sex partners (Gossett, 1994). These programs are usually referred to as "domestic partnership" benefit programs. Opposition to such programs often turns on the fear of significant increases in costs to the employer, although in practice cost increases have been very limited (Hostetler and Pynes, 1995).

Though most of the jurisdictions adopting the domestic partnership benefit programs treat unmarried opposite-sex partnerships the same way they treat same-sex partnerships, a few have proposed limiting access to benefits only to same-sex partners on the theory that opposite-sex partners have the option of marriage while same-sex partners do not. Private corporations that offer domestic partnership benefits to their employees often limit such benefits to same-sex couples. Although there is some logic in this latter position, a public entity that adopts it is open to criticism as discriminating against heterosexuals and creating "special rights" for homosexuals alone. Of course, this argument can be countered by saying that this different treatment is only offered because civil marriage is a "special right" only available to opposite-sex partners (Horne, 1994; Donovan, 1998). As the number of private-sector companies offering such benefits increases, whether or not a public-sector employer offers them may also become an issue in the competition for the best employees (Herrschaft, 2000).

Diversity Training. In recognition of the changing composition of the American workforce, a number of employers, public as well as private, have begun to focus on ways of utilizing workforce diversity to facilitate achievement of the organization's goals. Diversity training is one approach that employers take to teach workers and supervisors to deal with cultural and value differences among their co-workers and subordinates. Such training hopes to eliminate dysfunctional friction at the worksite and to train supervisors to recognize, avoid, or properly handle discriminatory treatment so as to minimize legal actions against the employer. Sexual orientation, however, is a topic ignored in many discussions of diversity (Cox, 1993; Caudron, 1995).

In organizations governed by laws or policies that prohibit discrimination on the basis of sexual orientation, inclusion of this issue in diversity training courses flows naturally from the official policy. This does not mean, however, that sexual orientation will be a particularly comfortable or easy topic to address in such training. When there is no protection against discrimination, handling the issue of sexual orientation can be quite explosive and even threatening, given that self-revelation by lesbians and gay men may lead to dismissal or harassment. On the other hand, avoiding the topic may defeat the purpose of much diversity training that is aimed at making people tolerant and understanding of important differences among co-workers which, in turn, builds trust and facilitates the work of the organization (McNaught, 1993; Winfeld & Spielman, 1995; Zuckerman & Simons, 1996).

Other Issues. Personnel offices are frequently assigned responsibility for addressing a variety of other workplace-related issues in addition to the core personnel functions. Many of these tasks can be grouped under the very broad heading "Quality of Work Life" (QWL). The presence of lesbian, gay male, and bisexual employees in the workforce is not often addressed in the existing QWL literature, but personnel officials who wish to ensure inclusive work environments need to be aware of how certain actions affect nonheterosexual employees.

Lesbians and gay men are often accused of "flaunting" their sexuality whenever it becomes known to other workers; they have violated the presumption of heterosexuality that pervades most organizations. If the employee simply made a statement about his or her sexual orientation, discussed his or her social activities over the weekend with a person of the same sex, displayed a picture of his or her family on the desk, or appeared at an office function with the person he or she lives with or is dating, many employees are scandalized and find such behavior inappropriate in a work setting. Yet, if any of these situations had involved a heterosexual employee, no notice would have been taken. If the organization is committed to equal treatment regardless of sexual orientation, managers and their advisers in the personnel office must be able to distinguish unacceptable behavior from unexpected behavior. Standards concerning appropriate levels of discussion or knowledge about an individual's life outside the office need to be consistent, although, of course, every employee is entitled to determine the amount of personal information shared for him- or herself.

"Celebrating diversity" is a somewhat recent addition to the responsibilities of the personnel office and is considered part of maintaining organizational morale. In the public sector, events such as Black History Month may be even more important than in the private sector because they also reinforce the idea that the government is there to serve all of the people. Activists are working to establish a "Gay, Lesbian, and Bisexual History Month" in October (Jennings, 1994). For the past several years, October 11 has been celebrated as "Coming Out Day" when lesbians, gay men, and bisexuals are encouraged to identify themselves in some way to their families, friends, and co-workers (http://www.hrc.org/ncop/). Late June is traditionally the time for gay pride celebrations. Again, to the extent that personnel offices are responsible for making all employees feel that the organization respects and values the contributions any group makes, they must be knowledgeable about events and times of the year that have special meaning to each particular group.

Employee recognition is often an important part of an organization's traditions. Annual award dinners, employee appreciation picnics and parties, holiday parties, and other similar activities frequently fall to the personnel office to organize. Many times these events are designed to include family members in appreciation of the important role that family life plays in support of the productivity of each worker. Invitations to "husbands" and "wives" are likely viewed as limited only to legally married partners of employees; more inclusive invitations to "your guest" or "your partner" will indicate that the partners and family members of lesbian and gay male employees are welcome.

Occupational safety and health is another responsibility often assigned to the personnel office. Although there are no occupational injuries or diseases that are unique to lesbian and gay male employees, the high incidence of acquired immune deficiency syndrome (AIDS) among gay men has created a volatile workplace issue that must be addressed by personnel officers. (See Chapter 10 in this volume.) Effective education about how AIDS is and is not transmitted has become one of the most important occupational safety issues during the last ten years.

Many organizations have antinepotism provisions in their personnel policies, and the question of how these policies apply to lesbian and gay male partners who work for the same organization presents a quandary. In organizations that provide for the registration of domestic partners and treat such partnerships in a manner similar to the way marital partnerships are treated with respect to employee benefits, for example, application of antinepotism rules to homosexual partners would seem to be appropriate. But if the organization does not recognize such partnerships in any other way, "legitimizing" the relationship through the application of antinepotism rules would undercut the rationale for not recognizing the partners for other purposes.

TRANSGENDER ISSUES

This chapter has principally dealt with the issue of lesbian and gay male employees in the public sector workforce. These employees are often considered a subset of a larger group, sometimes collectively referred to as sexual minorities. Included in the broader category are transgendered persons, namely those persons whose biological sex at the time of birth does not match the psychological gender identity that emerges subsequently. This group includes transsexuals (i.e., persons who have had or are preparing to have surgical alteration of their biological sex to match their gender identity) and cross-dressers or transvestites (i.e., persons who choose to dress as a member of the opposite sex, either on a regular basis or only occasionally, but do not plan to surgically alter their bodies) (Bornstein, 1995; Garber, 1992; Green, 2000). Transgendered persons may or may not also be lesbian or gay males. If so, they face many of the same problems as other lesbians and gay men. If they are heterosexual in their sexual orientation, they are still likely to face discrimination in the workplace (Green, 2000). The state of Minnesota and about twenty local governments have adopted laws that prohibit discrimination on the basis of gender identity in addition to sexual orientation (van der Meide, 2000). This is an emerging issue for which personnel specialists must prepare themselves.

CONCLUSION

Public-sector organizations in the new century have three options available for addressing issues pertaining to lesbians, gay men, and bisexuals who currently, or may potentially, work for them. Historically, government agencies actively sought to identify and remove such employees; to some extent, this is still the policy of the United States military. A second option is simply to ignore the fact that the organization has nonheterosexual employees and omit the issue of sexual orientation from personnel policies or practices. This probably describes the current situation in most public-sector organizations. Finally, governments can choose to recognize, appreciate, and attempt to find advantages in the diversity of sexual orientations to be found in its workforce. A minuscule but increasing proportion of the 83,000 governmental units in the United States have chosen this strategy. Though only a few cities and counties have adopted this approach, those that have include some of the country's largest municipal jurisdictions, so, in practical effect, many public employees work in places that officially forbid discrimination on the basis of sexual orientation (van der Meide, 2000).

Regardless of which strategy any particular organization currently applies to the issue of sexual orientation and the workplace, the pressures for a policy change will confront every public-sector organization in the next few years. Whether it is simply to remove a policy of automatic exclusion of homosexuals, as in the military, or to provide the protection of a nondiscrimination law, or to treat domestic partnerships in the same way that marriages are treated for employee benefits, the demands for change are unlikely to subside.

NOTES

1. In recent years, the term *sexual orientation* has become more common. Older laws still use the term *preference*. The change is due largely to both scientific findings and political pressures that argue that to whom one is sexually attracted is less a matter of choice than of biological predisposition. (Burr, 1993)
2. The federal Civil Service Retirement System, for example, allows an unmarried employee to show that a third party is financially dependent on the retiree, and provision for a survivor annuity can be made for that person. However, if the employee died before actually retiring, such a dependent third party, unlike a spouse and/or minor children, would not be eligible for an annuity. There is no requirement that spouses or children actually be financially dependent on the retiree to receive a survivor's annuity.

REFERENCES

Able v. United States 1998. 155 F. 3d 628; 1998 U.S. App. LEXIS 23359.

Acanfora v. Board of Education of Montgomery County 1974. 491 F. 2d 498.

Aspin, Les. 1993. Memorandum to Secretaries of the Army, Navy, Air Force, and Chairman of the Joint Chiefs of Staff, July 19.

Badgett, M.V. Lee. 1995. "The wage effects of sexual orientation discrimination." *Industrial & Labor Relations Review* 48 (4):726–739.

Bayer, Ronald. 1987. *Homosexuality and American Psychiatry: The Politics of Diagnosis.* Princeton: Princeton University Press.

Bornstein, Kate. 1995. *Gender Outlaw: On Men, Women, and the Rest of Us.* New York: Vintage Books.

Burr, Chandler. 1993. "Homosexuality and Biology," *The Atlantic Monthly,* March, pp. 47–65.

Button, James W., Barbara A. Rienzo, and Kenneth D. Wald. 1997. *Private Lives, Public Choices: Battles over Gay Rights in American Communities.* Washington, DC: Congressional Quarterly Press.

Caudron, Shari. 1995. "Open the Corporate Closet to Sexual Orientation Issues," *Personnel Journal* (74) August, pp. 42–55.

Chibbaro, Jr., Lou. 1995. "Clinton: Being Gay Is 'Not a Security Risk'," *The Washington Blade* [Washington, DC], August 4, p. 1+.

Chibbaro, Jr., Lou. 1993. "Sodomy Law Repealed." *The Washington Blade* [Washington, DC], September 17, p. 1.+

Colker, Ruth. 1993. "A Bisexual Jurisprudence." *Law & Sexuality.* 3:127–137.

Cox, Jr., Taylor. 1993. *Cultural Diversity in Organizations: Theory, Research & Practice.* San Francisco: Barrett-Koehler Publishers.

D'Amico, Francine. 2000. "Sex / uality and Military Service." in Craig A. Rimmerman, Kenneth D. Wald, and Clyde Wilcox, eds. *The Politics of Gay Rights.* Chicago: University of Chicago Press.

District of Columbia. "Human Resources Policy," 1990.

Doe v. City of Belleville. 1997. 119 F. 3d 563; 1997 U.S. App. LEXIS 17940.

Donovan, James M. 1998. "An Ethical Argument to Restrict Domestic Partnerships to Same-Sex Couples." *Law & Sexuality.* 8:649–670.

Duberman, Martin. 1993. *Stonewall.* New York: Dutton.

Dyer, Kate, ed. 1990. *Gays in Uniform: The Pentagon's Secret Reports.* Boston: Alyson Publications.

Garber, Marjorie. 1992. *Vested Interests: Cross-Dressing and Cultural Anxiety.* New York City: HarperPerennial.

Gossett, Charles W. 1994. "Domestic Partnership Benefits: Public Sector Patterns." *Review of Public Personnel Administration* 14. Winter, pp. 64–84.

Government versus Homosexuals. 1975. New York: Arno Press.

Green, Jamison. 2000. "Introduction to Transgender Issues." in Paisley Currah and Shannon Minter, *Transgender Equality.* New York City: National Gay and Lesbian Task Force.

Hamer, Dean and Peter Copeland. 1994. *The Science of Desire.* New York City: Simon & Schuster.

Harbeck, Karen M. 1992. "Gay and Lesbian Educators: Past History/Future Prospects." In Karen M. Harbeck, ed.. *Coming Out of the Classroom Closet.* New York: Harrington Park Press, pp. 121–140.

Harvard Law Review Association, eds. 1989. *Sexual Orientation and the Law.* Cambridge, MA: Harvard University Press.

Herrschaft, Daryl. 2000. "A Trend Towards Fairness." *HRC Quarterly.* Winter:16–17.

Holman v. Indiana. 2000. 211 F. 3d 399; U.S. App. LEXIS 8532.

Horne, Philip S. 1994. "Challenging Public- and Private-Sector Schemes Which Discriminate against Unmarried Opposite-Sex and Same-Sex Partners." *Law & Sexuality.* 4:35–52.

Hostetler, Dennis, and Joan E. Pynes. 1995. "Domestic Partnership Benefits: Dispelling the Myths." *Review of Public Personnel Administration* (15) Winter, pp. 41–59.

Human Rights Campaign. 2000. Worknet-Discrimination-State and Local Governments. http://www.hrc.org/

Jennings, Kevin. 1994. "Why We Need a Lesbian and Gay History Month," *TWN* [Miami, FL], October 19, p. 6.

Katz, Jonathon Ned. 1995. *The Invention of Heterosexuality.* New York: Dutton.

Katz, Jonathon Ned. 1992. *Gay American History: Lesbians and Gay Men in the U.S.A.* Revised Edition; New York: Meridian.

Kauth, Michael R., and Dan Landis. 1996. "Applying Lessons Learned from Minority integration in the Military." In Gregory M. Herek, Jared B. Jobe, and Ralph M. Carney, eds. *Out in Force: Sexual Orientation and the Military.* Chicago: University of Chicago Press.

Keen, Lisa. 1995. "Despite Setbacks, Sodomy Law Challenges 'on a Roll.'" *The Washington Blade* [Washington, DC], June 30, p. 1+.

Keen, Lisa. 1992. "Military History: Blueprint for Bias." *The Washington Blade* [Washington, DC], December 11, p. 1+

LeVay, Simon. 1993. *The Sexual Brain.* Cambridge, MA: MIT Press.

Lewis, Gregory B. Forthcoming. "Barriers to Security Clearances for Gay Men and Lesbians." *Journal of Public Administration Research and Theory.*

Lewis, Gregory B. 1997. "Lifting the Ban on Gays in the Civil Service: Federal Policy Toward Gay and Lesbian Employees since the Cold War." *Public Administration Review.* 57(5):387–395.

McCaffery, Robert M. 1992. *Employee Benefit Programs: A Total Compensation Perspective.* 2nd ed. Boston: PWS-Kent Publishing Company.

McNaught, Brian. 1993. *Gay Issues in the Workplace.* New York: St. Martin's Press.

Murray v. Oceanside Unified School District. 2000. 79 Cal. App. 4th 1338; 2000 Cal. Appl LEXIS 298.

Nice, David C. 1994. *Policy Innovation in State Government.* Ames, IA: Iowa State University Press.

Norton v. Mary, 417 F. 2d 1161(1969).

Oncale v. Sundowner Offshore Services. 1998. 479 U.S. 806.

Paetzold, Ramona. 1999. "Same-Sex Sexual Harassment Revisited." *Employee Rights and Employment Policy Journal.* 3:251

Personnel Administrator v. Feeney, 422 U.S. 256 (1979).

Price Waterhouse v. Hopkins, 490 U.S. 228, 104 L. Ed. 2d 268, 109 S. Ct. 1775 (1989).

Reckard, E. Scott. 1993. "Hollywood Moving Forward on Recognizing Needs of Gay Employees." *Bay Windows* [Boston, MA], July 8, p. 5–6.

Riccucci, Norma M., and Charles W. Gossett. 1996. "Employment Discrimination in State and Local Government: The Lesbian and Gay Male Experience." *American Review of Public Administration* 26(2):175–200.

Rienzo, Barbara A., James W. Button, and Kenneth D. Wald. 1999. "Conflicts over Sexual Orientation Issues in the Schools." In Elaine B. Sharp, *Culture Wars & Local Politics.* Lawrence, KS: University Press of Kansas.

Rutledge, Leigh W. 1992. *The Gay Decades: From Stonewall to the Present.* New York: Plume Books.

Shahar v. Bowers, 70 F. 3d 1218 (1995).

Shahar v. Bowers, 836 F. Supp. 869 (1993).

Shelton v. Tucker, 364 U.S. 479 (1960).

Sherman, Suzanne, ed. 1992. *Lesbian and Gay Marriage.* Philadelphia: Temple University Press.

Shilts, Randy. 1993. *Conduct Unbecoming: Lesbians and Gays in the U.S. Military: Vietnam to the Persian Gulf.* New York: St. Martin's Press.

Simonton v. Runyon. 2000. 232 F. 3d 33; 2000 U.S. App. LEXIS 21139.

Singer, Bennett L., and David Deschamps, eds. 1994. *Gay and Lesbian Stats: A Pocket Guide to Facts and Figures.* New York: The New Press.

Singer v. United States Civil Service Commission. 1976. 530 F.2d 247 (1976); *vacated,* 429 U.S. 1034.

Sullivan, Andrew, ed. 1997. *Same Sex Marriage: Pro and Con.* New York City: Vintage Books.

Turner, Ronald. 2000. "The Unenvisaged Case, Interpretive Progression, and Justiciability of Title VII Same-Sex Sexual Harassment Claims." *Duke Journal of Gender Law and Policy.* 7:57.

van der Meide, Wayne. 2000. *Legislating Equality.* New York City: National Gay and Lesbian Task Force.

Winfeld, Liz, and Susan Spielman. 1995. *Straight Talk about Gays in the Workplace.* New York City: American Management Association.

Woods, James D. 1993. *The Corporate Closet.* New York City: The Free Press.

Zalesne, Deborah. 2001. "When Your Harasser is Another Man." *The Gay and Lesbian Review,* 8 (1):19–21.

Zuckerman, Amy J., and George F. Simons. 1996. *Sexual Orientation in the Workplace.* Thousand Oaks, CA: Sage Publications.

Chapter 9

Revisiting the Reinvented Public Union

George T. Sulzner

An appropriate starting point for consideration of the task facing labor unions in the United States is the following observation by John Hoerr (1991: 31):

> Unions must reinvent themselves much as some companies are trying to do. The United States industrial relations system cannot be reinvigorated unless unions carve out a new role for themselves. They must develop a vision of how workers should help shape the technological and social revolution that is transforming the workplace. They must identify new "leverage points" for union influence. Finally, they must improve their own human resources to help put labor's new vision into practice.

This is certainly a difficult assignment, especially in the private sector, but its validity holds, as well, for public-sector unions.

The distinctions between private- and public-sector unionism are gradually eroding. The boundaries between them are blurring. As cases in point, the early development of public labor-relations systems was modeled on private-sector practices. Increasingly dispute resolution procedures developed for the special problems of government unions have spilled over into the private sphere. The list of "mixed" public-private sector unions is growing. The arrival of competition in the communication, service, and transportation sectors of the private economy is becoming a more prominent feature of the governmental landscape. For, example, Massachusetts has contracted out nearly all its human service delivery to private contractors. A number of large cities have done this as well with respect to their public education systems, and it probably is the norm in most government jurisdictions now for maintenance services to be provided by private contractors. With more and more governments trying to reinvent themselves, downsizing, rightsizing, and reengineering have become buzzwords in the public sector along with consequent reductions in the public workforce. Further, the dramatic decline in the number of unionized workers in the private sector and their corresponding loss of political influence in Washington and the state capitols have recently had a negative impact, as well, on public-sector unions. Solidarity, with fewer private-sector brethren in alliance, has been weakened. The antiunion sentiment of the populace has washed across the public terrain as well. In short, while the climate for public-sector unionism is not likely to contain as many storm warnings as forecast for the private sector, it behooves its movers and shakers to think about reinventing the public union. The task ahead will not be accomplished without difficulties and risks for public unions. They can, however, build upon current trends, accentuate present strengths, and correct evident deficiencies. Public unions need to accept the reality that efforts to reinvent themselves cannot be postponed; they must begin now.

MICROINITIATIVES AT THE TABLE AND AT THE WORKPLACE

The first matter on the agenda is relating positively to what Hoerr has characterized as the technological and social revolution that is transforming the workplace. The record of public-sector unions is already substantial on this front. They have compiled a list of accomplishments with regard to pay equity for women. They have brought large numbers of women and visible minorities into the leadership ranks of public unions. They have initiated numerous innovations with regard to work schedules and employee services that have benefited their diverse constituencies.[1] Representing large numbers of professional employees, public unions have also been leaders in the accommodation of new technologies into the workplace (Klingner, 1993; Sulzner, 1985). Much, however, still needs to be accomplished. Unions should be more aggressive in publicizing the findings of a significant amount of research that shows that productivity gains are greater in unionized workplaces than in nonunion workplaces. The common explanation relates to the higher motivation and skill of union workers and the greater stability of the work environment. Because of favorable wages and benefits, worker morale is higher, turnover and absenteeism is lower, job security and process continuity is greater, and management practices are more professional (Freeman and Medoff, 1984; Kelly and Harrison, 1992; Roberts and Bittle, 1981; Sulzner, 1983). This experience provides a solid footing for further union initiatives in the area of increasing worksite efficiencies.

PARTICIPATIVE DECISION-MAKING SCENARIOS

Vehicles for collaborative problem solving are being advocated nearly universally by analysts of the modern workplace. Additionally, a recent national survey in the United States reveals that a majority of workers surveyed, including those in a unionized setting, desire a greater voice in deciding what happens at work (Freeman and Rogers, 1995). These various forms of participative decision making (the most common types being quality circles, process improvement teams, and labor-management committees) have been functioning at all levels of government for more than a decade. Contributions to productivity, job satisfaction, and employee commitment to the enterprise seem to be associated more with on-line work reorganization experiments than with off-line participatory forms such as labor-management committees (Batt and Appelbaum, 1995). Many of the new schemes for employee participation have been introduced by management as substitutes for marginalized union influence as in the United States and France, but also in countries, such as Germany or Australia, where unionism is firmly embedded in statute or institutional structures. Unions in the United States and elsewhere have reluctantly accepted these collaborative mechanisms, recognizing, perhaps, as Berndt K. Keller observes (1995: 35) that "Unions will definitely not be able to reverse these dominating trends; careful acceptance of the new models of more direct employee involvement, not straightforward opposition, is the only viable alternative."

An approach that seems to have worked well in Australia is for unions to accept these participatory mechanisms as an extension of a union's traditional role of representation at the workplace. Apparently there, some unions have developed close cooperation with progressive management in the processes of change. They have done so to promote their members' interests with respect to present and future training needs and the development of new and additional skills (McLean, 1995). Following this tack might also enable public unions to make a difference with regard to the effects of the development of a dual labor market. Government employers increasingly differentiate between "asset" employees in a primary labor market, consisting of skilled managerial, professional, and technical positions that carry high pay and benefits, status, and job security; and "cost" employees in a secondary market, consisting of less-skilled laborer and service positions filled on a temporary or part-time basis with low pay and no benefits, no status, and no job security (Johnston and Packer, 1987; O'Rand, 1986). Interestingly, we are seeing this differentiation emerging even within the professional and managerial ranks where key personnel—whether they be professors, managers, or social workers—are working with growing numbers of temporaries who are disconnected from the ongoing life of the institution and workplace. Forestalling the creep of the secondary market and the opening up of primary market opportunities for their members is likely to be one of the important future agendas of public-sector unions.

Arguing that public unions should not ignore the opportunity to utilize cooperative mechanisms to their advantage does not preclude taking into account the risks involved for the unions. First, these participatory vehicles have been initiated primarily by employers in a unilateral fashion on a more or less voluntary basis, motivated for the most part by purely economic objectives and a desire to introduce "union-free" processes of representation. This is not an encouraging context for unions. Most of the research evaluating collaborative decision making has focused on the impact of new forms of representation on different economic outcomes such as firm or organizational performance, cost reduction/productivity, efficiency, and product or service quality. Much less attention has been directed toward employee-related outcomes such as material rewards, improvements in working conditions, the humanization of work, and organizational democracy (Keller, 1995). In brief, prior to entering into cooperative arrangements, unions must ask whether the results will matter for employees as well as for their employers and under what specific conditions cooperation will occur.

Second, the union representatives must be cognizant of and make clear to all that a broad and general consensus on participation by both sides does not necessarily imply that there are no more differences of interest. What are the exact subjects to be probed within these cooperative forums? Are different forums merely consultative, or can they become substantive/delegative? Do they or could they possibly challenge the well-established scope of managerial prerogatives? For example, Kelly and Harrison report that successful collaboration requires the possibility that employees may "achieve outcomes that also empower them" (Kelly and Harrison, 1992: 277). The literature highlights the fact that there seems to be a large difference between a comparatively far-reaching delegation of autonomy in personnel/operational task-related matters and much less participation in strategic decisions. Participation on whose terms is the key question. The answer will determine whether it is symbolic or real.

Third, unions need to think ahead with regard to the nature of the future relationship between collective bargaining as a form of interest representation and the different new forms of employee participation and consequent interest representation. Can they coexist? Certainly this seems to be the case in certain situations. Will participative forms further erode the legitimacy of unions and assist in their withering away? There is evidence that indicates this result also occurs in particular situations (Keller, 1995; Kelley and Harrision, 1992). Strategic thinking is obviously a necessity for public unions as well as for public agencies. Fourth, unions need to be aware of the fact that worker participation has the potential for widening rather than for reducing the gap between the primary and the secondary labor market. There may be a tendency toward further segmentation or even dualization between winners and losers, between key groups and marginalized workers in these participation schemes. After all, logic would dictate that in the overwhelming majority of organizations, not all employees would be given the opportunity to participate because the returns on investment in human capital are likely to differ significantly and the costs would ultimately outweigh the benefits. Moreover, it is also reasonable to assume that at least some of the participative forms were launched as potential instruments of workplace rationalization designed to lower labor costs.

The above commentary illustrates that endorsing the new forms of participation holds out the risk that the union might be co-opted by management. The external environment of law and politics also contains hazards for public unions that are engaged in participatory decision-making formats. Here, the risk is that even with mutual good will existing on the part of labor and management, outcomes will be blunted by the lack of flexibility and receptivity in the political system. Currently there are a number of legal and procedural impediments to the successful implementation of participative schemes. Management rights, particularly at the federal level, are too entrenched in statute or in contract, and thus the scope of bargaining is too narrowly defined for collaborative negotiations to occur on substantive matters. Position classification schemes are too rigid, and performance appraisal systems are too individualistic to reward group enterprise and to facilitate team building in the workplace. Moreover, labor relations boards' or commissions' interpretations of public collective-bargaining statutes have tended to favor centralized decision processes that are far removed from the point of service delivery, that zone of action that seems most amenable to joint endeavors. The Supreme Court's decision in *NLRB v. Yeshiva University* (1980), which struck down collective bargaining for faculty at private-sector universities, was also thought to have a chilling effect on efforts to encourage participative decision making. Perhaps the most difficult obstacle to overcome, however, as Kearney and Hays (1994: 48) note is the short-term focus of public actions. Sustained commitment of time and effort to implement participative decision making is a necessary element for accomplishment. As they state, "[t]runcated time horizons are serious enough in the private sector, but tend to be even more common and confounding in the public sector, where elected officials and their political appointees enter and depart government with startling rapidity and where budget shortfalls can disrupt even the most peaceful labor relations setting." Why should public unions move toward endorsing cooperative problem solving when the probability of failure is perhaps greater than the likelihood of success? Because, when the ship of state is sinking, the only way it can continue afloat is for all the passengers (labor and management) to accept their common plight and to work together to bail out the excess water and plug the leaks.

REPRESENTING THE VOICE OF THE MEMBERS AT THE WORKPLACE

The voice function of unions has received a lot of attention since Freeman and Medoff wrote their book *What Do Unions Do?* Freeman and Medoff (1984, 8) refer to voice as "the use of direct communication to bring actual and desired conditions closer together." They further observe that in industrialized economies and large enterprises, "A trade union is the vehicle for collective voice—that is, for providing workers as a group with a means of communicating with management" (Freeman and Medoff, 1984: 8). The notion of communicating the collective voice of the workers as an essential element of unionism is an old one. Beatrice and Sidney Webb highlighted the importance of voice for industrial unions in their classic study *Industrial Democracy*, published in 1902. They held that it was a requirement that unions as institutions provide mechanisms to hear the voices of their members and use those mechanisms to ascertain and advance the will of their constituents. Moreover, Sen. Robert Wagner, the principal author of the National Labor Relations Act, passed in 1935, claimed that "the [workers'] struggle for a voice in industry through the process of collective bargaining is at the heart of the struggle for the preservation of political as well as economic democracy in America (Gross, 1985: 10). Greenfield and

Pleasure (1993), in their comprehensive study of worker's voice, spotlight a troubling tendency in the empirical examinations of the voice function, following the work of Freeman and Medoff. They write, "In the burgeoning literature on employee voice, however, a significant, consistent and troubling underlying assumption appears: that voice is desirable primarily or solely insofar as it creates or contributes to the efficiency of the firm" (Greenfield and Pleasure, 1993: 170). We have already commented about a similar flaw in the research on participative decision making, obviously an activity associated closely with the exercise of voice. Greenfield and Pleasure (1993: 172) assert that this is a misplaced emphasis. "In a particular time, place, union, or industry," they observe, "voice may be directed to the improvement of production; in another context it may be the establishment of a particular system of industrial justice. Goals may vary over time and issue and multiple objectives may exist." The key point is that the legitimacy of voice does not derive from its object but from its source, the voices of the workers themselves.

Public unions, as previously noted, have incorporated the voices of an increasingly diverse workforce in their contractual, judicial, and legislative initiatives. They have, in this sense, been out in front of their private sector colleagues. More should be done, however, and this may be an activity that public unions can practice and in so doing regain some political leverage. Donald Klingner (1993: 23) argues that "what public unions must do, if they can, is to rebuild their political constituency by championing broad public interests. . . ." He thinks current social and economic conditions present public unions with some potent issues for their function of voice, that is, supportive career opportunities for a diverse workforce; organizational democracy in the allocation of benefits, training, and participation; organizational justice with regard to the continuity and solvency of retirement and health-care plans. Public unions, he claims, need to step up and articulate how they, as the chosen representatives of workers, can address these matters constructively.

The impact of unions in communicating that effective voice is demonstrated by Weil's (1992 & 1995) research on the role of unions in enforcement of the Occupational Safety and Health Act (OSHA). He found that unionized workplaces are more likely to be inspected by OSHA, that inspectors give greater scrutiny to inspections of unionized workplaces, and that union workplaces pay higher penalties for health and safety violations. Weil's studies highlight the fact that unions are credible agencies for the voice of workers. Unions have the ability to listen, articulate, and implement the interests of an increasingly diverse workforce in public organizations. Their success in shaping the social revolution at the worksite will depend on their willingness to engage this challenge.

Improving the Instruments of Industrial Justice: The Grievance Arbitration Process

The grievance process, culminating if necessary in contract arbitration, is also an aspect of employee voice in that it provides a well-established mechanism for workers to give reasoned expression to their complaints. Lewin and Mitchell

(1992) observe that similar to studies of other agencies of voice, recent research on grievance procedures has evaluated their utility in terms of their contribution to the productivity of the firm. Again, as Greenfield and Pleasure have emphasized, this focus is slanted toward an imposed value. The grievance arbitration process was not originally designed or incorporated to enhance the efficiency of an organization. That end may be a by-product, but the grievance arbitration system was implemented at worksites as a form of industrial justice to guarantee due process for handling employee discipline and other operational problems. Many questions are being raised currently with respect to the practice of the grievance arbitration process and its continuing effectiveness in handling complaints dealing with the administration of collective bargaining agreements.

The primary role of local unions in the labor-management system in the United States is protecting the integrity of the contract through the grievance arbitration procedure. The day-to-day problems of employees that in numerous other countries would be dealt with by works councils, labor courts, or job actions are the responsibility of locally elected union officers in the United States. Inadequate resolution of these work-related problems can erode the agreement, undermine the authority of the local union representatives, and in the minds of members, raise questions about the utility of having a union represent them.

Among contemporary unionists, there are a number of dissatisfactions with the operation of the grievance arbitration procedure (Roberts, 1994). Generally speaking, complaints relate to the process becoming too time consuming, unpredictable, and costly. Concern has arisen about the delays in the process. From start to finish (filing a grievance to an arbitrator's decision), it can easily take 12 to 18 months. This obviates one of the major intended attributes of the grievance arbitration process: to bring closure to problems at work before they fester and grow from molehills into mountains. Part of the difficulty is the reluctance of the parties to accept relatively inexperienced arbitrators. Relying on busy, experienced arbitrators adds to scheduling difficulties and concurrent delays. The time for resolution is also stretched out by the apparent growing reluctance on the part of management to settle disputes at the earlier stages of the grievance process. Increasingly, it seems, management is prepared to "just say no" at every step short of arbitration forcing the union to either arbitrate or accept management's position on the grievance.

The impact and value of precedent with regard to compliance with decisions throughout the process has also declined. Virtually all collective bargaining contracts have, at the end of the section outlining the grievance procedure, the declaration that the arbitrator's decision is "final and binding." In the past, this statement, with the exception of a small fraction of cases, was honored by the parties. No more. Traditionally, rarely did either party go to court to adjudicate an arbitrator's decision. Rather, they were committed to the system as the vehicle for resolving conflicts at work. They also knew that the courts were reluctant to overturn arbitrators' decisions, generally deferring to the private law of the workplace. Now, management is more disposed to sue and the courts are more disposed to intervene with decisions based on a judge's view of the contract. Litigation, of course, can add years of delay to final decisions. Further, the past practice of accepting the finality of an arbitrator's decision as binding on a particular matter until the next set of contract negotiations is fading away. Management practice currently is more likely to force the union to grieve and arbitrate the same or similar issues each time they arise if the original arbitration has not gone management's way. Needless to state, this pattern adds to the frustration of the unions with the process and lowers the morale of workers.

Finally, the process of arbitration has become rather costly. Insistence on briefs, official transcriptions, and representation by attorneys, all formalizations of the hearing format, have raised the cost of arbitration. Typically, arbitration costs each side between $1,200 and $2,000 per case. For most organizations this is a negligible expense, simply another cost of operations even if they appeal the decision to the courts. Unions fund the costs from membership dues. If the dues collected decrease, so does the union's ability to exercise its option to arbitrate and adjudicate. In this context, unions increasingly accept managements' solution to workplace problems. Looking at the contemporary situation, unionists are fully aware that access to financial resources can bias the grievance arbitration process. Companies and governments, for the most part, have much deeper pockets than unions, and by exercising their financial leverage, they have tilted the outcomes of the grievance arbitration process in their direction.

From the public unions' point of view, what can be done? They can advocate in the literature, in the legislature, and at the table for incremental changes in the process that would level the playing field, for example, expedited arbitration, establishment of a panel of arbitrators assigned to their occupational domain, or experimentation with mediation to resolve grievances. All and each of them would reduce costs and lessen the delays in reaching decisions on grievances. Unions can highlight the negative effect on the morale of employees of the current attempts by management to manipulate the grievance arbitration system to its advantage. After all, even hardball strategies under some circumstances may have diminishing returns. The United States Postal Service is an example. True, homicides at the worksite are extreme examples, but they reflect an environment at work in which problems festered for too long without resolution. Recently, the service has been engaging in various experimental practices with arbitration to expedite the backlog of grievance cases, and they have been significantly reduced.

Public unions might also decide to engage in job actions, such as work-to-rule, to get management's attention relative to their dissatisfaction with the present operation of grievance arbitration procedures. After all, the grievance arbitration system was introduced during World War II as an alternative to job actions and work stoppages by labor as expressions of their dissatisfactions with management practices. Perhaps what is needed to restore its integrity is a new version of union militancy at the workplace.

Public unions should also push hard at the table for the expansion of the scope of the grievance process. Public unions are prohibited from negotiating many important aspects of employment such as position classifications, job restructuring, work assignments, and agency organization. Although they can often negotiate or demand consultation about the impact of these decisions, by then it is often too late to represent the members' views effectively on these matters. Yet, as has been often pointed out (Kearney, 1995), if government is to be reinvented, unions will have to be part of the decision process. John Sturdivant, then president of the American Federation of Government Employees (AFGE), bluntly declared, "There will be no reinventing government . . . only bureaucratic tinkering around the margins—without fundamental changes in the union's role in the workplace" (Sturdivant, as quoted in Walters, 1993: 28). It remains to be seen whether the unions will have enough political leverage or member militancy to expand the general scope of negotiable matters. Regardless, a first step might be to expand the scope of the grievance process to include position classifications and job assignments. These can be grieved in the private sector, and some unionized public employees in Canada (Chodos and Sulzner, 1995) have the right to grieve position classifications. Expanding the scope of the grievance process along these lines at public worksites would increase the relevancy of unions for their members as public employees adjust to new management initiatives with regard to the rationalization of work processes.

Finally, though, it must be recognized that all of these potential reactions by public unions to the dilution and erosion of the legitimacy of the grievance arbitration process, while important, are marginal. What is truly needed is a return to an attitude by management that a willingness to make the procedures work is in their interest as well as that of the unions. After World War II, Roberts (1994: 396) relates management in the United States followed a "kind of implied policy of accommodation" relative to industrial unions. Thinking that unions were here to stay, management agreed to a mutually beneficial trade-off; companies would not try to oust unions, and unions would not try to push bilateralism into vital areas of corporate decision making. The key to holding the policy together was the growing membership of unions and their corresponding gains in economic and political power. Today, with unionism practically disappearing off the map in the private sector and just holding its own in the public realm, management has been freed up to reject accommodation with unions. They believe that unions are not here to stay and that management's long-term interest lies in getting rid of established unions and resisting the attempts of unions to organize nonunion work facilities. Moving from the present hostile environment into a more cooperative context in the future seems to be dependent on unions regaining a significant independent power base. Given current trends in the United States, this will take some doing on the part of both public- and private-sector unions.

MACRO-INITIATIVES IN THE PUBLIC ARENA

The most significant challenge for public unions has been the difficult adjustment to an era of fiscal restraint. Because most public services are highly labor intensive, the response to budget shortfalls has been to cut personnel, freeze hiring, eliminate some agencies and services, and privatize a number of services traditionally performed by regular government employees. In fact, as Kearney (1995: 180) observes, the "principal victim of government retrenchment has been public employees." These steps have been taken by elected chief executives of both major parties, proving once again that regardless of party ideology, political regimes in their role as employer act in similar fashion. Beyond the damage to the economic well-being of individual government workers, the labor-management system as a whole has suffered. In many instances, pay freezes and furloughs of employees have been established by executive order or through legislation. In other instances, political executives have made it clear they are not able to put any additional monetary items on the table. Often, they are only prepared to talk about reductions in the existing wage and benefit package. When pay is finally negotiated a year or two later, increasingly, there is no retroactivity. All of these actions, in effect, leave the essence of the collective bargaining process in limbo, in a form of suspended animation. When this happens, the legitimacy of the process is eroded, and the negative effect spills over into all the other dimensions of the labor-management relationship. Amelioration of the situation is inherently limited, however, if the only resort is to the bargaining table. Unions must enter the public arena if they wish to redress the opposing forces that confront them currently.

A possible approach is to litigate. The American Federation of State, County, and Municipals Employees (AFSCME) won watershed court decisions dealing with pay equity for women (Cook, 1991). Recently, they, along with the Massachusetts Teachers Association, successfully challenged a priori actions by Governor Weld of Massachusetts in furloughing state employees and increasing their individual contributions to health plans without an opportunity for negotiation. The National Treasury Employees Union (NTEU) has been noteworthy for its success in litigating disputed matters at the Federal level of labor-management relations. It is likely that we will witness even more litigation on the part of public unions as they attempt to restore rights or benefits that are the object of take-away actions by public executives and/or legislatures. Litigation, though, is basically a defensive action on the part of unions to restore elements of the status quo. To turn around present conditions, unions need to explore, as Hoerr (1991) claims, new "leverage points" for union influence in the public arena.

One new source of leverage might be the marketing of public unionism. More and more governmental agencies are engaging in systematic public relations, adding staff to assist in putting their best foot forward. Unions are late arrivals to this activity, but they urgently need to market their mission—persuading the public that governmental service is a must, at least in the areas of health, education, welfare, transportation, and the protective services, and that public unionized employees deliver it efficiently and effectively. Messages along these lines reflect the underlying motivations of public employees. For the most part, they sought public employment originally because they wanted to promote the common good rather than private greed. Unions need to demonstrate that they do not exist solely to enhance the private interests of their members. Citizens have a residue of good will for the individual acts of service performed daily by public employees.

That feeling can be turned to good advantage by public unions. AFSCME has sponsored a series of informational television spots throughout the northeast to good effect. Other unions should follow their example. The current explosion in the number of cable channels offers abundant opportunities for public unions to get the message across to the citizenry. At a minimum, community public-access television should be utilized more than it is presently. Unions could organize programming which, in part, features local governmental innovation in the provision of service and in approaches to problem solving that capitalize on the expertise of their members. Public unions seem uniquely situated to engage the prevailing political culture that is so opposed to collective action by governments and unions. Public service is a noble calling, and public unions have a responsibility to get the message out to the taxpayers who fund them.

Public unions also have to adapt better than they have to the era of government by referendum. It is no longer enough to lobby the executive and legislative branches and turn out the members to campaign for particular elected officials. Today, the boundaries of the domain of governments are being set by referenda, and, in this medium, the antiunion constituencies so far seem to have the upper hand. Decades after Proposition 13 in California, governments are still trying to live within the restrictive confines of referendum revenue limitations set by the voters. Last year, unions—both public and private—formed an alliance with other human-service organizations to defeat an additional revenue limitation by referendum in Massachusetts. These kinds of associations should be retained and promoted for future ballot initiatives in the public interest as defined by progressive rather than regressive coalitions. The thirteen ballot questions approved by the attorney general of Massachusetts for the 1996 general election, however, are not products of any progressive coalition (*Boston Globe*, September 7, 1995: 30). One problem, of course, is that a variety of needs have to be met by a given and shrinking pool of public funds. As the largesse from the federal government continues to decrease, state and local governments face additional burdens in meeting the perceived crises in health care, corrections, and public education. All of these concerns leave less money for public-employee wages, benefits, and jobs (Kearney, 1995). It is hard to build solidarity among diverse interests under these circumstances, but public unions, because they represent employees in all these service areas, could be the instrument for unified collective action at the polls. Further, even though the battle seems uphill—business interests spent, for example, five times as much on the nine referendum ballot questions as spent by labor and nonprofit interests in Massachusetts in 1994 (*Boston Globe*, May 24, 1995: 32)—there are some positive signs. Polls have indicated that citizens support designated tax increases, especially in the areas of health, education, and corrections. Unions should explore sponsoring referenda that set aside tax increases for specific purposes. The effect would be to reduce the present cutthroat competition for shares of the general fund of revenues where supporting one worthy cause means opposing another.

Along these same lines, public unions must, even in these difficult financial times, put more resources into research. They need to enter the policy fray more positively—not just opposing change, but presenting their own reasonable alternatives to deal with pressing matters on the government agenda. The economic expertise of unions must be increased so that they can go head-to-head with the policy recommendations of governmental budget and finance agencies. They also should rely more on the expertise of their members relative to the line operations of government. Managers, as we know, are listening more to their staff with regard to ways in which service can be improved in both content and delivery. Unions could do much more then they have done to utilize this advice in developing counterproposals that address problems but do not exclusively rely on personnel reductions as the most favored solution.

PROSPECTS

A crucial question that should be asked is the following one: Even if unions decided to try to reinvent themselves, are they capable of doing it? Public unions are labor-intensive organizations. They are very dependent on the human resources of their members and staff for accomplishment. Ninety percent of union officials are part-time voluntary representatives, and 90 percent of them are located in union locals throughout the United States (Roberts, 1994). Nearly all are elected and serve at the pleasure of the members. This grass-roots structure assures that the union will be in touch with the voice of the workers they represent. It also works against the leadership becoming entrenched in office and isolated from their constituents. Further, it typically means that changes in the way unions operate at the workplace cannot be implemented without the support of the membership. If leaders want to redirect scarce union resources, they must spend the time and energy to persuade and educate the members regarding the merits of the proposals. The flip side of this situation is that "as the local goes, so goes the union." If the local unit is not up to the job, the union as a whole suffers. Unfortunately, too often the performance of locals is inadequate.

Virtually all union constitutions and bylaws mandate an array of officers and committees to perform the separate tasks of the organization. Usually there will be four or five principal officers, an executive board made up of regular members to oversee the officers, and two or three committees charged with particular assignments. Typically, none of the individuals serving in these capacities will have received any training for the union positions. Their respective talents are those they bring from their primary occupations. Under these circumstances, it is rather important that locals sustain a critical mass of members from which they can draw leaders and activists. Union business is generally conducted after working hours or, in part, during regular hours of work. If union officers leave their regular duties to engage in union business, either lost wages are paid from union dues or, more commonly in the public sector, contracts contain clauses that permit union officials a "reasonable amount" of paid agency time to deal with work-related problems. Presently, though, given the pressures for efficiency in governmental operations, there has been a consistent narrowing of managements' view of "reasonable." The net effect often is "catch as catch can" with respect to fulfilling union responsibilities at the job site.

Few locals have any pool of expertise that they can resort to with respect to research or advice in the areas of law, economics, education, or politics. For that kind of assistance they must rely on their respective state or national organizations. This dependency is also present, though perhaps to a lesser degree, when collective-bargaining agreements are negotiated or arbitrated. What level of support can local unions expect from their regional, state, and national organizations? The amount and quality of assistance obviously varies from union to union, but one constant exists—unions are only as strong as their membership and consequent financial and political resources permit.

The contemporary situation for public sector unions is a mixed bag. The traditionally weak federal unions are even weaker today as the Clinton administration moves forward, toward its goal of reducing the number of employees by 272,000 persons (see Postscript). Union membership has always been low, (around 25 percent of those eligible), and it obviously will decline further, greatly reducing the ability of federal unions to provide services to their members. Federal unions appear to be an "endangered species." The picture is brighter at the state and local level. Although only one state, New Mexico in 1992, has enacted a collective-bargaining law since Ohio and Illinois in 1984, the number of public employees covered by collective-bargaining agreements has been growing. For example, in 1992, 90,000 employees were added to the ranks of those represented by unions, which was nearly double the number of new state and local government positions created in 1992. As might be expected, gains did not occur in uniform fashion around the country. New Jersey and Pennsylvania had a high degree of organizing, whereas in California, Massachusetts, and Michigan there was very little (Bronfenbrenner and Juravich 1994). Regardless of the level of organizing, it is a fact that public-employee rolls have declined in the Northeast and the Midwest, those areas where public unionization took root. Although the overall numbers show a slight increase in unionization at the state and local levels of government, many states in the above regions show a decline. For most states where public unionization is embedded in statute and in the personnel systems, the present situation regarding membership is stagnant, with marginal increases in some years offset by marginal declines in other years. Political and financial resources have not grown, and it is likely in many circumstances that union revenues have barely kept even with the rate of inflation. In a number of instances, they have probably fallen below the rate of inflation. Generally, public unions, if they wish to launch new initiatives or add to their quotient of expertise, are looking at reallocations of existing resources. Public unions, like other public organizations, have turned to their payrolls to reduce costs. Whether the reductions in staff are applied at headquarters or in the field, the net result to union locals is a cutback in service from the regional, state, or national organization and a corresponding obligation to be more self-reliant. The problem is that relying on the indigenous talents of the local organization will not enable public unions to reinvent themselves.

What can be done to free up resources for the future viability of public unions? Perhaps it is time to reduce competition and for a go-it-alone approach. More joint organizing efforts are called for, as well as consolidation of unions in the public sector. Why should the American Federation of Teachers and the National Teachers Association remain independent of each other or, for that matter, why should the various fraternal orders of police officers? With the same goals for their organizations, consolidation would cut organizing costs and reduce administrative overhead, releasing funds for more strategic purposes. They should follow, perhaps, the lead of the International Brotherhood of Machinists, the United Auto Workers, and the United States Steel Workers who are currently exploring the possibility of a major consolidation. All of the public unions, moreover, might seek affiliation with the AFL-CIO. Some public unions now play a major role in its councils, and bringing more into the fold would give them an even greater voice. Further, affiliation with the AFL-CIO would provide access for many public unions to the institution-building facilities already operating within the confines of the AFL-CIO. These would include the Organizing Institute, a new training program to centralize and upgrade the organizing efforts of its affiliates; the Labor Institute for Public Affairs, charged with improving labor's overall public image; the George Meany Center for Labor Studies, charged with educating union personnel broadly in terms of organized labor's current concerns as well as with specific programs dealing with human resource utilization; and the Union Privilege Benefit Program, which is tied to the associate membership recruiting program of the AFL-CIO. This is not to say that public unions do not have similar programs, but none are as comprehensive or as well funded. Public unions would not just be drawing benefits from this association; they would also be bringing expertise to the AFL-CIO regarding their experience in servicing a workforce that is representative of the kind that will occupy future job sites. Given the limitations on resources that all unions face, pulling together in common avoids costly redundancies and increases the critical mass of talent that public unions need to counter the prevailing civic culture and government policies. "Going it alone" or "doing your own thing," it seems pretty evident, are not prescriptions that will provide an adequate sense of direction for handling the multiple tasks that lie ahead for public unions.

POSTSCRIPT

Reviewing the chapter from the distance of four years, what is apparent is continuity in the environment for public unions. The legal framework at the national level and in the states is unchanged. Union representation has dropped at the federal level as a result of the 355,000 employees who were removed from government employment during the Clinton administration, while the numbers represented by unions at the state and local level of government in the United States remained about the same at 30.5 percent and 43.4 percent of the respective workforces (U.S. Bureau of Labor Statistics, 1998). The public unions at all levels of government continue to represent a diverse workforce, with women, African-Americans, and Hispanic workers showing an increasing propensity to support unionization (U.S. Bureau of Labor Statistics, 1999). Public unions have continued to promote pay equity and comparable work treatment for female employees, and to date about 20 states have comparable worth policies in place (Kearney with Carnevale, 2001: 153). Gains were made in enrolling health care workers into a union, and this area of employment continues to be a possible, rich proving ground for union organization as well as for correctional officers in prisons. (Kearney with Carnevale, 2001: 42–43). The success of the "Justice for Janitors" organizing campaign in southern California enlarged the Hispanic segment of public unions, however, Hispanics remain a difficult minority to unionize (Kearney with Carnevale, 2001: 22). Public unions have entered the fray of referendum politics at the state level, but the rising costs of that enterprise have deterred extensive involvement (Kearney with Carnevale, 2001: 79). John Sweeney, as president of the AFL-CIO, has allocated intensive resources for national election campaigning and voter registration efforts. Although the number of legislators oriented to economic justice and social equity concerns in Congress has increased, the administration of President Bush shows early signs of a positioning on labor policy that will set unions back on their heels and place them in a defensive mode of holding onto the status quo.

In fact, shortly after assuming office, President Bush revoked Bill Clinton's Executive Order 12871 (1993), as amended, which had established the National Partnership Council and required federal agencies to form labor-management partnerships for management purposes. President Bush's Executive Order 13203, which he signed on February 17, 2001, immediately dissolved the National Partnership Council. It is not immediately clear what impact this will have on the many partnership councils that had been created within agencies.

Reaction to this decision was immediate. On the one hand, Bush's acting director of the U.S. Office of Personnel Management (OPM), Steven Cohen, stated that abolishing the NPC will have no significant effect on labor-management relations in the federal government (Labor Relations Press, cyberFEDS).

Federal employee unions, however, saw Bush's action quite differently. For example, the head of the largest independent union for federal employees, the National Treasury Employees Union (NTEU), said that Bush's executive order represents a step back for meaningful labor relations in the federal government and risks a return to a more adversarial-based relationship between labor and management that is costly and unproductive. The president of NTEU, Colleen M. Kelley, said that "The president's decision is extremely disappointing, given the success NTEU has had with its agency partners in improving service to taxpayers throughout the federal government. . . . Working in partnership allows agency management and federal employees to work together to solve problems that hinder effective delivery of federal services" (National Treasury Employees Union, 2001).

Kelley also noted that there has been a recognition, over the years in both the public and private sectors, that the involvement of front-line employees is critical to an organization's success in carrying out its mission (National Treasury

Employees Union, 2001). The NTEU represents some 150,000 employees in twenty-five federal agencies and departments across the country.

In 1991, the General Accounting Office (GAO) reported that federal labor-management relations were "too adversarial, and bogged down by litigation over procedural issues and minutiae." After the initial seven years of partnership, the Office of Personnel Management (OPM) under the Clinton administration concluded that there "has been a sizable shift toward labor-management cooperation and away from the mutually destructive, adversarial relationships common in the past" (National Treasury Employees Union, 2001).

A very good example of a partnership success story is the reorganization and modernization of the Internal Revenue Service (IRS). Since Congress, in 1998, called for the agency to undergo the largest reorganization of a federal agency in our nation's history, the ability for all employees to have predecisional involvement in reorganization decisions has led to the smoothest transition on record. In the midst of this massive reorganization, U.S. taxpayers have experienced increased customer service throughout two filing seasons (National Treasury Employees Union, 2001).

Not surprisingly then, leaders of several federal employee unions expressed their dismay about Bush's abolishment of the NPC. For example, a spokesperson for the American Federation of Government Employees (AFGE) stated that Bush's executive order will "embolden managers who never wanted to work with unions" but pointed out that "agencies are still allowed to retain and develop policies that support labor-management collaboration and union input" (Labor Relations Press, cyberFEDS). Bobby L. Harnage, president of the AFGE, stated that "In one day, President Bush has torn apart what has taken years to craft—the development of a government workplace that is people-driven, highly flexible, creative and responsive to the changing needs of the American people. It is the American taxpayers who will suffer as a result of Bush's actions. Partnerships have led to increased efficiency and service to the public" (American Federation of Government Employees, 2001).

Harnage went on to say that "Bush's hasty and foolhardy actions give no time for new Cabinet officials to review the benefits of partnership and the billions of dollars that have been saved through partnership. This is not sound management based upon any effort to serve the public efficiently and effectively. It is a giant step backward, to years of adversarial relations between federal workers, their unions and the government which we hoped we had moved past. This is a divisive act and one that says he's more bully than peacemaker" (American Federation of Government Employees, 2001).

The effects of Bush's executive order that abolishes the NPC will take some time to unfold, but they certainly signal a desire on the part of the administration to return to a top-down decision-making management style. Bush's appointees may prefer this. However, the NPC was something supported by both the managers and the workers in the trenches who did the actual partnering to improve government productivity, efficiency, and ultimately the delivery of public services. It remains to be seen whether those grass-roots partnerships can survive in the current political environment.

It should also be noted that wage gains in the decade of the 1990s, for public unions did not reflect the increase of prosperity during the last six years of the decade. The Bureau of Labor Statistics reported that wages averaged about 3.5 percent, slightly above the level of inflation (U.S. Bureau of Labor Statistics, 1998). This reflects a trend that seems to be developing in which there is a stabilization of financial relationships among the bargaining parties over time. The monetary outcomes of collective bargaining are becoming more predictable as governments exert predominant influence over the economic package and as both sides have a clearer grasp of the financial parameters that constrain the process. Collective bargaining in the public sector has decreasing utility with regard to the determination of increments of pay and benefits (Kearney with Carnevale, 2001: 177; Sulzner, 1998). Public unions, operating within an environment that holds little likelihood for breakthrough advances on the macro level of public-sector labor relations have increasingly turned their attention to bargaining vehicles that may improve their ability to create favorable impacts on conditions that affect the workplace, that is, issues of process and productivity, health and safety, workload and schedules, training and technologies, and communication. Chief among these are the practices of "interest-based bargaining" and "grievance mediation."

Interest-based bargaining is contrasted with position-based bargaining. Similar to what Walton and McKersie called "integrative bargaining," this type of negotiation focuses on handling common concerns, is continuous in practice, operates best at the operational level of service delivery, and rests on an attitudinal foundation that recognizes the equality of the parties as "partners in problem solving". Kearney places interest-based bargaining within the broad framework of participative decision making. He notes that it "promotes the kind of work climate consistent with teamwork" and "had the potential to make collective bargaining a strategic asset in organizations as it pushes to the surface numerous problems management may not know exist" (Kearney with Carnevale, 2001:136). In the public sector, one of the particular realms where interest-based bargaining takes place is matters relating to personnel policy and practice. Much of this activity is driven by the need to adapt current personnel policies and practices to a diverse workforce. Employers and unions are being forced to consider a range of concerns, dealing with employee training and development, day care and elder care, maternity and paternity leaves, and accommodations for older workers. Some examples of union training and development efforts are:

AFSCME District 37 in New York City administers an education fund that offers to members skills-improvement courses and assistance in preparing for promotion exams;

SEIU Local 100 in California helped develop a career ladder program for nurses;

AFSCME Local 1776 at the University of Massachusetts at Amherst negotiated an apprenticeship program for janitors so they could train to be electricians, painters, plumbers, and carpenters (Kearney with Carnevale, 2001:200).

Managers and union officials have developed partnerships at the federal level of government founded on interest-based processes that have engaged contract and workplace disputes. There are further reports of successful interest-based programs in Wisconsin, Missouri, and Maine. Additionally, in site-based management in K–12 education, administrators and teachers jointly determine policies, rules, and procedures in expanding nationally (Kearney with Carnevale, 2001:342). Undoubtedly, these joint efforts will grow in number as the economic payoffs from collective bargaining diminish.

Grievance mediation is also becoming more common in unionized work facilities and is the second leg, along with interest-based bargaining, in a participative climate at work locations. Part of the drive to initiate grievance mediation as a dispute resolution procedure is a general recognition among the parties and neutrals that arbitration dockets have too many cases that should have been resolved at earlier steps in the grievance process. Their presence at the arbitration stage adds to the general delay in obtaining decisions from the arbitrators and to the costs of dispute resolution systems. Similar to interest-based bargaining, grievance mediation is premised on the idea that the parties can be equals in problem solving and attempts, through the facilitation of a mediator, to identify the "real" interests in dispute and identify alternative ways by which they might be resolved satisfactorily for all the involved participants. The process is not one where adversaries face off against each other. Rather, emphasis is placed on understanding the other party's perspective and, in so doing, finding common ground for conciliation of the dispute. The outcomes are not precedents for any future contests and typically are not embodied in any official form. Its use is spreading throughout the states with a unionized workforce, most notably in the United States Postal Service in its handling of EEO complaints (Kearney with Carnevale, 2001:321). The Canadian public service has just completed a year-long experiment in which adjudicators (arbitrators) of the Public Service Staff Relations Board have functioned as grievance mediators in federal labor-relations disputes. Although the final evaluation of the experiment is not yet completed, early indicators point to considerable success (Sulzner, 2001). Many contract disputes, as well as disciplinary cases that involve the ending of employment, need the final judgment of an arbitrator. Grievance mediation, however, can be an important vessel of intervention, which can produce settlement where disputes occur and where practical remedies that have some hope of staying power can be developed.

The attention of public-sector labor relations seems to be moving toward a more decentralized location. This places more stress on the competency of local managers and union officials where human resources may already be stretched rather thin. Concerns are offset, however, by the parties' day-to-day knowledge of processes, conditions, hindrances, and lubricants that effect relationships at work. A host of surveys in the past several years confirm that employees are increasingly concerned about working conditions at the facilities where they are employed. It is in the interest of both management and the public unions to zero in on these matters and to attempt to address them effectively. Ultimately, though, both sides share a common interest in raising the economic package for public employees.

When minimal gains result from the period (the 90s) of unprecedented growth in revenues at the national and state levels of government, this task appears to be particularly daunting as the nation in the spring of 2001 faces steep declines in the economy and in the resulting revenues. Public unions will likely maintain a steady state of well being in the short term. Reinvention is still, however, a necessity for the long-term future of public unionism.

NOTE

1. Not all public unions have welcomed women and people of color into their ranks. Public safety unions (police, fire, and corrections) in particular have responded in many instances only after intervention by the courts. See Riccucci (1990).

REFERENCES

American Federation of Government Employees (AFGE). Press Release. "Bush Halts Federal Partnerships: Tough Luch Taxpayers!" February 16, 2001. http://www.afge.org/REALEAS/1-021601.htm.

Batt, Rosemary, and Eileen Appelbaum. 1995. "Worker Participation in Diverse Settings: Does the Form Affect the Outcome, and If So, Who Benefits?" Paper presented at the Tenth World Congress of the International Industrial Relations Association. Washington, D.C., May 31–June 4.

Boston Globe. May 24, 1995: 32, and September 7, 1995: 30.

Bronfenbrenner, Kate, and Tom Juravich. 1994. *The Current State of Organizing in the Public Sector: Final Report.* Amherst, Mass.: Labor Relations & Research Center.

Chodos, Philip, and George T. Sulzner. 1995. "The Public Service Reform Act of Canada and Federal Labor Relations." *Journal of Collective Negotiations in the Public Sector,* 24(2): 97–110.

Cook, Alice H. 1991. "Pay Equity: Theory and Implementation." In Carolyn Ban and Norma M. Riccucci, eds., *Public Personnel Management: Current Concerns—Future Challenges.* New York: Longman.

Freeman, Richard B., and James L. Medoff. 1984. *What Do Unions Do?* New York: Basic Books.

Freeman, Richard B., and Joel Rogers. 1995. "Worker Representation and Participation Survey: First Report of Findings." *Proceedings of the Forty-Seventh Annual Meeting of the Industrial Relations Research Association,* January 6–8. Washington, D.C., 336–45.

Feuille, Peter. 1992. "Why Does Grievance Mediation Resolve Grievances?" *Negotiation Journal* 8, no. 2: 131–145.

Greenfield, Patricia A., and Robert J. Pleasure. 1993. "Representatives of Their Own Choosing: Finding Workers' Voice in the Legitimacy and Power of Their Unions." In Bruce E. Kaufman and Morris M. Kleiner, eds., *Employee Representation: Alternatives and Future Directions.* Madison, Wisc.: Industrial Relations Research Association.

Gross, James A. 1985. "Conflicting Statutory Purposes: Another Look at Fifty Years of NLRB Law Making." *Industrial and Labor Relations Review* 39(1): 7–18.

Hoerr, John. 1991. "What Should Unions Do?" *Harvard Business Review* 69(3): 30–40.

Johnston, William B., and Arnold H. Packer. 1987. *Workforce 2000: Work and Workers for the 21st Century.* Indianapolis: Hudson Institute.

Kearney, Richard C. 1995. "Unions in Government: Where Do They Go From Here?" In Steven W. Hays and Richard C. Kearney, eds., *Public Personnel Administration: Problems and Prospects,* 3rd ed. Englewood Cliffs, N.J.: Prentice Hall.

Kearney, Richard C., and Steven W. Hays. 1994. "Labor-Management Relations and Participative Decision Making: Toward a New Paradigm." *Public Administration Review* 54(1): 44–51.

Kearney, Richard C., with David G. Carnevale. 2001. *Labor Relations in the Public Sector,* 3rd ed. New York: Marcel Dekker, Inc.

Keller, Berndt K. 1995. "Emerging Models of Worker Participation and Representation." *Proceedings of the Tenth World Congress of International Industrial Relations Association.* Washington, D.C., May 31–June 4, 32–38.

Kelly, Mary Ellen R., and Bennett Harrison. 1992. "Unions, Technology, and Labor-Management Cooperation." In Lawrence Mishel and Paula B. Voos, eds. *Unions and Economic Competitiveness.* New York: M.E. Sharpe, Inc.

Klingner, Donald E. 1993. "Public Sector Collective Bargaining: Is the Glass Half-Full, Half-Empty, or Broke." *Review of Public Personnel Administration* 13(3): 19–28.

Labor Relations Press, cyberFEDS. "Managing Today's Federal Employees," vol. 2, issue 10. http://www.feds.com/nll_lib/mtfe/mtfe0210.htm.

Lewin, David, and Daniel J.B. Mitchell. 1992. "Systems of Employee Voice: Theoretical and Empirical Perspectives." Paper presented at the Forty-Fifth Annual Meeting of the Industrial Relations Research Association. New Orleans, La.: January 3–5.

McLean, Greg. 1995. "Reform—Unions' Future." Paper presented at the Tenth World Congress of the International Industrial Relations Association. Washington, D.C., May 31–June 4.

National Labor Relations Board v. Yeshiva University, 444 U.S. 672 (1980).

National Treasury Employees Union (NTEU). Press Release. "Bush's Decision Is a Step Back for Meaningful Labor-Management Relations." February 16, 2001. http://www.nteu.org/

O'Rand, A. 1986. "The Hidden Payroll: Employee Benefits and the Structure of Workplace Inequality." *Sociological Forum* 1: 657–683.

Riccucci, Norma M. 1990. *Women, Minorities and Unions in the Public Sector.* Westport, Conn.: Greenwood Press.

Roberts, Higdon C., Jr. 1994. "Contemporary Perspectives and the Future of American Unions." In Jack Rabin, Thomas Vocino, W. Bartley Hildreth, and Gerald J. Miller, eds. *Handbook of Public Sector Labor Relations.* New York: Marcel Dekker, Inc.

Roberts, M., and W.E. Bittle. 1981. "The Union Contract: A Solid Investment." *Federationist* 88(5): 8–10.

Sulzner, George T. 1983. "Productivity and Job Security: The Issues of the 1980s in United States Public Sector Labor Relations." *Journal of Collective Negotiations in the Public Sector* 12(2): 79–86.

———. 1985. "Public Sector Labor Relations: Agent of Change in American Industrial Relations?" *Review of Public Personnel Administration* 5(2): 70–77.

———. 1998. "The Implementation of the Labor-Management Sections of the 1992 Public Service Reform Act and the Future of Federal Labor-Management Relations in Canada." *Journal of Collective Negotiations in the Public Sector* 27, no. 2: 131–148.

———. 2001. "Arbitrators Doing Mediation: An Experiment in Dispute Resolution at the Public Service Staff Relations Board of Canada." Unpublished manuscript.

USA Today. September 1, 1995, 5a.

U.S. Bureau of Labor Statistics. 1998. *Public Employment by Level of Government 1955–1998,* Washington, D.C.: Government Printing Office.

———. (BLS) 1999. "The Employment Situation: October, 1–25."

Walters, Jonathan. 1993. "The Chastening of Public Employees." *Governing* 6(4): 26–30.

Webb, Sidney, and Beatrice Webb. 1902. *Industrial Democracy.* London: Longmans, Green and Co.

Weil, David. 1991. "Enforcing OSHA: The Role of Labor Unions." *Industrial Relations* 30(1): 20–36.

———. 1992. "Building Safety: The Role of Construction Unions in the Enforcement of OSHA." *Journal of Labor Research* XIII(1): 121–32.

———. 1995. "Mandating Safety and Health Committees: Lessons From the States." *Proceedings of the Forty-Seventh Annual Meeting of the Industrial Relations Research Association,* January 6–8. Washington, D.C.: 273–81.

Chapter 10

Chronic Health Challenges and the Public Workplace

James D. Slack

In both the public and the private sectors, the American workplace currently faces two kinds of health care challenges.[1] The first kind can be described as "acute," and these include routine health issues such as colds and influenza as well as such reparable damages to the body as broken bones, ergonomics, and migraine headaches. These acute, or short-term health conditions represent a challenge to the workplace because they result simultaneously in a drop in productivity and an increase in the utilization of the organization's health care package.

Although acute health challenges are problematic, chronic health conditions represent a far greater challenge to the workplace. This challenge includes long-term and recurring health conditions that in many cases, are either irreparable or terminal. These include physical impairments such as cancers, dysfunctional organs, and paralysis, as well as such mental impairments as depressive disorders, schizophrenia, and anxiety disorders. Because chronic health issues do not always present a healing remedy, they tend to place a greater burden on the organization's benefit package. They also require greater investments in thought and resources in finding remedies to the resulting disruption to the workflow. Moreover, the challenge of chronic health issues is that management must find ways to protect the workplace rights of affected employees as well as maintain the collective health rights of the entire workforce. As a result, chronic health issues tend to be subject to increasing litigation, and this represents the greatest cost to the workplace. This chapter focuses on what public personnel managers need to know about the legalities surrounding chronic health issues that affect the workplace.

DISABLED AMERICAN EMPLOYEES

Disabilities are chronic health conditions. In the United States and other developed countries, they are caused by a wide variety of physical and mental factors as well as by adverse behavioral patterns. Although chronic health conditions have a direct impact on the ability to work, none of the top causes of disabilities stem necessarily from workplace accidents or workplace conditions but from the employee's personal environment. The top ten causes for disabilities are reported in Table 10.1.

TABLE 10.1 Top Ten Causes of Disabilities in the U.S. and Developed Nations

Ranking	Cause of Disability
1	ischaemic heart disease
2	unipolar major depression
3	cerebrovascular disease
4	road-traffic accidents
5	alcohol use
6	osteoarthritis
7	trachea, bronchus, & lung cancers
8	dementia/other degenerative & hereditary central nervous system disorders
9	self-inflicted injuries
10	congenital abnormalities

SOURCE: Christopher J.L. Murray (ed.). 1996. *Global Health Statistics.* Cambridge, MA: Harvard University Press. Also see "The Numbers Count," National Institute of Mental Health @ www.nimh.nih.gov/publicat/numbers.cfm (January 2001).

In the United States, there are more than 86 million disabled persons—31 percent of the total population. According to the U.S. Centers for Disease Control and Prevention (2001), there are approximately 42 million people with physical impairments. More than 7 million use assistive technology devices (ATD) because of mobility impairments, and almost 5 million use ATDs for orthopedic impairments. As reported in Table 10.2, the vast majority of Americans with physical disabilities are of working age, and most do not require prolonged absences from the job. Table 10.3 reports that these disabilities significantly affect both men and women, as well as European and African Americans.

The National Institute of Mental Health (2001) estimates that nearly 45 million adult Americans suffer from at least one form of mental impairment.[2] Within this total there are 18.8 million adults with depressive disorders, 2.2 million with schizophrenia, 19.1 million with anxiety disorders, and 4 million with Alzheimer's disease. Adult women are nearly twice as vulnerable as men in acquiring depressive disorders, and it appears that depression is occurring at increasingly younger periods of life for many Americans. Posttraumatic stress disorder from rape and sexual abuse is also prevalent among adult women (Valentine, 2000). The U.S. Surgeon

TABLE 10.2 Number of Selected Reported Chronic Conditions per 1,000 Persons by Working Age Categories

Disability	18–44 Years in Age	45–64 Years in Age
diabetes	11.8	58.2
prostrate disease	2.2	14.7
female genital disease	24.2	20.7
heart disease	39.3	116.4
high blood pressure	49.6	214.1
arthritis	50.1	240.1
visual impairment	24.0	48.3
hearing impairment	41.9	131.5
speech impairment	7.8	6.6
paralysis of extremities	5.1	13.5
orthopedic impairment	122.4	177.8

SOURCE: U.S. Center for Disease Control, National Center for Health Statistics, January 2001 (www.cdc.gov/nchs/fastats).

General (U.S. Department of Health and Human Services, 1999) estimates that approximately 15 percent of all American adults seek mental health services each year. This amounts to approximately 200 million workdays lost annually (*US Newswire*, 2000; Dewa and Lin, 2000). In the 1990s, psychiatric claims filed with the U.S. Equal Employment Opportunity Commission (EEOC) more than doubled—to approximately 3,000 per year (Forster, 2000). By the year 2020, major depressive disorders is expected to replace heart disease as the number one cause of disabilities among adults in the United States and other developed nations (Murray and Lopez, 1996). Work-related factors, such as economic hardship, role conflict, work

TABLE 10.3 Number of Selected Reported Chronic Conditions per 1,000 Persons by Age Group (45–64) and by Race and Gender

Disability	Race		Gender	
	White	Black	Male	Female
diabetes	55.8	121.4	56.9	59.4
prostrate disease	16.2	23.0	30.4	—
female genital disease	28.5	37.8	—	40.0
heart disease	126.9	93.2	133.5	100.3
high blood pressure	207.8	344.7	214.8	213.3
arthritis	234.2	250.2	193.0	284.0
visual impairment	45.6	67.9	61.0	36.4
hearing impairment	155.1	71.9	183.4	82.9
speech impairment	7.2	15.7	7.9	5.4
paralysis of extremities	7.3	7.0	16.8	10.3
orthopedic impairment	179.9	156.4	187.5	168.6

SOURCE: U.S. Center for Disease Control, National Center for Health Statistics, January 2001 (www.cdc.gov/nchs/fastats).

overload, and stress, is expected to contribute greatly to the rise in depressive disorders among adult men and women (McCurry, 2000; U.S. Department of Health and Human Services, 1999).

Disabled Americans can be found in all segments of society; they are rich and poor, Anglo and non-Anglo, men and women. Some have chronic conditions that are very apparent to everyone, and others suffer from conditions that are not so immediately apparent; still others have disabilities that may not be evident at all. Whether or not one can actually see the infliction, people with chronic physical or mental impairments are considered to be disabled.

PROTECTING DISABLED WORKERS

Disabled Americans need protection because society makes them vulnerable in at least three ways. First, historically we have neglected the needs of disabled people. It was not until the early 1970s that the first piece of legislation was enacted in the United States that actually dealt with the issue of providing disabled people with access to fundamental social and community activities, such as entering public buildings or using the bathrooms in those buildings. By ignoring their needs for nearly two hundred years, we also denied them meaningful participation in society. Second, various disabilities are often misunderstood and, as a result, the capabilities of disabled individuals are frequently underestimated. Our initial tendency is to assist the paraplegic person in the wheelchair or to refrain from directing too many questions to the person with a speech impairment. By wanting to help them in this fashion, we often make the assumption that disabled people cannot participate meaningfully in our society. Third, disabilities can make us feel uncomfortable, and we therefore tend not to want disabled individuals around us. The history of cancer certainly reflects this feeling. Uncomfortableness is sometimes pronounced when it comes to being around people with contagious diseases, such as hepatitis or the human immunodeficiency virus (HIV) that causes acquired immunodeficiency syndrome (AIDS). Our own fears about disabilities can block opportunities for meaningful participation on the part of the disabled person.

Two pieces of federal legislation, the 1973 Rehabilitation (Rehab) Act and the 1990 Americans with Disabilities Act (ADA), protect the workplace rights of disabled employees. Although the two laws have many similarities, there are four factors that separate them (Slack, 1998). The first difference is jurisdiction. The 1973 Rehabilitation (Rehab) Act protects individuals who are employed in federal programs or those who are employed in agencies that either receive federal contracts or direct federal funding. Hence, state and local governments, as well as many nonprofit organizations, are covered by Rehab. The ADA, on the other hand, is much broader in jurisdiction because it covers organizations that affect commerce and that do not receive federal funding. Congress defined *affecting commerce* broadly to include the public and private sectors. While the vast majority of businesses are covered under ADA—organizations that employ fifteen or more full-time employees for most of the year—state and local governments and nonprofit organizations may also fall under the jurisdiction of the ADA if they have programs that do not receive federal funding.[3] Hence, public human-resource specialists must be aware that employees in their organizations may be protected by both Rehab and the ADA.

The second difference deals with selection expectations. Rehab requires management to be "disability sensitive." It requires managers to take affirmative action with disabled individuals in the hiring, promotion, and retention processes. The ADA, on the other hand, requires management to be "disability-blind" when it comes to those matters. It prohibits managers from using affirmative-action practices in selecting disabled individuals. Public and nonprofit human-resource specialists must, therefore, be aware as to which law applies to which selection process because Rehab can invite litigation from disabled persons and the ADA can invite litigation from those who are not.

The third difference between Rehab and ADA deals with enforcement mechanisms. Seeking remedy against an employer is a bit more complex under Rehab, requiring the involvement of the EEOC, the federal department responsible for funding the particular program, and the U.S. Department of Justice. The ADA, however, simply requires notification through the EEOC.

Fourth, the laws differ in terms of permanent physical modification expectations, with architectural requirements being much stricter under Rehab. Employers "must accommodate" the disabled in removing office barriers. Hence, the organization is expected, regardless of cost and inconvenience, to do such things as install wheelchair ramps, provide braille instructions in elevators, and make restrooms handicap-accessible.[4] In contrast, the ADA only requires permanent structural modifications to be made only when those accommodations are "readily achievable" in terms of expense and effort.

From all other perspectives, Rehab and the ADA are identical. Each is designed to protect the workplace rights of disabled Americans or, in the case of Rehab, "handicapped-Americans."[5] An employer cannot discriminate against a disabled employee if the employee is otherwise qualified to perform the essential functions of the job with or without reasonable accommodations. In providing protection from workplace discrimination, both Rehab and the ADA use the same three-pronged definition of *disability*. A person can claim to be protected under either law if he or she:[6]

1. has a physical or mental impairment that substantially limits one or more of the major life activities; or
2. has a record of such an impairment; or
3. is regarded as having such an impairment.

The second and third prongs of the definition are intended to prevent speculation on the part of the employer as to what employee-related costs the future might bring to the organization. They are especially important in combating subtle and clever disability-based discrimination in the workplace. The second prong protects a person from either being denied employment or being terminated from employment as a result of fear that additional costs might be borne at the end of the impairment's remission. *Cleveland v. Policy Management System* (1999) and *Sheehan v. Marr* (1st Cir. 2000) underscore that, although an employee may be deemed as "totally disabled" through another law (such as, the Disabled Veterans Act), management is prevented from presuming automatically that the employee cannot perform the essential functions of the job and, hence, is unprotected under Rehab and the ADA.

The third prong protects those individuals with impairments that might never manifest, yet might present the possibility of someday adding to the organization's health care and workplace expenses. A series of court decisions *(School Board of Nassau County v. Arline, Murphy v. United Parcel Services, Inc.,* 1987 and *Sullivan v. River Valley School District, 1999),* make it very clear that employees must be judged on actual abilities to perform the essential functions of the job. They cannot be judged on the basis of financial fears or social bigotry.

DISABILITIES COVERED AND NOT COVERED

Even though all chronic health conditions are viewed as disabilities, the federal government has been relatively careful in delineating specifically which disabilities are protected under the ADA and Rehab. Physical impairments include physiological disorders, cosmetic disfigurements, and anatomical losses or dysfunctions that affect at least one of the major body systems.[7] Mental impairments include such psychological disorders as emotional or mental illness, specific learning disabilities, mental retardation, and organic brain syndrome.[8]

Some physical and mental impairments are not protected. For instance, EEOC guidelines do not recognize certain physical characteristics, such as age, pregnancy, normal ranges of weight and muscle tone, height, and hair color. Personality traits, for example, poor judgment and hot tempers, are also not considered impairments.[9] Congress made it very clear that certain lifestyles and behaviors are not protected under either Rehab or the ADA: homosexuality, transsexualism, transvestism, pedophilia, exhibitionism, voyeurism, kleptomania, compulsive gambling, pyromania, to name a few.[10]

Past abuse of addictive drugs and alcohol is considered a protected disability, but *current* abuse is not protected under either Rehab or the ADA. In *Collings v. Longview Fibre* (9th Cir. 1995), "current" use of addictive drugs was defined as being a matter of months prior to detection and discharge. In *Conley v. Village of Bedford Park* (7th Cir. 2000), the court ruled that recovering alcoholics are protected under Rehab and the ADA as long as they are actually "recovering" and as long as they can perform the essential functions of the job. The reason for distinguishing between past and current problems with drugs and alcohol is that Congress acknowledges the right of employers to maintain a safe workplace. Employers can demand that employees' blood and urine be free from drugs and alcohol at the workplace (Colbridge, 2000). In *Newland v. Dalton* and *Williams v. Widnall* (9th Cir. 1996), the courts ruled that employers do not have to tolerate disruptive behavior or insubordination of recovering addicts (drugs or alcohol) even if the behavior is the result of the addiction.

Finally, the courts have also limited correctable chronic health conditions that are protected under the ADA and Rehab. In a series of rulings in 1998 and 1999, the Supreme Court determined that many correctable impairments—such as poor eyesight or high blood pressure—are not protected. As Justice Sandra Day O'Connor noted, "If the impairment is corrected it does not 'substantially limit' a major life activity."

SUBSTANTIALLY LIMITING MAJOR LIFE ACTIVITIES

Disabilities covered by both Rehab and the ADA must substantially limit major life activities. Rehab and the ADA take a broad view on what constitutes "major life activities": walking, seeing, hearing, performing manual tasks, or caring for oneself. All or a combination of these activities are central to performing anyone's job. In *Bragdon v. Abbot* (1998), the Supreme Court underscored the fact that protection under these two laws do not necessitate a "total" limitation but only a "substantial" limitation. However, in *Sutton v. United Air Lines, Inc.* (1999), the Court ruled that decisions regarding substantial limitations must be made on a case-by-case basis and not simply on a diagnosis of an impairment. To be deemed "substantially limiting," Rehab and the ADA require the disability to be severe in nature, long-term in duration, and permanent in terms of impact on major life activities.

NOTIFICATION AND DOCUMENTATION REQUIREMENT

The ADA and Rehab are similar to other pieces of civil rights legislation in that the burden of proving membership within the protected class belongs solely to the individual seeking protection. Hence, it is the responsibility of the disabled employee to provide management with clear notification and accurate documentation about the chronic health condition. Because many kinds of disabilities are not readily apparent, this requirement typically means the submission of a note or report from either a physician or a mental health counselor.

The notification and documentation requirement may seem benign albeit "bureaucratic," but it can have serious impact on persons with certain kinds of disabilities. People tend not to want to "publicize" personal health conditions and, given the social stigma attached to some chronic illnesses, many employees are afraid of ridicule or retribution. Mental depression or past drug abuse, for instance, may not be issues about which one wants to talk with a supervisor, and given the stigma that still surrounds HIV/AIDS, providing documentation remains risky business for many people infected with the retrovirus (Slack, 2001A; 2001B). For employees with HIV/AIDS, the requirement means presenting *official* documentation that directly links the retrovirus to him- or herself. An anonymous blood test will not satisfy the notification requirement.

The fact is that Rehab and the ADA make the topic of chronic health conditions far less personal, and they change the very nature of confidentiality in the workplace (Slack, 1998; 1996). Especially in circumstances where reasonable accommodations are requested, the circle of entities that may need to know *something* (yet *not necessarily everything*) about an employee's health condition may extend well beyond the confidence of the immediate supervisor: human resource specialists, other supervisors (in case of job transfer), co-workers and union stewards (in case of job modifications), the legal staff (for guidance on applying Rehab and the

ADA), the insurance staff (for purposes of benefit consultation and processing pharmaceutical claims), the organization's first-aid staff (in case of emergencies), the medical staff (for purposes of verifying the disability), and the Employee Assistance Program (EAP) staff (for counseling, intervention, and crisis management.)

Ultimately the employee is faced with the dilemma of either not notifying the employer—out of fear of ridicule, ostracization, or discrimination—or placing trust in that the employer will comply with the tenets of either law and be sensitive to the changing nature of confidentiality as well as reactions to social stigmas that may be attached to specific chronic conditions. In both the private (Scheid, 1998) and public (Slack, 1998) sectors, management's compliance *with* the law tends to come part and parcel with understanding *of* the law. Similarly, it appears that disabled employees' tendency to exercise rights covered by both laws increases with added education and training about protections provided by the laws (Granger, 2000). Without proper notification and documentation, however, disabled workers cannot make claims and management bears no responsibility in protecting workplace rights.[11]

MANAGEMENT'S RESPONSIBILITIES

Chronic health conditions present tremendous challenges to workplace and personnel managers. Some of the more critical issues include (1) redefining job descriptions, (2) determining the agency's capacity to provide reasonable accommodations, (3) controlling costs, (4) curtailing the spread of contagious diseases at the workplace, and (5) developing strategies to train staff and employees to better prepared them to handle effectively situations involving disabilities.

Job Descriptions.   Rehab and the ADA protect disabled workers as long as they can perform the essential functions of their jobs. Although required in neither Rehab nor the ADA, it is wise to reanalyze each job description within the organization so that tasks deemed to be "essential" in nature can be distinguished from tasks that are "marginal." Doing so permits management to determine—and to document in court, if necessary—whether a disabled job applicant or employee is otherwise qualified to perform the essential functions of a job. It is especially important to modify job descriptions prior to beginning the selection process because they are the basis for most job announcements and will be central to counter litigation.

Reasonable Accommodations.   Rehab and the ADA require management to provide reasonable accommodations to otherwise qualified employees and job applicants with disabilities if such accommodations are needed in performing the essential functions of the job. Both laws also require management to do so only in response to requests by the employees for such accommodations. Although management cannot impose reasonable accommodations on employees or job applicants, it should be prepared to enter into a discussion about specific workplace accommodations.

What is reasonable accommodation? From management's point of view, it is important to provide disabled employees with reasonable accommodations for at least two reasons. First, reasonable accommodation constitutes a significant form of health intervention. *Early intervention* can keep disabled employees healthier and, therefore, more productive for a longer period of time. Second. adoption of reasonable accommodation strategies can be submitted in court as evidence that the organization is attempting to comply with both the letter and spirit of Rehab and the ADA.

But what constitutes a reasonable accommodation? Reasonable accommodations can and should take a variety of forms. Recognizing that reasonable accommodation is very much in the eye of the beholder, Congress suggests three types: (1) physical or structural changes, such as modifying buildings to ensure wheelchair accessibility; (2) job modification, such as removing marginal tasks from the job description, acquiring assistive technology devices (ATDs), flextime utilization, job transfer, or filling of vacancies; and (3) modification of selection and training materials and processes, such as using special readers or interpreters or changing the size of print on examinations.

Management must recognize that each worksite—indeed, each set of essential functions, type of disability, stage and level of disability, and individual capability—constitutes a unique situation and thereby calls for unique accommodations. Hence, what is needed for one disabled American to perform the essential functions of a particular job in a specific workplace will not be identical to what is needed for another disabled American in either the same or a different place of employment. A case-by-case approach is required, and this means that human resource specialists and workplace supervisors must gain familiarity with the chronic health conditions present in the particular workforce.

In many ways, devising reasonable accommodations for physical disabilities is more straightforward than building strategies to deal with employees with mental disabilities. Certainly there are exceptions; some physical disabilities, especially those with few outward manifestations, can be very problematic in finding accommodations that are acceptable and reasonable. Contagious physical illnesses, such as hepatitis or HIV-related illnesses, are causes for concern, especially in improperly trained workforces or ill-equipped workplaces. For the most part, however, it is somewhat simpler to deal with an employee who is paraplegic or perhaps one who has a hearing or sight loss. Assuming the necessary reexamination of job descriptions, one can determine if the employee is otherwise qualified to perform the essential functions of the job. One can also determine if reasonable accommodations are needed to enable the employee to perform the essential functions.

Providing reasonable accommodations for mental impairments is a much harder task, one that workplace supervisors and human resource specialists least understand. (Schwartz & Post, 2000; Wimbiscus, 1996–97; Meltsner, 1998) This had led to a growing number of lawsuits. One employee with a mental impairment was denied the use of accrued paid leave time, as well as unpaid leave, to deal with psychiatric problems (*Schmidt v. Safeway, Inc.,* 1994). Another was called derogatory names by supervisors (*Owens v. Archer Daniels Midland,* 1999), and another suffered from a hostile work environment (*Disanto v. McGraw-Hill,* 1998).

One organization denied a mentally disabled employee's request for accommodations in the form of medication breaks, restroom breaks, and technical assistance during training sessions (*Barton v. Tampa Electric Co.*, 1997). In each of these instances, the organization lost in litigation and was directed to compensate the employee with millions of dollars.

Stephen Sonnenberg (2000a; 2000b) offers a variety of suggestions on how to deal effectively with employees who suffer from mental disabilities. Five of his suggestions are listed below:

1. Review and revise job descriptions to include references to employees' ability to cope with stressful circumstances.

The job description should protect both the organization and the employee. If stressful activities are central to the job, coping with stress should be listed as an essential function.

2. If an employee appears or claims to have a mental impairment, scrupulously avoid generalizations or stereotypes about mental illness. Resist the temptation to play armchair psychologist.

Much of the litigation pertinent to mental impairments results from managers and human resource specialists attempting to solve mental health problems on their own. Management should have in place a referral system to handle these issues.

3. If an employee complains that working with his supervisor is too stressful and causes emotional problems, elicit a written admission that he will be able to perform essential job duties only if he has a different supervisor or works in a different location.

This will help protect the organization from litigation. Neither Rehab nor the ADA requires reasonable accommodation, in this case a job transfer, simply because of difficulty in working with either a supervisor or a co-worker (Goldman, 1999). Reasonable accommodation is permitted only in cases where the employee is substantially limited in his or her ability to perform the essential functions of the job. The organization is further protected if the job description includes the statement of "ability to work in stressful conditions" as an essential function.

4. Consider even vague requests for accommodation from employees, their family members, or their representatives as triggering a duty to engage in an interactive process with the employee.

The request for reasonable accommodation may not always be clear and precise. This is especially true in the case of employees with mental health conditions (Noe, 1997). Because reasonable accommodations are always on a case-by-case basis, the employee may not even know what is needed to keep him or her able to perform the essential job tasks. Management must listen closely.

5. A psychiatric diagnosis is not determinative.

The decision to provide reasonable accommodation is never a function of a medical opinion. It is always a function of law. Rehab and the ADA, and subsequent court decisions, are the basis for determining who is protected and who is accommodated. The psychiatric diagnosis is only the first step in making these determinations.

Controlling Costs. If employers dislike Rehab and ADA, it is primarily because of a fear of cost. With few exceptions, however, providing individualized and reasonable accommodations prove to be one of the least expensive activities. The Job Accommodation Network (2001) estimates that most reasonable accommodations will cost under $300 per case and, in the vast majority of cases, will cost under $100. Some examples of relatively inexpensive accommodations might include flextime for medical appointments or work breaks to apply medication. For employees with suppressed immune systems or mental disabilities, a relatively inexpensive accommodation might involve an occasional five-minute "stress time-out." For employees with special diet needs, especially diets needed for specific medication, vendors can provide specialized machine foods at no cost to the employer.

But the expense of accommodation is a legitimate concern for the work organization and so the question remains: How far do you have to go to provide reasonable accommodation? In *Alexander v. Choate,* the court underscored the need for accommodations to be *reasonable.* Organizations do not have to endure undue hardships in providing accommodations. They do not have to operate in the red, nor do they have to lay off employees. Private businesses are expected to make profit, and public and nonprofit organizations are expected to continue service delivery activities.

What determines undue hardship? As in the case of accommodations, undue hardship is seen through the eye of the beholder and is determined on a case-by-case basis. Rehab and the ADA provide the following guidelines to assist organizations and the courts in determining whether specific accommodations are "reasonable" in particular work organizations: (1) The nature and cost of the specific accommodation, (2) the financial resources of the specific organization, (3) whether the organization is a part of a larger organization with greater financial resources, and (4) the nature (indoor/outdoor, temporary/permanent) of the worksite.[12]

The cost of group insurance packages is a continuing concern of employers and is a primary issue in the area of undue hardship. Unlike other kinds of accommodations, the group health package represents a "collective" accommodation; therefore, the cost of it is not eased terribly by the size of the organization. In a series of decisions (*Chrysler v. DILHR*, 1976, *Western Weighing Bureau v. DILHR, McDermott v. Xerox*, 1977) rendered even before the passage of the ADA, the courts have ruled consistently that a work organization cannot discriminate against employees based on either knowledge about current costs or speculation about future costs. Yet the courts have also recognized the right of work organizations to consider the issue of expense in purchasing insurance policies and health care packages for employees. This seems especially true in the case of mental impairments.(Serritella, 2000) In *Weyer v. Twentieth Century Fox Film Corp.* (9th Cir. 2000), the court held that a more limited plan of coverage, specifically a shorter term of coverage, for mental disabilities was permissible to help reduce costs and thereby avoid undue hardship. In *Hess v. Allstate Ins. Co.* (2000), the court found that work organizations and insurers cannot be held liable for offering less health care coverage for mental disabilities than it does for physical disabilities. In essence, the court is continually searching for balance between protecting disabled Americans in the workforce and ensuring that the workplace does not suffer unduly. Debate over group health insurance is central to the search for balance.

Curtailing the Spread of Disease at the Workplace.   In protecting the rights of disabled employees, management must also be concerned with guarding the health of all employees. A fundamental fear is the transmission of contagious physical impairments, particularly blood-borne pathogens like HIV and hepatitis, through workplace activities. While the threat of infection by blood-borne pathogens is most prevalent among service providers in health care agencies, transmission can also occur quite readily among employees in a variety of public safety organizations. Furthermore, the potential of contagion is very real in any workplace because every employee "carries" blood that can "spill" by simple cuts and tears on the skin. Whether in the municipal budget office or the county hospital's emergency room, the workplace is not as safe as it once was. It is management's responsibility to minimize the amount of workplace contact with blood, as well as to establish protective procedures for instances when it occurs. The Occupational Safety and Health Administration (OSHA) and the National Institute for Occupational Safety and Health (NIOSH) provide employers both procedural regulations and technical assistance in meeting this responsibility.[13]

Training.   It is management's responsibility to develop and implement strategies to train staff and employees to better prepare the workplace to handle effectively situations involving chronic health conditions. This involves training on how to implement Rehab and ADA as well as on how to protect the health of all employees. It also entails acquiring a basic and preliminary understanding of the types of mental and physical impairments found in the particular workplace. Not providing such training simply increases vulnerability to litigation as a result of inappropriate workplace actions and behavior. Litigation is always the most expensive workplace cost.

Especially in the public sector, employee and staff training tends to take a back seat to other budgetary priorities. Richard L. Schott (1999) notes that this is especially true when it comes to providing training programs in the area of mental health. Stephen Sonnenberg (2000a; 2000b) reminds us that the effectiveness of mental health training depends on developing relationships with mental health professionals. To gain a better understanding of both physical and mental impairments, it is quintessential to incorporate a variety of external expertise into the training strategy.

For management to send an unambiguous message as to the importance of employee disabilities, training must be mandatory, workplace specific, and periodic. It should include such topics as (1) Rehab, ADA, and OSHA regulations; (2) workplace-specific procedures that management will follow when an employee seeks to provide notification and documentation about a disability, (3) the changing nature of confidentiality under Rehab and the ADA and its application to the specific workplace; (4) services provided by the organization, including concrete but preliminary sketches of possible "individualized" reasonable accommodations; (5) undue-hardship issues pertaining to the specific workplace; and (6) with the help of external experts, familiarization with disabilities and health issues potentially facing the organization. In addition to the periodic formal training sessions, routine staff meetings should include relevant topics, such as updates on pertinent court cases, web-based information, and circulation of relevant information found in outlets like NIOSH or the *Report on Disability Programs*.[14]

CONCLUSION

One thing is abundantly clear about the American workplace: Healthy people are less expensive and more productive than sick people. Two things are equally evident about the American work force: Individually, we are aging and thereby incrementally becoming less healthy; collectively, we are facing a greater number (and a wider variety of kinds) of chronic health challenges. Because Rehab and the ADA prohibit the exclusion of persons with many types of mental and physical impairments from the workplace, management must do whatever it can to keep them healthy and productive. Whether it is a result of humanitarian feelings of compassion for the employee or businesslike concerns about profit and productivity, it is in management's best interest to develop a workplace environment that supports the needs of disabled employees as well as guards the health of all employees. Building a positive workplace environment—one where employees with chronic health conditions feel comfortable in exercising their rights under the law and where supervisors feel encouraged in the application of those rights—remains a challenge for management and human resource specialists in the new century.

NOTES

1. I want to thank Mark Feeser, a graduate assistant in the Department of Government and Public Service at the University of Alabama at Birmingham, for his help in the preparation of this manuscript.
2. Diagnoses of mental illness in the United States is based on standards set by the American Psychiatric Association. *See:* American Psychiatric Association. *Diagnostic and Statistical Manual for Mental Disorders,* 4th ed. (DSM-IV). Washington, DC: American Psychiatric Press, 1994.
3. Several types of organizations are exempt from both pieces of legislation: the federal government, Native American tribes, private clubs, and in certain situations religious organizations.
4. The laws also differ in terms of appropriate references to chronic health conditions. Rehab refers to persons with chronic health conditions as being "handicapped." ADA refers to these persons as being "disabled." Hence, public human resource specialists should use the term *handicap* in referring to Rehab and *disability* when referring to the ADA.

5. For the sake of clarity throughout the rest of this chapter, only the term *disability* will be used.
6. 29 CFR section 1630.2(h)(1).
7. 29 CFR section 1630.2(h)(2).
8. 29 CFR section 1630.2(h)(2) and 29 CFR section 1630, App., 1630.2(h).
9. 42 USCA section 12211(b).
10. 56 Fed. Reg. 35,748, July 26, 1991.
11. Ibid.
12. 42 U.S.C. 12111 section 101(10)(B) (1995).
13. The website for OSHA is www.osha-slc.gov. The website for NIOSH is www.cdc.gov/niosh.
14. *Report on Disability Programs* is a newsletter published by Business Publishers, Inc., 8737 Colesville Road, Suite 1100, Silver Spring, MD 20910-3928. (301) 589-5103. www.bpinews.com. It is published 25 times a year.

REFERENCES

Alexander v. Choate, 469 U.S. 287 (1985).
Barton v. Tampa Electric Company, 6 AD Cases 1179 (M.D. Florida 1997)
Bragdon v. Abbott, 118 S. Ct. 2196 (1998).
Chrysler v. DILHR, 14 Fair Empl. Prac. Cases (BNA) 344 (Wis.Cir.Ct. 1976)
Cleveland v. Policy Management Systems Corp., 526 U.S. 795 (1999).
Colbridge, Thomas D. 2000. "Defining Disability Under the Americans with Disabilities Act." *FBI Law Enforcement Bulletin* 69, no. 10 (October):28–32.
Collings v. Longview Fibre, 63 F 3d 828 (9th Cir. 1995), cert. denied, 116 S. Ct. 711 (1996).
Conley v. Village of Bedford Park, 2000 WL703806, (7th Cir. Ill. 2000).
Dewa, Carolyn S., and Elizabeth Lin. 2000. "Chronic Physical Illness, Psychiatric Disorder, and Disability in the Workplace." *Social Science and Medicine* 51, no. 1. (July):41–51.
Disanto v. McGraw-Hill, 8 AD Cases 1147 (S.D. New York 1998).
Forster, Julie. 2000. "When Workers Just Can't Cope." *Business Week* (October 30):100–101.
Goldman, Charles. 1999. "Recognizing When Stress Results from Covered Disability." *ADA Compliance Guide* (July).
Granger, Barbara. 2000. "The Role of Psychiatric Rehabilitation Practitioners in Assisting People in Understanding How to Best Assert Their ADA Rights and Arrange Job Accommodations." *Psychiatric Rehabilitation Journal* 23, no. 3 (Winter):215–214.
Hess v. Allstate Ins. Co., 19 NDLR 28 (D. Me. 2000) (No. 99–384–P–C).
Job Accommodation Network. 2001. www.janweb.icdi.wvu.edu 918 Chestnut Ridge Road, Suite 1, Morgantown, WV 26506-6080. Phone: (800) ADA-WORK.
McCurry, Patrick. 2000. "Disabling Depression." *Director* 54, no. 2 (September):34–38.
McDermott v. Xerox, 65 N.Y.2d 213, 480 N.E. 2d 695,491 N.Y.S. 2d 106 (1985).
Meltsner, Samuel. 1998. "Psych. Disabilities: What's Real, What's Protected." *Business and Health* (June):46–53.
Murphy v. United Parcel Service, Inc., 119 S. Ct. 2133 (1999).
Murray, Christopher J.L., and Alan D. Lopez. (eds.) *Summary: The Global Burden of Disease: A Comprehensive Assessment of Mortality and Disability from Diseases, Injuries, and Risk Factors in 1990 and Projected to 2020.* Cambridge, MA: Harvard School of Public Health, Harvard University Press, 1996.

National Institute of Mental Health, U.S. National Institutes of Health, January 2001, www.nimh.nih.gov/publicat/numbers.cfm

Newland v. Dalton, 81 F.3d 904 (9th Cir. 1996).

Noe, Samuel R. 1997. "Discrimination Against Individuals with Mental Illness." *Journal of Rehabilitation* (January–March):20–26.

Owens v. Archer Daniels Midland Co., 30 F. Supp.2d. 1802 (C.D., Illinois 1999).

Scheid, Teressa L. 1998. "The Americans with Disabilities Act, Mental Disability, and Employment Practices." *Journal of Behavioral Health Services and Research*. 25, no. 3:312–325.

Schmidt v. Safeway, Inc. 561 F. 3d. 302 (C.D., Illinois 1994).

School Board of Nassau County v. Arline, 480 U.S. 273 at 284 (1987).

Schott, Richard L. 1999. "Managers and Mental Health: Mental Illness and the Workplace." *Public Personnel Management*, vol 28, no. 2 (Summer):161–184.

Schwartz, Robert H., and Frederick R. Post. 2000. "The ADA and the Mentally Disabled: What Must Firms Do?" *Business Horizons* 43, no. 4 (July/August):52–56.

Serritella, Diane. 2000. "Disability and ADA: Employers and Insurers Not Obligated by the ADA to Provide Equal Benefit Plans for Physical and Mental Disabilities." *American Journal of Law and Medicine* 26, no. 4:112–115.

Sheehan v. Marr, 207 F.3d 35 (1st Cir. 2000).

Slack, James D. 2001A. "Zones of Indifference and the American Workplace: The Case of Persons with HIV/AIDS." *Public Administration Quarterly* (forthcoming.)

Slack, James D. 2001B. "The Americans with Disabilities Act and Reasonable Accommodations: The View From Persons with HIV/AIDS." *Policy Studies Journal* (forthcoming.)

Slack, James D. 1998. *HIV/AIDS and the Public Workplace: Local Government Preparedness in the 1990s*. Tuscaloosa, AL: University of Alabama Press.

Slack, James D. 1996. "Workplace Preparedness and the Americans with Disabilities Act: Lessons from Municipal Government's Management of HIV/AIDS." *Public Administration Review*, vol. 56, no. 2 (March/April):159–167.

Sonnenberg, Stephen P. 2000a. "Coping with Mental Disabilities in the Workplace: Tips for Employers." *Employee Benefit News* 14, no. 7 (June):78–81.

Sonnenberg, Stephen P. 2000b. "Mental Disabilities in the Workplace." *Workforce* 79, no. 6:142–144.

Sullivan v. River Valley School District, 194 F.3d 1084 (10th Cir. 1999).

Sutton v. United Air Lines, Inc., 119 S.Ct. 2139 (1999).

U.S. Centers for Disease Control and Prevention, National Center for Health Statistics, January, 2001. (www.cdc.gov/nchs/fastats/disable; www.cdc.gov/nchs/fastats/aids-hiv.)

U.S. Department of Health and Human Services. 1999. *Mental Health: A Report of the Surgeon General*, Rockville, MD: U.S. Department of Health and Human Services, Substance and Mental Health Services Administration, Center for Mental Health Services, National Institutes of Health, National Institute of Mental Health. See especially Chapter 4, "Adults and Mental Health."

US Newswire. 2000. "International Labor Organization Report Examines Mental Health in the Workplace." (October 10).

Valentine, Pamela V. 2000. "Traumatic Incident Reduction I: Particulars of Practice and Research." *Journal of Offender Rehabilitation*, vol 31, no. 3/4:1–5.

Western Weighing Bureau v. DILHR, 21 Fair Empl. Prac. Cases (BA) 344 (Wis.Cir.Ct. 1977).

Weyer v. Twentieth Century Fox Film Corp., 198 F.3d 1104 (9th Cir. 2000).

Williams v. Widnall, 79 F. 3d 1003 (10th Cir. 1996).

Wimbiscus, Mark. 1996–97. "Responsibilities of Employers Toward Mentally Disabled Persons Under the Americans with Disabilities Act." *Journal of Law and Health*, 11:173–193.

Chapter 11

Public Employees' Liability for "Constitutional Torts"

David H. Rosenbloom
Margo Bailey

Every person who, under color of any statute, ordinance, regulation, custom, or usage, of any State or Territory or the District of Columbia, subjects, or causes to be subjected, any citizen of the United States or other person within the jurisdiction thereof to the deprivation of any rights, privileges, or immunities secured by the Constitution and laws, shall be liable to the party injured in an action at law, suit in equity, or other proper proceeding for redress. For the purposes of this section, any Act of Congress applicable exclusively to the District of Columbia shall be considered to be a statute of the District of Columbia.

Civil Rights Act of 1871, as amended and
codified in 42 U.S. Code, Section 1983 (1982).

INTRODUCTION

Ever since the establishment of the Republic, public employment in the United States has been considered a "public trust." The concept that public employees have special obligations to the political community has prompted a variety of restrictions on their constitutional rights. For instance, the Constitution prohibits federal employees from being electors in the electoral college and from accepting gifts, offices, emoluments, or titles from foreign governments without the consent of Congress. The document also requires them to swear or affirm their support for it. As early as 1801, President Jefferson sought to restrict the First Amendment rights of federal employees to engage in electioneering because he deemed such activities ". . . inconsistent with the spirit of the Constitution and [their] duties to it" (Rosenbloom, 1971, 39–40). Over the years, public employees have faced limitations not only on their political and economic activities, but also on their residency, privacy, speech and association, and general liberties (Rosenbloom, 1971; Rosenbloom and Carroll, 1995). Beginning in the 1970s, they also became potentially liable for "constitutional torts," which has had the effect of requiring public administration to comport more fully with constitutional law and values. The development of this additional legal obligation, its scope, and its consequences for public personnel management in the United States are the subjects of this chapter.

Constitutional torts are acts committed by public officials or employees, within the frameworks of their jobs, that violate individuals' constitutional rights in ways that can be appropriately remedied by civil suits for money damages. For instance, the violation of an individual's Fourth Amendment right to privacy through an unconstitutional search is such a tort. So is a public employee's unconstitutional act of racial discrimination. Civil liability for money damages for constitutional torts can now be potentially attached to most federal, state, and local government employees. In general, they are vulnerable to both compensatory and punitive or exemplary damages. Under Eleventh Amendment interpretation, state governments and agencies cannot be sued in federal court for money damages for their constitutional torts (though other remedies for their unconstitutional acts are available). By extension, state employees cannot be sued as surrogates for state governments in such cases (*Will v. Michigan Department of State Police*, 1989). However, state employees can be sued in their *personal* capacities for constitutional torts committed while exercising official authority (*Hefer v. Melo*, 1991). Similarly, federal employees, but not agencies, can be sued for money damages in constitutional tort suits (*FDIC v. Meyer*, 1994). Local governments, which enjoy no Eleventh Amendment immunity and are treated as "persons" in this area of the law, can be sued for compensatory but not for punitive or exemplary damages for constitutional torts caused directly by their policies (*Pembaur v. City of Cincinnati*, 1986; *City of Newport v. Fact Concerts*, 1981). Even public employees who never deal directly with members of the public may face liabilities for violations of their subordinates' constitutional rights.

This chapter focuses public employees' *personal* liability for constitutional torts, which makes "constitutional competence" a matter of basic job competence by requiring public personnel to know the constitutional law that governs their official actions (Rosenbloom, Carroll, and Carroll, 2000: chapter 2). For human resource managers, personal liability for constitutional torts requires knowing how the Constitution pertains to public employment and to building constitutional protections into administrative systems for recruitment, selection, employee development, promotion, adverse actions, reductions in force, equal opportunity, labor relations, background investigations, drug testing, and assisting employees with addictions and other problems.

PUBLIC OFFICIALS' ABSOLUTE IMMUNITY: THE TRADITIONAL APPROACH

Until the 1970s, under federal judicial interpretations, public employees at all levels of government generally held absolute immunity from civil suits stemming from the exercise of their official functions. Under this approach, when public officers are acting within the outer perimeter of their authority, they cannot be sued personally for violating individuals' constitutional rights. For example, in *Stump v. Sparkman* (1978), a state judge who enjoyed absolute immunity was shielded from a damage suit even though he authorized the sterilization of a "mildly retarded" female high school student under circumstances that failed to protect her constitutional right to due process of law. Moreover, the judge acted without specific legal authorization but not beyond the ultimate scope of his office. The rationales for granting legislators, judges, executive branch officials, and rank-and-file employees absolute immunity are all somewhat different, but at their root is the belief, developed in common law interpretations, that the activities of governmental functionaries should not be controlled by individuals' actual or threatened lawsuits. As the Supreme Court stated the principle in *Spalding v. Vilas* (1986: 498), the first case on official executive immunity to reach it:

> In exercising the functions of his office, the head of an Executive Department, keeping within the limits of his authority, should not be under an apprehension that the motives that control his official conduct may, at any time, become the subject of inquiry in a civil suit for damages. It would seriously cripple the proper and effective administration of public affairs as entrusted to the executive branch of the government, if he were subjected to any such restraint.

This approach drew some of its legal strength from the ancient principle of "sovereign immunity," which is derived from the notion that "the king can do no wrong." It precludes suing the federal and state governments in some types of cases unless they have given their permission to be sued through a tort claims act or other legal device (*United States v. Lee*, 1982).

GENERAL LEGAL TRENDS RELATED TO OFFICIAL LIABILITY

Whatever the strength of the legal rationales for public employees' absolute immunity, by the 1970s judicial support for the idea had clearly weakened, apparently as a result of two major legal trends. First, there had been an expansion of legal liability generally throughout the American legal system. As Peter Schuck (1988: 4) observes, "On almost all fronts and in almost all jurisdictions, liability has dramatically expanded. It does not seem to matter what kind of party is being sued. Doctor or public official, landlord or social host, government agency or product manufacturer—all are more likely to be held liable today." Although the number of suits initiated per capita may be no larger at present than in colonial times and other periods in United States history (Galanter, 1988: 19), plaintiffs appear more apt to win or receive satisfactory settlements because of contemporary judicial interpretations. Schuck, a leading student of "suing government" (1982), summarizes the underpinnings of contemporary tort law:

> Although the new judicial ideology of tort law is complex and multifaceted, four elements stand out: (1) a profound skepticism about the role of markets in allocating risk; (2) a shift in the dominant paradigm of causation [from determinant to probabilistic causal relationships]; (3) a tendency to broaden jury discretion; and (4) a preoccupation with achieving broad social goals instead of the narrower, more traditional purpose of corrective justice between the litigants (Schuck, 1988: 6).

The second trend toward greater liability for public administrators is rooted in the vast changes in constitutional doctrines initiated by the Warren Court (1953–1969). Beginning in the 1950s, the federal judiciary demonstrated a continuing propensity to afford individuals greater constitutional protections vis-à-vis public administrative action (Rosenbloom and O'Leary, 1997). Whole categories of persons who formerly had very few constitutional protections when interacting with public bureaucracies were granted greater substantive, privacy, procedural, and equal protection rights under the First, Fourth, Fifth, Eighth, and Fourteenth Amendments. For instance, public employees were afforded substantial due process protections in dismissals, greater freedom of speech and association rights (including such activities as whistle-blowing and joining labor unions), and much stronger claims to equal protection of the laws. Clients or customers who receive welfare or public housing gained clear procedural due process protections of these benefits for the first time. The courts reinterpreted the equal protection clause to overturn the "separate but equal" doctrine that had previously permitted public services, such as education, to be racially segregated. Prisons were also desegregated under the Fourteenth Amendment and drastically reformed to reduce overcrowding and brutal conditions under the Eighth and Fourteenth Amendments. Individuals confined to public mental health facilities were granted a constitutional right to treatment or habilitation. The constitutional rights of persons accused of crimes were expanded to include "Miranda warnings" (*Miranda v. Arizona*, 1969) and other safeguards. The privacy and due process rights of persons engaged in "street-level" encounters were also enhanced, though somewhat modestly (Lipsky, 1980; *Terry v. Ohio*, 1968; *Delaware v. Prouse*, 1979; *Kolender v. Lawson*, 1983). More recently, property rights have been strengthened against administrative "takings" by zoning regulations (*Dolan v. City of Tigard*, 1994) and forfeitures (*United States v. James Daniel Good Real Property*, 1994). Taken together, these developments brought about a revolution in the relationship of the federal courts to public administration at all levels of government. It is no longer unusual to find a federal judge deeply involved in the management of a state or county prison or local school system. A substantial "juridical" element was added to federalism (Carroll, 1982), and the courts have become far more salient to such public administrative matters as budgeting and personnel (Rosenbloom and O'Leary, 1997; Horowitz, 1983; *Missouri v. Jenkins,* 1990, 1995).

When individuals possessed few constitutional rights in their encounters with public administrators, constitutional torts would necessarily be limited in number. Certainly police brutality or violations of the Fifteenth Amendment's guarantee of the right to vote regardless of race might have been the basis of suits, but by and large it was difficult for public administrators to violate individuals' constitutional rights simply because the public held so few substantive, procedural, and equal protection guarantees in their interactions with government agencies. However, once the courts articulate rights for public employees, clients/customers, prisoners, public mental health patients, individuals engaged in street-level encounters, and property owners, the potential number and scope of constitutional violations becomes substantial. Consequently, some enforcement mechanism is necessary to enable individuals to preserve and vindicate their new protections against unconstitutional administrative action. Enter liability.

FROM ABSOLUTE TO QUALIFIED IMMUNITY: THE RISE OF LIABILITY

As late as 1959, a plurality on the Supreme Court, in *Barr v. Matteo* (p. 571), continued to adhere to the principle that:

> It has been thought important that officials of government should be free to exercise their duties unembarrassed by the fear of damage suits in respect of acts done in the course of those duties—suits which would consume time and energies which would otherwise be devoted to governmental service and the threat of which might appreciably inhibit the . . . administration of policies of government.

However, once the public was gaining an array of constitutional protections in their dealings with administrators and liability law was becoming more expansive, the courts sought to establish a better balance between the governmental requirement of efficient and effective administration, on the one hand, and the need to deter violations of individuals' rights and to compensate for them, on the other. In fact, so remarkable had been the changes in liability and constitutional law that by the 1970s the concept of "absolute" immunity for most public officials was clearly out of place.

During that decade, the Supreme Court used two legal vehicles to redefine the liability of public administrators. First, in *Bivens v. Six Unknown Named Federal Narcotics Agents* (1971), the Court held that federal officials could be liable, directly under the Constitution, for breaches of individuals' Fourth Amendment rights. In essence, the Court reasoned that the Fourth Amendment gives victims of unconstitutional federal searches and seizures a constitutional right to sue the officials involved for money damages. Subsequently, the Court ruled that similar rights to redress exist under the Fifth and Eighth Amendments (*Davis v. Passman,* 1979; *Carlson v. Green,* 1980). Under ordinary circumstances, individuals can bring suits against federal officials under the First Amendment as well (see *Bush v. Lucas*, 1983, for an exception).

Second, the Supreme Court dramatically reinterpreted the standards for liability regarding state and local public administrators and officials. The Court resurrected the Civil Rights Act of 1871, which is now codified as 42 U.S.C. section 1983 and is generally called section 1983. The relevant portion of the act is quoted in the epigraph to this chapter. Although well conceived in the Reconstruction Era as a means of providing federal judicial protection to former slaves, the act was rendered virtually moribund by a number of judicial interpretations and doctrines that drastically restricted its coverage (Rosenbloom and O'Leary, 1997; "Section 1983 and Federalism," 1977). In terms of liability, the courts refused to interpret literally the act's explicit application to "every person who." Instead, the judiciary reasoned that in writing "every person," Congress could not have intended to override the long-standing absolute immunity at common law enjoyed by many state and local government officials, such as legislators and judges, from civil suits for damages. Consequently, even though such officials might be directly responsible for the violation of individuals' federally protected rights, they could not be sued effectively under the act. It was through the redefinition of official immunity during the 1970s that the act became a major force in public administration and American law.

The Supreme Court departed from past interpretations in *Scheuer v. Rhodes* (1974) when it abandoned the concept of absolute immunity for officials who exercise executive functions. Instead, it opted for a "qualified immunity" that afforded many public officials immunity from civil suits for money damages only if they acted in good faith and reasonably. A year later, in *Wood v. Strickland* (1975: 321–322), *reasonably* was interpreted to mean whether the official "knew or reasonably should have known that the action he took within his sphere of official responsibility would violate the constitutional rights" of the individuals affected.

Bivens, Scheuer, and *Wood* opened the door to many suits against public administrators by individuals seeking money damages. Under the standard for the qualified immunity they developed, these suits could allege that the administrators failed to act in good faith by displaying malice or a reckless disregard of individuals' rights. In practice, defending against such a charge proved burdensome for the public officials involved. The issue of "good faith" is considered a matter of fact that may be submitted to juries for determination. Consequently, suits could be drawn out and very expensive to defend. Under such conditions, the process itself was punishment, and public officials were consequently under substantial pressure to settle out of court, without strict regard to the merits of the charges against them. In an age of crowded dockets, elaborate trials in liability suits against public officials also took a toll on the courts. The Supreme Court sought to reduce these pressures in *Harlow v. Fitzgerald* (1982), which established the current standard for public administrators' qualified immunity and liability.

The *Harlow* decision "completely reformulated qualified immunity along principles not at all embodied in the common law" (*Anderson v. Creighton*, 1987: 645). The new standard for qualified immunity eliminated the issue of good faith from suits for compensatory damages: "government officials performing discretionary functions, generally are shielded from liability for civil damages insofar as their conduct does not violate clearly established statutory or constitutional rights of which a reasonable person would have known" (*Harlow v. Fitzgerald*, 1982: 818). For the most part, motives become irrelevant. The key question is whether the conduct violated clearly established constitutional rights of which the administrator should reasonably have known. This is a matter of law that can be decided by a judge in a truncated legal proceeding called a summary judgment. The judge grants qualified immunity if he or she concludes that the law was not clearly established or that an administrator could not reasonably have known that the conduct involved would violate a constitutional right.

The great advantage of the *Harlow* approach is that summary judgments are far quicker and much less burdensome than jury trials. The immunity is from suit, not just a defense against liability (*Mitchell v. Forsyth*, 1985). The *Harlow* construction applies to federal officials directly under the Constitution and to local officials under section 1983.

THE LOGIC OF LIABILITY: DETERRENCE AND JUDICIAL INFLUENCE ON PUBLIC ADMINISTRATION

When the courts do something as dramatic as overturning the effects of centuries of common law, one is impelled to consider their rationale and the effects of the change. The logic of rejecting absolute immunity in favor of qualified immunity (or liability) is clear. First, the liability under consideration here is personal liability, not the liability of agencies or government entities. Personal liability is viewed by the Supreme Court as an excellent enforcement mechanism. In the Court's words, ". . . the *Bivens* remedy [that is, official liability], in addition to compensating victims, serves a deterrent purpose" (*Carlson v. Green*, 1980: 21), and the general point has been to "create an incentive for officials who may harbor doubts about the lawfulness of their intended actions to err on the side of protecting citizens' constitutional rights" (*Owen v. City of Independence*, 1980: 651–652).

The deterrent effect of liability is magnified greatly by the potential assessment of punitive or exemplary damages against public administrators. In *Smith v. Wade* (1983), the Supreme Court had an opportunity to require the federal courts to apply a tough standard for subjecting public administrators to such damages. Historically, there have been two general standards for these damages: One is whether the individual found liable acted with malice in violating the other party's rights, that is, displayed "ill will, spite, or intent to injure" (*Smith v. Wade*, 1983: 37); the other standard is recklessness, or a "callous disregard of, or indifference to, the rights or safety of others" (*Smith v. Wade*, 1983: 37). The Supreme Court allowed the lower courts to use recklessness, which is the weaker of the two. It reasoned that "the conscientious officer who desires . . . [to] avoid lawsuits can and should look to the standard for actionability in the first instance," that is, whether the action violated clearly established rights of which a reasonable person would have known (*Smith v. Wade*, 1983: 50). In other words, a finding that compensatory damages are appropriate will often support the assessment of punitive or exemplary damages as well because conduct at issue will manifest at least an indifference to the rights of the injured party. Reliance on recklessness rather than malice makes it easier to use damages to punish public administrators financially and to deter similar unconstitutional behavior on the part of others. Although punitive damages may trigger due process concerns, they are largely open ended and are not technically required to bear a tight relationship to the injury involved (*BMW of North America v. Gore*, 1996). Consequently, in cases where qualified immunity is not granted, plaintiffs may allege malice in the hope of recovering greater damages.

A second aspect of the logic of liability is more complex. The way that the courts constructed public officials' qualified immunity enables them to exercise considerable direction over public administration. In effect, the Supreme Court has made knowledge of constitutional law a matter of job competence for public administrators. As it stated in *Harlow* (1982: p. 819), "a reasonably competent public official should know the law governing his conduct." But what is that law? In the words of former Supreme Court Justice Lewis Powell, "Constitutional law is what the courts say it is" (*Owen v. City of Independence*, 1980: 669). Consequently, public administrators must take direction from judges, who determine how the Constitution bears upon their jobs. Moreover, despite the qualifier in *Harlow* that the rights involved must be "clearly established," the Supreme Court has not limited liability to instances where a similar or identical administrative action was already ruled unconstitutional (*Pembaur v. City of Cincinnati*, 1986). Rather, the concept of "clearly established" extends to constitutional values and principles that should be known by a reasonably competent public official. Even if the constitutionality of some particular act has never been litigated, a public administrator engaging in it may be liable if he or she reasonably should have understood that it would violate the Constitution.

Overall, therefore, public administrators' liability promotes two judicial objectives: It is a strong tool for enforcing the constitutional rights that the judiciary has established for individuals in their interactions with public administrators, and it also enables the courts to exercise greater direction over public administration. The latter judicial interest has also been manifested in the courts' willingness to entertain suits seeking very broad reforms of administrative institutions or processes, such as public mental health facilities, public schools, and public personnel systems (Rosenbloom and O'Leary, 1997; Chayes, 1976; Horowitz, 1977, 1983).

THE IMPACT OF LIABILITY

It is difficult to assess comprehensively the impact of the change from absolute to qualified immunity. There is a lack of systematic knowledge about this area of the law. It is clear that thousands of suits have been brought against public employees, but less is known about their resolution (Lee, 1987; Farley, 1989). The likelihood of a public administrator losing a constitutional tort suit and paying damages personally appears relatively slim.[1] Nevertheless, public managers have been very concerned with potential liability and the costs of legal defense, settlements, and judgments (Friel, 1998; Rivenbark, 1998).

Even if more were known about case resolutions, settlements, and damages, however, it would still be very difficult to assess the overall impact of liability upon public administrative practices. Part of the intent of liability is to change public administrators' behavior to assure that it complies with constitutional requirements. To the extent that qualified immunity is successful, public administrators will be less likely to violate constitutional rights, and there will be fewer grounds for suing them. For example, police today routinely do recite Miranda warnings, and social service and personnel agencies have built constitutional due process into their standard operating practices. It would be surprising to find many constitutional violations in these areas. Nevertheless, there are surely many instances in which individuals whose rights are violated by public administrators fail, for one reason or another, to bring cases. Consequently, only limited inferences can be drawn from the number of cases filed, the absence of more filings, and the outcomes of cases. But clearly liability law is not a dead letter, and the best defense is to know and respect individuals' constitutional rights.

EXCEPTIONS TO THE GENERAL PATTERN OF PUBLIC OFFICIALS' LIABILITY

There are some exceptions to the current standard for qualified immunity and to the availability of compensatory damages as a remedy for injuries. When public employees are engaged in adjudicatory or legislative functions, they are likely to retain absolute immunity, as do judges and elected legislators (*Butz v. Economou, 1978; Tenny v. Brandhove,* 1951). It is important to remember that absolute immunity pertains to the function, not to the official position description. For instance, an administrative law judge will have qualified rather than absolute immunity when hiring or disciplining subordinate employees. Necessarily, the functional approach results in some ambiguity, and even some public employees engaged in adjudicatory functions, such as public defenders and members of prison disciplinary committees, do not enjoy absolute immunity (*Tower v. Glover,* 1984; *Cleavinger v. Saxner,* 1985).

In *Bush v. Lucas* (1983), the Supreme Court held that liability suits were inappropriate remedies in cases brought by federal employees, alleging that they had been subjected to illegal or unconstitutional personnel actions. The Court reasoned that federal personnel law provides for elaborate remedies, including hearings before the Merit Systems Protection Board, for such employees. Therefore, in the Court's view, because Congress explicitly created these remedies, it would be improper for the judiciary to fashion additional ones through constitutional interpretation. The *Bush* ruling does nothing, however, to prevent non-federal government employees from using section 1983 as a means of seeking compensatory and punitive damages for personnel actions taken against them in violation of their federally protected constitutional or statutory rights.

THE CONSTITUTIONAL RIGHT
TO DISOBEY

Public administrators' potential liability for constitutional torts has generated a concomitant nascent constitutional right to disobey unconstitutional directives. In *Harley v. Schuylkill County* (1979: 194), a federal district court explained that:

> The duty to refrain from acting in a manner which would deprive another of con-
> stitutional rights is a duty created and imposed by the constitution itself. It is logi-
> cal to believe that the concurrent right is also one which is created and secured by
> the constitution. Therefore, we hold that the right to refuse to perform an uncon-
> stitutional act is a right "secured by the Constitution. . . ."

The Supreme Court has not had occasion to consider the constitutional right of public employees to disobey unconstitutional orders. However, the district court's conclusion appears to be supported by strong policy reasons as well as by constitutional imperative. As Robert Vaughn (1977: 294–295), points out: "Con-gress and the courts have already adopted the concept of personal responsibility by providing penalties for the wrongful acts of public employees. The courts now have the opportunity to vindicate the concept of personal responsibility by accept-ing the right of public employees to disobey under appropriate circumstances." To prevail in asserting a constitutional right to disobey unconstitutional directives, the employee may have to show: (1) that the refusal to obey was based on a sincere belief that the action at issue was unconstitutional and (2) that he or she is correct in his or her legal analysis.

In practice, of course, disobedience is likely to be a last resort. Public employ-ees also have a constitutional right to seek to eliminate unconstitutional practices through whistle-blowing (*Pickering v. Board of Education*, 1968; *Givhan v. Western Line Consolidated School District*, 1979). In modern personnel and management sys-tems, employees will also have the opportunity, to discuss with a supervisor their reasons for not wanting to carry out an order, and some resolution short of litiga-tion is highly likely.

CONSEQUENCES FOR PUBLIC
PERSONNEL ADMINISTRATION

Public employees' liabilities for constitutional torts have several important conse-quences for public personnel administration. First, although such liability conveys great benefits by helping to protect constitutional rights, it also adds to the cost of government. The potential to be sued for constitutional torts makes public employment less desirable. Public personnel management is now infused with constitutional law and potential liability. In the past two decades or so, the Supreme Court decided several cases involving public employees' challenges to personnel actions that allegedly violate freedom of speech or association, Fourth Amendment privacy rights, procedural due process, and equal protection.[2] The government plainly could have avoided some of the suits it lost by paying greater attention to clear constitutional doctrines in the first place.[3] However, in some cases the law may appear clear to a judge but not necessarily so to a personnel manager. For example, affirmative action became deeply ingrained in the 1980s and 1990s and is still widely practiced in public personnel systems, even though judges relying on the Supreme Court's reasoning in *Adarand Constructors v. Pena* (1995), might well find most instances of it unconstitutional.[4] In other cases, the law itself may be so unclear that it affords little or no useful guidance. *Waters v. Churchill* (1994), which involved public employees' freedom of speech, is probably the preeminent example of just how fuzzy constitutional law can be (Rosenbloom, 1994). The key standard in Justice Sandra Day O'Connor's plurality opinion was that "only procedure outside the range of what a reasonable manager would use may be condemned as unreasonable" (*Waters v. Churchill*, 1994: 678), to which, Justice Antonin Scalia responded that "it remains entirely unclear what the employer's judgment *must* be based on" (*Waters v. Churchill*, 1994: 693).[5] Although such unclarity would seem to relieve public personnelists of liability under the *Harlow* standard, they still need to follow and comply with the case law as it develops in the federal district and circuit courts.

Many public personnel systems protect their employees in liability suits by providing them with legal representation, legal insurance, and/or indemnification. These approaches go a long way toward eliminating the risk of being harmed financially in a lawsuit arising out of one's performance in public office. Nevertheless, sufficient insurance can be costly, the availability of legal representation may depend on the specific circumstances involved, and indemnification may be incomplete or unavailable for punitive or exemplary damages. Moreover, any significant lawsuit will engulf one's time, attention, and energy. Consequently, liability remains an aspect of the public service that may be viewed as a drawback by prospective and current public employees.

Ironically, though, outsourcing public personnel functions may not reduce this problem. With the exception of the Thirteenth Amendment's ban on slavery and involuntary servitude, the Constitution does not ordinarily apply to interactions between private parties. However, the Constitution may control the behavior of private organizations and individuals when they take on public functions or become so deeply enmeshed with government that they are indistinct from it (that is, when they engage in "state action"). For instance, private physicians on part-time contracts to provide health care to prisoners and privately employed prison guards can be held liable for violating the Eighth Amendment's ban on cruel and unusual punishment (*West v. Atkins*, 1988; *Richardson v. McKnight*, 1997). Moreover, they have no immunity—either absolute or qualified—in such suits (*Richardson v. McKnight*, 1997). Unfortunately for those making human resource management decisions, the law regarding state action is notoriously unclear (*Lebron v. National Railroad Passenger Corporation*, 1995). There is a great deal of uncertainty regarding the personnel functions or public-private partnerships that might make the Constitution apply to outsourcing arrangements. Perhaps the leading candidate for triggering state action doctrine is background investigations, which can involve Fourth Amendment privacy concerns.

Second, public personnel systems will have to take greater responsibility for teaching public servants to be constitutionally competent (Rosenbloom, Carroll, and Carroll, 2000). The public administrator's best defense against liability for constitutional torts is reasonable knowledge of the constitutional rights of those individuals on whom his or her official actions bear. Universities can teach broad constitutional principles, values, and reasoning in their Master of Public Administration programs, but they are not well suited for teaching the detailed constitutional law that controls specific jobs, such as that of a social worker, police officer, or prison guard. Constance Horner, former director of the U.S. Office of Personnel Management, recognized the important role that personnel agencies can play in constitutional education by calling for "constitutional literacy" among higher-level federal employees (Horner, 1988). Even in the absence of a commitment by personnel agencies, continual training in constitutional matters is highly desirable because, under the Supreme Court's decision in *City of Canton v. Harris* (1989: 390), a local government may be held liable for violations of constitutional rights caused by its failure to take "reasonable steps to train its employees."

Third, education and training in personnel and human-resources management for the public sector should specifically and comprehensively cover the constitutional rights of public employees and applicants. Public servants have extensive constitutional rights to freedom of speech, association, privacy, due process, equal protection, and liberty (Rosenbloom, 1971; Rosenbloom and Carroll, 1995; Rosenbloom and O'Leary, 1997). Therefore, virtually any public administrator who engages in hiring, promoting, disciplining, or evaluating subordinates may potentially violate an individual employee's constitutional rights. Traditional personnel policies based on managerial values, such as efficiency as "axiom number one" (Gulick and Urwick, 1937: 10, 192), must now be revised substantially or even abandoned in favor of policies that recognize the importance of public employees' constitutional rights. Personnelists who are poorly trained in the constitutional aspects of public employment will not be well positioned to develop policies that secure the due process, equal protection, privacy, and other constitutional rights of public employees.

Finally, contemporary liability doctrine has major implications for the practice of strategic human-resources management (SHRM) within governmental entities. SHRM integrates human-resource planning into an organization's strategic management processes. Public employees' liability for constitutional torts strongly suggests that government SHRM models are incomplete if they do not articulate clearly personnelists' responsibilities for helping their organizations to guard against breaches of constitutional rights.

Under SHRM, human-resource organizations are expected to balance the roles of strategic partner, employee champion, change agent, and administrative expert (Ulrich, 1997). These roles give human resource professionals the opportunities to plan for and react to management decisions. As a strategic partner, human-resource professionals have gained a "seat at the table." This allows them to work directly with executives to develop recruitment, compensation, performance management, and other resource practices to achieve strategic goals. In their roles as employee champions, human resource professionals help managers understand and carry out their responsibilities for increasing employee commitment. The change-agent role requires human resource professionals to help both managers and employees cope with changes occurring within their organizations. It is within the role of administrative expert that human resource professionals will find their traditional responsibilities for establishing, implementing, and enforcing personnel rules. Encompassed within this role is basic legal compliance.

The general framework of strategic partner, employee champion, change agent, and administrative expert may limit the effectiveness of government human-resource offices because it may not result in a comprehensive strategy for adhering to constitutional tenets and obligations. There may be a tendency to isolate the analysis of constitutional compliance to staff attorneys or others with specific responsibility for legal matters. This would be a mistake for two reasons. First, it ignores the responsibilities of those carrying out other strategic human-resource roles to ensure constitutional compliance. For example, strategic partners must be able to explain the constitutional consequences of outsourcing human-resource activities to the organization's executives. Employee champions must work closely with managers to help them understand their responsibility to protect employees' freedom of speech, religious freedom, and privacy rights—even when administrative convenience or expedience alone might dictate some other course. In addition, employee champions can help employees fulfill their obligation to protect the constitutional rights of the individuals to whom they provide goods and services. During reengineering activities, change agents should help management and employees to establish new practices that uphold constitutional protections, as well as to promote increased efficiency and effectiveness. Periodic "constitutional audits" are a useful approach for reviewing practices and official guidelines to ensure that they are current with the ever-changing constitutional law of public administration. To be most effective in the personnel context, human-resource managers should participate on audit teams, along with legal experts, employee representatives, and program managers.

Second, the current SHRM framework does not promote constitutional competence for government executives, managers, and employees. The *Harlow* decision requires public employees to make decisions that reflect reasonable knowledge of clearly established constitutional rights. Clearly, legal compliance is paramount not only because it is a basic requirement for democratic constitutional government, but, more mundanely, because failure to protect constitutional rights adds substantially to the financial costs of government. This cost can be reduced substantially if government human-resource professionals incorporate a role for constitutional compliance into their SHRM activities. In their SHRM roles as strategic partner, employee champion, change agent, and administrative expert human-resource professionals gain access to the entire organization.

Therefore, they are well positioned to educate managers and employees about the most effective methods to protect constitutional rights as they carry out their responsibilities.

Training human-resource professionals to assess constitutional compliance across their different SHRM roles will help governments reduce the costs of public employees' liability. They will be more knowledgeable about how current case law impacts human-resource activities and able to apply their knowledge when carrying out their responsibilities. This will help organizations establish practices that minimize the potential for litigation related to violations of constitutional rights. They can teach managers and employees how to reduce their liability for constitutional torts, perhaps with the added benefit of making public employment more desirable because managers and employees are given the opportunities to increase their constitutional competence.

NOTES

1. Yong Lee (1987) identified approximately 1,700 cases in the odd years from 1977 to 1983. This figure pertains only to reported cases. The number of unreported federal district court decisions in official liability cases is unknown but presumably substantial. From 1993 to 1998, 7,000 federal employees sought legal representation by the Department of Justice, but only 14 were ultimately found personally liable in court (Friel, 1998, 1). Lee (1987, 169) lists the mean awards as follows: 1977, $48,552; 1979, $14,711; 1981, $63,031; 1983, $92,411.

2. Successful First Amendment challenges include: *Chicago Teachers Union v. Hudson* (nonunion employees in bargaining unit cannot be coerced to pay for a union's nonrepresentational activities, including political activities, and a procedure for resolving amounts in dispute is required); *Rankin v. McPherson* (remark by probationary employee in constable's office expressing hope that next assassination attempt on President Ronald Reagan is successful is constitutionally protected and cannot be the basis for dismissal); *Rutan v. Republican Party of Illinois* (partisan affiliation or support is an unconstitutional basis for personnel actions involving ordinary public employees' promotion, training, assignment, and similar actions, as well as hiring and firing); *Waters v. Churchill* (speech-related dismissals require reasonable belief that employee made alleged remarks); and *United State v. National Treasury Employees Union* (provision banning federal employee acceptance of pay for non-job-related published and other expression violates free speech/press). Fourth Amendment decisions include: *O'Connor v. Ortega* (administrative searches and seizures in public workplace must be reasonable in inception and scope if employee meets threshold test of having a reasonable expectation of privacy under the circumstances involved); and *National Treasury Employees Union v. Von Raab* (suspicionless drug testing of some categories of customs employees is constitutional). For a case that involves a procedural due process violated by dismissal from civil service job without prior notice and opportunity to respond, see *Cleveland Board of Education v. Loudermill*. For a case on the Equal Protection Clause that prohibits dismissal of nonminority in violation of seniority rights to further equal employment opportunity/affirmative action, see *Wygant v. Jackson*.

3. *Cleveland Board of Education v. Loudermill* is the clearest example of an instance in which a minimal, almost costless procedure could have obviated a suit. *Wygant v. Jackson* occurred

because a school board agreed to race-based dismissals that would almost certainly result in litigation and, in high probability, loss as well. The statutory ban in *United States v. National Treasury Employees Union* was exceptionally broad, and the administrative rules pursuant to it were so complex as to appear irrational and arbitrary.

4. In *Adarand*, the Supreme Court held that all racial classifications are constitutionally suspect and subject to strict judicial scrutiny. To be constitutional, they must serve a compelling governmental interest in a narrowly tailored fashion.

5. The question was whether a public employee could be disciplined for what her supervisor thought she said or only for what she actually said. There was no majority opinion on the Supreme Court, but the guiding principles appear to be that (1) the employer must reasonably investigate what the employee may have said, and (2) the employer must really believe the employee said it before imposing discipline.

REFERENCES

Adarand Constructors v. Pena, 515 U.S. 200 (1995).

Anderson v. Creighton, 483 U.S. 635 (1987).

Barr v. Matteo, 360 U.S. 564 (1959).

Bivens v. Six Unknown Named Federal Narcotics Agents, 403 U.S. 388 (1971).

BMW of North America v. Gore, 517 U.S. 559 (1996).

Bush v. Lucas, 462 U.S. 367 (1983).

Butz v. Economou, 438 U.S. 478 (1978).

Carlson v. Green, 446 U.S. 14 (1980).

Carroll, James D. 1982. "The New Juridical Federalism and the Alienation of Public Policy and Administration." *American Review of Public Administration*, 16 (Spring):89–105.

Chayes, Abram. 1976. "The Role of the Judge in Public Law Litigation." *Harvard Law Review*, 89:1281–1316.

Chicago Teachers Union v. Hudson, 475 U.S. 292 (1986).

City of Canton v. Harris, 489 U.S. 378 (1989).

City of Newport v. Fact Concerts, 453 U.S. 247 (1981).

Cleavinger v. Saxner, 474 U.S. 193 (1985).

Cleveland Board of Education v. Loudermill, 470 U.S. 532 (1985).

Davis v. Passman, 422 U.S. 228 (1979).

Delaware v. Prouse, 440 U.S. 648 (1979).

Dolan v. City of Tigard, 512 U.S. 374 (1994).

Farley, John J. 1989. "The Representation and Defense of the federal Employee by the Department of Justice." U.S. Department of Justice, Spring (mimeograph).

FDIC v. Meyer, 510 U.S. 471 (1994).

Friel, Brian. (1998). "Managers Rarely Found Liable in Lawsuits," *Government Executive (The Daily Fed)*, May 19:1.

Galanter, Marc. 1988. "Beyond the Litigation Panic." In Walter Olson, ed., *New Directions in Liability Law*. New York: Academy of Political Science, pp. 18–30.

Givhan v. Western Line Consolidated School District, 349 U.S. 410 (1979).

Gulick, Luther, and L. Urwick, eds. 1937. *Papers on the Science of Administration*. New York: Institute of Public Administration.

Harley v. Schuylkill County, 476 F. Supp. 191 (1979).

Harlow v. Fitzgerald, 457 U.S. 800 (1982).

Hefer v. Melo, 116 L.Ed. 2d 301 (1991).

Horner, Constance. 1988. "Remarks on FEI's [Federal Executive Institute's] 20th Anniversary Dinner," Charlottesville, VA, Oct. 14, p. 14.

Horowitz, Donald. 1977. *The Courts and Social Policy.* Washington, DC: Brookings Institution.

Horowitz, Donald. 1983. "Decreeing Organizational Change: Judicial Supervision of Public Institutions." *Duke Law Journal*, 88, 3: 1265–1307.

Kolander v. Lawson, 461 U.S. 352 (1983).

Lebron v. National Railroad Passenger Corporation, 513 U.S. 374 (1995).

Lee, Yong. 1987. "Civil Liability of State and Local Governments: Myths and Reality. *Public Administration Review*, 47 (March/April):160–170.

Lipsky, Michael. 1980. *Street-Level Bureaucracy.* New York: Russell Sage.

Miranda v. Arizona, 384 U.S. 436 (1966).

Missouri v. Jenkins, 494 U.S. 33 (1990); 515 U.S. 70 (1995).

Mitchell v. Forsyth, 472 U.S. 511 (1985).

National Treasury Employees Union v. Von Raab, 489 U.S. 656 (l989).

O'Connor v. Ortega, 480 U.S. 709 (1987).

Owen v. City of Independence, 445 U.S. 622 (1980).

Pembaur v. City of Cincinnati, 475 U.S. 469 (1986).

Pickering v. Board of Education, 391 U.S. 563 (1968).

Rankin v. McPherson, 483 U.S. 378 (1987).

Richardson v. McKnight, 521 U.S. 399 (1997).

Rivenbark, Leigh (1998). "Protection Needed Against Lawsuits," *Federal Times*, July 20:3.

Rosenbloom, David H. 1971. *Federal Service and the Constitution.* Ithaca, NY: Cornell University Press.

Rosenbloom, David H. 1994. "Fuzzy Law from the High Court," *Public Administration Review*, 54 (November/December):503–506.

Rosenbloom, David H., and James D. Carroll. 1990. *Toward Constitutional Competence: A Casebook for Public Administrators.* Englewood Cliffs, NJ: Prentice Hall.

Rosenbloom, David H., and James D. Carroll. 1995. "Public Personnel Administration and Law," in Jack Rabin, Thomas Vocino, W.B. Hildreth, and Gerald Miller, eds., *Handbook of Public Personnel Administration.* New York: Marcel Dekker, pp. 71–113.

Rosenbloom, David H., James Carroll, and Jonathan Carroll 2000. *Constitutional Competence for Public Managers: Cases and Commentary.* Itasca, IL: F. E. Peacock Publishers.

Rosenbloom, David H., and Rosemary O'Leary 1997. *Public Administration and Law.* New York: Marcel Dekker.

Rutan v. Republican Party of Illinois, 497 U.S 62 (1990).

Scheuer v. Rhodes, 416 U.S. 232 (1974).

Schuck, Peter. 1982. *Suing Government: Citizen Remedies for Official Wrongs.* New Haven, CT: Yale University Press.

Schuck, Peter. 1988. "The New Judicial Ideology of Tort Law." In Walter Olson, ed., *New Directions in Liability Law.* New York: Academy of Political Science:4–14.

"Section 1983 and Federalism." 1977. *Harvard Law Review*, 90:1133–1361.

Smith v. Wade, 461 U.S. 31 (1983).

Spalding v. Vilas, 161 U.S. 483 (1896).

Stump v. Sparkman, 435 U.S. 349 (1978).

Tenny v. Brandhove, 341 U.S. 367 (1951).

Terry v. Ohio, 392 U.S. I (1968).

Tower v. Glover, 467 U.S. 914 (1984).

Ulrich, Dave (1997), *Human Resource Champions: The Next Agenda for Adding Value and Delivering Results.* Boston, MA: Harvard Business School Press.

United States v. James Daniel Good Real Property, 510 U.S. 471 (1994).

United States v. Lee, 106 U.S. 196 (1882).

United States v. National Treasury Employees Union, 513 U.S. 454 (1995).

Vaughn, Robert. 1977. "Public Employees and the Right to Disobey." *Hastings Law Journal,* 29:261–295.

Waters v. Churchill, 511 U.S. 661 (1994).

West v. Atkins, 487 U.S. 42 (1988).

Will v. Michigan Department of State Police. 491 U.S. 59 (1989).

Wood v. Strickland, 420 U.S. 308 (1975).

Wygant v. Jackson, 478 U.S. 267 (1986).

Chapter *12*

Hiring in the Federal Government: The Politics of Reform

Carolyn Ban

Hiring is one of the most critical personnel functions in any organization, and all organizations—public, private, and nonprofit—have adapted their hiring procedures to reflect the changing needs of the organization, the changing workforce, and new technology. But change in the public sector has been more difficult because of the political nature of the issues involved and because of the political process necessary for reform. This chapter will examine the various attempts at reform from a political perspective, focusing on the conflicts of values and of political interests involved, on the range of political actors, and on the results, to date, of reform efforts. It will also look at how managers use the system as it currently exists and at the impact of demographic and technological changes on the hiring process.

THE POLITICIZATION OF HIRING

Many people tend to see personnel management as essentially a technical field, but, at least in the public sector, it is squarely in the middle of many of the key political debates of our time. One of those debates concerns the appropriate role and size of government. As a result, the size of the federal workforce has been politicized for at least the past twenty years. Ronald Reagan's first act as president, in 1980, was to sign a retroactive hiring freeze (later found to be illegal), and Clinton's reinvention of government focused as much on shrinking the size of the federal workforce as on improving the management of government. In fact, "[f]rom January 1993 to January 2000, the Federal Government civilian workforce was reduced by 384,000 employees" (U.S. Office of Personnel Management, 2000a). But, especially in the Clinton administration, this desire to take credit for reducing the size of government was not linked to a political vision of a smaller role for government, so there was no parallel

166

reduction in the number or scope of federal programs. The result was, in effect, a shell game, in which federal ranks shrank while the number of employees working for the federal government as contractors continued to swell.

It has been hard, within this politicized environment, to have a rational debate about the size the federal workforce should be to meet its many missions or about the most effective ways to bring in new workers, because so much energy was directed in the opposite direction of encouraging people to leave through early retirement packages or even laying employees off (in federal parlance, through Reductions in Force, or RIFs).

CONFLICTS OF VALUES AND INTERESTS

Attempts to reform the hiring process are complex as well because they reflect debates about core values of public service and public management. On the one hand, the civil service was based, from its founding, on the concept that employees should be selected on the basis of merit, rather than on party affiliation, inside contacts, or nepotism. On the other hand, both scholars and political activists have argued over what we mean by merit and how best to assess who is most meritorious.

The civil service system is also expected to reflect values of openness and equity and to be representative of the country's diverse population. In the early years of the civil service, that meant geographic representation, and state of residence was explicitly taken into consideration in hiring. More recently, the focus has been on demographic characteristics, such as gender and race or ethnic origin.

Further, since the Civil War, the system has been designed explicitly to reward military service, and veterans still receive preference in hiring, but that value can be seen as conflicting with the goals of merit and equity.

The challenge is not only balancing sometimes conflicting social goals, but also the need to meet management goals, especially speed and efficiency. From the standpoint of good management, the ideal system would be cost-efficient to operate, would allow the public sector to identify and hire good candidates quickly, and would give managers flexibility to hire the people they identify and to offer them pay and benefits competitive with the market, thus providing incentives to managers to recruit aggressively for the best employees. But meeting these management goals while upholding the social goals discussed above is difficult to impossible.

THE POLITICS OF REFORM: THE KEY POLITICAL ACTORS

Each of the values above is reflected in the interests of the many actors who have been directly or indirectly involved in the ongoing cycles of reform of the hiring process. They include career managers, political appointees and rank-and-file employees, as well as interest groups representing specific groups, including veterans, women, African Americans, and Hispanics. The reform process may take place via administrative reform, but major reforms require legislative approval, and proposals are revised and shaped during the legislative process. The courts, too, have, over the past twenty years, played a central role in reshaping hiring in the federal government. Reforms, thus, have taken place through the give and take of the political process, as well as through the judicial process. The net result is a system that has moved from simplicity to complexity, from centralization to extreme decentralization, and, in the process, is still struggling to reconcile conflicting values.

TWENTY YEARS OF REFORM: WHAT HAVE WE LEARNED?

To understand how the current system has evolved, it is useful to review briefly the major reforms of the past twenty-plus years. They include a major legislative reform (the Civil Service Reform Act of 1978), an ongoing judicial reform (the Luevano consent decree), and a more recent series of administrative reforms (the National Performance Review).

If we take as our baseline the system in place prior to passage of the Civil Service Reform Act of 1978, central to that system was a standardized examination called the PACE exam that was administered centrally by the Civil Service Commission and was used to select new employees for entry-level positions in more than 100 classes of jobs (Ban and Ingraham, 1988). That system was based on a core value, the merit system, but defined merit in a narrow way, as results on a single test. PACE was an expensive system to operate because the number of applicants was far greater than the number of positions available. The large number of applicants meant that, although a 70 was, in theory, a passing score, people who scored lower than the high 90s were rarely selected for jobs. This raised some troubling questions. One was the issue of test validity. This system was seen as relying strictly on merit, but merit came to be defined exclusively as high scores on the test. Although the test was carefully validated using psychometric methods, even those who developed it did not argue that a person who received a 98 would necessarily be a more successful and productive employee than one who received a 97, or even a 95. Tests cannot tell us whether the job applicant is motivated, whether he or she gets along well with others, and, in the case of a general test like PACE, how quickly he or she can master the skills needed for a specific job.

PACE was an open system, in the sense that it was a clear and well-known route into government, and it was an apolitical system, in that only those who scored highly on the test could be considered for positions. But it probably had adverse impact (that is, it may have discriminated against African Americans and Hispanics).

LEGISLATIVE REFORM: THE CSRA

President Carter's Civil Service Reform Act (CSRA) had the goal of modernizing the federal personnel system, making it more efficient, and thus improving management and productivity of the civil service as a whole. Although the teams planning the reform critiqued the slowness and inflexibility of the federal system for hiring, the bill itself included only modest reforms in this area. They focused on decentralizing the hiring process for those positions not covered by the PACE exam, giving agencies more control over the process with the assumption that in-house hiring processes would be faster and more responsive to managers' needs.

Why, given the lofty goals, were the reforms so narrowly drawn? One explanation lies in the political process and in the strength of some of the political actors mentioned above. For example, early drafts of the reform proposals included limiting veterans preference, but the veterans groups were so well organized that it quickly became obvious that Congress would not support any change in this area (Ingraham, 1984).

Even this modest reform did not last long. Reagan's first appointee as director of the Office of Personnel Management (the successor agency to the CSC), Don Devine, moved to withdraw delegations of hiring authority in a number of cases. As a result, the net effect of the CSRA was minimal (Ban and Marzotto, 1984).

Judicial Reform: The Luevano Consent Decree

Far more radical reform resulted from the political process as played out in the courts. Late in President Carter's term, a group of Hispanic organizations brought a lawsuit against the federal government, charging that the PACE examination had adverse impact on minority groups and demanding that the federal government abandon its use. One of the last acts of the Carter administration was to sign what is called the Luevano Consent Decree (named for one of the parties of the suit) agreeing to do just that (Ban and Ingraham, 1988). Many of the most important changes in the federal system flow from that Consent Decree and from the continued involvement of the courts in deciding what are fair and equitable ways for the federal government to select its employees. Abandoning the PACE examination forced a complete overhaul of the process for hiring entry-level professional employees, and the continued involvement of the courts in overseeing the implementation of the consent decree continues to shape the hiring process, sometimes with unintended consequences, as we will see below.

Administrative Reform: The NPR

The National Performance Review (later renamed the National Partnership for Reinventing Government), headed by Vice President Gore, was a dramatic attempt to improve the quality of management throughout the federal government. While it covered virtually all aspects of federal management, it espoused a model of dramatic change in the federal personnel system, focusing on three key themes: deregulation, decentralization, and delegation. The NPR report on Human Resources (National Performance Review, 1993) advocated dramatic reform of the federal personnel system, but, once again, the political process limited the opportunity for fundamental reform. Many of the reform proposals would have required legislation, but the Democrats lost control of Congress in 1994, dooming the chances for passing any civil service reform legislation.

Still, the NPR is a case study of the impact that can be made via administrative reform, without going through Congress. First, the NPR eliminated the Federal Personnel Manual, the 10,000 page guideline to personnelists on how to implement Title 5 (the law governing the civil service system) and the Code of Federal Regulations (the official regulations implementing that law). A second focus of the NPR recommendations was decentralization. In particular, the NPR recommended that OPM abandon its traditional role of gatekeeper of the civil service system. OPM would no longer conduct exams centrally and maintain central registers. Instead, it would delegate authority to agencies to do all their own examining, expanding a movement begun as a result of the Civil Service Reform Act of 1978 (Ban and Marzotto, 1984). Third, the NPR called for delegating more responsibility for managing the human resource function to line managers themselves. Giving managers more authority in hiring, classifying, and assessing the performance of their employees was seen as an integral part of breaking through the traditional culture of control that characterized the civil service system (Ban, 1998).

The Clinton administration used the planned deregulation of the civil service system to justify dramatic cuts in the size of the human resources workforce, arguing that a simpler system would reduce staff needs. "From 1992 to 1996, the number of people employed in personnel occupations declined by 18 percent" (Ban, 1998). While this argument was probably specious (especially absent legislative reform), the reduction in HR staff levels forced managers to take a more active role in the process and forced HR offices to find more efficient ways to carry out their work.

CURRENT APPROACHES TO HIRING: INCOMPLETE REFORM?

Decentralization of the Hiring Process

For more than twenty years, various groups have attempted to reform the hiring system through political, legal, and administrative efforts. What has the net effect been? First, the current system is extremely decentralized. The federal government has abandoned the PACE exam and has also delegated hiring authority for virtually all positions directly to the agencies. Decentralization has great advantages but also considerable costs. No longer does the person looking for a federal job apply centrally through the Office of Personnel Management. Rather, an agency posts its own jobs, and applicants apply directly to the agency. From the agency's perspective, this means that applicants are likely to be genuinely interested in working in that agency, something that was not always the case when the application process was centralized. It also means that, for most positions, agency HR staff, who are likely to understand the work of the agency and its specific needs, are reviewing applications. That knowledge should increase the odds that the applicant's fit for the specific job is being assessed correctly, and decentralized hiring can, in many cases, be faster than a more centralized process.

The negative aspects of a decentralized approach are twofold. First, it increases the effort required by the applicant, who must now search for openings across agencies rather than simply submitting a single application. Second, particularly for small organizations, there are significant costs in recruiting and reviewing applications. Centralization provides economies of scale that are lost in a decentralized system.

Movement Away from Written Tests

The new system is also considerably more complex than the old PACE examination and far less reliant on written examinations. In response to the Luevano Consent Degree, the Office of Personnel Management developed a battery of six examinations, each validated for a group of related occupations and known collectively as the Administrative Careers with America (ACWA) examinations. OPM clearly intended ACWA to be a "major vehicle for college graduates and other candidates with equivalent experience to obtain federal employment" (U.S. General Accounting Office, 1994: 2). Although OPM spent a great deal of time and effort validating these examinations, ACWA as a system was largely a failure. Managers found it overly time-consuming and were dissatisfied with the quality of applicants. As a result, they proceeded to use every route possible to avoid hiring via ACWA. The net effect is that written tests have virtually been abandoned as part of the federal hiring process. As Table 12.1 makes clear, OPM's ACWA exams were used for less than one percent of new hires from fiscal year 1991 through fiscal year 1998. Only about 10 percent of hiring was through OPM non-ACWA examining.

TABLE 12.1   Entry Level Hires: Professional and Administrative Positions
FY 1991–FY 1998

Hiring Method	FY 91	FY 92	FY 93	FY 94	FY 95	FY 96	FY 97	FY 98	Total
OPM ACWA Examining	481	338	238	66	131	63	119	97	1,533
Outstanding Scholars	3,186	1,839	1,432	1,416	1,842	1,640	1,822	1,677	14,854
Noncompetitive Appointments/ Direct Hires	11,772	6,995	4,151	3,624	3,466	3,796	3,772	3,823	41,396
OPM non-ACWA Examining	3,464	2,374	1,878	1,628	2,355	2,530	2,415	2,847	19,491
Agency Delegated Examining	3,817	1,995	1,179	1,233	1,762	1,332	1,957	3,060	16,335
Agency Merit Promotion	13,167	10,797	8,913	8,974	10,085	8,991	8,659	9,040	78,644
Cooperative (Co-Op) Education Program (SCEP) Conversions	1,152	1,248	1,288	1,299	1,020	755	582	533	7,877
Presidential Management Interns	214	152	189	104	130	101	249	272	1,411
Totals	37,253	25,708	19,286	18,344	20,791	19,208	19,575	21,349	181,514

SOURCE: National Academy of Public Administration, 1999, p. 2.

Heavy Reliance on Internal Promotion

In fact, by far the largest source of entry-level hires into professional and adminis-trative positions was internal promotion, accounting for 43 percent of new hires. To some extent, this figure reflects the impact of years of hiring freezes and cutbacks in the size of the workforce. Unable to bring in new people from outside, agencies often moved staff up from technical and clerical positions to professional and administrative occupations, sometimes through formal professional-development programs but also as the only way to fill critical shortages. Merit promotions still require an open, competitive process with formal vacancy announcements and ranking of candidates. NAPA's study found that 70 percent of managers rated the quality of these internal candidates as excellent or above average, but that "[a]gen-cies expressed some concern that these employees may not possess the level of ana-lytical and writing skills needed to perform successfully in most of the jobs for which they were selected" (National Academy of Public Administration, 1999). NAPA does not provide information on the percent of these hires who have a bach-elors or advanced degree compared to those hired through other sources. It will be important to track these employees over time and to compare their promotion rate to those of candidates hired externally to see whether they have the potential not only to perform well in their current jobs but to grow into higher-level positions.

Reliance on Noncompetitive Hiring Methods

The last twenty years can be seen as proof that managers will always look for routes within the system, or around it, to meet their needs for speed in hiring and for the flexibility to hire people they have recruited. Previous research has shown that, even under the more formal hiring systems, managers are creative in finding informal ways around the system. These include (Ban, 1997; Ban, 1995; Ospina, 1992; Jorgansen, 1996):

- use of provisional appointments (sometimes lasting for years)
- converting positions from classified (i.e., competitive) to exempt
- "tailoring" (i.e., fitting the job description for the vacancy to the specific skills of the individual the manager wants to hire)
- "soliciting a declination" (i.e., talking people ranked higher on a civil ser-vice list into withdrawing from consideration so as to reach a preferred candidate either by making the job sound unattractive or by promising consideration for a future position)

Some of these strategies are quite legal; others (such as tailoring) are on the edge ethically, while soliciting a declination is clearly illegal. It is important to stress that, even if these approaches violate the spirit of the law, the intent is not necessarily corrupt. Although it is possible to use these approaches to hire friends or political cronies, typically managers report that gaming the system is necessary to get talented people on board as quickly as possible.

At the formal level, over the past twenty years, there have been a series of hiring authorities that opened up considerable flexibility, at least for a time. Each system was, in turn, embraced by astute managers. The first was in response to the crisis created by the Luevano Consent Decree, which forced the federal government to cease use of the PACE examination immediately. The consent decree gave OPM three years in which to develop a new "examination procedure which is designed to examine for that particular job category" (*Luevano et al. v. Alan Campbell*, 1981, para. 13). In the meantime, agencies were permitted to hire under Schedule B, which is a noncompetitive hiring authority that had previously had quite limited use. During the transition period, OPM approved wider use of Schedule B for agencies that certified that they were unable to fill positions by other means (Ban and Ingraham, 1988: 711).

Opening the door to the use of Schedule B resulted in a dramatic change in the hiring process and in the role of managers in recruiting and hiring. It decentralized the process so that applicants had to apply to a specific agency for a specific position, and it rewarded managers for actively recruiting (typically through university placement offices and job fairs) because they were much more likely to be able actually to hire promising candidates they had identified

Once managers had firsthand experience of a more flexible approach to hiring that empowered them in the process, it was very hard to gain support for moving back to a more centralized and more "hands-off" process, but that is exactly what OPM attempted to do in developing the new ACWA examinations. It is not surprising, then, that managers were unenthusiastic about the new tests and that they looked for new ways to recreate the hiring flexibility they had lost. They moved first to take advantage of what is technically known as direct hire authority. This hiring authority required OPM to identify hard-to-fill occupations and to approve agency requests to use a special authority to fill positions in those fields noncompetitively if the candidate met the basic qualifications for the job. This authority enabled managers to go to campuses or to job fairs, for example, and to hire qualified applicants on the spot. Table 12.1 shows the heavy use of direct hire (second only to internal merit promotion) in 1991. Unfortunately, from the point of view of managers, in late FY 1991, OPM changed the rules and delegated authority to agencies to determine their shortage-category occupations. But it set such stringent requirements that use of direct hire fell significantly in following years (National Academy of Public Administration, 1999). Direct hire also became somewhat less direct and more burdensome when OPM declared that veterans preference needed to be applied, requiring recruiters to bring resumes back and have them rated and ranked rather than being able to hire immediately.

Direct hire is not the only noncompetitive hiring authority available. A second special hiring method, the bilingual/bicultural appointing authority, resulted from the Luevano Consent Decree and was targeted to improving hiring of Hispanics. Under this authority, job applicants who meet the minimum qualification requirements for a job, including the language or cultural requirement, can be hired without further competition. In addition, there are provisions for noncompetitive hiring for former Peace Corps volunteers and for congressional staff. The range of noncompetitive authorities helps explain why, in spite of the limits placed on the use of the direct hire authority, for FY 98, use of various noncompetitive appointments, including direct hire, was still second only to merit promotion as a means for filling professional and administrative positions (see Table 12.1).

Another popular noncompetitive hiring authority that was developed as a direct result of the Luevano Consent Decree is the Outstanding Scholar Program, which allows agencies to hire applicants noncompetitively, based on their undergraduate grade point average. If the applicant has an undergraduate GPA of 3.5 or higher or is in the top 10 percent of his/her graduating class, her or she can be hired immediately without taking a test. Use of the Outstanding Scholar Program has been heavy because it meets managers' desire for speed and flexibility in hiring, but the program is controversial, first, because it has not been particularly effective in meeting the original goal of increasing minority representation. NAPA reports that, "of all the hiring methods, . . . outstanding scholar appointments produced the lowest percentage of minorities hired into the professional and administrative positions" (National Academy of Public Administration, 1999:15). In fact, it is most often used to hire white women, who are not covered under the Luevano decree. There is also a lively debate concerning its validity as a selection method. The U.S. Merit Systems Protection Board has questioned whether GPA or class standing are effective predictors of on-the-job performance, particularly because neither the quality of the institution nor the program of study is considered, and has argued that this process "has little more than speed of hiring to recommend it" (U.S. Merit Systems Protection Board, 2000: 17).

In short, in the current decentralized environment for hiring, those managers who participate most actively in the recruiting process are also likely to have learned how to find their way through the hiring system and to want to make use of all the legally available flexibilities. It is important to note that this is not typically out of the desire to abuse the system by hiring based on inappropriate criteria, but rather out of a genuine desire to fill positions quickly with new employees who meet managers' sense of the skills needed (Ban, 1995).

BARRIERS TO REFORM: VETERANS PREFERENCE AND THE RULE OF THREE

Even though the process for hiring in the federal government has changed dramatically over the past twenty years, two policies that have not changed are veterans preference and the Rule of Three. It is important to understand why they are problematic from management's perspective to understand the steps managers have taken in response.

By law, the federal government is required to give preference to veterans in hiring, a tradition that dates back in law to the Civil War, but informally all the way to George Washington, who "occasionally gave preference to officers of the Revolutionary Army" (U.S. Civil Service Commission, 1973: 7). Veterans are given five extra points on civil service exams, and disabled veterans or surviving spouses of veterans are given ten points. That means that a nonveteran could score 100 on a test but be passed over for a veteran with a lower score.

It is interesting that, although consideration of race or sex in hiring has been highly controversial, there has been little if any public discussion of the implications of veterans preference, even though it obviously takes into consideration a factor other than strict merit, as defined by test scores or ranking of qualifications. As discussed above, veterans organizations have worked hard to protect veterans preference, and courts have upheld its legality, even in the case of states where absolute veterans preference is the policy (that is, where any veterans who pass the test must be hired before any other candidates, no matter how high the other candidates' test scores). But from a managerial perspective, veterans preference is dysfunctional because managers may be required to hire someone who they really do not think is the best qualified. To pass over a veteran at the top of the list requires written justification, which may or may not be approved. As a result, some managers have sometimes "gamed the system," finding various routes around a veteran who is "blocking the list" (Ban, 1995). OPM describes one such technique: announcing positions at multiple grade levels "so they may choose a candidate from one list while failing to consider a veteran who appears on another list" (U.S. Office of Personnel Management, 2001: 2). OPM reported that most agencies were complying with the requirements for veterans preference. Nonetheless, many mangers feel that veterans preference impedes attempts to streamline the hiring process.

The Rule of Three is another traditional aspect of the hiring process that is overdue for change. Under the Rule of Three, managers are given a list of the top three scorers on a test and must make their appointment from that rather narrow group. Managers see this as giving them an overly limited pool from which to choose, and they question the ability of written tests or evaluation of experience to make such fine distinctions among candidates. The Rule of Three has deep roots; along with veterans preference, it goes back to the Grant administration (U.S. Merit Systems Protection Board, 1995), and the effect of the two is cumulative; that is, the Rule of Three, combined with veterans preference, "may restrict managers' choices to fewer than three candidates. This can occur when the certificate of eligibles is headed by a single veteran or a pair of veterans, a situation that makes the veterans listed first the only possible choices unless they decline a job offer or can be passed over" (U.S. Merit Systems Protection Board, 1995: 7).

The impact of the Rule of Three is particularly great in the federal government, as compared to some states, because it has been interpreted to mean three names, not three scores on a test. In some jurisdictions, tie scores result in all those with the same scores being placed on the list, but the federal government uses tie breakers to narrow the list to three people. Veterans preference is the first tie breaker. The second is "name requests," that is, a request by the hiring manager to include a specific individual if his or her score is high enough. Finally, ties are broken by use of random numbers. That is the most common method of breaking ties (U.S. Merit Systems Protection Board, 1995), and it is certainly no guarantee that the best candidates will be on the list.

AGENCY REFORM STRATEGIES

In the absense of comprehensive reform that addresses these problems, individual federal agencies have found their own ways to introduce reform. A few agencies have taken advantage of the provision of the civil service law (Title 5) that permits agencies to conduct demonstration projects that try out new approaches to human resources that require suspension of existing civil service law or regulations. One of the more innovative in the hiring area is the U.S. Department of Agriculture (USDA) Personnel Management Demonstration Project, begun in 1990. Among its key initiatives were authorizing direct hiring for shortage categories and implementing an alternative candidate assessment method, using categorical groupings instead of numeric scores. Specifically, rather than ranking people by test scores, those evaluating job candidates put those who met qualifications into two categories: quality and eligible. Managers can then select from the entire pool of those ranked qualified, rather than from only the three top scorers on a test. If the quality group has only one or two candidates, those in the eligible list may also be referred to as the candidate. Although this demonstration obviously suspends the Rule of Three, it does not suspend veterans' preference; in fact, it gives veterans in the quality group absolute preference. Nonveterans can be selected only if all veterans are disqualified or if the agency approves a request to pass over the individual. The USDA demonstration project also gives managers the option of paying cash recruitment incentives and of reimbursing travel and transportation expenses for new hires (U.S. Office of Personnel Management, 1992).

It is important to understand, however, that demonstrations were not intended to fix individual agency problems, but rather as a way to test and evaluate new models that could then be implemented across the system. The demonstration provision has not lived up to that expectation; none of the demonstrations, including USDA, have yet led to systemwide change (Ban, 1988–89; Ban, 1992). Rather they have become one more way for individual agencies to opt out of the system by asking to have their demonstration project made permanent. So, for example, USDA has received permission to move permanently to the system created by their demonstration, as has the navy for its demonstration, but the flexibilities created by those demonstrations are not available to other agencies.

Some agencies have taken an even more drastic approach—literally opting out of the system. They have given up hope that the "standard" federal personnel system embodied in Title 5 of the U.S. Code will be changed any time soon and have convinced Congress to let them opt out of Title 5 and set up their own personnel systems. As a recent OPM report pointed out:

> In the Federal Government, the trend toward flexibility has manifested itself in a number of ways, including the attempt by a number of agencies to move away from the specific requirements of Title 5. Full or partial exemption from Title 5 is of course nothing new. Agencies such as the Tennessee Valley Authority and the Federal Reserve Board have been outside Title 5 for decades. But the movement in that direction has gained momentum, to the extent that nearly half of Federal civilian

employees are now outside some aspect of Title 5 coverage (The U.S. Postal Service, with over 800,000 employees, constitutes the majority of the Title 5-exempt work force) (U.S. Office of Personnel Management, 1998b:1).

This strategy is controversial. Some fear "Balkanization," and it is true that having a large number of different systems might make it more difficult for individual employees to move easily across government. Others argue that seeing the federal workforce as a single employer is unrealistic, as agencies have different missions and cultures, and that HR systems should be designed to meet their specific needs (Ban 1995; Marzotto, 1988). In fact, OPM found that leaving Title 5 did not necessarily lead to dramatic changes. They "found few differences in [non-title 5 agencies'] recruitment, hiring, and promotion practices with the important exceptions of the 'Rule of Three' and veterans preference. None of the organizations exempt from Title 5 staffing regulations follow the 'Rule of Three' unless they are obligated also to apply veterans preference" (U.S. Office of Personnel Management, 1998b:5).

Increased use of contractors may also reflect managers' frustrations with the lack of flexibility in hiring. Of course, contracting out may be the only choice when hiring freezes and ceilings make it difficult to hire new employees, especially from outside government. That has led to a dramatic increase in dependence on contractors to do the work of government (Light, 1999). Many managers bemoan this reliance on contractors and would gladly take fewer workers if they were full-time employees (Ban, 1995). But others use contracting to get around some of the rigidities of the personnel system. They may be able to bring in contractors more quickly than they can get through the hiring system, they may have more flexibility in what they can pay, and they know that they can terminate a contract or ask the contractor to replace workers who are not doing well (See Chapter 16).

HIRING IN THE FEDERAL GOVERNMENT: FUTURE CHALLENGES

The failure of comprehensive reform poses challenges for the future. First, the number of current employees eligible to retire is increasing rapidly (Kauffman, 2001a). Of course, not all of them will leave as soon as they are eligible. Still, higher turnover is likely at a time when federal agencies are having more trouble competing with the private sector, especially in technical areas, including information technology. The relatively slow federal process, combined with uncompetitive salaries, is presenting problems both for recruitment and for retention of high-quality employees, and the federal government is required to hire only U.S. citizens, so it cannot follow the strategy used by many private-sector firms faced with staff shortages in technical areas—recruiting abroad and hiring noncitizens.

The position of the Bush administration on these issues is not yet clear. On the one hand, calls for dramatic reform of the hiring system continue to be heard from outside government (Kauffman, 2001a). But it is not yet clear that the Bush administration has an agenda or plan for how to deal with workforce issues, including hiring. In an article entitled "Work-Force Measures Will Wait," the *Federal Times* reported on remarks by Sean O'Keefe, the deputy director of the Office of Management and Budget, at a conference sponsored by the National Academy of Public Administration (Kauffman, 2001b: 3). Although he stated that OMB "recognizes the government's significant work-force challenges and will propose steps to help agencies tackle those problems . . ." he also said that "he does not believe comprehensive civil service reform is the answer."

Sweeping reform is unlikely, but several changes have improved the system, albeit incrementally. First, the increasing use of the web to advertise vacancies has, at least to some extent, reduced the information costs to job applicants caused by decentralization. It has become far easier for job seekers to find vacancies in the fields, agencies, or locations that interest them. OPM has made provision of "timely, accurate, and complete employment information" via USAJOBS a priority in its 2000 strategic plan (U.S. Office of Personnel Management, 2000a: 22) Increasing use of technology, not only to recruit, but also to test and rank candidates, will also speed the hiring process and reduce the workload for HR staff.

Another new approach to hiring was introduced by President Clinton. In July, 2000, he signed Executive Order 13162, "authorizing the Federal Career Intern Program as a tool to attract 'exceptional men and women to the federal work force who have a variety of experiences, academic disciplines and competencies' " (U.S. Office of Personnel Management, 2000b). Unlike the Presidential Management Internship program, this new internship program is decentralized. Each agency can decide whether to create an internship program that will provide a vehicle for recruiting new employees, typically at the GS-5,7, or 9 level, for a two-year program that will provide interns with formal training and developmental opportunities. At the end of the two years, interns can, at the discretion of the agency, be converted to the competitive career service (i.e., to permanent jobs). Because the regulations were only issued recently (*Federal Register*, 2000), it is too early to tell to what extent the Bush administration will support creation of new internship programs and push agencies to implement them.

CONCLUSIONS

There is a growing realization that the federal government may be facing a human capital crisis. David Walker, the comptroller general of the General Accounting Office, has taken the lead in identifying the problems. As he has stated, "[S]erious human capital shortfalls are eroding the ability of many federal agencies—and threatening the ability of others—to economically, efficiently, and effectively perform their missions" (U.S. General Accounting Office, 2001). The increased recognition that human capital is essential for achieving agency mission is reflected in OPM's strategic plan, which plans to measure the strategic outcome of "high workforce quality" by the extent of agreement among HR directors and staff, and by staff and line managers, "that their workforce enables their agency to meet its mission" (U.S. Office of Personnel Management, 2000a: 15). However, in spite of the Clinton administration's attempts to deregulate and decentralize HR processes, many managers and supervisors feel that their ability to hire high-quality staff is still being impeded by "archaic and overly complex systems" and that delegation has sometimes not been delegated within agencies "down the chain of command to managers and first-line supervisors" (U.S. Office of Personnel Management, 1998a, ii).

Without more major reforms, what we are likely to see in the near future is probably not a train wreck. The federal government is still an attractive employer for enough people so that most jobs will be filled. What we can expect, however, is more use of contracting out to meet the need for highly skilled technical employees and more agencies attempting to leave the standard federal system, embodied in Title V, to set up their own, more flexible personnel systems. Both trends reflect the fact that, in the eyes of many managers, and some political leaders, the Title V personnel system is broken. Unless political leaders are willing to tackle some of the hard issues raised by the need to balance conflicting values and interests, the politics of hiring will leave us with a system that is overly complex and far from optimal in helping agencies bring in and retain the life-blood of their organizations: outstanding employees.

NOTE

1. Technically, an examination or selection method is said to have adverse impact on a specific group if the pass rate for the group is less than 80 percent of the pass rate for whites. In the case of the PACE exam, "in 1978, about 42 percent of whites taking the test passed at 70 percent or higher, compared to only about 5 percent for blacks and 13 percent for Hispanics" (Ban and Ingraham, 1988: 709).

REFERENCES

Ban, Carolyn. 1988–89. "Q.E.D.: The Research and Demonstration Provisions of the Civil Service Reform Act," *Policy Studies Journal* 17 (2):420–34.

Ban, Carolyn. 1992. "Research and Demonstrations under CSRA: Is Innovation Possible?" In Patricia W. Ingraham and David H. Rosenbloom, eds. *The Promise and Paradox of Civil Service Reform.* Pittsburgh: University of Pittsburgh Press.

Ban, Carolyn. 1995. *How Do Public Managers Manage? Bureaucratic Constraints, Organizational Culture, and the Potential for Reform.* San Francisco: Jossey-Bass.

Ban, Carolyn. 1998. "Reinventing the Federal Civil Service: Drivers of Change," *Public Administration Quarterly.* 22 (1):21–34.

Ban, Carolyn, and Patricia Ingraham. 1988. "Retaining Quality Federal Employees: Life After PACE." *Public Administration Review* 48 (3):708–18.

Ban, Carolyn, and Toni Marzotto. 1984. "Delegations of Examining: Objectives and Implementation." In Patricia W. Ingraham and Carolyn Ban, eds. *Legislating Bureaucratic Change: The Civil Service Reform Act of 1978.* Albany: State University of New York Press.

Federal Register. 2000. Vol. 65, No 241, Thursday, December 14: 78077–78079.

Ingraham, Patricia W. 1984. "The Civil Service Reform Act of 1978: Its Design and Legislative History." In Patricia W. Ingraham and Carolyn Ban, eds. *Legislating Bureaucratic Change: the Civil Service Reform Act of 1978.* Albany: SUNY Albany Press.

Jorgensen, Lorna, Kelli Fairless, and W. David Patton. 1996. "Underground Merit Systems and the Balance Between Service and Compliance." *Review of Public Personnel Administration* xvi (2):5–20.

Kauffman, Tim. 2001a. "Work-Force Restructuring Must Top Agenda," *Federal Times*, January 1:7.

Kauffman, Tim. 2001b. "Work-Force Measures Will Wait," *Federal Times*, April 9:3.

Light, Paul. 1999. *The True Size of Government*. Washington, D.C.: The Brookings Institution.

Luevano et al. v. Alan Campbell. 1981. Consent Decree, as amended. U.S. District Court for the District of Columbia (No. 79-0271).

Marzotto, Toni. 1988. "The Fragmentation of the Federal Workforce." Paper presented at the Annual Conference of the American Political Science Association.

National Academy of Public Administration (NAPA). 1999. *Entry-Level Hiring and Development for the 21st Century: Professional and Administrative Positions* (HRM Series V). Washington, D.C.: NAPA.

National Performance Review. 1993. *Reinventing Human Resources Management*. Washington, D.C.: U.S. Government Printing Office.

Ospina, Sonia. 1992. "'Expediency Management' in the Public Service: A Dead-End Search for Managerial Discretion." *Public Productivity and Management Review* xv (4):405–21.

U.S. Civil Service Commission: 1973. *Biography of an Ideal: A History of the Federal Civil Service*. Washington, D.C.: U.S. Government Printing Office.

U.S. General Accounting Office. 1994. *Federal Hiring: Testing for Entry-Level Administrative Positions Falls Short of Expectations*. GAO/GGD-94-103.

U.S. General Accounting Office. 2001. *Human Capital: Meeting the Governmentwide High-Risk Challenge*. Statement of David M. Walker, comptroller general of the United States. Testimony before the Subcommittee on Oversight of Government Management, Restructuring, and the District of Columbia. Committee on Governmental Affairs. U.S. Senate. February 1. GAO-01-357T.

U.S. Merit Systems Protection Board. 1995. *The Rule of Three in Federal Hiring: Boon or Bane?* Washington, D.C.: USMSPB.

———. 2000. *Restoring Merit to Federal Hiring: Why Two Special Hiring Programs Should be Ended*. Washington, D.C.: USMSPB.

U.S. Office of Personnel Management. 1981. *Manager's Handbook*. Washington, D.C. U.S. Government Printing Office.

U.S. Office of Personnel Management. 1992. *U.S. Department of Agriculture Personnel Management Demonstration Project: First Annual Evaluation Report*. OS92-7. Washington, D.C. USOPM.

U.S. Office of Personnel Management. 1998a. *Deregulation and Delegation of Human Resources Management Authority in the Federal Government*. Washington, D.C. Office of Merit Systems Oversight and Effectiveness, USOPM. July. MSE-98-3.

U.S. Office of Personnel Management. 1998b. *HRM Policies and Practices in Title 5-Exempt Organizations*, Washington, D.C. Office of Merit Systems Oversight and Effectiveness, USOPM. August. MSE-98-4.

U.S. Office of Personnel Management, 2000a. *Federal Human Resources Management for the 21st Century: Strategic Plan, FY 2000-FY 2005*. September 30.

U.S. Office of Personnel Management. 2000b. *OPM's Interim Rules on Federal Career Intern Program to Help Agencies Build Future Work Force*. OPM News Release. December 14.

U.S. Office of Personnel Management. 2001. *Veterans: Getting Their Preference?* Washington, D.C. Office of Merit Systems Oversight and Effectiveness, USOPM. March.

Chapter *13*

Employee Performance Appraisal and Pay for Performance in the Public Sector: A Critical Examination

J. Edward Kellough

In the most general sense, it is the task of management to help ensure that effective organizational performance is achieved. Toward that end, managers bring together material resources and personnel, coordinate and direct their utilization, and set policies and procedures aimed at enhancing productive activity. Of course, a focus on performance rests on a presumption that superior (or inferior) performance will be recognized when it is accomplished. Clearly, management's ability to move an organization toward optimal productivity will be frustrated if satisfactory and unsatisfactory levels of performance cannot be identified. But for that to take place, an adequate means of performance appraisal is necessary. In some instances it may be possible to assess organizational productivity or performance comprehensively, or if that is not an option, the productivity of specific organizational subunits might be scrutinized. More often, however, attention is focused on the productivity or performance of individual employees, and a presumption is made that greater individual productivity will accrue to the benefit of organizational performance generally. From this point of view, it would appear that a "key to improving productivity and quality services in the public sector is accurately measuring and controlling the performance of each worker" (Nigro and Nigro, 2000: 134). This chapter examines the concept of individual-level performance appraisal in the public sector. The central concern will be on questions of (1) what precisely is appraised, (2) how, more generally, are appraisals conducted, and (3) how are the results of performance appraisals utilized. Difficulties that may be encountered in each of these areas of concern are addressed as the discussion proceeds.

IDENTIFYING PERFORMANCE CRITERIA AND STANDARDS

If we are interested in measuring job performance, it would appear that our criteria for assessment should reflect the quality of work outcomes or results; that is, we should focus ideally on what it is that the worker produces and how well it is produced. An understanding or knowledge of job content, developed through systematic job analysis, would be essential for identifying and specifying such criteria. Job analysis provides insight into the various tasks essential for the job, and work outcomes could be defined in terms of those tasks. Results-oriented measures could include such outcomes as the number of projects completed, number of forms processed, or the number of clients served. Work output measures by themselves, however, are of obviously limited utility. Allowance would have to be made for variation in the quality of product or service delivered, and variation in the level of difficulty of specific tasks would certainly have to be considered as well. As a result, selection of criteria for performance evaluation is only half of the problem. The other half is determining appropriate standards of performance for each specified task. Such standards should reflect reasonable expectations of what is actually possible in terms of accomplishments. Those kinds of expectations, of course, could come only from an understanding of the nature and context of the jobs under analysis that have been developed through long experience and the documentation of previous levels of output or the utilization of time and motion studies (Carroll and Schneier, 1982: 131–134; Murphy and Cleveland, 1995: 154–156).

Clearly, the development of performance-appraisal systems based on results-oriented criteria and well-conceived performance standards may not be easily accomplished. In some instances, meaningful work outcomes at the level of individual employees are difficult to identify. What, for example, should be specified as measurable work outcomes for a county road-maintenance crew worker whose specific tasks vary from day to day and are, at least in part, a function of weather and a variety of other factors that may not be easily predictable? Work products of numerous other types of employees in the public sector may also be difficult to ascertain. Consider, for example, a clerk in a local tax commissioner's office or a receptionist in a state agency whose specific duties will vary with fluctuations in public demand for the services of their respective units. Similarly, consider individuals such as budget analysts or program auditors who often work in teams: What work outcomes are appropriately specified for their jobs when the fact is that much of what they do is dependent upon the work of others? Certain products or services may be identified for which the individual employee may be held accountable in each of these instances, but those outcomes may not capture the full extent of the responsibilities of the individual; in addition, reasonable performance standards may prove to be elusive, especially when the nature of particular tasks varies in unpredictable ways. In such circumstances, appraisal may be skewed toward the assessment of work outcomes that are most easily measured, even if they are not necessarily the most meaningful. Performance appraisals based on the quality and quantity of work outcomes produced by an individual are best developed when the individual's tasks are routine and are focused almost exclusively on the production of tangible work products. Performance criteria and standards for individual employees whose tasks are diffuse, whose work depends on the actions of numerous other individuals, and whose effort is directed toward the production of less-than-tangible services or products may not always be readily identifiable.

For these reasons, performance appraisal is often based on other types of criteria that may not represent actual work product or outcomes but are nonetheless judged to be prerequisites for successful performance. Certain employee behaviors deemed to be essential for effective performance are used as such criteria. For example, the timely completion of required paperwork or reports; efforts to assist co-workers; respectful, courteous, timely, and tactful interaction with agency clients; and the ready acceptance of direction and feedback from supervisors are all examples of behavioral criteria that could form the basis for the performance appraisal of individual workers. The advantage of behaviorally based performance-assessment systems is that for many jobs, specific criteria—that is, presumably effective job behaviors—are more easily identified than are work products or results for which the individual can be reasonably held accountable. It is also likely that similar behaviors may be relevant to a number of jobs so that separate criteria will not need to be developed for every distinct job and that employee behaviors should be relatively easy to observe and evaluate. A focus on behavior is not the same thing, however, as a focus on work product or actual employee accomplishments, and that is the major disadvantage of behavior-based criteria. An employee may complete a report on time, but that obviously is not a productive activity if the report contains errors or is otherwise of poor quality. In other words, the presence of desired behaviors by themselves may not be sufficient if the connection between those behaviors and work outcomes is tenuous. Nevertheless, behavior-based approaches to performance appraisal are common. In the early 1990s, for example, the state of Georgia spent many months and an enormous amount of resources developing a new employee performance-management system known as *GeorgiaGain* that rests largely (although not entirely) on behavioral criteria for individual performance (Nigro and Kellough, 2001).

A third approach to developing criteria for employee performance is to specify particular traits or personal characteristics presumed to be associated with effective performance. Employees may be evaluated in such systems on the basis of traits such as "dependability," "cooperativeness," "honesty," "diligence," or "initiative." Such evaluation systems are easily developed. It is not difficult to identify a set of presumably positive traits that are desirable as characteristics of employees. Trait-based approaches have been widely used in the past, and they can be used across a wide range of jobs, but their use is now typically discouraged because the linkage between apparent possession of particular traits and actual performance on the job may be quite weak, and the determination of the extent to which an individual employee exhibits an individual trait is highly subjective (Carroll and Schneier, 1982: 37; Tompkins, 1995: 252–253). In addition, trait scales typically do not provide the kinds of specific information necessary to structure effective employee training and development efforts (Latham and Wexley 1994: 38). Actual job behaviors and work outcomes (if they are specified) are typically much easier to observe and will better identify training and developmental needs.

CONDUCTING THE APPRAISAL

Although there are a variety of specific approaches, including narrative essays written by supervisors and ranking or comparison methods (Cardy and Dobbins, 1994: 64–67), performance appraisal is most often accomplished, regardless of whether the criteria are job outcomes, behaviors, or traits, through the use of a rating scale on which the person conducting the evaluation indicates the observed level of performance, generally by simply placing a checkmark in an appropriate box. For each performance criterion specified, for example, four or five performance levels may be identified. It is not uncommon to find performance levels defined as "unsatisfactory," "minimally satisfactory," "satisfactory," "highly satisfactory," "outstanding," or some variation of that scheme. The performance levels specified are assumed to reflect relevant standards for performance, but obviously the actual definition or meaning of those standards will be determined by the judgment of the raters involved, and that judgment may well vary from one person to another. In other words, satisfactory performance on a particular criterion or job dimension may to a considerable extent rest in the eye of the beholder. To the degree that this is the case, an employee's appraisal can be as much a function of the rater's attitude and perception as it is actual performance.

To reduce this problem, it is necessary that performance levels be accompanied by at least brief narrative definitions. Trait- and behavior-based rating scales, for example, often utilize performance levels tied to behavioral anchors. Behaviorally-anchored rating scales (BARS) do not rely simply on ambiguous performance levels defined as satisfactory or unsatisfactory and various other gradients thereof. Instead, each level of performance is defined in terms of clearly articulated behaviors that are intended to be easily observable and are relevant to the particular job being performed. This procedure narrows somewhat the range of interpretative discretion exercised by the rater and thus helps to ensure consistency or uniformity in the application of the rating scale, although some discretion will necessarily remain in the hands of the evaluator. In instances where job outcomes or results are utilized as performance criteria, specific standards representing different levels of quality or quantity of work product should be specified. As noted earlier, these standards are unique to the tasks associated with each job and are developed through an analysis of the nature of the job and experience with the kinds of levels of productivity that are possible. But even in instances where meaningful individual-level work outcomes and performance standards tied to those outcomes can be defined, some judgment exercised by the rater will still be necessary.

In many, or perhaps most, organizations, individual performance ratings are conducted on an annual basis, although other schedules are certainly possible. Regardless of the schedule, however, the results must be reported back to the employee. This communication can be accomplished simply by distribution of a copy of the rating sheet, but it is far more desirable to take advantage of the opportunity that this stage of the process provides for counseling and direction from the employee's supervisor, designed to provide the employee with information, not only about how well he or she performed, but also about what might be changed or altered so that performance can be improved (Carroll and Schneier, 1982: 177–181; Daley, 1992; Klein and Snell, 1994). These appraisal interviews or briefing sessions may, in fact, be the most crucial aspect of the appraisal process. It is here that the supervisor may be able to explain the basis for judgments made in the evaluation and offer suggestions for employee improvement. In some systems grounded on the concept of Management by Objectives (MBO), the supervisor and employee will set goals to be achieved during the upcoming performance cycle (Carroll and Schneier, 1982: 143). The individual goals are based on previously articulated organizational objectives, and it is assumed that directing employee efforts toward specific job-related goals tied to those objectives is one way of effectively promoting organizational productivity. Additionally, a substantial body of literature suggests that employee participation in the establishment of realistic yet challenging goals will enhance employee commitment to the organization and motivation to perform (Locke, 1983; Locke and Latham, 1984; Murphy and Cleveland, 1995: 215–224; Roberts and Reed, 1996). Ultimately, however, the effectiveness of the goal-setting exercise and the appraisal interview itself will hinge on the skill, ability, and commitment of the supervisor involved.

It should be clear, then, that there may be a number of obstacles to effective performance appraisal. The process can never be entirely objective. Judgment must be exercised in the selection of criteria for appraisal, the definition of performance standards, and the application of those standards to individual employees. A substantial commitment from the organization is necessary for performance criteria and standards to be defined adequately and for raters (usually supervisors) to be trained adequately in the proper application of the system. It is also important that sufficient time be allowed for effective counseling of employees during the performance briefing or interview, although that may be difficult to accomplish when supervisors are confronted with numerous other pressing demands on their time. In short, substantial organizational resources must be devoted to the performance-appraisal process if it is to be made effective.

Because rater judgment is such a critical aspect of the appraisal process, some concern must be focused on the possibility of bias or error in the exercise of that judgment. Bias would occur, of course, when performance ratings are altered to conform to the rater's personal views of individual employees that are unrelated to work productivity. Bias can also obviously be the product of prejudice based on factors such as race, ethnicity, gender, age, or disability. Clearly, such considerations have no place in the appraisal process, and evaluations made on such bases are legally proscribed. But in addition to bias, error can occur as a result of less invidious, but still unacceptable, processes. A supervisor, for example, may have friends or "favorite" employees who are rated more generously than others. Several common errors are identified in the literature (e.g., see Cardy and Dobbins, 1994: 27–33,

Carroll and Schneier, 1982: 39–41; Latham and Wexley, 1994: 100–104). A discussion of some of the most important types of errors follows.

The Halo Effect.   Evaluators will often rate an employee, who performs well on one dimension of a job, high on all other aspects of the job. In this situation, it is as if the employee can do no wrong—hence the label "halo effect," but the process can also operate in the opposite direction. For example, poor performance in one area of work may lead the rater to judge the employee harshly in other areas. In general, the problem occurs whenever a rating in one dimension or aspect of a job (whether good or bad) is generalized to other dimensions.

The First-Impression Error.   Raters, especially supervisors, may base subsequent performance appraisals on the impressions they formed of an individual employee when that person first came on the job. In other words, initial impressions, whether favorable or unfavorable, influence subsequent evaluations of performance. Information that is not consistent with the first impression formed is suppressed or discounted. For example, if during the first month on a job an employee had difficulty and performed poorly, the impression such behavior leaves with a manager may lead that manager to give the employee low performance ratings during later evaluations even though the employee's performance improved.

The Similar-to-Me Effect.   Performance evaluators may tend to judge more favorably employees whom they perceive as exhibiting behaviors or values similar to their own. In other words, "the more closely the employee resembles the rater in terms of attitudes or background, the stronger the tendency of the rater to judge that person favorably" (Latham and Wexley, 1994: 103).

Comparison or Contrast Effects.   It may frequently be the case that employees are evaluated relative to each other rather than relative to actual job performance standards. An employee who is quite good, for example, may be rated as average simply because he or she is compared to others who are exceptional performers. Alternatively, an employee who is only average in performance may be rated highly because by comparison he or she looks good next to his or her mediocre colleagues. In either situation, an error occurs because performance is not judged relative to the actual requirements and standards set for the jobs at issue, but the reliance on employee contrasts or comparisons as a basis for performance appraisal is driven in part by the view of many managers that the appraisal process should produce a distribution of ratings that resemble a normal or bell-shaped curve (Latham and Wexley, 1994: 101; Lane 1994).

The Central Tendency Error.   This error is one of the most common in performance appraisal, occurring when the rater judges all employees as average or slightly above average. This problem may have the effect of limiting the usefulness of performance appraisal for some purposes, but the fact is that the dynamics of the appraisal process often lead managers or supervisors into this difficulty. Typically, there is no particular incentive in the process for a rater to judge a subordinate extraordinarily high. If such judgments are made in a few cases, the supervisor risks alienating the bulk of employees who may feel resentment that some are favored at their expense. If higher ratings are given to numerous employees, upper management will undoubtedly question the rater's judgment and demand documentation to support that judgment. Alternatively, if employees are rated below satisfactory, the supervisor will risk the hostility of affected employees and will again need substantial documentation to support the judgment when it is challenged. In this situation, one can see readily that the path of least resistance for raters is to judge most employees as satisfactory or slightly above satisfactory unless truly extraordinary circumstances occur. As a result, there may be little variation in ratings among large numbers of employees, and actual scores will not reflect fine gradations in the quality of performance.

Bias and error may never be completely eliminated from the appraisal process, but it can be reduced if raters are adequately trained in the application of the appraisal system and are sensitized to the kinds of problems that can occur and when clearly defined behavioral or results-oriented performance standards are established (Latham and Wexley, 1994: 104–107). Additionally, error may be minimized when appraisal information is collected from a variety of sources; that is, supervisory appraisals may be supplemented with information from self-appraisals as well as with ratings by an employee's subordinates, peers, or customers (Campbell and Lee, 1988; deLeon and Ewen, 1997; Edwards and Ewen, 1996; Lathan and Wexley, 1981: 79–98; Murphy and Cleveland, 1995: 133–142). Because these multi-rater approaches involve the collection of data from a number of points of view relative to the employee being evaluated, they are often referred to as 360 degree evaluations (Bracken et al. 1997, Tornow and London, et al. 1998). Ratings by subordinates, peers, customers, and self appraisals can provide useful supplements to the judgment of a supervisor who may not always be sufficiently familiar with an employee's work or who may not observe an employee often enough to render an informed judgment (Murphy and Cleveland, 1995: 123–124). Of course, the expansion of the appraisal process to include other evaluators in addition to a supervisor can make the process more cumbersome, time-consuming, and expensive.

THE UTILIZATION OF PERFORMANCE-APPRAISAL RESULTS: AN UNCOMFORTABLE LOOK AT PAY FOR PERFORMANCE

Performance appraisals are conducted because it is believed that their results will be helpful in the process of improving individual employee performance and ultimately organizational performance. As noted above, the appraisal interview, if conducted effectively, provides an opportunity for the supervisor to guide employee behavior in productive ways. When an appraisal uncovers areas of performance that need improvement, they can be pointed out to employees and instructions as to how to improve can be provided (Roberts and Reed, 1996). In addition, in every organization some employees will be promoted while others will not, some will face adverse actions, some will be provided training opportunities that others will be denied, and some will receive larger pay increases than others. Ideally, we would have some rational basis to guide those decisions so that the process of distributing organizational rewards and sanctions actually promotes productive activity. Individual-based performance appraisal is the tool we rely on to provide that foundation (Murphy and Cleveland, 1995: 88–95). Obviously, however, the decisions made on that basis are only as good as the appraisal process itself.

The use of performance-appraisal ratings to determine annual employee pay increases is an interesting and important case in point. During the 1980s and 1990s, pay-for-performance systems enjoyed an enormous popularity in the public sector (Ingraham, 1993; Kellough and Lu, 1993; Kellough and Selden, 1997). In one approach, often known as merit pay, annual pay increases were tied to the outcomes of individual-level performance appraisals. An alternative approach was to use the outcomes of the individual-level appraisal process to award financial bonuses rather than increases in base pay. Merit-pay systems were by far the most common pay-for-performance schemes. The federal government experimented with merit pay from 1981 to 1993, and numerous state and local government jurisdictions continue to rely on such systems. At a basic level, the concept of pay-for-performance has an appealing logic: One must simply determine which employees are superior performers and reward them with increased pay. Presumably, such a policy would prevent the resentment or alienation of the best employees that could result when their superior contributions are not recognized and they receive the same pay as their less-productive colleagues. At the same time, poorer performers are offered an incentive to improve their levels of productivity.

The argument for merit pay rests closely on the principles associated with a set of ideas about worker motivation known as equity theory (Adams, 1965; Mowday, 1983; Rainey, 1997). According to that perspective, individual employees will adjust their behaviors at work depending on their perception of how equitably they are being treated. In other words, employees' perceptions of equity at work will affect their levels of motivation. A superior performer who receives the same compensation as a much less-productive co-worker would perceive inequity, for example, and would over time adjust his/her output downward until the perceived inequity is no longer present. Such an employee could easily question why the extra effort necessary to achieve higher levels of productivity should be sustained if it is not recognized and rewarded (Schay, 1988). In fact, equity theory would suggest that the best way to ensure that top performers will continue to be productive is to find ways to acknowledge their higher levels of productivity—such as pay differentials.

Additional theoretical support for pay-for-performance systems may be found in expectancy theory (Vroom, 1964; Porter and Lawler, 1968). This theory specifically addresses the psychological or cognitive processes associated with the development of motivation, rather than questions of what incentives or motives are most effective. According to this view, individuals will be motivated to behave in productive ways, depending upon their perceptions of the extent to which such behavior is possible, and if it is accomplished, it will lead to valued rewards. More specifically, expectancy theory suggests that an individual will be most highly motivated to perform when he or she expects that (1) their effort will lead to higher levels of performance (the effort-performance expectation), (2) higher performance will lead to specified outcomes (the performance-outcome expectancy), and (3) the outcomes are desirable or valuable. Because higher pay would appear to be valuable to most, if not all, employees, proponents of pay for performance suggest that all that management must do to enhance employee motivation to perform is to offer financial incentives (either as bonuses or increases to base pay), encourage employees to believe that they can perform, and demonstrate that performance will be recognized and rewarded. It sounds like a simple idea, but in practice it does not appear to work as advertised.

In the early 1990s, after more than a decade of experimentation with pay for performance in government, examinations of the empirical literature could find little evidence that employee motivation or productivity was actually enhanced by such systems (Kellough and Lu, 1993; Milkovich and Wigdor, 1991). Difficulties with the concept of pay for performance arise in a number of ways. Consider, for example, the notion from expectancy theory that employees must believe that their levels of effort will lead to effective performance if they are to be motivated to perform. In many circumstances, it will be difficult for management to promote that view among workers. Employees typically do not labor in isolation. Organizations are systems in which workers' efforts must be coordinated, and it is often the case that there are interdependencies among employees. A given individual's level of performance will, therefore, frequently depend on the productivity of others in the organization. Other employees may make decisions or perform a variety of operations that will influence a specified individual's task difficulty and probability of success. Individuals in such situations will recognize this dilemma and will perceive that when this occurs, their own level of effort may make little difference in their ability to perform.

It is also essential, again from the view of expectancy theory, that employees perceive that performance is explicitly linked to pay, if pay-for-performance systems are to motivate workers. The issue referred to here is the performance-outcome expectancy. The difficulty at this point obviously lies largely in the performance-appraisal process. As demonstrated earlier, individual-based performance appraisal is never entirely objective. Ultimately, the appraisal process rests on rater judgment. Employees recognize this characteristic of the process, and as a result, there is often a tendency for employees to question the accuracy of appraisal outcomes, especially when their performance is not rated as highly as they think it should be rated (Hamner, 1983). Efforts to base pay on the outcomes of performance appraisal have the effect of raising the stakes and increasing employee sensitivity to appraisal outcomes, and it should be stressed that employee perceptions of accuracy can have little to do with whether or not the appraisal outcome is in fact accurate. Ego involvement and a desire to rationalize unfavorable ratings may be more than sufficient to lead employees to question rater judgment, especially when pay is affected. Because employee perceptions are important determinants of employee motivation—that is, expectancy theory requires that employees perceive that good performance is recognized for the performance-outcome expectancy and subsequent motivation to be high—perceptions that the appraisal process is less than fair will undermine the motivational potential of pay for performance.

Clearly, the dynamics of performance appraisal can exacerbate this difficulty. It should be recalled that it is often the case that raters, especially supervisors, are reluctant to draw sharp distinctions between employees. Low ratings and high ratings each require justification. The rater must be prepared to defend the judgments rendered, and such effort will divert time and energy away from what may be seen as tasks more instrumentally associated with the organization's mission. As a result, variation in appraisal outcomes is constrained and the perceived legitimacy of the process can be further undermined. Efforts to link pay to the outcomes of such a process would appear to invite employee alienation.

An additional difficulty is associated with the levels of pay increases or bonuses offered under pay-for-performance systems: The assumption that higher pay (as opposed to lower pay) is valued by public employees, which is also a necessary part of the foundation of pay for performance, seems reasonable on its face, but the motivational potential of pay increases or bonuses is surely linked to the size of those increases or bonuses. For two reasons, this points to an additional difficulty, especially in the public sector. The first point is that there is a tendency, noted above, for there to be relatively little variation in the outcomes of performance appraisal processes. In addition, research has shown that when performance ratings are intended for use in making administrative decisions, including pay decisions, raters tend to be even more lenient than usual (Murphy and Cleveland, 1995: 96). As a result, the money available for distribution to employees under a pay-for-performance system is typically spread among a wide group so that, especially in the case of increases to base pay, most employees usually receive awards that are not much different than they would have received under an across-the-board distribution. Very few are denied increases, and few receive substantial increases. In some organizations, outstanding ratings are actually rotated among employees to counter this problem, but, of course, that further undermines the perceived legitimacy of the system. The second point is that the difficulties caused by the frequently small average pay increases under pay-for-performance systems in the public sector are often made worse because of an unwillingness on the part of many jurisdictions to fund such systems adequately. As a result, the amount of money available to reward performance may be relatively small. Typically, it is the case that payroll totals under pay for performance are not allowed to exceed what would have been available under a traditional pay system. Although that approach may be understandable from a budgetary perspective, the effect is that larger pay increases for some employees must be offset by smaller pay increases for other workers—a fact that operates to constrain variation further in pay outcomes and limit the motivational potential of the system.

It should be acknowledged also, that even if pay-for performance mechanisms could succeed in increasing employee motivation, improvements in employee and organizational productivity may not follow. In other words, there are additional considerations beyond a failure to boost motivation that may lead to little observed impact of pay for performance on individual productivity. One factor, of course, is that such approaches to pay administration can lead to dysfunctional activities among employees. Effort might be directed toward tasks that are most easily measured, regardless of their relevance to organizational outcomes, and competition among employees for performance-based incentives can undermine the teamwork and cooperation often necessary for organizational success. It is also the case, however, that even if motivation is increased as a result of pay for performance, motivation alone may not be sufficient to boost productivity. Employees must also have an understanding of what is expected, the opportunity to perform, and the ability to perform. Shortcomings in any of those areas of concern can undermine individual productivity, regardless of the level of employee motivation.

CONCLUSION

Performance appraisal is intended to be a tool through which management may direct individual behavior within organizations into productive channels. Appraisal outcomes are used also as the basis for a number of administrative decisions regarding training, promotions, adverse actions, and even pay. Although the appeal of individual-based performance appraisal may be great from a managerial perspective, we have seen that there are a number of difficulties with the concept. The use of performance appraisal as a basis for allocating pay incentives is particularly troubling, and given the record in that area of activity, such action should be approached with caution. With respect to the appraisal process itself, at a minimum, an organization must be willing to commit substantial managerial time and other resources to the activity if there is to be any hope of its effective implementation. In fact, some observers, especially proponents of Total Quality Management (TQM), have argued that the problems with individual-based performance appraisal are so substantial that we would be better off to abandon the idea and focus on measuring the productivity of meaningful work units or larger organizational subdivisions or systems (Bowman, 1994; Deming, 1986; Juran, 1964). Such an approach may have the effect of allowing us to avoid the problem that individual performance is often a function, at least in part, of factors beyond the individual's control (Fox and Shirkey, 1997), but other performance-measurement problems associated with identifying appropriate performance criteria and standards will remain at such levels. In the end, we should approach individual-based performance appraisal guardedly. It may at times be a useful managerial tool, but our view must be tempered by a knowledge of the limitations inherent in the process.

REFERENCES

Adams, J. S. 1965. "Inequity in Social Exchange." In L. Berkowitz, ed., *Advances in Experimental and Social Psychology.* Orlando, FL: Academic Press.

Bowman, James S. 1994. "At last, An Alternative to Performance Appraisal: Total Quality Management." *Public Administration Review,* Vol. 54, No. 2 (March April):129–136.

Bracken, David W., et al., 1997. *Should 360-Degree Feedback Be Used Only for Developmental Purposes?* Greensboro, NC: Center for Creative Leadership.

Campbell, D. J., and C. Lee. 1988. "Self Appraisal in Performance Evaluation." *Academy of Management Review,* Vol. 13:187–196.

Cardy, Robert L., and Gregory H. Dobbins. 1994. *Performance Appraisal: Alternative Perspectives.* Cincinnati, OH: South-Western Publishing Company.

Carroll, S. J., and C. E. Schneier. 1982. *"Performance and Review Systems: The Identification, Measurement, and Development of Performance in Organizations.* Dallas: Scott, Foresman, and Company.

Daley, Dennis M. 1992. *Performance Appraisal in the Public Sector.* Westport, CT: Quorum Books.

deLeon, Linda, and Ann J. Ewen. 1997. "Multi-Source Performance Appraisals." *Review of Public Personnel Administration,* Vol. 17, No. 1 (Winter):22–36.

Deming, W. Edwards. 1986. *Out of the Crisis.* Cambridge, MA: MIT Press.

Edwards, Mark R., and Ann J. Ewen. 1996. *360° Feedback: The Powerful New Model for Employee Assessment & Performance Improvement.* New York: American Management Association.

Fox, Charles J., and Kurt A. Shirkey. 1997. "Employee Performance Appraisal: The Keystone Made of Clay." In Carolyn Ban and Norma M. Riccucci, eds., *Public Personnel Management: Current Concerns, Future Challenges,* 2nd ed. New York: Longman, pp. 205–220.

Hamner, W. Clay. 1983. "How to Ruin Motivation with Pay." In Richard M. Steers and Lyman W. Porter, eds., *Motivation and Work Behavior.* New York: McGraw-Hill, 264–275.

Ingraham, Patricia W. 1993. "Of Pigs in Pokes and Policy Diffusion: Another Look at Pay for Performance." *Public Administration Review,* Vol. 23, No. 3 (July/August):348–356.

Juran, J. M. 1964. *Managerial Breakthrough.* New York: McGraw Hill.

Kellough, J. Edward, and Haoran Lu. 1993. "The Paradox of Merit Pay in the Public Sector." *Review of Public Personnel Administration,* Vol. 13, No. 2 (Spring):45–64.

Kellough, J. Edward, and Sally C. Selden. 1997. "Pay for Performance in State Government: Perceptions of State Agency Personnel Managers." *Review of Public Personnel Administration,* Vol. 17, No. 1 (Winter):5–21.

Klein, H. J., and S. A. Snell. 1994. "The Impact of Interview Process and Context on Performance Appraisal Interview Effectiveness." *Journal of Management Issues,* Vol. 6:160–175.

Lane, Larry M. 1994. "Public Sector Performance Management: Old Failures and New Opportunities," Vol. 14, No. 3 (Summer):26–44.

Latham, G. P. and K.N. Wexley 1994. *Increasing Productivity Through Performance Appraisal,* 2nd ed. Reading, MA: Addison-Wesley Publishing Company.

Locke, Edwin A. 1983. "The Ubiquity of the Technique of Goal Setting in Theories of and Approaches to Employee Motivation." In Richard M. Steers and Lyman W. Porter, eds., *Motivation and Work Behavior.* New York: McGraw-Hill, 81–90.

Locke, E. A., and G. P. Latham. 1984. *Goal Setting: A Motivational Technique That Works.* Englewood Cliffs, NJ: Prentice-Hall.

Milkovich, G. T., and A. K. Wigdor., eds. 1991. *Pay for Performance: Evaluating Performance Appraisal and Merit Pay.* Washington D.C.: National Academy Press.

Mowday, Richard T. 1983. "Equity Theory Predictions of Behavior in Organizations." In Richard M. Steers and Lyman W. Porter, eds., *Motivation and Work Behavior.* New York: McGraw-Hill, 91–113.

Murphy, Kevin R., and Jeanette Cleveland. 1995. *Understanding Performance Appraisal: Social, Organizational, and Goal-Based Perspectives.* Thousand Oaks, CA: Sage Publications.

Nigro, Lloyd G., and J. Edward Kellough. 2001. "Civil Service Reform in Georgia: Findings of a Survey of State Employees' Views About GeorgiaGain and Act 816," paper presented at the 62nd National Conference of the American Society for Public Administration, March 10–13, Rutgers University, Newark, NJ.

Nigro, Lloyd G., and Felix A. Nigro. 2000. *The New Public Personnel Administration,* 5th ed. Itasca, IL: F. E. Peacock Publishers.

Porter, L. W., and E. E. Lawler III. 1968. *Managerial Attitudes and Performance.* Homwood, IL: Dorsey Press.

Rainey, Hal G. 1997. *Understanding and Managing Public Organizations,* 2nd ed. San Francisco: Jossey-Bass.

Roberts, Gary E., and Tammy Reed. 1996. "Performance Appraisal Participation, Goal Setting, and Feedback." *Review of Public Personnel Administration,* Vol. 16, No. 4, (Fall):29–60.

Schay, Bridgette W. 1988. "Effects of Performance-Contingent Pay on Employee Attitudes." *Public Personnel Management,* Vol. 17:237–250.

Tompkins, Jonathan. 1995. *Human Resource Management in Government: Hitting the Ground Running.* New York: HarperCollins.

Tornow, Walter W., and Manuel London. 1998. *Maximizing the Value of 360-Degree Feedback: A Process for Successful Individual and Organizational Development.* San Francisco: Jossey-Bass.

Vroom, V. 1964. *Work and Motivation.* New York: Wiley.

Chapter

Understanding Training in the Public Sector

Ronald R. Sims

"Once, land and capital were the key strategic resources. Now, knowledge is our key strategic resource and learning is our key strategic skill."

Vice President Al Gore,
Lifelong Learning Summit (January 2000)

INTRODUCTION

It is important for public personnel management (PPM) professionals to be familiar with training in the public sector because the industrial age has shifted to the knowledge age, and the workforce is increasingly diverse and transforming from the physical to the virtual domain. PPM professionals must realize that careers are becoming fluid with the expansion of the contingent workforce; outsourcing of jobs; and the appearance of the free agent in federal, state, county and local agencies. Today, agencies are competing as much for talent as for financial resources. For example, while nearly all government agencies have become technology-savvy, efforts to recruit and retain staff amid skill shortages is even more difficult in the public sector than among private companies. Government agencies cannot offer the high salaries or stock options that lure workers to their private counterparts (Cunningham, 2000). However, some government organizations like Fairfax County in Virginia, the state government of Missouri, and California's state Department of Corrections in efforts to recruit and retain quality information technology (IT) employees, have increasingly turned to the creative use of benefits, developed recruitment ads to resemble private-sector ones, and formed coalitions with private companies to develop IT training programs.

Technological innovations, increased efficiency, and good people are not enough, however, to make an agency excel in today's demanding environment. Competitiveness and survival require learning. The distinguishing feature between agencies that succeed and those that fail lies in the ability to learn and adapt to the environment more effectively. Workplace learning has never been more important, and one strategy for surviving and thriving is continuous employee and organizational learning.

Marquardt observes that "A learning organization, systematically defined, is an organization which learns powerfully and collectively and is continually transforming itself to better collect, manage and use knowledge for organizational success" (1996: 19). Knowledge is doubling every two or three years, and communication media such as the Internet make it possible to exchange information as quickly as it is created.

Learning is a powerful vehicle for fostering organizational improvement and success, and like their private sector counterparts, public sector organizations are increasingly recognizing that one way of cultivating it is through formal employee training and development. For example, the Federal Aviation Administration (FAA) has recently undertaken efforts to become a learning organization. One of the ways the FAA is addressing learning is in its Materiel Management function, where they have recognized that a planned and determined effort to create a learning organization based on proven business principles requires a clear understanding of (1) the critical competencies that employees must develop to achieve the agency's mission and goals and (2) the agency's responsibility for providing the learning, training, and development for employees to close performance gaps (Federal Aviation Administration, 2000). Within the Department of Energy (DOE) complex, both Sandia and Los Alamos national laboratories have been engaged in knowledge management projects that include organizing written documentation as well as interviewing employees to capture their nuclear weapons knowledge base, both of which are important in becoming a learning organization (Ashdown and Smith, 1999).

According to data collected by organizations such as the American Society for Training and Development (ASTD) about leading-edge companies, one of the components that gives these companies an edge is commitment to and investment in learning. The AST reports that 2,000 corporate formal training expenditures in the United States totaled $54 billion. It is estimated that U.S. organizations spend more than $200 billion annually on human-resource-development (HRD) interventions (*Training,* 2000) that include not only training, but also performance management, career development, and organizational development. These estimates do not account for lost time, which adds another $200 billion to $300 billion to the overall training investment (Robinson and Robinson, 1998). Federal, state, county, and local governments also invest substantially in training and development. For example, estimates on how much the government spends on federal-employee training range from $15 billion to $30 billion a year (one estimate has the figure as high as $45 billion a year), covering everything from desktop applications to air traffic-control policies and purchasing rules (Merrill, 1999).

Research also shows that high-impact companies, public-sector agencies, and other institutions attribute much of their front-runner status to recognition of the importance of including training as a key element in their strategic planning process. In recent years, public-sector agencies have increasingly recognized that training the workforce is a win-win strategy for organizational success (Sims, 1998).

The purpose of this chapter is to discuss how those responsible for public-sector training have and must continue to respond to increased calls for accountability and change in their agencies. The first section offers a discussion of the traditional role of training.

The next section reviews federal policies and programs that have driven changes in training over the years. The third section looks at the changing role of public-sector training. Finally, the chapter attempts to answer the question "What will the future of public-sector training look like?"

THE TRADITIONAL ROLE OF TRAINING

Historically, the purpose of learning and development (hereafter referred to as training) programs in the federal government has been to assist in achieving an agency's mission and performance objectives by improving employee and organizational performance. Until recently, it was not unusual to hear that government offices were not aware of the best ways to develop their employees and thus protect their major investment and primary asset—human capital. Further, leaders often did not know how much or what kind of training was directed toward their organization's real priorities. For example, in the traditional agency approach, government offices as varied as the procurement policy office and the Pentagon, as well as key congressional members and staff, did not treat human capital as fundamental to the strategic management of their operation (Burman, 2000b).

The classroom approach to training at the heart of traditional training (and employee development) initiatives is ill-suited to today's government organizations. Customers of training want performance improvement; the traditional training mode offers instruction with no guarantee of job transfer. Customers want individualized help; the traditional training orientation gives them one-size fits all. They want help on the job; they want to control the time, place, and content. They want highly specialized service; training simply cannot provide enough of it in a classroom mode where the economics work against small class sizes. They want contact with a wide range of experts and practical examples; the traditional training paradigm gives them an agency trainer or two and a small collection of case studies. An example of the changing demands of training' customers is the experience of the Department of Labor (DOL).

In response to the changing training needs, the Department of Labor recently awarded a contract to Learn2.com, a provider of online learning solutions, and partner Innovative Management and Technology Approaches Inc. (IMTAS) to provide online training to up to 16,000 DOL employees nationwide (*EDP Weekly's IT Monitor,* 1999). Chief reasons for Learn2.com and IMTAS being awarded this contract was their nontraditional approach to training, ability to offer specialized, customized training, and their willingness to develop a partnership with the DOL to facilitate the DOL's Life Long Learning Initiative. In short, they were sensitive to the needs of their customer, DOL, and willing to work closely with them to meet their desired training goals.

Training in government learning must be strategically managed to achieve the objectives of the agency and to ensure the full utilization of the workforce. Particularly in times of constrained resources and the introduction of new policies and programs like those discussed below, training dollars must be targeted for the biggest payoffs. Agencies must avoid the traditional approach to budget constraints—freezing hiring and eliminating training—and recognize that such an approach runs counter to the new vision of government employees, a vision that, according to Comptroller General David Walker (Government Accounting Office), is "simply recognizing the importance of people as human capital" (Burman, 2000b).

PUBLIC-SECTOR TRAINING POLICY AND PROGRAM DRIVERS

Various legislation and programs aimed at improving government accountability, quality, and effectiveness have served and will continue to serve as important drivers for change in training efforts in public-sector organizations. This section highlights several of these drivers.

Government Employees Training Act (GETA).   GETA, which became law on July 7, 1958, is the governmentwide authority for training federal employees (Title 5, U.S. Code, Ch. 41). The act recognized the importance of federal employees' self-development and found it "necessary and desirable in the public interest that self-education, self-improvement, and self-training by such employees be supplemented and extended by government-sponsored programs."

The basic authority was reinforced by Executive Order (EO) 11348 in 1967, which states that it is the policy of the United States "to develop its employees through the establishment and operation of progressive and efficient training programs, thereby improving public service, increasing efficiency and economy, building and retaining a workforce of skilled and efficient employees, and installing and using the best modern practices and techniques in the conduct of government's business." EO 11491 issued in 1969 added the requirement to train personnel and management officials in labor management relations. The Equal Employment Opportunity Act of 1972 required the establishment of training and education programs to maximize opportunity for employees to advance so as to perform at their highest potential. The Civil Service Reform Act of 1978 addressed the development of candidates for the Senior Executive Service (SES) and the continuing development of senior executives.

The March 1994 amendments to GETA broadened the purpose of training and aligned it with agency performance objectives, making training a management tool responsive to the current and future needs of agencies. The legislation recognized that HRD had evolved from traditional training activities to include workplace learning, education, career management, organizational development, and performance improvement.

Section 624 of the Treasury, Postal Service, and General Government Appropriations Act, 1997. Prohibiting use of appropriated funds for training that is offensive to federal employees and unnecessary in the execution of their official duties, this section forbids training associated with religious or quasi-religious and "new age" belief systems, training that includes high levels of stress unrelated to the employees' work environments, and training meant to change employees' personal values or lifestyle outside the workplace.

Policies like those above contributed to changes in agency training over the years. An important outgrowth of these and other policies has been the recognition that the responsibility for performance-based individual and organizational learning is shared by the employees, the supervisor, agency management, and the agency' HRD office. At the IRS, employees, managers at all levels, and the training staff are all responsible for performance-based employee training and organizational learning (Internal Revenue Service, 2001). More-recent policies developed under the Clinton administration continue to have a dramatic impact on federal training.

Government Performance and Results Act (GPRA). Congress's determination to make agencies accountable for their performance lay at the heart of two landmark reforms of the 1990s: the Chief Financial Officers (CFO) Act of 1990 and the GPRA of 1993. With these two laws, Congress imposed on federal agencies a new and more businesslike framework for management and accountability. More fundamentally, GPRA requires agencies to set goals, measure performance, and report on their accomplishments. For example, over a recent five-year period the Department of Transportation's (DOT) application of both GPRA and NPR has occurred in a succession of stages so that each stage derives from or acts upon the product of the preceding stage. Thus, the goals and outcomes in the strategic plan cascade to the performance plan, from the performance plan to the budget, and from the budget to annual performance agreements. This formal structure has been institutionalized and is now understood by DOT's appointed and career managers to be the blueprint for action and setting priorities in day-to-day operations (Brzezinska, 2000).

Executive Order (EO) 13111. President Bill Clinton provided pivotal direction to government leaders about workforce learning and development in January 1999 through EO 13111, *Using Technology to Improve Training Opportunities for Federal Government Employees.* The EO embodies many tenets that federal executives could use to harness the power of training; for example, learning should be an integral, planned part of doing business as opposed to an afterthought. Further, every agency's strategic plan should identify training and education as a means for achieving goals. The business strategy espoused by EO 13111 makes sense.

EO 13111 specifically called on agencies to include a set of goals to provide effective training opportunities and allied performance measures as part of the annual budget process. Further, agencies are expected to identify the resources needed to achieve the accomplishment of those goals in their annual performance plans. Additionally, EO 13111 encourages innovation through agency demonstration projects and makes full use of best commercial practices when purchasing instructional software. Under EO 13111, agencies must also work with business, academia, and other appropriate entities to foster a competitive market for electronic instruction.

The Department of Housing and Urban Development's (HUD) Community Connections' Community 2020 planning software CD-ROM training is an example of innovation resulting from reforms mandated by EOs and other recent government legislation. The Community 2020 planning software CD-ROM was a winner of *Government Executive* magazine's eighth annual Government Technology Leadership Awards. The Community 2020 planning software helps states, localities, and government organizations spend their federal dollars more wisely in achieving their overall missions. The training package guides the user through a community with characters that take the shape of buildings, a mailbox, a traffic light, and a bus. The package includes six modules and a final test, called the 2020 Challenge (Anonymous, 1999).

Executive Order 11348. In January 1999, the White House released a memorandum updating EO 11348, titled *Providing for the Further Training of Government Employees,* establishing a President's Task Force on Federal Training Technology. As EO 11348 states, "A coordinated federal effort is needed to provide flexible training opportunities to employees and to explore how federal training programs, initiatives and policies can better support lifelong learning through the use of learning technology." As part of their annual budget requests, federal agencies will be required to submit goals for providing improved training to their employees by using the latest available technology. For example, one of the FY 2000 goals of the U.S. Department of Energy, Albuquerque Operations Office (US DOE/AL) Human Resources and Training Division, Training and Development Branch (HRDTD/T&DB) was to (Department of Energy, 2000):

> Manage training costs by enhancing partnering and general cost avoidance/saving activities in regards to efficiency of operations and utilize technology supported learning to meet organizational/individual learning.

THE CHANGING ROLE OF PUBLIC-SECTOR TRAINING

Today there is every indication that the pressure on government to transform itself and do more with less will continue in the years to come as skilled and experienced government workers become increasingly scarce. Yet, drivers of accountability and change, like the 1993 National Performance Review (NPR, often called the Gore Report because former Vice President Gore chaired the NPR) may not be around during the Bush administration. In fact, the office of the NPR has been shut down by President Bush, and Bush also revoked the National Partnership Council, which was established by the NPR.

The NPR was a comprehensive reappraisal of the way the federal government works, and it set in motion an unprecedented wave of organizational change. In response to the NPR, agencies found ways to reinvent their business processes using several principles (cutting back to basics, reengineering business processes, putting the customer first, cutting red tape, and empowering employees to get results) found in successful public- and private-sector organizations (Federal Human Resource Development Council, 1997). As noted, however, the Bush administration has not been supportive of the NPR, thus making it very likely that NPR initiatives will either cease or be abolished.

In addition, the Office of Personnel Management (OPM), which administers the GETA and other HRD programs and initiatives, no longer provides direct training to government agencies, but it administers the Management's Training and Management Assistance (TMA) program, developed in 1982. This is a contracting vehicle that helps federal, state, and local government agencies design and manage large and complex training and resource development projects. In partnership with government agencies and private-sector firms, TMA provides its customers immediate access to highly qualified, competitively selected contractors that can design and develop a wide range of learning and human-resource management solutions.

AGENCIES AS LEARNING ORGANIZATIONS

The concept of the "learning organization" has received steady attention since the 1990 publication of Peter Senge's book *The Fifth Discipline: The Art and Practice of the Learning Organization* (1990). Public sector organizations are now being pressured to realize unprecedented performance through the application of learning-organization principles to change their internal processes. It is expected that, in becoming learning organizations, agencies will be able to meet the increased demand for better products and services and a more customer-oriented focus. Public organizations are increasingly recognizing that, as learning organizations, they must enhance the capacity to learn, adapt, and change. Many agencies have adopted what is known as high-leverage training (Carnevale, 1990). High-leverage training is linked to strategic agency goals and objectives, uses an instructional-design process to ensure that training is effective, and compares or benchmarks the agency's training programs against programs in other agencies and companies.

ALIGNING TRAINING WITH AGENCY OBJECTIVES: BEING A STRATEGIC PARTNER

Today's agencies are required to identify training requirements based on their strategic and performance plans. The strategic plan and annual performance plans called for in the GPRA provide a blueprint for transforming an agency's current performance into the desired future state. The performance plans include incremental goals that lead toward the achievement of the longer-term strategic goals.

At this point, it is critical to analyze strategic goals to determine short-term and long-term training requirements. The performance plans are tools that can be used to help agencies identify the human, information/technological, and other resources to achieve the desired future performance.

Today, training must ensure that any competency gaps within the workforce are addressed so that the agency can achieve its future performance goals. For example, the Department of Energy's Office of Advanced Automotive Technologies (DOE OATT) participated in customized team training through the Federal Executive Institute (when the office grew from eight to thirty engineers) to address employee competency gaps better and to meet their mission—to research and develop technologies for vehicles of the future that will have several times the fuel economy of today's vehicles (Werth, 1999).

Traditional Versus Customer/Client Orientation

Those responsible for training in the public sector have had to rethink how they are adding value in their customers' eyes, meaning that they have had to move from an expert focus to a customer focus. PPM professionals are expected to engage customers in developing direction, rather than announcing training decisions. Today, this expectation has to be harmonized with the overarching legislative demands and policies that are placing demands on agencies. The need for collaboration between PPM professionals responsible for training and customers ensures that the training products and services are coordinated so that the whole training issue or the whole client can be the focus. Clearly, training in the public sector has to be focused on the need for training goals and standards, visions, and results to guide their activities so that they can support the bigger agency picture. For example, OPM provides assistance to federal agencies to help them achieve their strategic goals through a multimillion-dollar contract-based Training and Management Assistance Program designed to improve human resources management (Office of Personnel Management, 2000).

A customer orientation in training is always looking for ways to involve customers by asking them what they want, when they want it, and how training can better meet their needs. Like their parent agencies, training functions step back and ask the question, How can we get closer to the customers and bring them further into the work, learning, and training design and deliver processes? In answering this question, PPM professionals begin by partnering with customers to ensure that all training is indeed seen by the customers as adding value. Table 14.1 offers a comparison of the traditional versus customer/client orientation.

The Shift from Training to Learning

Learning in the workplace is continuing to shift from formalized, short-term instruction by an expert to informal, strategically focused learning facilitation by stakeholders and internal employees. This change parallels the just-in-time (JIT) manufacturing movement. JIT learning is evident in the development of learning organizations and action learning teams in private and public sector organizations.

TABLE 14.1   A Comparison of Traditional Versus Customer/Client-Oriented
Training Approaches

Characteristic	Traditional Training Approach	Customer/Client-Oriented Training Approach
Starting Point	Training Function	Client/customer understanding
Focus	Programs/services on hand	Customer business issues
Training Means	"Selling"—or "You take what I offer"; "Choose from our menu"	Customer-oriented practices; customized programs and services
Training Ends	Number of participants enrolled; number of courses available and offered; budget variance	Client /customer satisfaction; bottom-line or agency results impact
Agency Ends	Skill development	Customer's goal attainment and impact
Revenue	Central budget (through number of courses and/or participant days)	Client provides revenue based on alignment with needs and satisfaction with deliverables
Planning Horizons	Short term	Long-term—position for the future
Operating	Getting employees and management to take what is offered	Understanding customer business needs and meeting those needs

Training in public organizations is also becoming more closely linked with organization strategy. This trend is expected to continue and become more important when the results of training are being measured.

Training in today's agencies is increasingly aimed at delivering just-in-time learning and development services. This approach puts the focus on learning, not training, and this puts the learner at the center. The new approach allows customization to the individual and breaks down the boundary that classifies some training materials, situations, and settings as appropriate for learning while others are not. For example, the City of Scottsdale, Arizona in their efforts to train departmental systems users on financial system changes and procedures recently decided to use computer-based training (CBT). The training allows users to have complete control over their learning experience. Users navigate through the course material at their own pace and focus on training that is most relevant to their needs (Clifford, 2000). Table 14.2 highlights the key elements of the shift from training to learning.

TABLE 14.2 Key Elements of the Shift from Training to Learning

From Training	To Learning
Focus on short term	Focus on lifelong learning/development
Skill based	Core competency based
Driven by individual request	Driven by agency strategy
Concentrates on managers and executives	Concentrates on all employees
Assessment done by HR and/or management	Assessment done by affected individuals
Training happens on site	Learning happens anyplace
Training is scheduled periodically	Learning happens in real time
Training is based on knowledge delivery	Learning based on creating new meaning about sharing experiences in workplace
Instructor driven; designed by specialists	Self-directed
Generalized, prescriptions	Specific, trainees/learners determine
Trainers deliver, trainer centered	Facilitated jointly, learner centered

Role of Technology in Training

Changes in technology, like other changes that have an impact on agency training, require that the training function offer a wider array of products and services for a broader array of customers; for example, only a few years ago, training functions were viewed as responsive when they offered basic skills training such as introductory word-processing, spreadsheet, and database courses. New technologies are influencing training.

Not only is the goal of the federal training technology initiative to advance lifelong learning, but also to reduce the cost of federal training by helping to develop a market for technology-mediated forms of instruction, thereby encouraging private-sector investment. This is also one of the benefits identified in the DOD's ADL initiative. Federal agencies which have been known to develop their own training at great expense and considerable duplication, could then have easy access to the highest quality of training.

THE FUTURE OF TRAINING (AND DEVELOPMENT) IN THE PUBLIC SECTOR

What will the future of training in the public sector look like? Managing training strategically in the future is critically important if federal, state, county, and government investment is to pay off. Along with the strategic orientation of training there are several important trends in training in the public sector that are important to emphasize, including the role of training and development in government change, which has and will continue to precipitate the development of agencies as learning organizations. The remainder of this chapter discusses some of the trends that will continue to impact public-sector training.

INCREASED ROLE OF TRAINING AND DEVELOPMENT IN PUBLIC-SECTOR CHANGE

The training function in government has the job of building the agencies' capacity to embrace and capitalize on change. It will make sure that change initiatives that are focused on creating high-performing teams or agencies are defined, developed, and delivered in a timely way. Training functions can also make sure that new visions for their agencies get transformed into specific behaviors by helping employees figure out what work they can stop, start, and keep doing to make the vision real. In a sense, this new view of government training means that training will increasingly be viewed as a catalyst for change. This point is highlighted in the OPM *FY 2000-FY 2005 Strategic Plan,* in which the agency recognizes the important role that human resource development (HRD) or training must play in helping other government agencies change and meet their strategic goals and objectives (Office of Personnel Management, 2000).

Currently, an increasing number of states use their training systems to help change or redesign their agencies to meet contemporary realities; for example, states like Alabama, Florida, Georgia, Kansas, Utah, and Wisconsin offer management training programs, often referred to as Certified Public Managers Programs, as tools of new strategic deployment, transmitting and supporting new management styles, technology, and workforce systems (Paddock, 1997). In taking on a more active role as change agents in the years to come, agency training personnel are in a prime position to help their agencies respond to change and to realize increased employee performance and productivity.

INCREASED INTEGRATION OF TRAINING IN ACHIEVING AGENCY STRATEGIES

One of the traditional problems of training in public-sector organizations was that in spite of the investment of money and time, little change resulted over time. Clearly, this is no longer acceptable. As we move further into the twenty-first century, training must be appropriately linked to the agency's strategy, its mission, and vision and must have a future focus.

A future focus will increase the likelihood that the training strategy will be an outgrowth of the agency's overall strategy and that it will more likely receive the required support and resources. To be consistent with the GPRA guidance, agency training goals must continue to focus on target levels and performance indicators.

Increased Interagency Collaboration/Sharing and Benchmarking

The move toward increased interagency collaboration/sharing and benchmarking should continue in the future as agencies try to make their training dollars go further and learn from each other's experience. Many government training functions and agencies have realized that sharing training resources can help them save money while offering employees high-quality training that would otherwise not be available; for example, the DOE's Albuquerque Operations HRTD generated $61,000 in FY 2000 cost-avoidance through partnering and sharing as part of the Federal Inter-Agency Training Council (FIATC) (Department of Energy, 2000).

Rather than doing training evaluation internally, more and more agencies will be expected to benchmark measures of training that are compared from one agency to others. To benchmark, those responsible for agency training will need to gather data on training and compare it to data on training at other agencies within and outside of government. For example, the U.S. Forest Service has used the services of the Brookings education center through their database and field trips to benchmark and customize its training against other state, local, federal, and private organizations.

In the years to come, training functions will have to be more fully engaged with training functions in other public and private organizations. Consortiums of federal, state, and local agencies, especially the smaller agencies, will be essential to furnish the talent and capital needed to support advanced technological applications in training. For example, General Accounting Office (GAO) acquisitions officials share their missions among contracting and program personnel at other government and private organizations, using integrated project teams to focus outcomes, adopting balanced-scorecard techniques to identify gaps and successes, and finding better metrics to demonstrate progress to achieving the agencies' bottom-line results (Burman, 2000b).

Increased Role of New Technology in Real or Just-in-Time Training

New technologies are going to provide increased opportunities for agencies to rethink how they deliver education, or what some call "learning solutions," for the employees. The traditional remedial-focused, skill-based training model will continue to be shattered by these changes. According to Hyde (1999), we are likely to see tremendous innovations in web-based learning, distance learning, interactive learning centers, and new forms of collaborative learning for individuals and teams that involve the exchange of information and expertise across agency boundaries. All of these technological innovations will increase the move toward a "real-life" orientation of all government training.

A major benefit of new training technology is that it can save time, lost productivity, and travel costs so that funds can be reinvested to enhance learning quality in agencies. One example of benefits of new training technology is the Department of Defense (DOD) Distributed Learning (DL) training initiative that fostered inter-service collaboration, precluded redundant efforts, and showed total savings of $346,000 in executing readiness training, using DL versus traditional resident training courses.

INCREASED ACCOUNTABILITY AND RESULTS-ORIENTED MEASURES OF TRAINING

With resource constraints at all levels of government, the pressure will continue for agencies to produce results in all of their activities, which extends to their training programs. An authority in training evaluation says that the ability to demonstrate results, or rather impacts (e.g., productivity gains or quality improvements) is the ultimate feat for today's training (Kirkpatrick, 1996). Gone are the days in which agency training could rely solely on "smile sheets," referring to the simple evaluation forms, with which we are very familiar, which ask us whether we got what we wanted out of the training or whether we liked the instructor. The IRS Office of Chief Counsel embraces comprehensive training evaluation models like those suggested by Kirkpartick (Internal Revenue Service, 2001). The IRS's training-evaluation approach recognizes the interrelationship of the employee and organizational functions and achievement of results.

Werth (1998) suggests that theoretically it could be argued that the closer to "reality" training becomes, the easier to identify the impact of training; for example, if the training itself includes actual or simulated job experiences, it should be easier to relate any change in the learner's behavior on the job and ultimately any agency change or impact to the training itself.

> Agencies will need to continue to build the business case for training by incorporating information like the following in their business cases:

- How training will advance the agency's strategic and performance goals.
- The competency gaps that will be addressed.
- Clear identification of the potential benefits to be realized if the competency gap is closed (tangible and intangible benefits).
- The training strategies considered.
- The training strategy selected and reasoning.
- The total life-cycle costs of developing and implementing the training.
- A cost-benefits comparison/analysis.
- The consequences to the agency's strategic and performance goals if training is not conducted.

Those responsible for agency training must continue to strive to get a return-on-investment for agency training efforts. The tools, techniques, and a reliable process *are* available to measure the ROI in agency training, and PPM professionals will be expected to use them.

Increased Importance of Training in Countering the Effects of Downsizing and Rightsizing

As government agencies increasingly realize that the key competitive difference in the twenty-first century will be its people, training must be given increased priority if agencies are to overcome the damage often done by unending downsizing, streamlining, and rightsizing; for example, the GAO in predicting that by 2004, 40 percent of all U.S. capital investment will be in information technology has recognized that failure to hire and train competent employees despite the recent downsizing trends in government will lead to ineffective acquisition staff that purchase inadequate equipment (Burman, 2000b). Clearly, training departments (and their staff) cannot play a significant role in helping their host agencies achieve their strategic objectives if there are fewer and fewer resources—both human and dollar—available to them, nor can agencies successfully achieve expected results.

The challenge for agencies, managers, and PPM professionals is how to make sure that training does not take a back seat to the day-to-day operational concerns of managers and employees. Despite what appears to be a number of major hurdles for those remaining in PPM offices, they must find ways to redouble their efforts to get agency managers to both recognize and follow through on training and development plans for their employees. The challenge of trying to get agencies to recognize the long-term importance of training may appear to be daunting. However, agencies like the U.S. Coast Guard (e.g., see for example, the Coast Guard 2020, Ready Today planning document), the Department of Veterans Benefits Administration, and the National Park Service among others at the federal, state, and local levels are making impressive strides in providing cost-effective, just-in-time, quality training for their employees while they continue to wrestle with new legislation and various reform initiatives.

CONCLUSION

Government is changing at the local, the state, and especially the federal level. Like other organizations, agencies are experiencing the impact of the knowledge-based economy, dramatic advances in technology, increased emphasis on results, and rising expectations of their customers. The government workforce is also changing, demanding more opportunities for learning, becoming more diverse, and expecting more flexibility and support in the workplace, and the pace of this change—in the work agencies do, the way they do it, and the workforce available to do it—is accelerating.

Learning will be increasingly important as agencies are pressured to change and to respond to technological advances, and as the skills needed by employees constantly change and increase. Intense interest in agencies as learning organizations is not a mere coincidence or fad; it is an accepted reality that learning is key to sustaining future agency survival and continuous improvement. Strategically driven training is one response agencies must increasingly use to meet the new demands being placed on them.

Senior administrators need to continue to demand more of PPM and the training function. They need to invest in training as if it were a business, and they must get beyond the traditional stereotype of agency training professionals as incompetent value-sapping support staff.

As we look to the future, increased training in government may be the only solution to ease the pain of reforms in government. As Deidre Lee, former administrator of the Office of Federal Procurement Policy recently noted (Burman, 2000a):

> A trained workforce is critical to adapting to changes and recognizing the importance of a competitive process. Similarly agencies must provide training to ease the shift toward commercial-style business management. Agencies also need the tools to recruit, retain and promote employees with the necessary leadership ability to further these reforms. Investment in human capital offers the greatest payoff. This is about people. (p. 91).

Public-sector organizations and PPM professionals must continue to unleash training's full potential.

REFERENCES

Anonymous. 1999. "HUD: Community 2020 Planning Software CD-ROM Training Package." *Government Executive* (December): 60.

Ashdown, B., and K. Smith. 1999. "Managing Knowledge—One Step Up on the Information Chain." http://www.osti.gov/inforum99/papers/orgknowl.pdf.

Bethoney, H. 1999. "Spec Unites Learning Systems." *PC Week.* (June 28): 40–41.

Brzezinska, D. 2000. "Effects of GPRA at the DOT, 1994–2000," *The Public Manager* (Spring): 23.

Burman, A.V. 2000a. "A Legacy of Reform." *Government Executive* (May): 90–91.

Burman, A.V. 2000b. "Investing in People." *Government Executive* (June): 105–106.

Carnevale, A.P. 1990. "America and the New Economy." *Training and Development Journal* (November): 31–52.

Clifford, C. 2000. "Computer-based Training for Financial Management Systems: The City of Scottsdale Experience." *Government Finance Review* (February): 35–37.

Cunningham, C. 2000. "Reeling in IT Talent in the Public Sector—Forget Stocks; It's Benefits, Flexibility, and a 40-hour Week that Lure IT Pros to Government Jobs." *InfoWorld* (May 15): 78–83.

Department of Energy. 2000. *FY 2000 AL Annual Training Summary Report.* (Washington, D.C. Department of Energy).

EDP Weekly's IT Monitor. 1999. Learn2.com to Provide Online Training for Up to 16,000 Labor Dept. Workers: Award Supports Executive Order On Technology-Enhanced Training. (November 8): 3.

Esterson, L.L. 2000. Training Online: Staff Development Moves to the Web." *Washington Business Journal* (September 22): 73–74.

Federal Aviation Administration. 2000. *A Competency-based Learning and Development Program (Briefing Handout).* http://www.opm.gov/hrd/lead/FALLFEST/OPMBRI~1.htm.

Federal Human Resource Development Council. 1997. *Getting Results Through Learning.* (May). Washington, D.C.: Federal HRD Council.

Green-Gilliam, J.M. 2000. "City Hall Fights Back." *Human Resources Professional* (May/June): 16–18.

Gore, A. 1993. *From Red Tape to Results: Creating a Government That Works Better and Costs Less, Report of the National Performance Review.* Washington, D.C.: U.S. Government Printing Office.

Hyde, A.C. 1999. "Can the Classroom Survive the Millennium?" *The Public Manager* (Summer): 57–58.

Internal Revenue Service. 2001. "Tax Professionals Career." *The Digital Daily* (March 5), Section 5-Training, p. 5.

Kirpatrick, D.L. 1996. "Great Ideas Revisited." *Training and Development Journal* (January): 54–59.

Marquardt, M. 1996. *Building the Learning Organization.* New York: McGraw-Hill.

Merit Systems Protection Board. 1995. "Leadership for Change: Human Resource Development in the Federal Government." (July).

Merrill, K. 1999. "Federal Task Force Scrutinizes the Future of Government Education." *Computer Reseller* (May 10): 73–74.

National Commission on the Public Service (Volcker Commission). 1989. *Leadership for America: Rebuilding the Public Service.* Washington, D.C.: U.S. Government Printing Office.

Office of Personnel Management. 2000. *Federal Human Resources Management for the 21st Century: Strategic Plan FY 2000-FY 2005.* (September 30). Washington, D.C.: United States Office of Personnel Management.

Paddock, S.C. 1997. "Benchmarks in Management Training." *Public Personnel Management* (Winter): 44–49.

Robinson, D.G., and J.C. Robinson. 1998. *Moving from Training to Performance: A Practical Guidebook.* San Francisco. Berrett-Koehler.

Senge, P. 1990. *The Fifth Discipline: The Art and Practice of the Learning Organization.* New York: Doubleday.

Sims, R.R. 1998. *Reinventing Training and Development.* Westport, Conn.: Quorum.

Training. 2000. *Training Industry Report* (October): 33–41.

Werth, J.B. 1999. "Training for Reality: How the Public Sector is Making Training Programs Come Alive." *The Public Manager: The New Bureaucrat* (Fall): 27–29.

Chapter 15

Human Resource Management and Capacity in the States

Patricia Wallace Ingraham and Sally Coleman Selden

INTRODUCTION

Public management reform in the United States is a nearly constant process. Decades ago, Herbert Kaufman described it as an unending cycle; more recently, Paul Light turned to the vastness of the ocean for a comparison, describing constant reform efforts as an inexorable tide (Kaufman, 1969; Light, 1998). Yet management reform, while seemingly endemic, is most often viewed and analyzed through a federal lens. At that level, different agency missions, functions, structures, and sizes allow for some comparative analysis; such broad differences, however, also impede the lesson learning so critical to the long term effectiveness of reform (Thompson, 1999).

A different set of experiences is provided by examination of the U.S. states. The federal emphasis on devolution in the 1990s, the extensive infatuation with the concept of "reinventing government," and new expectations for performance at all levels of government focused attention on state governments and their capacity to be effective. States vary dramatically in both existing capacity and success in changing it (Burke and Wright, 2000; Berry, Wechsler, and Chakerian, 1999). Nonetheless, the experience of the fifty states with management reform provides the opportunity for systematic comparison and a rich and underutilized information pool for lesson learning.

This is particularly true of human resource management. The federal government has seen some movement away from the structural and procedural rigidities that flow from Title V, USC, but, since the Civil Service Reform Act of 1978, there has been little fundamental reform of the legislative base for the federal personnel system. The states, on the other hand, have civil service systems that range from highly centralized and tightly structured (New York) to very decentralized (Texas). One state (Georgia) has abolished the civil service system altogether and another (Florida) is considering that action. Reforms have recently been enacted in Virginia,

Wisconsin, and Missouri, but they have addressed different issues in each setting. Generally, states have experienced few of the recruiting difficulties encountered by the federal government, but they have devised creative recruiting, training, and development strategies to ensure that their human resource needs are met.

This chapter draws upon the experience of the states as documented by the Government Performance Project (GPP), which analyzed state management systems in 1998 and again in 2000. The GPP proceeds from the assumption that human resource management systems are critical and integral components of states' management abilities and capacities. A state (or other government) that does not have the right people and expertise to perform critical functions is not likely to be effective in delivering services and meeting other citizen expectations. Human Resource Management is one of four systems analyzed by the GPP. The others are Financial and Capital Management, Information Technology Management, and Managing for Results. The analytical model employed by the GPP explicitly argues that integration among these models is likely to contribute to improved capacity and will likely enhance performance as well (Ingraham and Donahue, 2000). This component of the model is very important for human resource management systems because they have traditionally been associated with rigidly impermeable civil service structures and were explicitly designed to limit external influence, and, thus necessarily integration with other systems. Human resource management systems were assessed according to the following criteria, which are the product of extensive research and expert advising:

- Clear and understandable personnel policies and procedures
- Timely hiring
- Education, training, and development of the workforce
- Necessary skills and good workforce planning to achieve the right mix
- Effective compensation, motivation, and reward systems
- Effective discipline and termination policies and procedures
- Agency and managerial flexibility in hiring, rewarding, and disciplining.

In this chapter, we have four objectives: to describe the range of experience, systems, and practices currently in place in the fifty states; to describe the broad models of reform and reform strategies that can be extracted from the descriptive analysis; to draw distinctions between high capacity and low capacity states in terms of how they look and how they do business; and to draw lessons where possible about how to effectively create human resource management capacity. The broader intent is to demonstrate the extent to which state governments—often called the laboratories of democracy—are laboratories for management reform as well.

STATES AS LABORATORIES FOR MANAGEMENT

Drawing upon data collected in 1998 and 2000, this section describes trends and innovations in state human resource management systems. We do not seek to exhaustively review trends and innovations across the full range of human resource management functions. Rather, we examine trends and innovations related to recruiting and retaining employees, with a focus on hiring, compensation, and training.

Personnel Authority: The Shift to Shared Responsibility

In a traditional civil service system, the authority to administer personnel-related functions rests with a central personnel office (CPO). Advocates of centralization believe that this arrangement ensures equitable treatment of employees, consistency in the delivery of human resource services, efficiency gains through economies of scale, and clearly delineated roles between the CPO and agencies. In recent years, however, many scholars and practitioners have suggested that states would be better served by decentralized systems in which agencies and managers have broader authority over core personnel practices (for example, see Thompson, 1995). The diversity of practice and systems in the states allows for analysis of these assertions.

In 1998, the GPP asked states to describe the extent to which classification, recruiting, testing, hiring, and performance-appraisal procedures were centralized (under the control of the central personnel agency) or decentralized (managed by individual agencies). Responses varied from completely centralized to completely decentralized across the key personnel functions (see Selden, Ingraham, and Jacobson, forthcoming). Two years later, the GPP asked states to indicate who has primary responsibility—central HR staff, agency HR staff, agency managers, contractors/vendors, state budget offices—for thirty-five different human resource functions. Figures 15.1 and 15.2 present data on ten of these functions in the areas of classification, performance appraisals, recruiting, testing, and appointment decisions. Figure 15.1 demonstrates that, in 2000, the development of classification systems was largely centralized: forty-one states indicated that the classification system was developed centrally. The state delegated this authority to agency HR staff in seven states—Idaho, Indiana, Louisiana, Maryland, Minnesota, Missouri, and Mississippi. In two states, Georgia and Texas, the agency HR staff and agency managers share responsibility for developing the classification system.

Comparison of 1998 and 2000 data suggests that in the area of classification, states are moving toward more central involvement rather than less. In 1998, eight states had decentralized authority to agencies and managers for classification. In 2000, only two states decentralized authority for developing the classification system. In terms of individual job classifications and reclassifications, however, states are more willing to share authority.

Figure 15.1 also demonstrates that the same pattern holds true for performance appraisal. States are more likely to delegate authority to agencies and their managers to administer performance appraisals than to develop the instruments. More states place sole responsibility for developing performance appraisal instruments in the state's central HR office (n = 18) than administering them (n = 1). Compared to

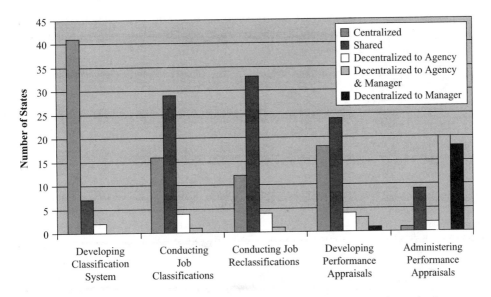

FIGURE 15.1   Responsibility for Classification and Preformance Appraisal

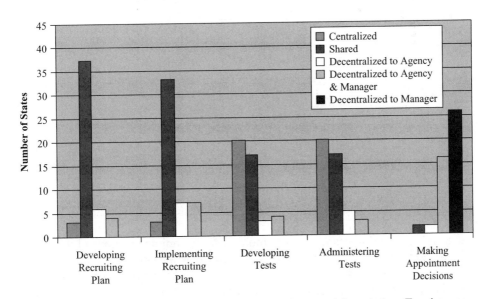

FIGURE 15.2   Responsibility for Recruiting, Testing, and Appointing Employees

data collected in 1998, CPOs formally delegate less authority to agencies and managers in this area; rather, they partner with agency actors to implement the performance appraisal system (see Table 15.1).

TABLE 15.1   Developing Performance Appraisals: A Comparison of Authority in 1998 and 2000

Locus of Authority	1998	2000
Centralized	25	18
Shared	6	34
Decentralized	17	9

As shown in Figure 15.2, the locus of personnel authority varies in the selection process—recruiting, testing, and hiring. First, responsibility for recruiting prospective employees is most often shared between the CPO and agencies. The number of states reporting that recruiting is centralized fell from nine states in 1998 to three states in 2000. The shift, however, is not toward decentralization but rather toward shared authority—eight states shared authority for recruiting in 1998 compared to thirty-seven states sharing responsibility for developing recruiting plans and thirty-three states sharing responsibility for implementing recruiting plans in 2000. Second, in the area of testing, the trend is also toward shared responsibility. In 1998, twenty-six states responded that a central authority conducts testing, but in 2000, twenty states maintain central control over developing and administering testing. Finally, consistent with the 1998 data, all but two states (Pennsylvania and Tennessee) grant complete authority to agencies and their managers to select a candidate for an open position. Within agencies, the amount of managerial discretion to select candidates varies. For example, managers in twenty-six states determine whom to hire.

The comparisons in Figures 15.1 and 15.2 demonstrate further that, although there is more sharing of personnel responsibility within government, very few states contract with third-party sources for those services. Exceptions include:

- Vermont contracts responsibility for job reclassification.
- North Carolina uses a contractor to develop performance appraisals.
- Florida, Louisiana, and Nebraska outsource test development.
- Florida and Virginia contract out administration of selected tests.

Hiring: The Search For Talent

State governments increasingly find themselves competing for highly talented workers (Ingraham, Selden, and Moynihan, 2000). Each year states must fill a considerable number of positions. For example, in 1999, Virginia had 40,000 vacancies, Texas 31,000, and North Carolina 27,292. Some of these positions are newly created, but most are vacant because employees leave voluntarily, retire, or are terminated. In 1999, voluntary turnover in state governments ranged from 2 to 20 percent.

Facing competition for skilled labor, open positions, and growing turnover, states implemented changes intended to eliminate practices that slow hiring; they also adopted technological innovations to improve the selection process. As a result, the period from 1998 to 2000 represents a period of significant change in the procedural requirements that govern hiring. Several states, such as Iowa, passed legislation to eliminate the "Rule of X" (three, seven, ten, etc.) or to expand the number of names or scores on the certified list. To keep that list fresh, Idaho shortened the length of time a register of eligible candidates is valid. Indiana decentralized hiring authority for entire occupational categories to agencies. Both Iowa and Indiana eliminated testing. Wisconsin repealed its residency requirement, repealed all restrictions on out-of-state recruiting, and eliminated the restrictions on the number of qualified candidates that can be interviewed.

Technological advances are also transforming state recruiting efforts. Currently, all states post job openings online, and 45 states offer state applications online. South Carolina's web site generates more than a million "hits" a month. Twenty-three states currently have technology that accepts state government applications online. Florida's web-based application system allows applicants to input and store their state employment application and apply for as many vacancies as they choose. The Tennessee Employment Application Monitoring System (TEAMS) allows applicants to conduct job searches, submit applications online, and take employment examinations. Job applicants receive their examination score that day. Nineteen states operate online resume banks, and twelve states use virtual job fairs. Maryland's approach to recruiting includes using its own web site, as well as commercial recruitment sites. In addition to these technological advances, fifteen states provide job information on kiosks located throughout the state.

Furthermore, states are using partnerships and other strategies to increase their applicant pools. North Carolina, for example, established a statewide recruitment network. Recruiters from agencies and universities work in partnership with the Office of State Personnel to identify the state's recruitment needs, to design a statewide recruitment plan, to promote the state as the employer of choice, and to maximize existing resources. Maryland state government launched a television campaign to highlight the valuable jobs state employees hold. Indiana's Brand or Image campaign promotes positive aspects of working for the state through print ads, radio ads, TV ads, brochures, web sites, and video.

Because of continued difficulty in filling positions, however, states are also using temporary employees to meet their needs. In 2000, Georgia employed the largest share of temporary employees (20 percent), followed by Mississippi and North Dakota (18 percent). South Carolina developed the TempO initiative to help state agencies meet short-term staffing needs. Similarly, Nebraska, in partnership with the Omaha Workforce Development Office, operates the Specialized Office Services program that serves as a "clearinghouse" for all temporary jobs in the state.

COMPENSATION: STRUCTURING MORE FLEXIBILITY AND DIVERSITY

Two patterns emerge when analyzing state responses to issues of classification and compensation: more flexible classification systems and more diversity in monetary reward programs. For example, in 1999, the Oklahoma Legislature passed legislation that reduced 100 pay grades to eighteen broader pay bands. It relaxed the statutory limitations of pay increases for Oklahoma State employees to allow for career progression, for interagency lateral transfers, for salary market adjustments, and for skill-based salary adjustment.

As shown in Table 15.2, four states indicated that they used broad banding for classifying all of their employees (Idaho, Massachusetts, West Virginia, and Wyoming). About 20 percent of states use broad banding for executives and managers. A number of states have broad-banded positions since 1998. For example, Virginia's pay structure for classified employees shifted from twenty-three pay grades with steps to nine pay bands without steps. In 1999, Washington banded all exempt employees. Indiana implemented a broad-banding program for executives that allows more opportunity to link compensation to organizational goals. Through this program, the state can make counteroffers, offer hiring bonuses, give project-management-based pay, and use gainsharing.

TABLE 15.2   Use of Broad Banding

All employees	8.2%
Executives	20.4%
Managers	20.4%
Specific agencies	8.2%
Specific classifications/occupations	26.5%
Other	16.3%

Most often states use broad banding for specific classifications or occupations. For example, Arizona broad-banded information technology (IT), engineers, and technical classes. Wisconsin's broad-banding program includes nonrepresented professional supervisors and professional staff, as well as IT, fiscal, and professional science occupational areas. This program gives agencies the flexibility to set original and subsequent appointment rates anywhere between the range minimum and the appointment maximum.

During the past two years, states have changed policies that limit flexibility in monetary recognition for performance, as well as diversified the ways they pay and reward employees. Louisiana, for example, addressed a long-standing problem with its compensation system by making employees who have been at the salary range maximum for three years with no wage increases eligible for a lump sum adjustment up to 4 percent of their annual base salary.

Virginia's overhaul of its system was more substantive. It replaced the traditional annual step-increase program with a threefold strategy. First, the role adjustment program allows agencies and managers to shift an individual's "role/job" to a higher-level pay band to maintain the position's competitiveness to the appropriate labor market. Second, based on individual or team performance ratings, performance-based adjustments are offered. Finally, pay bands are adjusted based on market conditions.

Although the most common remuneration program in state government continues to be an annual step increase to an employee's salary, many states now also rely on some form of pay-for-performance to allocate salary increases. In 2000, we found a dramatic increase from 1998 in the use of individual and group performance bonuses. In 2000, about 64 percent of states allow for individual performance bonuses and 38 percent use group bonuses. Those figures were 14.3 percent and 2 percent, respectively, in 1998 (Selden, Ingraham, and Jacobson, forthcoming).

As shown in Table 15.3, states utilize both skill pay and competency pay. Indiana, for example, allows agencies to customize their compensation strategy by selecting the appropriate strategies ranging from competency-based pay, to skill-based pay, to gainsharing, to pay-for-performance. An analysis of Indiana's Department of Financial Institution's workforce revealed that the majority of financial examiners were leaving between the four- and seven-year service mark. At this point, examiners had attained a highly technical skill set because the state had sent individuals to highly expensive training. The agency's investment was

TABLE 15.3 Forms of Remuneration Used

	Percent of States Using
Pay-for-Performance	74%
Individual performance bonuses	64%
Group performance bonuses	38%
Skill pay	54%
Competency pay	42%
Gain sharing	18%
Annual step increase	78%
Cost-of-living payments	66%

not paying off. As a result, the department structured a variable competency pay program to target employees at the four- to seven-year mark.

To attract candidates to state government employment, states adjusted their salaries to be more competitive with market wages, provided more flexibility in starting salaries, and allowed for signing bonuses. Florida conducts annual pay studies to determine where class salaries are in association with the labor market. Idaho routinely shifts the pay schedule to address market wages. Missouri has a long-term plan to move state employee salaries to the identified market rates of pay to improve recruitment and retention. Oregon developed a market pricing system for selected management benchmark jobs. Kentucky allows agencies to negotiate starting salaries; Virginia offers more flexibility in starting salaries depending on education, training, and experience (up to 15 percent above prior salary). Some states, such as Maryland, utilize hiring and retention bonuses to secure and retain employees in hard-to-fill positions.

TRAINING

Training is a critical component of a high performing workforce. Because new responsibilities, such as in the area of personnel, are now shared with managers, the need for training is particularly keen. Furthermore, in an increasingly competitive job market, it is essential that governments explore training as both an opportunity to retain employees and as a means to attract and develop new employees. Like most private and public sector organizations, state governments are facing tremendous challenges in developing workforces that have the necessary competencies for the current technology-driven workplace.

Although many states know more than ever about training because of the advances in information technology that track training, in 2000 we found that 22 states were unable to estimate their total or per-employee training expenditures. Reported spending ranged from $300,000 (Montana and Oregon) to $68,270,167 (Virginia). On average, spending per state employee ranged from a low of $30 in New Mexico to a high of $1,000 in Minnesota. The amount expended on management training was somewhat higher than that spent on state employees, with a range of $67 (Iowa) to $1,650 (Virginia).

Technology has infused training in many different ways. States have utilized web-based technology to disseminate training opportunities. Many state web pages include course catalogues, registration forms, and "learning links" to other educational and training sites. Massachusetts will place a training administration module on its network to track employee training statewide, link job competencies to employee training, and allow on-line employee requests for training.

States are delivering training in nontraditional mediums, such as CD-ROM, distance learning, and internet-based training to supplement more traditional training courses and institutes. Massachusetts operates six regional training centers; each is equipped with a videoconferencing system that is used for distance learning courses on management and supervision. Because of this new delivery structure, the commonwealth has greatly expanded both its course offerings and the number of employees served. Louisiana designs and delivers training over the web and on CD-ROM. Utah partners with Western Governor's University (WGU) to provide an employee development program for all employees. This partnership is unique because WGU is a competency-based, "virtual university" with an online course catalog, online student counseling, online bookstore, and online library.

States have worked to improve their employees' training programs. Some states such as Wisconsin and Pennsylvania have developed strategic training plans. Pennsylvania indicated that prior to 1997, training was authorized only if the curriculum was within the scope of an employee's current job duties. Now, the commonwealth authorizes training to further enhance employees' skills, particularly in areas in which the commonwealth is in need. Through a cooperative agreement with AFSCME, Illinois developed the Upward Mobility Program to provide career development opportunities for employees.

Finally, a common theme in many states' responses was leadership training. Missouri, for example, created a series of one-day programs for managers and supervisors. Pennsylvania offers a series of seminars to executives on the best contemporary management thinking. Working with Iowa State University, Iowa developed a leadership academy that offers an Executive Development Program and Certified Managers Program.

Another theme that emerged in leadership training is competency-based programming. Missouri's Executive Institute identified four executive competencies and addresses each in a separate two- to three-day workshop. Tennessee's Leadership Development Initiative is founded on a set of core competencies that all supervisors and managers are expected to master within their first eighteen months on the job. The core competencies are considered basic or fundamental for both private and public sector.

The Patterns of Change

All of these changes have occurred within a smaller set of broad patterns. The patterns fall on a continuum from the traditional, centralized, and hierarchic systems of New York and Pennsylvania to the very decentralized system of Texas. The middle of the continuum is represented by the increasing number of states that have moved from either strongly centralized or decentralized systems toward one that reflects shared responsibility between a central agency or authority, agencies, and managers. These patterns create different foundations for change and reform but also suggest different paths for further changing.

Traditional Centralized Systems. When many civil service systems were created, there was a strong belief that rigidly centralized systems were the only way to exclude undue partisan influence and pressure on public employment systems. Many of the components of the personnel systems that grew from this conviction had an interactive influence with centralization to create a hierarchical structure increasingly bounded by laws, rules, and regulations. Graded authority structures and public compensation systems, for example, reinforced principles of centralization and hierarchy. In their favor, centralized, hierarchical structures promoted standardization, stability, and predictability. They did not, however, create or support the discretion and flexibilities that many public organizations and their leaders now find critical to longer-term effectiveness.

One indicator of centralized hierarchy is central control of recruiting, testing, and hiring. The state's classification system and total number of classifications is important here because it reflects not only complexity of the hiring system and the extent to which it is flexible and responsive to changing employment demands, but also the extent to which standardization has yielded to some tailoring to individual agency needs and employment climates.

Even though some reform to this rigid model has occurred in those states that adopted it originally, many states continue to retain remarkable classification complexities. New York, for example, with about 158,000 employees, has 4,000 classification titles (down from an earlier high of about 7,000). Pennsylvania, a strong advocate of the centralized model, has 89,000 employees and 2,838 classification titles. Despite some decentralization, Minnesota retains 2,152 classification titles for its 33,773 employees. By contrast, South Carolina works with 452 classification titles for its nearly 72,000 employees.

Another indicator of strongly centralized systems is the continued reliance on central control of testing and on a narrow definition of "testing," that is, a written examination offered in a limited number of places at set periods of time. As with the complicated classification systems described above, compensation guidelines and procedures are complex and inflexible in the traditional centralized model. The practice of within-grade step increases for annual salary increases is a common mark of the traditional system. Because states falling at this end of the continuum are often highly unionized as well, the personnel system is further standardized and limited by labor/management agreements.

Decentralized Systems.   At the other end of the continuum—and essentially standing alone there—is Texas. Texas does not have a central personnel agency. Job classification is a central function but falls within the purview of the state auditor's office, which reports to the legislature. Although there was limited adoption of the purely decentralized model, several of its elements continue to be attractive. First, the model offers a system that is responsive to the different needs of different agencies and that allows agencies and managers the flexibility they need to adapt to changing circumstances. Second, the model provides clearer accountability for personnel and for hiring and firing. Central personnel authorities diffuse accountability by interceding in the relationship between agency, manager, and employee. A decentralized system links responsibility and accountability more tightly in that regard. Finally, proponents of decentralization argue that, in a decentralized personnel system, because it is more flexible and managers have more discretion, human resources will be better utilized because they will be better matched to real agency needs, better targeted, and better directed.

However, as the states moving away from decentralized models suggest, decentralization has several downsides for human resource management. First, in a strongly decentralized system such as that of Texas, it is difficult to monitor and assess personnel activities and needs. No central information gathering or evaluation is in place. Planning on a statewide basis is severely restricted, and incentives for better coordination are limited. Further, managing human resources in a decentralized system may place talent and skill demands on managers that they do not have. In the 1998 GPP survey, for example, many states noted that "managing" decentralization was an extremely difficult task.

Shared Responsibility Systems.   For all of the reasons noted above, many states have created human resource management systems that balance or share responsibility and authority between the central personnel agency and the other agencies of government. Within this "middle ground," there can be wide variation in the extent to which authority is formally delegated away from the center or to which it is shared in more informal and narrow arrangements. Such sharing allows continued consideration of broad governmental concerns such as equity but combines them with the HR customization necessary to better agency performance.

While the research reported here notes that the trend is away from either decentralization or centralization toward shared responsibility, it is important to note that it also reports "sharing" primarily in terms of implementation of systems designed centrally. In other words, strategic responsibilities and design and the continued protection of broad governmental values have a central focus; mission-specific strategies and implementation have an agency focus. Responsibility for the integrity of the system is shared.

South Carolina provides one example of this model: Within the state's broad HR framework, agencies are given substantial flexibility in creating reward and recognition programs and are given broad discretion in designing disciplinary policies. Indiana has applied the central strategy/agency choice model to compensation. Actual hiring decisions are delegated to agencies and managers in twenty-six states.

Lessons From High Performing States.   What does this tell us about what is likely to work and what are not? Do those states that have created high HR capacity have common characteristics and similar HR systems, or have they chosen different paths to effectiveness? Several significant lessons emerge from this analysis and from the broader GPP effort. First, there are clear differences between the states in their efforts to build human resource management capacity. States such as Virginia, South Carolina, Washington, Wisconsin, and Michigan have viewed their human resource management systems as important resources critical to the broader effectiveness of the state government. In all of these cases, the mission, the design, and the responsibilities of the HR system are now the product of careful planning and analysis of needs. This planning relates not only to workforce planning, which is key, but to evaluation of the needs and satisfaction levels of current employees, to the HR support needs of state agencies, and to information gathering to assess the quality of the state's workforce and the state as a workplace. Information is gathered in a variety of ways and from a variety of sources: 360 performance evaluations, citizen customer evaluations, benchmarking activities, employee suggestion programs, and broadly participative strategic planning are all a part of the efforts of high capacity states. Revamped HR information technology systems clearly play a major part in these activities.

Second, in the states that have built strong capacity, emphasis is on both the ability to target and recruit necessary new employees and the ability to provide excellent training and development opportunities for those who are already employees of the state. Again, diversity and flexibility in offerings and opportunities are the watchwords. Virginia, for example, conducts training needs assessments for the central state government, for state agencies, for job classification activities, and for individual training needs. It then provides many options for training, including management training, communication training, labor/management relations training, and alternative conflict resolution. Other leading states provide similar packages.

Flexibility is another common characteristic of high capacity states and reflects diversity in approaching functions such as recruiting, compensation, and performance appraisal. In compensation, for example, some state menus include skill-based pay, competency-based pay, pay for performance, gain sharing, and other group performance bonuses. Agencies and managers are given substantial discretion in their choice of incentives and options for recognizing performance. Several states have utilized strategic partnering to plan for and target flexibilities, as well as to think about the best ways to use them. As one example, Wisconsin state government, working with the Wisconsin State Employees Union, has created a project to identify best practices in labor/management relations and to apply them when possible to Wisconsin. North Carolina has partnered with state agencies and universities to create a statewide recruiting network to better match needs with opportunities and to use recruiting resources more flexibly and effectively.

Finally, there is increasing evidence that states are working with their legislators to create a firm statutory base for the flexibilities they are creating in their HR systems. As we noted earlier, the general pattern that is emerging in the states is not movement toward either end of the centralization/decentralization continuum but movement toward its middle. There are important exceptions to this generalization, however. Two major states, New York and Pennsylvania, have made some changes to their systems but remain firmly anchored to the centralized model of state HR administration. Two other states, Georgia and Florida, have either moved or are proposing to move essentially off the continuum. Georgia abolished its central state merit system in 1997. Florida is proposing to do so in 2001. One report to the governor advocating the Florida action observed that the intent was "... to change from unduly protecting Career Service employees to enabling their performance" (Florida Council, p. 5). Advocates of abolition of existing systems argue that it is not possible to operate anyplace along the continuum of existing structure and practice if excellent performance is the objective.

Georgia and Florida, however, represent unusual use of legislative authority to change and reform state HR management systems. More commonly, states have relied on smaller and more circumscribed legislative changes in their efforts to build additional HR capacity. Virginia rewrote its personnel law to permit greater flexibility in classification and compensation practices. Colorado and Iowa made substantial changes to hiring requirements, with Iowa eliminating both a required number of people on hiring lists and the testing requirement. Oklahoma and Washington created legislative authority for broad-banding their pay systems. Again, the pattern overall is to use legislation to change the most restrictive and obstructive components of the existing personnel structures but to leave the base in place.

THE STATES AS LABORATORIES FOR MANAGEMENT REFORM?

As even this brief survey discloses, the breadth of experience in human resource management provided by the states is substantial. That experience covers major structural models of HR systems, as well as new "start-from-scratch" models that argue the old ones cannot be fixed. The undeniable lesson here, however, is that even in states that continue to adhere to centralized, standardized models, some new flexibilities are replacing older rigidity. A larger number have made flexibility the cornerstone of their efforts.

There is virtually no innovative technique or practice that has not been tried or is not now in place in one of the states. The diversity of economic circumstances in which states marshal and allocate their resources allows comparison of similar reforms in different settings, and the states themselves are quick to learn from one another.

As all levels of government strive toward better and more effective utilization of their human resources, the experience of the states—most notably those that have made careful efforts to improve capacity and performance—can provide a rich learning resource. The examples in this chapter demonstrate clearly that the "laboratories of reform" are fertile ground for better understanding the complicated issues related to better managing people in a public environment.

REFERENCES

Berry, Francis, Barton Wechsler, and Richard Chakerian. 1999. "Reinventing Government: Lessons From a State Capital." In H. George Frederickson and Jocelyn Johnston, eds. *Public Management Reform and Innovation* Tuscaloosa: University of Alabama Press, 329–55.

Brudney, Jeffrey L., F. Ted Hebert, and Deil S. Wright. 1999. "Reinventing Government in the American States: Measuring and Explaining Administrative Reform." *Public Administration Review* 59: 19–30.

Burke, Brendan F., and Deil S. Wright. 2000. "Reviewing, Reassessing, Reconciling, and Reinterpreting Performance Indicators in the American States: Exploring State Administrative Capacity." Discussion Paper, University of North Carolina, Chapel Hill, N.C.

Florida Council Of 100. 2000. *Modernizing Florida's Civil Service System.* Tampa: The Florida Council of 100.

Ingraham, Patricia W., and Amy Kneedler Donahue. 2000. "Dissecting the Black Box Revisited: Characterizing Government Management Capacity." In Carolyn J. Heinrich and Laurence E. Lynn, Jr., eds. *Governance and Performance: New Perspectives* Washington, D.C.: Georgetown University Press, 292–318.

Ingraham, Patricia W., Sally Coleman Selden, and Donald P. Moynihan. 2000. "People and Performance: Challenges for the Future Public Service—the Report from the Wye River Conference." *Public Administration Review* 60: 54–60.

Kaufman, Herbert. 1969. "Administrative Decentralization and Political Power." *Public Administration Review* 29, 3.

Light, Paul. 1998. *The Tides Of Reform.* New Haven: Yale University Press.

National Comission on State and Local Public Service (Winter Commission). 1993. *Hard Truths/Touch Choices: An Agenda for State and Local Reform.* Albany, N.Y.: Rockefeller Institute of Government.

Riccucci, Norma. 1991."Apprenticeship Training in the Public Sector: Its Use and Operation for Meeting Skilled Craft Needs." *Public Personnel Management* 20: 181.

Selden, Sally Coleman, Patricia Wallace Ingraham, and Willow Jacobson, forthcoming. "Human Resource Practices in State Governments: Findings from a National Survey." *Public Administration Review.*

Thompson, James R. 1999. "Devising Administrative Reform That Works: The Example of the Reinvention Lab Program." *Public Administration Review* 59, 4: 283–92.

Chapter 16

Privatization and Human Resources Management

Sergio Fernandez, Carol E. Lowman, and Hal G. Rainey

Privatization of public services has been one of the most significant developments in public administration over the last several decades. Around the world, trillions of dollars worth of activities have been privatized or considered for it. In the United States and some other countries, much of this privatizing has taken the form of contracting out, and such arrangements have spread widely and rapidly. These developments have important implications for human resources management in government, and this chapter discusses many of the most important ones. After some background on the privatization trend, the discussion turns to general implications for public management. Then, the chapter addresses one of the main issues for human resources management, the skills and knowledge needed to manage contracting out and similar arrangements, and we enumerate many of these by identifying skill requirements for a well-developed contracting process. We discuss specific issues that privatization raises for human resources management, including organizational design issues and the professionalization of the procurement workforce (the experts on contracting and procurement) through education and certification requirements. Then the chapter covers one of the most important challenges, of managing relations with employees and unions in privatization situations, and discusses employee and union opposition to contracting out, its impact on employees' job security and wages, and how human resources managers and other officials need to address these issues to deal with such opposition and to treat employees fairly. Finally, the chapter reports on developments in a recent trend towards privatization or "outsourcing" of human resources management functions themselves. All these topics represent challenges for everyone involved in human resources management in government and reflect the imperatives to increase their capacity to respond to such challenges.

THE PRIVATIZATION TREND

Privatization as a service delivery method dates at least as far back as the sixteenth century during the reign of Elizabeth I (Kent, 1998) and in the United States predates the foundation of the republic. The practice, however, has spread widely in the last two decades, in many forms such as contracting out, load shedding, sale of state assets, vouchers, franchise agreements, deregulation, and other arrangements for transferring production of governmental goods and services into private hands. In the United States, governments have owned few commercial or industrial enterprises, so privatization in this country has commonly taken the form of contracting out. Contracted services in the United States have spanned the wide spectrum of governmental functions, from development and production of atomic weapons to the delivery of social services at the state and local level.

Governments have joined this privatization movement in pursuit of cost savings, better quality of service and better performance, and access to new alternatives and skills they need. They were pushed in this direction by economic problems in many nations in the 1970s and 1980s and by strong claims about the benefits of privatization from some academics and theorists. These theoretical rationales came from advocates of privatization representing perspectives such as neoclassical economics theory, liberal political philosophy, and public choice theory. Some economic theorists assert that, in the absence of competition and profit incentives, public agencies are unlikely to produce public goods or services at minimal cost (Pack, 1987, 527). According to Averch (1990), the quantity of output of a good or service produced by a budget maximizing public bureaucracy is "technically and allocatively inefficient" so that the public bureau will produce a level of output greater than the socially efficient level and for a higher than minimal cost (p. 60). Government can overcome this obstacle by allowing profit-maximizing businesses to bid competitively for the production of public goods and services. Similarly, Pack (1987) contends that, "competitive bidding by profit-maximizing firms for a well specified output guarantees that the product will be produced at the lowest cost" (p. 527).

From the perspective of liberal political philosophy, the coercive power of the state poses a grave danger to the personal freedom of the citizenry. Privatization therefore has value as a way of countering the power of the encroaching state that increasingly takes more of people's earnings and makes decisions about the use of this money in an unresponsive manner (Savas, 2000, 10).

Economists of the public choice school, such as Downs (1967) and Niskanen (1971), contend that bureaucrats, lacking a competitive market for their outputs and thus protected from competition, have more incentive to maximize their own budgets than to maximize efficiency or to be responsive to citizens. Privatization, then, becomes a way to break the monopolistic power of public bureaus and to force government to offer citizens more choices about government services.

Although one can debate these assumptions and assertions at length (e.g., Goodsell, 1993; Lowery, 1998; Moe, 1987), they gained wide acceptance during the 1970s and 1980s as economic woes and other developments fueled a trend in many nations toward regarding government as too big and too inefficient. Political leaders such as Ronald Reagan and Margaret Thatcher championed privatization as a solution for these problems. Savas (1987) published one of the most significant books about this movement, in which he concluded from a review of empirical research that the private sector, under contracts and other privatization procedures, delivered public services more efficiently and as effectively as did government.

The burgeoning privatization movement, however, elicited a response from authors and experts who challenged the view of privatization as a panacea for government's ills. By the end of the 1980s, a new stream of literature was enumerating the many problems posed by privatization, addressing the challenge of how best to manage it and to avoid its shortcomings (e.g., Donahue, 1989; Jennings, 1986; Kettl, 1993; Moe, 1987, 1996; Rehfuss, 1989). These authors tended to portray the strong claims for privatization as naïve in their assumptions that contracting out would automatically bring benefits and to point out that "successful privatization requires effective management by government officials" (Gill and Rainey, 1998, 1). Donahue (1989), for example, argued that for privatization to be successful, the government must be capable of specifying clearly the product or service it desires and must ensure the presence of effective competition if any gains in efficiency are to be realized. Government must also establish well-designed contract administration and monitoring systems to ensure accountability (p. 218). Concerning these requirements, Rainey (1997, 371) comments that "the chief irony of privatization is that proponents tout it as a cure for bad government, but it takes excellent government to make it work."

This latter current in the literature on privatization has focused on a number of different contingencies on which the success of privatization hinges. These include effective design of the contracting process (Wallin, 1997; Avery, 2000), improved contract management practices (Rehfuss, 1989; Kettl, 1993; Prager, 1994; Crawford and Krahn, 1998; Dicke and Ott, 1999), frameworks for deciding which functions to contract out (Ferris and Graddy, 1986; Donahue, 1989; Rehfuss, 1989; Moe, 1987), and methodological advice on how to make fair and accurate comparisons of public with private service delivery (Barnekov and Raffel, 1990; Prager and Desai, 1994; Sclar, 2000; Fernandez and Fabricant, 2000).

Part of this countertrend arose because the aggressive claims of privatization proponents have not been clearly supported by the available evidence. On the question of whether contracting out to private providers results in greater efficiency and higher quality of service, the results of empirical research are mixed. Savas (2000), for instance, reviews many studies comparing public with private service delivery in solid waste management, street sweeping, street paving, traffic-signal maintenance, bus transportation, administrative services, custodial work, tree maintenance, lawn maintenance, and corrections. He concludes that contractors selected through competitive bidding performed more efficiently than public agencies and performed work of equal quality (Savas, 2000, 153). Similarly, Siegel's (1999) review of research in about twenty local government service areas concludes that contracting improves efficiency and effectiveness and leads to cost savings in a number of service areas (p. 374).

On the other hand, many individual studies and examples have indicated problems with privatization. For example, Kamerman and Kahn's (1989) analysis of privatized child-care programs in North Carolina found that gains in efficiency were attained only through a reduction in the level of service provided, particularly by creaming off the easier and less costly cases. The news media have reported numerous horror stories about the corrupt or abusive behaviors of nonprofit or for-profit private organizations that provide services under contracts with government. Donahue (1989, 62) notes that one of Savas's own studies found that open competition among private garbage-collection services made the service more costly than either government provision or government contracting out of the service. Larger studies have also found evidence that privatization falls short of its proponents' optimistic claims. Hodge (1999) reports a meta-analysis of numerous empirical studies comparing public with private service delivery in different nations. He concludes that overall, contracting out produces cost savings, but that the savings actually concentrate in a few service areas such as garbage collection, cleaning, and maintenance (p. 467). Savings through privatization in other service areas were either much lower or nonexistent. In addition, no general difference could be ascertained between cost savings through contracting with the private sector and through contracting with other public-sector organizations (p. 464).

In sum, research on privatization has produced a controversy over its value. Most parties to the controversy, however, would almost certainly agree on several points. Privatization has been a strong movement and will continue to represent a major alternative for government decision makers. Privatization offers advantages and disadvantages, and even those skeptical of it see that it can provide useful strategic options for government, including such advantages as flexibility and the ability to attain skills and services not readily available in government. On the other hand, even those devoutly supportive of privatization tend to agree that the procedures and conditions for effective privatization have a significant bearing on its success, and hence the sound management of it becomes imperative. Sound management of any enterprise requires sound management of the human resources involved.

PRIVATIZATION AND PUBLIC MANAGEMENT

The increasing importance of privatization has raised important issues about the nature and role of public management in general. As contracting out spreads to new governmental functions and services, or increases in services where it has been present for a long time, more public managers and employees will find their working lives affected. Executives and managers of all types, including personnel and human resources managers, face challenges in preparing for this evolution.

As more services are contracted out, public managers will tend to have greater responsibility for activities and services actually performed by contractors. This will tend to strain the lines of authority and accountability (National Academy of Public Administration, 1989; Kettl, 1993). As Kettl (1993) puts it, the trend leads toward more sharing of power with nongovernmental actors. In some cases, he points out, contractors actually have been making important policy decisions and increasingly taking over important governmental functions. Other observers express related concerns that government and its leaders and managers may have reduced ability to defend values such as social equity and opportunity for the disadvantaged. One major issue concerns whether the role of public managers and employees will evolve from direct service providers to managers of contracts, with reduced influence over important processes and outcomes.

These concerns obviously apply to human resources management. For example, the experts exhort government agencies to engage in more "strategic human resources management," (e.g., McGregor, 1991), but how can they do so if private contractors control the workforce? On the other hand, with effective contract management, government managers can deal with this and other challenges; for example, the contract can specify that the government retain a role in major human resources decisions, such as retaining the right to approve hiring and firing of key personnel (Lawther, 1999, 29). Effective contracts can ensure fair treatment of employees (as later sections describe) and defend important values such as social equity. For example, under a contract, the government can retain the right to approve increases in user fees for services to make sure that such increases do not deny public services to indigent people. As all this and the preceding discussion shows, human resources management in government will require more and more attention to identifying, acquiring, and developing the persons, roles, and skills for effective contracting.

THE CONTRACTING PROCESS AND HUMAN RESOURCES NEEDS

No one has ever prepared a conclusive list of the human resources needs related to privatization because the skills, people, training, and other needs should be flexibly defined and will vary in different settings. One way of developing suggestions about such needs, however, involves examining a well-developed contracting process for indications. A well-developed process, such as the ones used in many federal agencies, includes three phases: the pre-award phase, during which the organization specifies its needs; a second phase involving evaluation of bids or proposals; and the post-award contract administration phase. Public employees and managers need knowledge and skills pertinent to each of the three phases.

The pre-award specification phase requires personnel with substantive knowledge of the program or function to be contracted out, as well as the analytical, communication, and writing skills necessary to draft clear contractual requirements and statements of work. Knowledge of the market, including such matters as the extent of competition between potential providers, is also crucial during this phase. Moreover, public managers must be capable of promoting effective communication and cooperation between the people in the procurement department (who are specialists in contracting and procurement procedures) and the people in the "user" departments (the operating units that want to contract out a function, and thus want to use the contractor and its services). These linkages, which are essential to ensuring that the contractor understands and meets the needs of the organization, require skillful management of integration devices, such as cross-functional teams, that come together to identify the organization's needs and draft technical requirements.

The evaluation phase of the contracting process demands personnel with the knowledge and skills to compare bids or proposals accurately and fairly. This includes substantive knowledge of the program or function being contracted out, financial skills such as cost-benefit analysis and marginal analysis, and some knowledge of microeconomic principles and transaction-cost economics.

Many authors have pointed to inadequate skills and training in contract administration as a serious problem in privatization processes (Moe, 1994; Kettl, 1988; Handler, 1996; Prager, 1994; and Wallin, 1997). To ensure that government gets what it pays for, contract administrators should be trained in the areas of quality assurance, project management, inspection, statistical sampling, accounting, auditing, and record keeping. Ideally, contract administrators should have skills in negotiation, persuasion, and conflict resolution and have sound knowledge of the law that applies to the contracting process.

For the phases of the contracting process just described, human resources managers and governmental personnel systems face decisions about how to design and deliver appropriate training. They also need to blend this training with other ways of acquiring needed skills, such as through hiring people or through still more contracting to meet those needs. In many instances, public organizations have contracted with consultants to draft technical specifications, with attorneys to provide legal advice related to procurement, and with large accounting or management firms to monitor other contracts. This creates an intricate web of external suppliers that can strain the lines of accountability and weaken the authority of public managers.

Also, as described below, privatization and contracting out can increase the need for knowledge and skills for which human resources managers in government already have responsibility. Contracting out may require a Reduction-in-Force (a "RIF") and may involve "Rights of First Refusal," "Veterans Preference," and governmental early retirement programs. These matters require knowledge of governmental laws, rules, and procedures about how to carry them out.

THE PROFESSIONALIZATION OF THE PROCUREMENT WORKFORCE

The skills and knowledge requirements for privatization are evolving, in part because governmental authorities such as legislative bodies are becoming involved in identifying them. At the federal level, Congress has taken action to enhance the professionalization of personnel involved in procurement and contracting out, in ways that increase their discretion and that make the required skills more open-ended. In the Federal Acquisition and Reform Act (FARA) and the Federal Acquisition Streamlining Act (FASA), Congress decreased and streamlined the elaborate regulations that previous legislation had imposed on federal procurement and contracting out. FARA and FASA increase contracting officers' discretion by allowing them to "exercise business judgment" and by allowing such changes as the use of oral proposals in place of written proposals in some instances.

In conjunction with this trend of providing for more professional discretion and skill in the procurement workforce, Congress has moved to professionalize these employees through increased requirements for education, training, and certification. The Defense Acquisition Workforce Improvement Act, for example, requires that procurement/acquisition personnel have a college degree or 24 hours of college credit in business topics, establishes certification requirements, and requires that certified personnel complete 80 hours of continuing education every two years. Additional legislation has strengthened such requirements and extended them to the entire federal procurement workforce. These developments reflect recognition in the legislative branch that more emphasis on privatization and contracting out will require corresponding increases in knowledge and skill on the part of government employees. Experts have sometimes cited limited expertise in contracting out as a problem for privatization in some state and local agencies (Chi, 1994), so this trend of seeking to enhance the professional preparation and certification of the personnel involved will disseminate to other levels of government.

ORGANIZATION DESIGN ISSUES: SEPARATING GOVERNMENT AND CONTRACT PERSONNEL

In addition to the need for acquisition of skills and personnel, increasing privatization raises still more challenges for government managers and personnel systems. Some of these involve issues of organizational design. One important example of this arises when government managers need to avoid mixing together government and contractor personnel. Government frequently contracts for services such as health, refuse collection, landscaping and janitorial services, where the government does not simply buy a product, but contracts for the knowledge and work of the contractors' personnel. At the federal level, the Federal Acquisition Regulation (FAR) forbids "personal services" contracts (with some exceptions) where the contractor's personnel appear to be, in effect, government employees (Federal Aquisition Regulation 37.101). The FAR forbids such contracts because government normally hires employees through Civil Service rules, and personal service contracts can bypass the Civil Service system. To prevent this, FAR requires that government managers avoid direct or even indirect supervision of the contractor's employees. [Federal Aquisition Regulation 37.104(d)(6)]. In some situations, government managers have to prevent these problems by physically separating the two types of employees, using various procedures (such as identification badges) to clearly identify the difference, and making sure that official documents such as organization charts emphasize the difference. Government managers may have to set up organizational designs that make sure that tasks and directions are relayed to contractor employees through the contractor's supervisory chain, not the government's, and specify the differences in duties and responsibilities in formal organizational documents. It is important to emphasize that such arrangements provide one example of the many issues and requirements that government managers may have to take into account. Actually, in many contracting-out situations, governmental and contractor employees unavoidably must work closely together with a lot of communication and interdependence. This can blur the lines of accountability between public and contractor employees and pose challenges for government managers that cannot readily be resolved by simply separating the two types of employees or relaying instructions through the contractor's chain of command.

PUBLIC EMPLOYEE AND PUBLIC UNION OPPOSITION TO PRIVATIZATION

The possibilities of reductions in force and of contractors' employees taking over governmental functions show why privatization gives public employees reasons to worry about their jobs and why public employee unions display tremendous concern about privatization. A study by the National Commission for Employment Policy concluded that, "by far the most contentious issue associated with contracting out is its impact on public sector workers" (1988, 11). Typically fervid in their opposition to privatization, public employees and public unions pose a formidable barrier to contracting out of services at all levels of government. This section discusses employee opposition to privatization; the various forms this opposition can take; empirical findings on the actual impact of privatization on public employment levels, wages, and benefits; and suggestions for public managers on how to cope with this important contingency when designing and implementing a privatization initiative.

Several studies have demonstrated the capacity of public employees and their unions to oppose contracting-out initiatives successfully. Ferris and Graddy (1986) found that the extent of public employee unionization had a significant negative effect on the likelihood that a city will contract out for a service. A Florida county considered privatizing mental health services. Concerns over the impact on their job security, wages, and benefits led county mental health employees to mount a successful campaign to block the initiative, despite a consensus among leading county administrators, mental health providers, client groups, and various community groups in favor of privatization (Becker et al., 1995). In addition, a large survey of sanitation collection services in U.S. cities with populations of more than 10,000 revealed that unionized cities were less likely to consider contracting out than nonunionized cities. The survey also found that opposition to contracting out was significantly higher in unionized cities than in nonunionized cities and that cities that considered contracting out but never did so reported significantly higher levels of opposition from both city employees and residents than cities that ultimately contracted out for sanitation collection services (Chandler and Feuille, 1991).

Public employee opposition to contracting out stems in large part from fears of job displacement and loss or reduction in wages and benefits. Opponents of privatization have also asserted that privatization does disproportionate harm to minorities employed in the public sector. In the Florida case study mentioned previously, the mere prospect of privatization sparked sufficient resistance among county employees to bring the initiative to a halt (Becker et al., 1995). The primary concern among most public employees was the loss of job security, but loss or reduction in benefits was also a significant barrier to privatization. Specifically, employees expressed outrage over the considerably lower retirement benefits and lower family health care coverage that the contractors offered (Becker et al., 1995). Interestingly, the issue of wages never became a stumbling block because the contractors offered salaries competitive with those of the county.

Public employees and public unions have employed various methods to influence or obstruct privatization initiatives. In many instances, public unions have mounted legal challenges to municipalities or agencies attempting to contract out a service. These legal challenges have contended that the decision was not taken to improve efficiency or effectiveness; that the decision was driven by political favoritism; that the agency or unit of government failed to bargain in good faith with unionized employees; and/or that the agency or unit of government acted in an unlawful, unilateral manner that caused it to violate its duty to bargain (Elam, 1997). Though public unions' success in the courts has varied in this regard (Naff, 1991), the mere threat of a lawsuit may convince decision makers to reconsider their decision to contract out. Moreover, the ability of public employees to obstruct privatization reaches beyond the courtroom. For instance, public employee unions have mounted both local and national public-relations campaigns against privatization to garner political support and public sympathy for their cause. Particularly at the local level, political opposition from public unions can pose a significant barrier to privatization. Local elected officials may be disinclined to antagonize public unions by proposing privatization because they depend on union members to deliver important services to constituents (National Commission for Employment Policy, 1988). Moreover, public employees tend to vote more frequently than the average citizen, and their collective voting power can influence the results of local elections significantly.

IMPACT OF PRIVATIZATION ON PUBLIC-SECTOR JOB SECURITY, WAGES, AND BENEFITS

Although the available empirical evidence on the impact of privatization on public-sector job security, wages, and benefits should allay some of the fears held by public employees and their unions, it seems to confirm others. Do many public employees become displaced when contracts are awarded to private or nonprofit firms? Although the evidence is not conclusive, it tends to refute the claim that contracting out results in layoffs of significant numbers of public employees. Based on a review of Department of Defense (DOD), General Accounting Office (GAO), and Office of Management and Budget (OMB) studies of military and civilian agency contracts, the National Commission for Employment Policy (1988) concluded that federal employee job displacement from contracting out was very low. Only about one in twenty federal workers in affected units became unemployed as a result of contracting out with the private sector. Moreover, the commission also conducted its own multiple-case study of seventeen city and county governments and found that few workers were laid off because of contracting out. In all but two of the seventeen cases, workers who were terminated were given opportunities for other jobs within government. Most of the cities established a "no lay-off" policy as a condition to awarding contracts. The findings from the multiple-case study, however, did reveal that former public employees subsequently hired by contractors tended to work for them for less than two years. Given the significance of this issue, further research is needed, particularly panel studies and other longitudinal studies to assess the long-term impact of privatization on public employees.

The same multiple-case study by the National Commission for Employment Policy (1988) found, as did Becker et al. (1995), that private contractors generally offered higher wages than cities and counties. However, other studies have shown that wages paid by private contractors were generally lower than those paid by cities and counties, sometimes by as much as half (National Commission for Employment Policy, 1988). On the impact of privatization on employee benefits, most of the available evidence confirms the concerns expressed by public employees and public unions about the considerably lower benefits packages offered by private contractors (National Commission for Employment Policy, 1988; Becker et al., 1995).

Concerning whether privatization does disproportionate harm to minorities employed in the public sector, the evidence is also mixed. Savas (2000) and the NCEP (1988) concluded that contracting out is not disproportionately harmful to minorities. Yet, when fiscal stress prompted the city of St. Louis to close down its public hospitals and enter into an agreement with a private provider, the city lost almost half of its African-American workforce (Stein, 1994). In 1979, the city's hospital division employed 3,344 workers, 74 percent of whom were black. By 1990, however, with both public hospitals closed, the same division employed only 178 workers, of whom only 39 percent were African American.

REDUCING BARRIERS TO PUBLIC EMPLOYEE OPPOSITION TO PRIVATIZATION

Even though the evidence on the impacts of privatization is mixed, public managers must treat public-employee and public-union opposition to privatization as a critical contingency when implementing privatization. The literature on the topic provides valuable advice on how to cope with public-employees' and public-unions' resistance. First, public managers can take steps to minimize the number of employees who lose their government jobs as a result of privatization (National Commission for Employment Policy, 1988; Eggers and O'Leary, 1994). Municipalities or agencies can contract out only for new or expanding services or can establish a "no lay-off" policy when contracting out for existing services. Employees can also be transferred to other departments or given hiring preference for new job openings in the municipality or agency. Reductions in workforce through attrition, by means such as early retirement incentives, can also help persuade employees to leave voluntarily. Finally, in some instances, public employees have been granted the right to bid for those services being contracted out.

For those public employees who become displaced, measures can be taken to assist them in securing alternate employment in the private sector or elsewhere (National Commission for Employment Policy, 1988; Eggers and O'Leary, 1994; Jackson, 1997). Resources can be directed toward employee assistance programs and services such as retraining, job placement, counseling, and reimbursement for lost pension and other benefits that can facilitate the transition to new jobs. Municipalities or agencies can also give preference to bidders who offer to hire displaced employees as part of their bid or proposal. Finally, contractors can be compelled to offer displaced public employees the right of first refusal to new jobs created as a result of privatization. In the federal government, many contracts for the purchase of commercial or industrial products and services fall under the authority of Office of Management and Budget Circular No. A-76 (Revised). The circular requires that, under certain circumstances, federal agencies must perform a cost comparison between providing goods and services in-house and through contract. When the results of the cost comparison suggest that private provision of goods and services is preferable to governmental provision, the circular mandates that resulting contracts contain the Right of First Refusal of Employment clause.

Under the Rights of First Refusal of Employment clause, the contractor who wins the cost comparison against the government must offer public employees affected by privatization the right of first refusal of any jobs on the contract for which they are qualified. Although this clause offers some protection for government employees, it by no means guarantees another job, because under certain conditions contractors are not required to offer the right of first refusal. Note that these conditions and the reference to this provision as a "right" make this right of first refusal a good example of how important it is for human resources managers to know about such conditions and specifications in the laws and rules, to ensure careful compliance with them, and to foster this knowledge and practice in other officials.

Another possible strategy for reducing barriers to privatization involves creating incentives to make privatization more acceptable to public employees (National Commission for Employment Policy, 1988; Eggers and O'Leary, 1994). Municipalities or agencies can tie pay levels to productivity improvements and efficiency gains to encourage support for privatization. Government organizations can create employee stock ownership plans (ESOPs) to offer public employees an ownership interest in new private enterprises that are created in privatization initiatives. A related strategy involves encouraging groups of employees to buy out government-service delivery operations and run them as employee-owned businesses. Governments can encourage such arrangements by transferring capital assets to the employee-owned business, granting the new business continued access to public facilities, providing financial and legal start-up assistance, and guaranteeing the initial contract award to the employee-owned enterprise.

Of course, one of the major reasons that government officials have to deal effectively with employee opposition to privatization arises from the possibility that public-employee unions can mount a legal challenge to the decision to contract out. As described earlier, unions have brought legal challenges claiming various improprieties in the contracting process. If the court finds that the government entity or the contractor acted improperly in making and implementing the decision, the court might award monetary damages for breach of contract by the contractor or award back pay to displaced public employees. Elam (1997) offers suggestions for overcoming the legal barriers to privatization that tend to address the points on which the legal challenges have been brought. First, state clearly the purpose for contracting out. Second, compile fact-based evidence with which to demonstrate that privatization will promote greater effectiveness or efficiency in service delivery. Third, draft clear specifications and performance requirements and employ competitive bidding (or other objective merit-based methods for selecting a contractor) to guard against claims of improper behavior or politically motivated contract awards. Fourth, seek legal counsel if considering refusal to bargain or negotiate. Finally, if contracting meets the criteria of mandatory negotiation, prepare to engage in extensive bargaining. This entails early acknowledgement of the duty to bargain; allowance of ample time for bargaining; notification to unions of the possibility of contracting (thereby initiating the formal bargaining process) no later than the day the agency announces its invitation for bids/solicitation for proposals; avoidance of unnecessary and burdensome time constraints; use of mediation when agreement cannot be reached; and the allowance of some concessions so as to maintain an atmosphere of good faith during the negotiations.

RUNNING A RIF: MANAGING REDUCTIONS IN FORCE

The suggestions for avoiding legal action show that although human resources managers and other officials in government need to consider many of the strategies and procedures described in previous sections, they must do so within a lattice of governmental statutes, laws, and rules that regulate the privatization process and related human resources practices. Knowledge and skill in these matters becomes another important resource that human resources managers need to provide or foster. Managing Reductions in Force—"RIFs"—provides another good illustration of this point.

As noted earlier, there is not much evidence that privatization displaces a lot of public employees, but it can still raise the possibility that a government entity will have to carry out a RIF. A substantial literature offers advice on managing the sensitive issues involved in "downsizing" or reducing employment in organizations of all types, through steps such as those described above in the discussion of dealing with employee resistance to privatization, such as finding new jobs for displaced employees. Governmental human resources managers, however, have to consider how to apply this advice within the context of governmental personnel systems.

Concerning the management of a RIF, for example, at the federal level the United States Office of Personnel Management (OPM) regulates the RIF process in accordance with Title 5 of the United States Code. The law designates a complicated process that agencies must follow in carrying out a RIF. It requires, for example, that when there are more than 50 government employees involved the agency must get the approval of Congress before beginning the process. The law also requires that agencies base decisions about which employees must leave or be moved to lower positions on factors such as the employee's type of appointment, status as a military veteran (veteran's preference), length of service and performance ratings. Agencies thus have to do careful analysis and planning of who the RIF will affect and how. Theses days the RIF plans are usually done with computer software, for which the human resources personnel provide a database on the agency workforce. The computer then identifies the employees that the RIF will affect, and in what way. Obviously, an understanding of this computerized process and of details involved, such as the nature of veteran's preference criteria, becomes important knowledge for human resources management personnel.

Once they have determined the impact of the RIF, human resources personnel have to send out RIF notices to all the employees affected, specifying the implications for them at least sixty days before the RIF takes effect. For example, an employee might be notified that he will be reduced by one grade, or that he will be reassigned to another organization. Sometimes labor agreements provide for longer notice periods and alter other details of how the RIF can be conducted, so human resources personnel have to be aware of the pertinent labor agreements and their legal requirements.

Since the RIF might involve voluntary separations or early retirement, human resources personnel at the federal level need familiarity with two incentive programs that Congress has created, the Voluntary Separation Incentive Pay (VSIP) and Voluntary Early Retirement Authority (VERA).[1] Personnel who are separated under the RIF may receive benefits under one of these programs, including pay for accrued leave time and lump sum amounts that take into consideration the employee's length of service, age, and other factors. All these procedures and calculations need to be handled accurately and properly.

Indeed, all the steps and procedures described here need accurate and proper management, because after the RIF is complete, all affected employees have various rights to grieve or appeal under either local labor agreements or under the auspices of the Merit System Protection Board. Thus, the running of a RIF serves to illustrate the various forms of expertise that privatization may require of governmental managers and personnel.

OUTSOURCING THE HUMAN RESOURCES FUNCTION

While expertise on the part of governmental personnel remains essential, one of the important recent developments in the area of human resources management has been the practice of outsourcing all or part of the human resources function. Private firms, which have customarily performed the human resources function internally, are now increasingly turning to external providers to perform human resources activities in an effort to reduce costs and to gain access to specialized knowledge and skills (Sunno and Laabs, 1994; and Csoiko, 1995, as cited in Klaas et al; 1999). Growing evidence also points to a significant incidence of this sort of outsourcing of the human resources function in the public sector. An International City Management Association (1989) survey of larger cities and counties conducted in 1988 found that approximately 8 percent of the respondents contracted out for personnel services. About ten years later, a similar survey of the 100 largest cities in America found that approximately 24 percent of the respondents reported contracting out for employment and training activities (Dilger et al., 1997, 22). Finally, a recent study of 22 federal agencies by the National Academy of Public Administration (NAPA, 1996; see also U.S. General Accounting Office, 1998) found that more than half outsource one or more human resources functions, most often with franchise programs (i.e., federal-agency administrative offices, which operate on a self-sustaining reimbursable basis by offering services to other public agencies). This and other evidence has prompted one author to characterize the outsourcing of the human resources function as "a trend that is more than transitory" (Siegel, 1999, 226).

Public agencies have at their disposal various types of alternative service providers with which to contract out for one or more human resources functions. These include private firms specializing in human resources services; central human resources offices from neighboring agencies or units of government; intergovernmental consortia that market their services to personnel departments in other agencies; and public-employee-owned enterprises such as Employee Stock Ownership Plans (ESOPs). The alternatives also include federal franchise programs like the U.S. Department of Treasury's Center for Applied Financial Management and the Office of Personnel Management's Personnel Resources and Development Center, which were set up to provide human resources services to other public agencies. According to Siegel (1999), except for outsourcing of training and development functions, governments tend to outsource human resources functions peripheral to core human resources management (i.e., drug-testing, health and benefits administration, or information systems operations), while private firms are more likely to outsource most human resources functions (p. 228). A NAPA (1997) study identified human resources functions that are not inherently governmental and for which competitive bidding is possible, as potential candidates for outsourcing. These functions include administrative and technical functions, employee development, staffing and classification, affirmative employment and diversity programs, employee and labor relations functions, human resources development, career transition services, employee assistance programs, organizational development services, management consulting functions, payroll processing, benefits administration, and health and safety services (pp. 29–35).

Why would a public agency consider outsourcing all or part of its human resources function? Outsourcing such functions offers public agencies several potential advantages over in-house provision. By contracting with larger firms that specialize in particular functions or services, a public agency may be able to take advantage of economies of scale to reduce the cost of service provision. Outsourcing can free up existing human resources staff, allowing them to focus on core competencies and play a more strategic role within the agency. Outsourcing may also enable an agency to procure services of higher quality from leading human resources providers. Finally, contracting out with external providers can enable an agency to procure specialized knowledge and skills not immediately available from within the agency. Dilger et al.'s (1997) survey of America's largest cities found that among the sixteen cities contracting out for one or more human resources functions, nine reported being satisfied to some extent with the services received, and seven were neither satisfied nor dissatisfied (p. 23). Beyond this study, however, little empirical evidence is available from the public sector on whether these potential advantages from outsourcing actually materialize in practice.

Outsourcing the human resources function is no panacea or "magic bullet" (National Academy for Public Administration, 1997; Siegel, 1999), for it requires effective management on the part of public managers and raises the sorts of challenges described earlier in this chapter. For example, contracting out requires that a public agency retain sufficient in-house knowledge and resources to monitor the performance of human resources contractors effectively and to ensure that the contract be designed with performance measures and incentives that encourage the contractor to behave in the best interest of the agency. Government officials also have to face the problem that contracting out the human resources function may result in loss of control over vital organizational functions such as recruitment, staffing, and training. In sum, successful outsourcing of human resources functions requires the sorts of knowledge and skill that this chapter has prescribed and illustrated for the management of privatization in general.

NOTE

1. Under the VSIP, the Government pays an employee a lump sum to leave civil service, up to a maximum award of $25,000, based on average pay, years of service, age and similar variables. Employees who choose the VERA incentive have the option of retiring before they have reached the age or length of service normally required for full retirement, although with a 2 percent penalty for every year short of retirement age.

REFERENCES

Averch, H. 1990. *Private Markets and Public Intervention: A Primer for Policy Designers.* Pittsburgh: University of Pittsburgh Press.

Avery, G. 2000. "Outsourcing Public Health Laboratory Services: A Blueprint for Determining Whether to Privatize and How." *Public Administration Review,* 60: 330–37.

Barnekov, T. K. and J. A. Raffel. 1990. "Public Management and Privatization." *Public Productivity and Management Review,* 14 (2): 35–152.

Becker, F. W., G. Silverstein, and L. Chaykin. 1995. "Public Employee Job Security and Benefits: A Barrier to Privatization of Mental Health Services." *Public Productivity and Management Review,* Vol. 19: 25–33.

Cayer, N. Joseph. 1995. "Merit System Reform in the States." In Steven Hays and Richard Kearney, eds. *Public Personnel Administration: Problems and Prospects, 3rd Edition.* Englewood Cliffs, N.J.: Prentice-Hall.

Chandler, T., and P. Feuille. 1991. "Municipal Unions and Privatization." *Public Administration Review,* Vol. 51: 15–22.

Chi, Keon. 1994. "Privatization in State Government: Trends and Issues." Lexington, Kentucky: The Council of State Governments.

Crawford, J. W., and S. L. Krahn. 1998. "The Demanding Customer and the Hollow State." *Public Productivity and Management Review,* 22: 107–118.

Csoko, L. S. 1995. Rethinking Human Resources: A Research Report. The Conference Board, Report No: 1124-95-RR: New York.

Dicke, L. A., and J. S. Ott. 1999. "Public Agency Accountability in Human Services Contracting." *Public Productivity and Management Review,* 22: 502–16.

Dilger, R. J., R. R. Moffett, and L. Struyk. 1997. "Privatization of Municipal Services in America's Largest Cities." *Public Administration Review,* 57: 21–26.

Donahue, J. D. 1989. *The Privatization Decision: Public Ends, Private Means.* New York: Basic Books.

Downs, A. 1967. *Inside Bureaucracy.* New York: Little, Brown.

Eggers, W. D., and J. O'Leary. 1994. "Overcoming Public Employee Opposition to Privatization." *Business Forum,* Vol. 19: 16–20.

Elam, L. B. 1997. "Reinventing Government Privatization Style: Avoiding the Pitfalls of Replacing Civil Servants with Contract Providers." *Public Personnel Management,* Vol. 26: 15–29.

Federal Acquisition Regulation, Subpart 7.3, "Contractor Versus Government Performance."

Federal Acquisition Regulation, Subpart 37.101, "Definitions."

Federal Acquisition Regulation, Subpart 37.104, "Personal Service Contracts."

Federal Acquisition Regulation, Subpart 52.207–3, "Right of First Refusal of Employment" (Nov. 1991).

Fernandez, S., and R. Fabricant. 2000. "Methodological Pitfalls in Privatization Research: Two Cases from Florida's Child Support Enforcement Program." *Public Performance and Management Review,* 24: 133–44.

Ferris, J., and E. Graddy. 1986. "Contracting Out: For What? With Whom?" *Public Administration Review,* 46: 332–44.

Gill, J. M., and H. G. Rainey. 1998. "Public Management, Privatization Theory and Privatization in Georgia State Government." Paper presented at the Annual Meeting of the American Political Science Association (Sept. 3–6).

Goodsell, Charles T. 1993. *The Case for Bureaucracy,* 3rd ed. Chatham, N.J.: Chatham House.

Handler, J. 1996. *Down from Bureaucracy: The Ambiguity of Privatization and Empowerment.* Princeton, N.J.: Princeton University Press.

Hodge, G. A. 1999. "Competitive Tendering and Contracting Out." *Public Productivity and Management Review,* 22: 455–69.

International City Management Association. 1989. *Service Delivery in the 90s: Alternative Approaches for Local Government.* Washington, D.C.

Jackson, C. Y. 1997. "Strategies for Managing Tensions Between Public Employment and Private Service Delivery." *Public Productivity and Management Review,* Vol. 21: 119–36.

Jennings, Edward T. 1986. "Public Choice and the Privatization of Government: Implications for Public Administration." In Robert T. Denhart and Edward T. Jennings, eds. *The Revitalization of the Public Service.* Columbia, Mo.: UMC Press, 157–75.

Kamerman, S. B., and A. J. Kahn, eds. 1989. *Privatization and the Welfare State.* Princeton: Princeton University Press.

Kent, J. 1998. "Elizabeth I and the Limits of Privatization." *Public Administration Review,* 21: 59–64.

Kettl, D. 1988. *Government by Proxy.* Washington, D.C.: Congressional Quarterly, Inc.

Kettl, D. F. 1993. *Sharing Power: Public Governance and Private Markets.* Washington, D. C.: Brookings Institution.

Klaas, B. S., J. McClendon, and T. W. Gainey. 1999. "HR Outsourcing and Its Impact: The Role of Transaction Costs." *Personnel Psychology,* 52: 113–36.

Kodrzycki, Y. 1998. "Fiscal Pressures and the Privatization of Local Services." *New England Economic Review,* January/February: 39–50.

Lawther, W. 1999. "The Role of Public Employees in the Privatization Process." *Review of Public Personnel Administration,* Winter 1999.

Lowery, David. 1998. "Consumer Sovereignty and Quasi-Market Failure." *Journal of Public Administration Research and Theory,* 8, 2 (April): 137–72.

McGregor, Eugene B. 1991. *Strategic Management of Human Knowledge, Skills, and Abilities.* San Francisco: Jossey-Bass.

Moe, R. C. 1987. "Exploring the Limits of Privatization." *Public Administration Review,* 47: 453–60.

Moe, R. 1994. "The 'Reinventing Government' Exercise: Misinterpreting the Problem, Misjudging the Consequences." *Public Administration Review,* 54 (2): 111–20.

Moe, R. C. 1996. "Managing Privatization: A New Challenge to Public Administration." In B. G. Peters and B. A. Rockman, eds. *Agenda for Excellence 2: The Administrative State.* Chatham, N.J.: Chatham House.

Naff, K. C. 1991. "Labor-Management Relations and Privatization: A Federal Perspective." *Public Administration Review,* 51: 23–30.

National Academy of Public Administration. 1989. *Privatization: The Challenge to Public Management.* Washington, D.C. NAPA.

National Academy of Public Administration. 1996. *Alternative Administrative Service Delivery: Improving the Efficiency and Effectiveness of Human Resources Services. Implementing Real Change in Human Resources Management, Phase II: Practical Applications.* Washington, D.C.

National Academy of Public Administration. 1997. *Alternative Service Delivery: A Viable Strategy for Federal Government Human Resources Management. Implementing Real Change in Human Resources Management, Phase III: Practical Tools.* Washington, D.C.

National Commission of Employment Policy. 1988. *Privatization and Public Employees: The Impact of City and County Contracting Out on Government Workers.* A Study prepared by Dudek and Company for the National Commission for Employment Policy.

Niskanen, W. A. 1971. *Bureaucracy and Representative Government.* Hawthorne, N.Y.: Aldine de Gruyter.

Pack, J. R. 1987. "Privatization of Public Sector Services in Theory and Practice." *Journal of Policy Analysis and Management,* 6 (4): 523–40.

PL 105-85, Section 1106 (National Defense Authorization Act for FY98).

Prager, J. 1994. "Contracting Out Government Services: Lessons from the Private Sector." *Public Administration Review,* 54: 176–84.

Prager, J., and S. Desai. 1996. "Privatizing Local Government Operations: Lessons from Federal Contracting Out Methodology." *Public Productivity and Management Review* 20 (2): 185–203.

Rainey, H. G. 1997. *Understanding and Managing Public Organizations.* 2nd Edition. San Francisco: Jossey-Bass.

Ravitch, F., and W. Lawther. 1999. "Privatization and Public Employee Pension Rights." *Review of Public Personnel Administration,* XX: 41–58.

Rehfuss, J. A. 1989. *Contracting Out in Government.* San Francisco: Jossey-Bass.

Savas, E. S. 1987. *Privatization: The Key to Better Government.* Chatham, N.J.: Chatham House.

Savas, E. S. 2000. *Privatization and Public-Private Partnerships.* New York: Chatham House.

Sclar, E. D. 2000. *You Don't Always Get What You Pay For: The Economics of Privatization.* Ithaca, N.Y.: Cornell University Press.

Siegel, G. B. 1999. "Where Are We on Local Government Service Contracting?" *Public Productivity and Management Review,* 22: 365–88.

Stein, L. 1994. "Privatization, Work-Force Cutbacks, and African-American Municipal Employment." *American Review of Public Administration,* Vol. 24: 181–91.

Sunno, B. P., and J. J. Laabs. 1994. "Winning Strategies for Outsourcing Contracts." *Personnel Journal,* 73: 69–76.

U.S. Code, Title 5, Sections 3501–3503.

U.S. General Accounting Office. 1998. *Management Reform: Agencies' Initial Efforts to Restructure Personnel Operations.* GAO/GGD-98-93. Washington, D.C.

U.S. Office of Personnel Management, Workforce Restructuring Office. 1999. *The Employee's Guide to Reduction in Force (RIF).* October, 1999 (Rev.).

Wallin, B. A. (1997). "The Need for a Privatization Process: Lessons from Development and Implementation." *Public Administration Review,* 57: 11–20.

Chapter 17

Human Resource Management in Nonprofit Organizations

Joan Pynes

Charitable nonprofits are private organizations that serve a public purpose. Because of their nondistribution constraint, they cannot pay dividends on profits to members or other individuals. If for some reason they must dissolve and no longer operate, their remaining assets must be distributed to a nonprofit organization. For those reasons, it is believed that they possess a greater moral authority than for-profit organizations. Nonprofits often perform public tasks that have been delegated to them by the state or perform tasks for which there is a demand that neither government nor for-profit organizations provide. They provide a myriad of services such as helping the disadvantaged, providing medical services, supporting museums and cultural activities, preserving the environment, and funding medical research. Many nonprofits are the recipients of government contracts and grants. Government has some influence on nonprofits through the conditions it may place on agencies that receive public funds, but it can quickly disassociate itself from programs when things go wrong.

Public and nonprofit organizations are similar in many respects. They define themselves according to their missions or the services they offer, and they are responsible to multiple stakeholders. Nonprofits are primarily responsible to supporters, sponsors, clients, interest groups, and government sources that provide funding and impose regulations; public agencies are primarily responsible to their respective legislative and judicial branches and to taxpayers, interest groups, cognate agencies, political appointees, clients, the media, and other levels of government.

There are, however, some interesting differences between public and nonprofit organizations in regard to issues that may influence human resource management practices. Some examples are provided below.

For four years, Wendy and her husband Gary Spearin served as lieutenants in the Salvation Army. They received a joint salary that was paid biweekly to Mr. Spearin. As a result, Wendy Spearin has no official tax records of her employment. Upon reaching retirement, she will not be eligible to receive the Social Security benefits that she would have accrued during her time working for the Salvation Army had she received a salary in her own name. The Salvation Army says its behavior is consistent with the law because Mrs. Spearin was an ordained minister at the charity.

The Boy Scouts of America claim that it is a voluntary association, with the First Amendment right to expressive association. As such, its policy to discriminate against homosexuals is lawful. As a result of this policy, the state of Connecticut has banned contributions to the Boy Scouts of America by state employees through a state-run charity. The state is also considering whether to block the scouts from using public campgrounds or buildings. In South Florida, Broward County has refused to provide $90,000 to the Boy Scouts. The Fort Lauderdale city commission denied a grant of $10,000, and the city of Miami Beach, the city of Wilton Manors, the Miami-Dade County school district, and the Broward County school district are investigating the possibility of severing their ties with the Boy Scouts.

One poster to recruit Girl Scouts troop leaders shows a girl with green hair and fingernails, and another poster shows a girl sporting a tattoo of the Girl Scout trefoil on her back. The message: "Sure we wear green. But a lot else has changed." The posters are designed to attract young single volunteers in their 20s and 30s, not the stay-at-home moms who anchored the volunteers corps since its inception (Wyatt, 2000).

On September 9, 2000, 250 striking workers at the Museum of Modern Art voted to return to work after a 134-day walkout. Archivists, assistant curators, librarians, bookshop workers, and other employees received an 18 percent wage increase over five years and promises to give jobs back to any union members furloughed when the museum is closed during its expansion and renovation.

This chapter will discuss four important differences: the role of bona fide occupational qualifications (BFOQs) in nonprofit HRM, the rights of nonprofits given their status as voluntary associations, the rights and responsibilities of nonprofit organizations in the management of volunteers, and collective bargaining and labor relations.

WHEN BONA FIDE OCCUPATIONAL QUALIFICATIONS (BFOQS) ARE LAWFUL

Most of us are aware that Title VII of the Civil Rights Act of 1964 forbids any employer to fail to hire, to discharge, to classify employees, or to discriminate with respect to compensation, terms, conditions, or privileges of employment in any way that would deprive any individual of employment opportunity due to race, color, religion, sex, or national origin. However, there are exemptions to Title VII that specifically state that employers may discriminate on the basis of sex, religion, or national origin if the characteristic can be justified as a "bona fide occupational qualification [BFOQ] reasonably necessary to the normal operation of the particular or enterprise" (Title VII Sec. 703e). The courts construe the BFOQ clause narrowly, and the burden of proving the BFOQ claim is on the employer.

In the above example, Mrs. Spearin filed a sex discrimination claim with the EEOC, charging that the Salvation Army's pay policy violates Title VII of the 1964 Civil Rights Act. The Salvation Army responded that Mrs. Spearin was an ordained minister at the charity, which is a religious organization. Therefore, it is exempt from Title VII in regard to how it compensates its ministers. In addition, Salvation Army officers typically view their work as voluntary service for which they receive an allowance (Williams, 2000, 26). Mrs. Spearin claims that the duties she performed were administrative and not spiritual and that the decision to discriminate was a business decision, not a religious one.

The Salvation Army has faced a similar situation in the past. A female officer took the charity to court after she was discharged for complaining that she received less compensation than did male officers of equal rank. The U.S. Court of Appeals for the Fifth Circuit ruled that the Salvation Army was a religious organization and that Congress did not intend for Title VII to regulate the employment relationship between a church and its minister (*McClure v. Salvation Army*).

The attorney representing Mrs. Spearin believes that the courts are more likely today to favor the equal treatment of women then they were almost 30 years ago. More recently, the U.S. Court of Appeals for the Ninth Circuit held that a Jesuit seminarian could bring a Title VII claim of sexual harassment against the Roman Catholic Church. The allowance of a lawsuit against a religious organization leads Mrs. Spearin's attorney to believe that she might be successful in her allegation of sex discrimination (Williams, 2000, 26).

Section 702 of Title VII permits religious societies to grant hiring preferences in favor of members of their religion. It states: "This title shall not apply to an employer with respect to the employment of aliens outside any State or to *a religious corporation, association, educational institution, or society with respect to the employment of individual of a particular religion to perform work connected with the carrying on by such corporation, association, educational institution, or society of its activities* (As amended by P. L. 92–261, eff. March 24, 1972).

Section 703 (e) (1), (2) provides exemptions for educational institutions to hire employees of a particular religion if the institution is owned, controlled, or managed by a particular religious society. The exemption is broad and is not restricted to the religious activities of the institution. These provisions permit the rejection of applicants because of their religion as long as the rejection can be shown to be a bona fide occupational qualification (BFOQ) "reasonably necessary" to the normal operation of the business.

In the public sector, the religion of an applicant or employee is irrelevant, and discrimination because of one's religion is prohibited. However, religiously affiliated nonprofits that provide services of a religious nature or educational institutions may in special circumstances discriminate against applicants or employees on the basis of their religion.

Why should the compensation practices of the Salvation Army be a concern to public administrators? More than half of the revenues of Catholic Charities and Lutheran Social Services comes from government grants and contracts (De Vita, 1999, 222), and religious institutions receive more than half of all private charitable contributions and account for a disproportionate share of the private voluntary effort (Salamon, 1999, 149).

Under the Charitable Choice provision of the Personal Responsibility and Work Opportunity Reconciliation Act of 1996 (PRWORA, Section 104 of P. L. 104–193) religiously affiliated nonprofits can compete for government contracts or accept vouchers on an equal basis without giving up the religious character of faith-based programs. The provision permits recipients of federal aid to require their employees to be of a particular faith, and it allows those groups to keep religious icons on their walls when providing social services paid for by the government. But the provision specifically prohibits the use of government dollars for proselytizing or for subsidizing the cost of running religious services (Moore & Williams, 2000). Will the greater influence of religious institutions in the provision of social/human/educational services serve to disadvantage women? As it now stands, women significantly contribute to their families' income, despite weekly earnings of only 76 percent of what men are paid (U.S. Department of Labor, Women's Bureau, 2000). The nonprofit sector has always been a predominantly female workforce. Of the 9.1 million paid employees of the nonprofit sector in 1994, 68 percent of the employees were women (Hodgkinson, Weitzman, Abrahams, Crutchfield, & Stevenson, 1996). One needs to question whether or not the increased participation of religious organizations in the provision of social or educational services will further depress the salaries of women working in the nonprofit sector (Steinberg & Jacobs, 1994).

While Title VII Sec. 703e permits employers to discriminate on the basis of sex, religion, or national origin if the characteristic can be justified as a BFOQ, it is silent on color or race. If a nonprofit organization such as Hispanic Services Council is permitted to use national origin as a BFOQ, are there circumstances when nonprofit employers should be able to use race as a BFOQ? Should nonprofits such as the NAACP and the Urban League be able to use race as a criterion in the recruitment and selection of their personnel?

THE VOLUNTARY AND LOCAL NATURE OF NONPROFIT ORGANIZATIONS

Nonprofits are referred to as voluntary organizations because they receive much of their financial support from private contributions and depend on volunteers to contribute their time and energies to serve charitable purposes. Because of their voluntary nature, which is reinforced by the First Amendment's protection of the freedom of association, nonprofits were often considered exempt from the application of nondiscrimination laws. The behavior and activities of voluntary associations were considered to fall within the sphere of private activity (Rosenblum, 1998, 161). This changed in 1984 when the United States Supreme Court ruled in *Roberts v. United States Jaycees* that local chapters of the Jaycees could admit women. The local St. Paul and Minneapolis chapters of the Jaycees sued their national organization. The national Jaycees had threatened to revoke the local charters because the local chapters had voted to admit women, a violation of the national organization's bylaws. The national Jaycees claimed that requiring them to admit women as regular members violated the organization's constitutionally protected freedom of association. By ruling in favor of the local chapters, the United States Supreme Court expanded the scope of a "public accommodation" to include voluntary associations like the Jaycees and limited their freedom of association when in conflict with the state's compelling interest to eradicate discrimination *(Roberts v. United States Jaycees)*.

Examples of public accommodations include but are not limited to hotels, restaurants, shops, hospitals, theaters, libraries, camps, swimming pools, meeting places, amusement and recreation parks, colleges, and universities. Three specific exemptions to public accommodations in most nondiscrimination laws are organizations that are "distinctly private," a religious institution or "an educational facility operated and maintained by a bona fide religious or sectarian institution," or the right of a natural parent, or the in loco parentis exception (in the place of a parent; acting as a parent with respect to the care and supervision of a child).

An organization's "expressive rights of association" refer to the right to associate for the purpose of engaging in those activities protected by the First Amendment: the right to speech, assembly, petition for the redress of grievances, and the exercise of religion. Any government intervention to regulate an organization's internal operations, such as membership or personnel policies, must be balanced against the organization's expressive rights of association. Nondiscrimination laws that force organizations to accept members whom they may not desire violate an organization's freedom of expressive association if the organization can demonstrate that these new members would affect in a significant way the group's ability to carry out its mission and express its private viewpoints *(Board of Directors of Rotary International v. Rotary Club; Hurley v. Irish-American Gay Group of Boston; New York State Club Association v. City of New York)*.

Another important characteristic of nonprofit organizations is their local orientation. Most social service agencies, schools, libraries, hospitals, museums, theaters, advocacy groups, foundations, clubs, and other common types of nonprofit organizations focus primarily on local constituencies and local issues. Even nonprofits linked with national organizations such as the American Red Cross are coordinated and run through local chapters with substantial local discretion. They raise and spend most of their money and employ most of their staff and volunteers through the local chapters (Oster, 1992; Young, 1989, 103).

Because of their local orientation, nonprofit managers must walk a thin line when defining and defending their membership and personnel policies. The complex environment that nonprofit administrators must operate in became exacerbated when the U.S. Supreme Court in a 5–4 decision held that the application of New Jersey's public accommodation law to the Boy Scouts violated its First Amendment right of expressive association *(Boy Scouts of America and Monmouth Council v. James Dale)*. The Boy Scouts argued successfully that, as a private organization, it has the right to determine criteria for membership. The Supreme Court heard this case on appeal from the Boy Scouts of America in response to the New Jersey Supreme Court's decision against its position.

The New Jersey Supreme Court held that the Boy Scouts of America is a place of "public accommodation" that "emphasizes open membership" and therefore must follow New Jersey's antidiscrimination law. The court further held that the state's law did not infringe on the group's freedom of expressive association *(Dale v. Boy Scouts of America and Monmouth Council Boy Scouts)*. The court reasoned that the New Jersey legislature, when it enacted the antidiscrimination law, declared that discrimination is a matter of concern to the government and that infringements on that right may be justified by regulations adopted to serve compelling state interests.

The New Jersey Supreme Court noted the BSA's historic partnership with various public entities and public service organizations. Local BSA units are chartered by public schools, parent-teacher associations, firehouses, local civic associations, and the United States Army, Navy, Air Force, and National Guard. The BSA's "learning for life" program has been installed in many public school classrooms throughout the country. Many troops meet in public facilities. The BSA in turn provides essential services through its scouts to the public and quasi-public organizations. This close relationship underscores the BSA's fundamental public character.

As the examples in the beginning of the chapter illustrate, the New Jersey Supreme Court's analysis of the public nature of the Boy Scouts is shared by many. The Boy Scouts of America's decision to exclude homosexuals has become controversial. In addition to Connecticut, the local governments and school districts in South Florida, Chicago, San Diego, and San Francisco told scouts troops they can no longer use parks, schools, or other municipal sites. Chase Manhattan Bank and Textron, Inc. have withdrawn hundreds of thousands of dollars in support, and many United Ways have cut off money (Zernike, 2000).

Nonprofit administrators must stay current with the changing and sometimes contradictory community norms and legal requirements across a diverse set of local communities and reconcile them with mandates from the national/parent organization.

This is especially true for sexual-orientation discrimination. When confronted with sexual-orientation discrimination, nonprofit managers find themselves in a complex legal environment. No federal legislation has been passed defining a national standard; thus, nonprofit managers face a patchwork of state and local laws, executive orders, and judicial and commission decisions barring such discrimination. The organizations that have withdrawn their support from the Boy Scouts have clearly stated that they cannot fund or support organizations that have policies that conflict with their own antidiscrimination policies. Despite the U.S. Supreme Court's ruling supporting the Boy Scouts of America's exclusionary policy, the stand of the Boy Scouts' National Council to refuse local councils to determine local policy has jeopardized their funding and support from *their* local communities. What does this mean? The U.S. Supreme Court upheld the right of voluntary associations to discriminate in regard to their employees and volunteers. The most appropriate policy, however, is for national nonprofit organizations to permit local chapters, sensitive to their community norms, to formulate their own nondiscriminatory policies.

This issue of local values is becoming more pronounced in the nonprofit sector. Just recently the president of the United Way of America announced that she was stepping down from her position approximately one year earlier than she had planned. Local United Ways were concerned over the United Way's governance structure. Many local United Way chapters withheld their dues in protest against the movement by the United Way of America to a more centralized structure. The local United Ways favor a structure that allows them to make most decisions. Joseph G. Calabrese, president of the United Way of Greater Rochester, stated the following, "We believe that being locally autonomous is the best way to succeed in the future" (Lewis, 2000, 47).

Managing Volunteers

There is a tradition of volunteerism in this country that began with churches, synagogues, and other religiously affiliated organizations. Today, a wide range of nonprofit organizations provide a variety of volunteer opportunities ranging from serving as board members to volunteering for one day. Volunteers are used to assist employees in meeting their agency's mission and thus become an important part of human resources management. Hodgkinson, Weitzman, Abrahams, Crutchfield, and Stevenson (1996, 13) report that, in 1994, 48 percent of American adults volunteered, at an average rate of four hours per week. In 1994, an estimated 89 million adults contributed more than 19 billion hours. In terms of full-time equivalent employment, this translated into 8.8 million employees whose assigned value was $182 billion.

Recruiting volunteers can be difficult. Brudney (1993) found that there has been an increase in competition among public and nonprofit agencies for volunteer talent. Contributing to the difficulty in recruiting volunteers is the nature of today's society. The United States ranks among the highest on a global scale in the percent of employees working fifty hours per week or more. Many workers are finding it difficult to balance job and family demands (Jacobs & Gerson, 1998) without adding volunteer work. Many Americans believe that the time pressures on working families are getting worse (National Partnership for Women & Families, 1998). The increased pressure on working adults with families has forced many nonprofits like the Girl Scouts to target new audiences for recruiting volunteers. Other nonprofits are rethinking the assignments they give to volunteers in terms of time, location, and length of commitment. Many communities have established volunteer banks where volunteers can be assigned to projects that do not require a long-term commitment to the agency or require volunteers to work scheduled hours each week.

The research on why individuals volunteer indicates that both intrinsic and extrinsic rewards motivate them. Intrinsic rewards include satisfaction, a sense of accomplishment, and being challenged, which result from the work itself. Extrinsic rewards are benefits granted to the volunteers by the organization. Many individuals use volunteering as a means for career exploration, others to develop skills that may enhance their paid positions. Some people volunteer because it provides them with the opportunity to meet new people. Some volunteer as a way to contribute and give back to the community. Others volunteer because they value the goals of the agency, and still others volunteer because they desire personal growth or external recognition.

There is no one reason that individuals volunteer. Therefore, the volunteer experience should attempt to provide satisfying and interesting opportunities and some form of external recognition. Nonprofit agencies need to recognize the different needs of volunteers and to be flexible in developing volunteer assignments and working hours.

Attention should be paid to the recruitment, selection, training, evaluation, and management of volunteers. Although volunteers can be a tremendous asset to any organization, they also present additional human-resources management challenges. Administrative responsibilities are increased as agencies must keep records and extend their liability insurance and worker's compensation policies to volunteers. Managing volunteer programs requires the development of personnel policies and procedures to assist with the integration of volunteers into the everyday operations of the agency. Paid staff, unions, and board members need to support the use of volunteers, oversight needs to be provided so that volunteers are properly utilized, and strategies need to be developed to motivate and retain volunteers.

One group of very important volunteers in nonprofit organizations is the governing board, often referred to as the board of directors or board of trustees. The governing board is responsible for developing policies relating to the nonprofit's management. It is the responsibility of the board of directors to make sure that the public purpose of the nonprofit organization is implemented. Some of the basic responsibilities of nonprofit boards include determining agency mission and purposes, selecting the executive director and evaluating her/his performance, participating in strategic and long-range planning, establishing fiscal policy and oversight, monitoring the agency's programs and services, promoting the agency in the community, and participating in the development of personnel/human resource management policies and strategies. Governing boards should not be involved in the day-to-day activities of the nonprofit, but instead should develop policies to guide the agency and provide oversight to ensure that it is fulfilling its public purpose. Because of the variety of knowledge and skills needed by nonprofit boards, agencies must make an effort to recruit board members who can assist the organization. The recruitment strategy includes seeking board members with diverse backgrounds and professional expertise. Nonprofit boards should be sensitive to the community and organizations they are serving. When possible, there should be a distribution of ages, gender, color, and representatives of the constituency being served by the organization. Expertise is needed in the following areas: personnel/HRM, finance, law, fundraising, and public relations.

Walt Mears, president of the National Writers Association, wrote a letter to the editor of *The Chronicle of Philanthropy* in which he admonished the publication for an article titled "Ensuring Service Delivery," published on August 24, 2000. In the letter, which was published on October 5 (p. 53), he takes issue with the article in its focus on managing volunteers and instead believes that volunteers are to be viewed as partners. Unlike employees who may have to withstand unpleasant working conditions until they can find other employment, volunteers are mobile. He also recognizes that board members, who are also volunteers, are often community leaders in their own right. In his letter, he recommends ten rules for working with volunteers:

1. You lead volunteers
2. You manage programs.
3. You do not insult the efforts of a volunteer by paying a staff member to do the identical job.
4. You do not use volunteers to replace paid staff and reduce expenses.
5. You recognize volunteers as a valued asset.
6. You manage programs in such a way that each volunteer can feel she exercised initiative and successfully carried out a plan which was, in part, at least, her creation.
7. You provide experienced, professional trainers when training is needed.
8. You know your volunteer and her other commitments.
9. You mutually understand and agree to the tasks planned to be undertaken by the volunteer.
10. You develop a conscious understanding of your mutual strengths and areas where each may need help.

Volunteers are critical to the success of most nonprofit organizations. Agencies should develop volunteer recruitment strategies to reach individuals whose interests and skills are likely to match the needs of the organization. To facilitate good staffing decisions, key staff should be involved in the development of the job descriptions for the volunteers they will supervise. This information will enable the agency to match the interest and skills of the volunteers with the positions in the organization. For example, a volunteer who wants to interact with other individuals would be unhappy working in isolation. Taking the time to match volunteer interests and skills with the needs of the agency in advance of their placement should help to minimize frequent turnover or absenteeism. The turnover rate and absenteeism of volunteers are some of the greatest challenges facing nonprofit administrators. Volunteers, like employees should also receive training on how to perform their tasks and on the performance standards of the agency.

LABOR RELATIONS AND COLLECTIVE BARGAINING

Nonprofit labor relations and collective bargaining are governed by the same laws that govern for-profit private-sector labor-management relations. They fall under the provisions of the National Labor Code, which consolidated the National Labor Relations Act of 1935, the Labor-Management Relations Act of 1947, and the Labor-Management Reporting and Disclosure Act, 1959. The National Labor Relations Board (NLRB) is the administrative agency responsible for enforcing the provisions of the laws. Until the 1970s, the NLRB excluded nonprofit employees from coverage. In 1974, Congress amended the National Labor Relations Act to bring nonprofit health care institutions under the law's coverage (P. L. 93–360, 88 Stat.395). The health care amendments indicated that Congress had no objection to bringing nonprofit employers under federal labor law. In 1976, the NLRB began to treat nonprofit and charitable institutions in the same way it treats businesses operated for profit. If a nonprofit employer has revenues that exceed certain amounts, then the NLRB can become involved in labor-management disputes. The NLRB has established a table of jurisdictional standards that provides the dollar amounts required for nonprofit organizations to come under its jurisdiction (National Labor Relations Board, 1997). For example, symphony orchestras fall under the NLRB's jurisdiction if they have gross annual revenues of $1 million or more. Employers who provide social services come under the NLRB standards if their gross annual revenues are at least $250,000; nursing homes, visiting nurse associations, and related facilities come under the NLRB standards if their gross annual revenues are at least $100,000.

Unlike federal government employees and some state and local public employees, nonprofit employees are permitted to negotiate over wages; they can also negotiate over hours and working conditions. Also, unlike many public employees, nonprofit employees are permitted to strike; not only have museum employees gone on strike, but the Florida Philharmonic Orchestra spent part of its fall 2000–2001 season on strike. Nonprofit employees in health care, social services, education, and even attorneys working for legal aid societies have gone on strike (Pynes, 1997). What is often neglected in discussions or cost-benefit analyses about the privatization of public services is the increased risk that critical services, provided by hospital emergency rooms or child protective services, may be disrupted by striking nonprofit employees.

The uncertainty of many workplace changes has shaken the confidence of many employees that their jobs are secure and that their wages will remain competitive. Professional employees are the fastest-growing group in the labor force, and unionization has been viewed as a mechanism to defend professional autonomy and improve working conditions. Unions have stepped up efforts to organize them. The old-line unions that historically represented blue collar workers have realized that, if they are to remain viable, they must follow the job growth. The projected job growth is in the service sector, for both higher paid technical and professional positions as well as low-paid service workers such as custodians, nursing assistants, and child care workers.

The impact of competition and organizational restructuring has become an issue in nonprofit organizations. Contracts have called for employers to notify employees of impending layoffs and to offer voluntary leaves of absences to employees before reducing their hours. In other circumstances, unions have been called on to defend professional autonomy and improve working conditions. Unions have sought to expand the scope of bargaining to include such issues as agency-level policy making, agency missions, standards of service, and professional judgment (Tambor, 1988). Other negotiated topics have included coverage for malpractice and professional liability insurance, legal representation of workers, workload issues, the provision of in-service training, financial assistance for licensing examinations, and remuneration for enhanced education (Tambor, 1988).

As more and more public services become privatized and former public employees enter nonprofit agencies, nonprofit managers can expect to see an increase in union activities. If nonprofit organizations wish to keep adversarial labor-management relations at bay, nonprofit administrators and boards of directors must work with their staffs to develop progressive and relevant human resource polices that respect employees. Employees must feel that their jobs are important and that they are contributing to the mission of the agency. Performance evaluations, promotions, and merit pay systems must be administered in an equitable and consistent manner. Career enrichment opportunities must be provided. Organizations that provide employees with the opportunity to participate in the decision-making process tend to have less labor strife (Peters & Masaoka, 2000).

FUTURE CHALLENGES

In today's robust economy, public, for-profit, and nonprofit organizations are competing with one another for talented and conscientious employees. Public and nonprofit organizations are also competing with one another for volunteers. If nonprofit organizations are going to be able to attract qualified employees and volunteers, they need to be flexible and have progressive HRM policies and programs in place. At one time, nonprofits could afford to be more complacent about HRM issues. Many nonprofits originated as a response to new societal needs, such as hospices for the terminally ill, rape crisis support organizations, domestic violence shelters, and daycare centers. They thus have missions that appeal to employees. Other nonprofits, such as museums, zoos, historical societies, and symphonies, are thought to be interesting places to work. However, interesting places to work can become less interesting, and employees' and volunteers' commitments to agency missions can erode if they are not treated with respect and allowed to grow professionally. Nonprofits must not only be innovative in how they treat and reward their employees and volunteers, but they also must be creative in how they recruit employees and volunteers. Nonprofits can employ individuals who possess the motivation to work in public service but who want to work in smaller, less bureaucratic organizations. Preston (1990) found that the opportunity to perform a variety of work and enhance one's skill development has been instrumental in attracting women to nonprofit organizations. Many women choose to work in nonprofits despite the often lower pay they provide so that they may take advantage of the opportunities the nonprofits offer. In this competitive environment, nonprofits need to be concerned not only about their compensation and benefit packages and their professional development opportunities, but also their antidiscrimination policies. Many potential employees and volunteers may choose to seek opportunities in organizations that are inclusive.

REFERENCES

Board of Directors of Rotary International v. Rotary Club, 481 U.S. 537, 544, 107 S.Ct. 1940, 1945, 95 L. ED. 2d 474, 483–84 (1987).

Boris, E. T., and C. E. Steuerle. 1999. *Nonprofits and Government: Collaboration and Conflict.* Washington, DC: The Urban Institute Press.

Boy Scouts of America v. Dale, No.99-699 U.S. Supreme Court, June 28, 2000. [On-line]. Available http://supct.law.cornett.edu/supct/html/99-699.zo.html[2000, June 28].

Brudney, J. L. "Volunteer involvement in the delivery of public services." *Public Productivity and Management Review*, Spring 1993, 16: 283–297.

Civil Rights Act of 1964, Title VII, Secs. 70

Dale v. Boy Scouts of America and Monmouth Council Boy Scouts, A–195/196–97, N.J. Sup. Ct. August 4, 1999. [On-line]. Available: http://lawlibrary.rutgers.edu/courts/supreme/a-195-97.opn.html.

De Vita, C. J. 1999. "Nonprofits and devolution: What do we know?" In E. T. Boris and C. E. Steuerle, *Nonprofits and Government: Collaboration and Conflict*. Washington, DC: The Urban Institute Press, 213–233.

Ellis, S. J. "Reverse discrimination: Volunteers vs. employees." *The NonProfit Times* 13 (15) October 1999: 16–18.

Hodgkinson. V. A., M. S. Weitzman, J. A. Abrahams, E. A. Crutchfield, and D. R. Stevenson. 1996. *Nonprofit Almanac 1996–1997 Dimensions of the Independent Sector*. San Francisco: Jossey-Bass, Inc.

Hurley v. Irish American Gay Group of Boston, U.S. No. 94–749 (1995).

Jacobs, J. A., and K. Gerson. 1998. "Who are the overworked Americans?" *Review of Social Economy*, 56 (4): 442.

Lewis, N. "United Way leader to depart earlier than expected." *The Chronicle of Philanthropy*, XII, October 5, 2000, (25): 47.

McClure v. The Salvation Army. No. 71-2270, 460 F.2d 553; 1972 U.S. app. LEXIS 10672, 1972.

Mears, W. "Keeping volunteers requires leadership." *The Chronicle of Philanthropy*, XII, October 5, 2000, (24): 53.

Moore, J. and G. Williams, "Report says 'Charitable Choice' is making a difference in delivery of social services." *The Chronicle of Philanthropy*, XII, May 18, 2000, (15): 27.

National Labor Relations Board. 1997. *A guide to basic law and procedures under the National Labor Relations Act*. Washington, D.C.: U.S. Government Printing Office.

National Partnership for Women & Families (1998). "Family matters: A national survey of women and men." [On-line]. Available: http:www.nationalpartnership.org/survey/survey8.htm. [August 23, 1999].

New York State Club Association v. City of New York. 108 S. Ct. 2234, 1988.

O'Neill, M. 1994. "The paradox of women and power in the nonprofit sector." In T. Odendahl and M. O'Neill, eds., *Women and Power in the Nonprofit Sector*. San Francisco: Jossey-Bass, pp. 1–16.

Oster, S. M. "Nonprofit organizations as franchise operations." *Nonprofit Management & Leadership*, 1992: 2: 223–258.

Peters, J. B., and J. Masaoka. "A house divided: How nonprofits experience union drives." *Nonprofit Management and Leadership*, 10, 2000, (3): 305–317.

Preston, A. E. "Women in the white collar nonprofit sector: The best option or the only option?" *The Review of Economics and Statistics*, 72, 1990: 560–568.

Pynes, J. E. 1997, "The anticipated growth of nonprofit unionism." *Nonprofit Management and Leadership*, 7, (4): 355–371.

Roberts v. United States Jaycees, 468 U.S. 609, 104 S.Ct. 3244, 82 L.Ed. 2d 462, 1984.

Rosenblum, N. 1998. *Membership and Morals: The Personal Uses of Pluralism in America*. Princeton: Princeton University Press.

Salamon, L. M. 1999. *America's Nonprofit Sector: A primer*, (2nd Ed.), New York: Foundation Center.

Steinberg, R. J., and J. A. Jacobs. 1994. "Pay equity in nonprofit organizations: Making women's work visible." In T. Odendahl and M. O'Neill, eds. *Women and Power in the Nonprofit Sector*. San Francisco: Jossey-Bass, pp. 79–120.

Tambor, M. 1988. "Social service unions in the workplace." In H. J. Karger, ed., *Social workers and labor unions.* New York: Greenwood Press.

U.S. Department of Labor, Women's Bureau. 2000. "Women's earnings as percent of men's, 1979–1999." October 25, 2000.

Williams, Gzant. "Rank and File: Former Salvation Army Officer Changes that Charity's Policy on Pay for Married Couples Violated her Civil Rights." *Chronicle for Philanthropy,* XII, 7 (January 27, 2000): 25–26.

Wyatt, K. "Girl scouts' recruiting drive tells old image to take a hike." The Associated Press. In *The Tampa Tribune,* October 25, 2000: 23.

Young, D. "Local Autonomy in a Franchise Age: Structural Change in National Voluntary Associations." *Nonprofit and Voluntary Sector Quarterly,* 1989, 18 (2): 101–117.

Zernike, K. "Policy on gays costing Scouts allies, money." *The New York Times,* August 29, 2000: 1, 3.

Index